XML: Extensible Markup Language

XML: Extensible Markup Language

Elliotte Rusty Harold

IDG Books Worldwide, Inc.
An International Data Group Company

Foster City, CA ◆ Chicago, IL ◆ Indianapolis, IN ◆ New York, NY

XML: Extensible Markup Language

Published by

IDG Books Worldwide, Inc.

An International Data Group Company

919 E. Hillsdale Blvd., Suite 400

Foster City, CA 94404

www.idgbooks.com (IDG Books Worldwide Web site)

Library of Congress Catalog Card No.: 98-70590

ISBN: 0-7645-3199-9

Printed in the United States of America

10 9 8 7 6 5 4 3 2 1

1B/RQ/QX/ZY/FC

Distributed in the United States by IDG Books Worldwide, Inc.

Distributed by Macmillan Canada for Canada; by Transworld Publishers Limited in the United Kingdom; by IDG Norge Books for Norway; by IDG Sweden Books for Sweden; by Woodslane Pty. Ltd. for Australia; by Woodslane (NZ) Ltd. for New Zealand; by Addison Wesley Longman Singapore Pte Ltd. for Singapore, Malaysia, Thailand, Indonesia, and Korea; by Norma Comunicaciones S.A. for Colombia; by Intersoft for South Africa; by International Thomson Publishing for Germany, Austria, and Switzerland; by Toppan Company Ltd. for Japan; by Distribuidora Cuspide for Argentina; by Livraria Cultura for Brazil; by Ediciencia S.A. for Ecuador; by Ediciones ZETA S.C.R. Ltda. for Peru; by WS Computer Publishing Corporation, Inc., for the Philippines; by Unalis Corporation for Taiwan; by Contemporanea de Ediciones for Venezuela; by Computer Book & Magazine Store for Puerto Rico; by Express Computer Distributors for the Caribbean and West Indies. Authorized Sales Agent: Anthony Rudkin Associates for the Middle East and North Africa.

For general information on IDG Books Worldwide's books in the U.S., please call our Consumer Customer Service department at 800-762-2974. For reseller information, including discounts and premium sales, please call our Reseller Customer Service department at 800-434-3422.

For information on where to purchase IDG Books Worldwide's books outside the U.S., please contact our International Sales department at 650-655-3200 or fax 650-655-3297.

For information on foreign language translations, please contact our Foreign & Subsidiary Rights department at 650-655-3021 or fax 650-655-3281.

For sales inquiries and special prices for bulk quantities, please contact our Sales department at 650-655-3200 or write to the address above.

For information on using IDG Books Worldwide's books in the classroom or for ordering examination copies, please contact our Educational Sales department at 800-434-2086 or fax 317-596-5499.

For press review copies, author interviews, or other publicity information, please contact our Public Relations department at 650-655-3000 or fax 650-655-3299.

For authorization to photocopy items for corporate, personal, or educational use, please contact Copyright Clearance Center, 222 Rosewood Drive, Danvers, MA 01923, or fax 978-750-4470.

is a trademark under exclusive license to IDG Books Worldwide, Inc., from International Data Group, Inc.

Credits

ACQUISITIONS EDITOR
John Osborn

DEVELOPMENT EDITOR
Denise Santoro

TECHNICAL EDITOR
Steven Champeon

COPY EDITOR
Eric Hahn

PROJECT COORDINATOR
Ritchie Durdin

BOOK DESIGNER
Jim Donohue
Kurt Krames

GRAPHICS AND
PRODUCTION SPECIALISTS
Linda Marousek
Hector Mendoza
E. A. Pauw

QUALITY CONTROL SPECIALISTS
Mick Arellano
Mark Schumann

PROOFREADER
Annie Sheldon

INDEXER
Liz Cunningham

COVER DESIGN
© mike parsons design

About the Author

Elliotte Rusty Harold is an internationally respected writer, programmer, and educator, both on and off the Internet. He got his start by writing FAQ lists for the Macintosh newsgroups on Usenet, and has since branched out into books, Web sites, and newsletters. Elliotte lectures about Java and object-oriented programming at Polytechnic University in Brooklyn. His Cafe au Lait Web site at `http://sunsite.unc.edu/javafaq/` has become one of the most popular independent Java sites on the Internet.

Elliotte is originally from New Orleans, where he returns periodically in search of a decent bowl of gumbo. He currently resides in the Prospect Heights neighborhood of Brooklyn with his wife Beth and cats Charm (named after the quark) and Marjorie (named after his mother-in-law). When not writing books, Elliotte enjoys working on genealogy, mathematics, and quantum mechanics. His previous books are *The Java Developer's Resource*, *Java Network Programming*, *Java Secrets*, and *JavaBeans*.

To David and Sherry Rogelberg

Preface

Welcome to XML. After reading this book, I hope you agree XML is the most exciting development on the Internet since Java, making Web site development easier, more productive, and more fun.

This book is your introduction to the exciting and expanding world of XML. In this book, you learn how to write documents in XML and use XSL style sheets to convert those documents into HTML so legacy browsers can read them. You also learn how to use document type definitions (DTDs) to describe and validate documents. This skill will become increasingly important as more browsers like Netscape and Internet Explorer 5.0 provide native support for XML.

XML: Extensible Markup Language is the first book to examine XML from the perspective of a Web page author, rather than a software developer. As a result, it doesn't spend a lot of pages discussing BNF grammars or parsing element trees. Instead, this book shows you how to use XML and existing tools today to produce powerful Web sites efficiently and productively.

Who You Are

This book is aimed squarely at Web site developers. I assume you want to use XML to produce Web sites that are difficult or impossible to create with raw HTML. You may be amazed to discover that in conjunction with XSL style sheets and a few free tools, XML enables you to accomplish tasks that previously required either custom software costing hundreds to thousands of dollars per developer or extensive knowledge of programming languages like Perl. No software in this book costs you more than a few minutes of download time and none of the tricks requires programming beyond the most basic cut and paste JavaScript.

XML builds on HTML and the underlying infrastructure of the Internet, however. To that end, I assume you know how to ftp files, send e-mail, and load URLs in your Web browser of choice. I also assume you have a reasonable knowledge of HTML at about the level of Netscape 1.0. When this book discusses newer, less common aspects of HTML such as Cascading Style Sheets or the <SPAN> and <DIV> tags, I cover these topics in depth.

I assume you have the following skills:

◆ You should be able to write a basic HTML page including links, images, and text using a text editor.

◆ You should be able to place that page on a Web server.

On the other hand, I do not assume you have the following skills:

◆ You do not need any knowledge of SGML. In fact, this preface is almost the only place in the entire book that mentions SGML. (Chapter 1 also briefly discusses SGML when you learn about the history of XML.) By design, XML should be simpler and more widespread than SGML, and these goals would be impossible if you have to learn SGML first.

◆ You needn't be a programmer of Java, Perl, C, or any other language, unlike the assumptions of many other XML books. XML is a markup language – not a programming language. You needn't be a programmer to write XML documents.

Knowledge in the following areas is not a prerequisite for this book, but is nonetheless helpful when you begin writing XML files:

◆ Web server configuration and the HTTP protocol

◆ JavaScript

◆ Database theory, particularly normalization rules

◆ SGML

◆ Some knowledge of international character sets

Just as in HTML, you don't need to have any of the preceding skills to learn to write XML files. Nonetheless, readers who understand these topics will find a few sections of this book more compelling than readers without this knowledge. If you are familiar with one or more of these topics, certain practices are easier to motivate and explain. If you aren't familiar with these topics, you'll just be asked to accept certain rules of XML that appear arbitrary on the surface.

This book assumes you're using Windows 95 or NT 4.0 or later versions. As a longtime Mac and UNIX user, I regret this assumption. Like Java, XML should be platform-independent. Also like Java, the reality falls somewhat short of the hype. Although XML code is pure text that can be written with any editor, some crucial tools are currently available only on Windows. In the not too distant future, I hope these tools will be available on the Macintosh and UNIX. Until then, XML development will remain primarily a PC-based activity.

What You'll Learn

This book has one primary goal: to teach you to write XML documents for the Web. Fortunately, XML has a decidedly gentle learning curve, much like HTML (and unlike SGML). As you learn a little XML, you can do a little XML. As you learn a little more XML, you can do a little more XML. Thus, the chapters in this book build steadily on each other and are meant to be read in sequence. Along the way, you learn the following:

◆ How semantic tagging makes XML documents easier to maintain and develop than their HTML equivalents

◆ How to post XML documents on Web servers in a form everyone can read

◆ How to make sure your XML is well-formed

◆ How to format your documents with XSL style sheets

◆ How to validate documents with DTDs

◆ How to use entities to build large documents from smaller parts

◆ How to attributes describe data

◆ How to use international characters like ζ and √ in your documents

◆ How to connect documents with XLinks and XPointers

◆ How to push Web sites with CDF

◆ How to develop a DTD from scratch

By the time you finish, you're ready to use XML to create compelling Web pages.

About This Book

Part 1: XML Basics

Part I introduces the purpose, structure, and syntax of XML and its associated style sheet language, XSL. Chapter 1, Introducing XML, provides you with the history and theory behind XML, the goals of XML, and some of XML's intriguing uses and applications. Chapter 2, Beginning XML, shows you some simple XML documents and teaches you how to write them with a text editor, how to render them into HTML, and how to serve them from a Web server. Chapter 3, Formalizing XML, discusses how XML gets its power through simplicity and extensibility – not a plethora of tags. XML predefines almost no tags at all, enabling you instead to define your own tags as needed. Chapter 4, XSL, focuses on how you present data with XSL style sheets, which describe how individual elements in your document should be formatted. This chapter shows how to use style sheets to provide custom appearances that unify a Web site's look and feel.

Part II: Advanced XML

Part II takes you beyond the basics to document type definitions (DTDs), international text, and the Extensible Linking Language (XLL). Chapter 5, Using DTDs in XML Documents, explores XML as a metamarkup language, which is defined via a document type definition. In this chapter, you learn how to design and create new markup languages for use in specialized domains such as music, mathematics, astronomy, electronics, genealogy, and any other field you can imagine. Chapter 6, Assembling Documents from Multiple Data Sources, shows you how a single XML document may draw both data and declarations from many different source entities and entity references. Chapter 7, Describing Elements with Attributes, shows you how to use and declare XML attributes inside XML tags. Attributes are intended for extra information associated with an element (like an ID number) used only by programs that read and write the file, not for the element content read and written by humans. Chapter 8, International Character Sets, explores how to write XML documents in languages other than English, how international text is represented in computer applications, how XML understands text, and how you can take advantage of the software you have to read and write in languages other than English. Chapter 9, XLinks and XPointers, introduces XLL (the eXtensible Linking Language), a new means of linking between documents. XLinks and XPointers transcend HTML's URL-based hyperlinks and anchors to provide additional features.

Part III: Practical XML

Part III introduces you to two practical uses of XML in different domains: Webcasting (a.k.a. push) and genealogy. Chapter 10, Pushing Web Sites with CDF, explores Microsoft's Channel Definition Format (CDF), which is an XML-based markup language for defining channels. This chapter also shows you how to convert your Web sites to CDF channels. Chapter 11, Developing a DTD from Scratch, leads you through the gradual development of several DTDs used for genealogical data. Along the way, you learn how to use XML tags as well as why and when to choose them.

Quick Reference

The Quick Reference provides a brief but complete list of all the various XML keywords and syntax used to construct prologs and DTDs. Use this section to look for the exact syntax of a tag.

Appendixes

Finally, four appendixes collect assorted useful material that doesn't fit into the main body of the book. Appendix A, International Text, contains detailed information about various different international character sets and their use in XML. Appendix B, The XML Specification, contains the complete XML 1.0 specification as published by the W3C. Appendix C, Additional Resources, suggests some resources for further exploration of XML, including mailing lists, specifications, and software. Appendix D, About the CD-ROM, describes the contents of the CD-ROM.

How to Use This Book

This book is designed to be read in sequence. Each chapter builds on the material in the previous chapters. Of course, you're always welcome to skim over familiar material.

I also hope you stop along the way to try some of the examples and write your own XML documents. You learn not just by reading, but also by doing.

Before you get started, please note the following grammatical conventions used in this book.

Unlike HTML, XML is case-sensitive. `<FATHER>` is not the same as `<Father>` or `<father>`. The father element is not the same as the Father element or the FATHER element. Unfortunately, case-sensitive markup languages have an annoying habit of conflicting with standard English usage. On rare occasion, you may encounter sentences that don't begin with a capital letter. More commonly, you'll see unexpected capitalization used in the middle of a sentence. Please don't be troubled by these instances – context usually explains the unusual capitalization.

Contacting Me

If you discover an error in this book or you would like to contact me about XML, send an e-mail to `elharo@sunsite.unc.edu`. You can also visit my Web site at `http://sunsite.unc.edu/xml//`.

Acknowledgments

The folks at IDG Books Worldwide have all been great. The acquisitions editor, John Osborn, deserves special thanks for arranging the unusual scheduling required to hit the moving target of XML. Denise Santoro shepherded this book through the development process. With poise and grace, she managed the constantly shifting outline and schedule required by a book based on unstable specifications and software. Copy editor Eric Hahn corrected many of my grammatical errors. Project coordinator Ritchie Durdin also deserves special thanks for putting up with the book's crazy schedule. Steven Champeon brought his SGML experience to the book and provided many insightful comments on the text.

WandaJane Phillips wrote the original draft of Chapter 10 on CDF and was instrumental in helping me almost meet my deadline. (Blame for the *almost* rests on my shoulders, not hers.) My brother Thomas Harold put his command of chemistry at my disposal when I was trying to grasp the Chemical Markup Language. Carroll Bellau provided me with parts of my family tree in Chapters 9 and 11, as well as some fascinating stories about my great-great-grandmother Domeniquette Baudean.

David and Sherry Rogelberg of the Studio B Literary Agency (`http://www.studiob.com/`) have been instrumental in making it feasible for me to be a full-time writer. I recommend them highly to anyone thinking about writing computer books.

As always, thanks go to my wife Beth for love and understanding throughout.

Contents at a Glance

Appendixes

Contents

Appendixes

Part I

XML Basics

Chapter 1

Introducing XML

IN THIS CHAPTER

- ◆ What is XML?
- ◆ Why is XML?
- ◆ The history of XML
- ◆ XML programs
- ◆ Related technologies
- ◆ XML applications

THIS FIRST CHAPTER introduces you to XML and some of its intriguing uses and applications. You learn how XML can be used for such diverse areas as chemistry, mathematics, push, multimedia arrangements, and more.

What Is XML?

XML stands for Extensible Markup Language (often misspelled as eXtensible Markup Language to justify the acronym). XML is a set of rules for forming semantic tags that break a document into parts and identify the different parts of the document.

XML Is a Metamarkup Language

XML isn't just another markup language like HTML or troff, which define a fixed set of tags describing a fixed number of elements. If your markup language of choice doesn't contain the tag you want or need, you're pretty much out of luck. You can wait for the next version of the markup language and hope that it includes the necessary tags, but you're really at the mercy of what vendors choose to include and support.

XML, however, is a metamarkup language, in which you make up the tags you need as you go along. These tags must be organized according to certain general principles, but they're quite flexible in their meaning. For instance, if you're working on genealogy and need to describe people, births, deaths, burial sites, families, marriages, divorces, and so forth, you can create tags for each of these elements. You don't have to try to force them to fit into paragraphs, list items, strong emphasis, or other very general categories.

The tags you create can be documented in a Document Type Definition (DTD). You learn more about DTDs in Part II of this book. For now, however, think of a DTD as a vocabulary and a syntax for certain kinds of documents. For example, Peter Murray-Rust's MOL.DTD describes a vocabulary and a syntax for the molecular sciences: chemistry, crystallography, solid state physics, and the like. This DTD can be shared and used by many different people in the field. Other DTDs are available for other disciplines, and you can create your own DTDs.

You may think that this approach is a nice idea in theory, but that in practice it's unlikely that Netscape and Internet Explorer will support thousands of different languages. The strength of XML, however, appears precisely when used as the template for these languages. XML defines a metasyntax that specific markup languages like CML, MathML, and others must follow. If an application understands this metasyntax, it automatically understands all languages built from this metalanguage.

A browser does not need to hard code each and every tag that may be used by thousands of different languages. Instead, the browser discovers the tags used by any given document as it reads the document or its DTD. The detailed instructions about how to render those tags are provided in a style sheet that's attached to the document.

For example, consider Schrodinger's equation:

$$i\hbar \frac{\partial \psi(r,t)}{\partial t} = -\frac{\hbar^2}{2m} \frac{\partial^2 \psi(r,t)}{\partial x^2} + V(r)\psi(r,t)$$

Scientific papers are full of these equations, but scientists have been waiting eight years for browser vendors to support tags needed to write such equations. Musicians are in a similar fix — Netscape and Internet Explorer don't support sheet music.

XML means you don't have to wait for the browser vendors to catch up with your ideas. You can invent the tags you need when you need them and tell the browsers how to display those tags.

XML Is a Semantic/Structured Markup Language

XML describes a document's structure and meaning. It does not describe the formatting of the elements on the page. Formatting can be added to documents through style sheets, but the document itself only contains tags that describe the contents of the document, not the appearance of the document.

By contrast, HTML encompasses both formatting, structural, and semantic tags. <B> is a formatting tag that makes its content bold. <STRONG> is a semantic tag that means its contents should be strongly emphasized. <TD> indicates that the contents are part of a table structure. In fact, some tags can have all three kinds of meaning. An <H1> header can mean the title of the page as well as "20 point Helvetica bold."

For example, a book in a list (you'll encounter this example in following chapters) could look like the following in HTML:

```
<dt>Java Secrets
<dd> by Elliotte Rusty Harold
<ul>
<li>Publisher: IDG Books Worldwide
<li>ISBN: 0-764-58007-8
<li>Pages: 900
<li>Price: $59.99
<li>Publication Date: May, 1997
<li>Bottom Line: Buy It
</ul><P>
The Java virtual machine, byte code, the sun packages, native
 methods, stand-alone applications, and a few more naughty bits.<P>
```

The book is described using a definition title, definition data, an unordered list, list items, and paragraphs. None of these elements have anything to do with a book. In XML, the same data could look as follows:

```
<book>
  <title>Java Secrets</title>
  <author>Elliotte Rusty Harold</author>
  <publisher>IDG Books Worldwide</publisher>
  <isbn>0-764-58007-8</isbn>
  <pages>900</pages>
  <price>59.99</price>
  <publication_date>May, 1997</publication_date>
  <recommendation>Buy It</recommendation>
  <blurb>
    The Java virtual machine, byte code, the sun packages, native
methods, stand-alone applications, and a few more naughty bits.
  </blurb>
</book>
```

Instead of generic tags like <dt> and <li>, this listing uses meaningful tags like <book>, <title>, <author>, and <price>. This approach has a number of advantages, not the least of which is that it's somewhat easier for a human reading the source code to determine exactly what the author intended.

XML markup also makes it easier for nonhuman, automated robots to locate all the books in the document. In HTML, robots cannot ascertain more than that an element is a <dt> — they have no means of determining whether <dt> represents a book title, a definition, or a designer's favorite means of indenting text. Indeed, a single document may contain <dt> elements with all three meanings.

XML element names can be organized to have extra meaning in additional contexts. For example, they may be the field names of a database. Not requiring a few fixed tags to serve all uses (as in HTML) makes XML far more flexible and amenable to varied uses.

Why Is XML?

Why are people excited about XML? What can you do with XML that you can't easily do with existing technology? Because of the X in XML (eXtensible), there are many different reasons why people like it. Which ones interest you depends on your needs. But once you learn XML, you're likely to find it as the solution to more than one problem with which you're already struggling.

This section investigates some of the generic uses to which XML can be put. Later, you'll see some of the specific applications already developed with XML.

Domain Specific Markup Language

By allowing professions to develop their own common markup languages, XML enables individuals in the field to trade notes, data, and information without worrying about whether the person on the receiving end has the particular proprietary payware used to create the data. They can even send documents to people outside the profession with a reasonable confidence that they can at least view (even if not understand) the document.

This process can take place without creating bloatware or unnecessary complexity for those outside the profession. You may not be interested in a general way of describing electrical engineering diagrams, but electrical engineers are. You may not need to include sheet music in your Web pages, but composers do. XML lets the electrical engineers describe their circuits and the musicians notate their scores without (for the most part) stepping on each other's toes. Neither field needs special support from the browser manufacturers or complicated plug-ins as is now the case.

Common Data Format

A lot of computer data from the last forty years is irretrievably lost — not because of natural disaster or decaying backup media (though those are problems too, ones XML doesn't solve) — but simply because nobody bothered to document how one reads the data media and formats. A Lotus 1-2-3 file on a ten-year-old 5 ¼-inch floppy disk may be effectively irretrievable in most corporations today without a huge investment of time and resources. Data in a less-known binary format like Lotus Jazz may be gone forever.

At a low level, XML is an incredibly simple data format. XML can be written in 100 percent pure ASCII text as well as a few other well-defined formats. ASCII is reasonably resistant to corruption. Removing bytes or even large sequences of bytes does not noticeably corrupt the rest of the text. This starkly contrasts with many other formats, such as compressed data or serialized Java objects, where corruption or loss of even a single byte can render the entire remainder of the file unreadable.

Furthermore, XML is well-documented. The W3C's XML specification and numerous paper books (such as this one) tell you exactly how to read XML data. There are no secrets waiting to trip up the unwary.

At a higher level, XML is self-describing. Suppose you're an information archaeologist in the 23rd century and you encounter this chunk of XML code on an old floppy disk that has survived the ravages of time:

```
<person id="p1100" sex="M">
  <name>
    <given>Judson</given>
    <surname> McDaniel</surname>
  </name>
  <birth>
    <date>21 Feb 1834</date>  </birth>
  <death>
    <date>9 Dec 1905</date>  </death>
</person>
```

Even if you're not familiar with XML you can tell this data describes a man named Judson McDaniel who was born on February 21, 1834 and died on December 9, 1905. In fact, even with gaps in or corruption of the data, you could still probably extract most of this information. The same cannot be said for most proprietary spreadsheet or word processor formats.

Data Interchange

Because XML is easy to understand, nonproprietary, and easy to read and write, it's an excellent format for interchange of data between different applications. One such format under development is the Open Financial Exchange Format (OFX). OFX is designed to let personal finance programs like Microsoft Money and Quicken trade data. The data can be sent back and forth between programs and exchanged with banks, brokerage houses, and so forth.

XML is a nonproprietary format unencumbered by copyright, patent, trade secret, or any other sort of intellectual property restriction. While designed to be very expressive, XML is also easy for both human beings and computer programs to read and write. Thus, it's an obvious choice for these exchange languages.

XML helps users avoid getting locked into particular programs simply because their data is already written in such a program, or because a correspondent only accepts that program's proprietary format. In computer book publishing, most publishers require submissions in Microsoft Word. As a result, most computer book authors have to use Word, even if they would rather use WordPerfect or Nisus Writer. It's extremely difficult for other companies to gain market share unless they can read and write Word files. Reverse engineering the undocumented Word file format is a significant investment of limited time and resources. Most other word processors have a limited ability to read and write Word files, but generally lose track of styles, revision marks, and other important features. Because Word's document format is undocumented, proprietary, and constantly changing, Word tends to end up winning by default, even when writers would prefer to use other, simpler programs. If a common word processing format was developed in XML, writers could use their program of choice rather than the program required by their publisher.

Structured Data

XML is ideal for large and complex documents. It not only lets you specify a vocabulary for the document, but also lets you specify the relations between elements. For example, if you're putting together a Web page of sales contacts, you can require that every contact has a phone number and an e-mail address. If you're inputting data for a database, you can make sure that no fields are missing. You can require that every book have an author. You can even provide default values to be used when no data is entered.

XML also provides a client-side include mechanism that can integrate data from multiple sources and display it as a single document. The data can even be rearranged on the fly. Parts of the data can be shown or hidden depending on user actions. This is all extremely useful when you work with large information repositories like relational databases.

A Brief History of XML

Like many standards, XML grew out of a lot of places around the same time. It's difficult to point to one person or time and say, "This is where XML started." Nonetheless, XML clearly has two main predecessors: SGML and HTML. Both were very successful markup languages, and HTML is probably the most widely used markup language in history. Nonetheless, both SGML and HTML have painfully obvious shortcomings, and a new approach was needed to combine their strengths without their limitations – XML.

The first impetus for XML was SGML, the Standard Generalized Markup Language. SGML is an international standard for semantic tagging of documents that's been around for a little over a decade. SGML is intended for semantic markup that assists computer cataloging and indexing, and can be extended in an infinite variety of ways to handle new data formats.

SGML is popular in the defense sector and various other industries that need to deal with large quantities of highly structured data. SGML is unbelievably complex, however, not to mention expensive. For instance, the standard version of Adobe FrameMaker costs about $850. Adobe FrameMaker+SGML starts at $1995 (I didn't omit a decimal point – that's one thousand, nine hundred, and ninety-five dollars), and that's one of the cheaper pieces of SGML software. SGML document management software routinely breaks into tens of thousands of dollars or more. Although SGML has its advantages, it is too complex and expensive for someone who wants to put their family tree on the Internet.

The second pot of soil out of which XML grew was HTML. Invented by Tim Berners-Lee at CERN in 1990, HTML was designed as a simple replacement for SGML that could be comprehended by mere mortals and written without the assistance of expensive authoring tools. It succeeded beyond his wildest expectations.

Unfortunately, HTML didn't scale very well. First of all, it was limited to a small fixed set of tags like <P>, <STRONG>, and <TITLE>. If the author needed a <BOOK>, <FATHER>, or <MOLECULE> tag, they were out of luck. HTML lacked the flexibility and adaptability of SGML.

In the early '90s, Marc Andreesen, Eric Bina, and a few others invented Mosaic at the University of Illinois, where they were working as cheap labor at NCSA for a few dollars an hour. Along the way, they added support for an <IMG> tag to HTML, and the Web took off. A couple of years later, Andreesen, Bina, and others, now at Netscape, began adding tags to Navigator at a furious rate, all of which became de facto standards with every new beta release. Throughout this process, however, no one worried about maintaining HTML's purity as an SGML application. In particular, semantic markup tags like <CODE>, <H1>, and <TABLE> were freely intermingled with stylistic markup tags like <CENTER>, <I>, and the notorious <BLINK>.

By 1996, the semantic roots of HTML had been thoroughly subverted by the needs of graphic designers. HTML tags no longer described the meaning of their content, but rather how the content would look when displayed by a Web browser. This approach posed significant challenges for indexing robots, disabled access, and many other uses. Interestingly these were all problems that SGML had solved years ago. At this point SGML user group meetings began to degenerate into long sour grapes sessions about how badly HTML sucked. Still SGML remained far too complicated and expensive for most uses.

In late 1994 and through 1995, Web sites began to grow. Old guard media companies like Time Warner and startups like c|net started to work on public Web sites on a previously unseen scale. Employees at large companies began putting more of their internal documents on private Web servers on the company LAN, simply because it was easier than distributing it on paper or in proprietary systems like Lotus Notes.

As these sites grew to hundreds of thousands of pages, many companies found themselves using large relational databases like Informix or Oracle to store Web content, which was then poured into templates using custom tags. Smaller sites began using products like Frontier or Cold Fusion to complete similar tasks. In essence, many different companies in different industries were growing into the realm where SGML-like solutions made sense, and they were all, more or less independently, reinventing their own version of SGML. In addition, these companies were paying tens of thousands of dollars or more to do this. Obviously, a new approach was needed.

Jon Bosak of Sun Microsystems started the W3C SGML working group (now called the XML working group) in the summer of 1996. The goal of the group was to create a sort of SGML lite that would bring SGML's strengths to the Web while still maintaining HTML's simplicity. Eventually, this goal would come to be called XML, though there were various arguments about the name. Other suggestions included MAGMA (Minimal Architecture for Generalized Markup Applications), SLIM (Structured Language for Internet Markup) and MGML (Minimal Generalized Markup Language) — in a few cases, the acronym seems to be more important than the full name.

XML is supposed to be a sort of SGML lite that retains the power and extensibility of SGML while being simple and cheap enough for mere mortals. To a large extent, this goal has been achieved. In regards to simplicity, the XML specification is an order of magnitude or more smaller than the SGML specification. In regard to power, there is little that can be done with SGML that can't be done with XML. In regard to cost, many free tools are already available for working with XML, with more anticipated soon. And Adobe has announced intentions to add XML support to FrameMaker — including the cheaper version.

Tim Bray was a prime mover in the development of XML and one of the two primary authors of the XML 1.0 specification. Bray had spent several happy years at "the best job in the world" managing the New Oxford English Dictionary Project. His experience with the OED informed his work on XML. In essence, he was trying to invent the markup language he wished he had back in 1987 when starting work on the OED. In particular, Bray wanted the following:

◆ a language simple enough for programmers to implement

◆ a language not limited to U.S. English

◆ documents easy for search engines to index

Tim Bray and C. M. Sperberg-McQueen of the University of Illinois wrote most of the original XML specification document. Many others contributed in one way or another.

A number of projects to produce markup languages for the Web for specialized domains occurred concurrently with the development of the official XML specification. The problems encountered by these languages heavily influenced XML's development. Peter Murray-Rust invented CML, the Chemical Markup Language, and the first general-purpose XML browser, Jumbo. At first, CML was supposed to be an SGML application, but it gradually transitioned to XML. Representatives of various companies involved in computer mathematics including Wolfram, IBM, Design Science, Waterloo Maple, the Geometry Center, and others contributed to the development of MathML for embedding mathematical equations in Web pages.

In November 1996, the first official draft specification for XML 1.0 was published, with numerous revisions over the next year.

April 1997 saw the first draft specification of XLL, the eXtensible Linking Language, primarily written by Eve Maler of ArborText and Steve DeRose of Inso Corp. and Brown University. Eve was also a major contributor to XML 1.0. XLL and its successors, XLink and XPointer, are discussed in Chapter 9. When fully implemented, XLL will allow more sophisticated and powerful linking than can be achieved with HTML and current browsers.

In July 1997, Microsoft released one of the first real applications of XML: the Channel Definition Format (CDF) for pushing Web pages to subscribers. CDF is part of Internet Explorer 4.0 and is discussed further in Chapter 10.

Because XML is purely a structural and semantic format, some means is needed of describing the formatting of individual elements. One possibility is HTML's cascading style sheets. Another possibility, first introduced by Microsoft and Inso Corporation in August 1997, is XSL (eXtensible Style Language), which is introduced in Chapter 2 and explored thoroughly in Chapter 4.

In January 1998, Microsoft released the MSXSL processor, a free tool used extensively in this book for combining XML documents with XSL style sheets to produce HTML pages that can be viewed in standard browsers like Netscape or Internet Explorer 4.0. Future versions of these browsers should be able to view XML files directly without the need for an intermediate conversion step.

In February 1998, the W3C gave its official stamp of approval to Version 1.0 of the XML specification. This book is based upon Version 1.0. Other projects, including further development of XSL and XLL, are moving forward with new projects on the horizon.

An XML-Data proposal has been submitted to the W3C to provide for more structured data with which both object-oriented programmers and relational database aficionados are comfortable. The inclusion of a namespace mechanism that enables different DTDs to merge without conflicts is now a virtual certainty.

In late March 1998, Netscape shocked the XML world by not only releasing the source code for Mozilla 5.0 but also including more support for XML than expected. The XML community has already begun tinkering with the code, and exciting developments are sure to come by the time you're holding this book.

Third parties are busy as well, building the tools that enable new sorts of XML-based applications. Scripting gurus Dave Winer and Larry Wall are rearchitecting Frontier and Perl, respectively, to work with XML. Microsoft may make XML the native format for future versions of Word.

XML is gathering steam and is likely to take off as soon as the first stable version of Netscape 5.0 is released, which may be in your hands by the time you read this book. At the same time, a lot is already known about XML, and you can get a good seat on the XML train by boarding it now. As you'll see throughout this book, you can gain a lot by writing your Web pages in XML, even if you have to convert them to HTML before posting them.

XML Programs

At the root, XML is a document format. It is a series of rules about what structures and text may appear in an XML document. The two levels of conformity to the XML standard are: well-formedness and validity. Part I of this book shows you how to write well-formed documents, while Part II shows you how to write valid documents. Part III shows you some applications of XML.

HTML is a document format designed for use on the Internet and inside Web browsers. XML can certainly be used for these purposes, as this book demonstrates. However, XML lends itself to far more general uses. It can be a storage format for word processors, a data interchange format for different programs, a means of enforcing conformity with intranet templates, and a way to preserve data in a human readable fashion.

Like all data formats, however, XML needs programs and content before it becomes useful. Thus, this book doesn't just discuss XML itself, which is little more than a specification for how data should be arranged. This book also discusses the programs you use to read and write data, and the content stored in XML. To understand XML, you also need to understand these.

XML documents are commonly created with an editor. This may be a basic text editor like Notepad or emacs that doesn't understand XML. It may be a WYSIWYG editor like Adobe FrameMaker that insulates you almost completely from the details of the underlying XML format. It may be something in between like JUMBO. For the most part, the fancy editors aren't useful yet, so this book concentrates on writing raw XML by hand in a text editor.

Other programs may also create XML documents. For example, Chapter 11 displays XML data straight from a FileMaker database. In this case, the data was first entered into the FileMaker database. Then, a FileMaker calculation field converted that data to XML. In general, XML works extremely well with databases.

In any case, the editor or other program creates an XML document. More often than not, this document is an actual file on some computer's hard disk, but this arrangement is not required. For example, the document may be a record or a field in a database or a stream of bytes received from a network.

An XML processor reads the document and verifies that the document's XML is well-formed. The processor may also check the validity of the document, though this test is not required. The exact details of these tests are covered in Chapter 3 and Chapters 5–8, respectively. Assuming the document passes the tests, the processor converts the document into a tree of elements.

Finally, the processor passes the tree or individual nodes of the tree to the end application. This application may be a browser like Netscape or another program that understands the data. A browser will display the data to the user. Other programs may also receive the data. For instance, the data may be interpreted as input to a database, a series of musical notes to play, or a Java program that should be launched. XML is extremely flexible and can be used for many different purposes.

All of these steps are independent and decoupled from each other. The XML document is the only connection between them. You can change the editor program independently of the end application. In fact, you may not always know what the end application is. It may be an end user reading your work, a database sucking in data, or an unknown future application. The data format is independent of the programs that read it.

HTML is also somewhat independent of the programs that read and write it, but it's really only suitable for browsing. Other uses, like database input, are outside its scope because HTML provides no way to force an author to include certain required content. For example, in HTML you have no way of requiring that every book has an ISBN number. In XML you can require this. You can even enforce the order in which particular elements appear. For example, you can require that <H2> headers must always follow <H1> headers.

Related Technologies

XML doesn't operate in a vacuum. Using XML as more than a data format requires interaction with a number of related standards. These standards include HTML for backward compatibility with legacy browsers; the CSS and XSL style sheet languages; URLs and URIs; the XLL linking language; and the Unicode character set.

HTML

Although Mozilla 5.0 provides some support for XML in the browser and Internet Explorer 4.0 includes code that can be used from inside a Java applet or a JavaScript program, neither is likely to be ready for prime time anytime soon. Furthermore, even when browsers are released with full and complete support for XML, it takes about two years before most users have upgraded to a particular release of the software. (In early 1998, my wife is still using Netscape 1.1.) Thus, you're going to need to convert your XML content into classic HTML for some time to come.

As a result, you should be completely comfortable with HTML before jumping into XML. You don't need to be a snazzy graphical designer, but you should know how to link from one page to the next, how to include an image in a document, how to make text bold, and so forth. Because HTML is the common output format of XML, a command of HTML leads to easier creation of desired effects.

On the other hand, if you're accustomed to using tables or single-pixel GIFs to arrange objects on a page, or if you begin a Web site by sketching out its appearance rather than its content, you need to unlearn some bad habits. XML separates the content of a document from the appearance of the document. The content is developed first, and then a format is attached to that content with a style sheet. Separating content from style is an extremely effective technique that improves both the content and the appearance of the document. Among other results, this approach increasingly enables authors and designers to work independently of each other. However, it does require a different way of thinking about the design of a Web site, and perhaps even different project management techniques when multiple people are involved.

CSS

Since XML allows essentially arbitrary tags to be included in a document, the browser cannot know in advance how each tag should appear. When you send a document to a user, you also need to send along a style sheet that tells the browser how to format individual elements. The first kind of style sheet you can use is a Cascading Style Sheet (CSS).

CSS was initially designed for HTML, but it works equally well with XML. CSS defines properties such as font size, font family, font weight, paragraph indentation, paragraph alignment, and other styles applied to particular tags. For example, CSS allows HTML documents to specify that all <H1> elements are formatted in 32 point centered Helvetica bold. Individual styles can be applied to most HTML tags that override the browser's defaults. Multiple style sheets can be applied to a single document, and multiple styles can be applied to a single element. The styles then cascade according to a particular set of rules. CSS style sheets and properties will be explored in detail in Chapter 4.

Applying CSS rules to XML documents is not hard either. Simply change the names of the tags to which you're applying the rules. Mozilla 5.0 directly supports CSS style sheets combined with XML documents, though at the time of this writing it crashes frequently.

XSL

The eXtensible Style Language, XSL for short, is a more advanced style sheet language specifically designed for use with XML documents. XSL documents are themselves well-formed XML documents.

XSL documents contain a series of rules that apply to particular patterns of XML elements. When a pattern is found, the rule outputs some combination of text. Unlike Cascading Style Sheets, this output text is close to arbitrary and not limited to the text of the element plus formatting information.

CSS can only change the format of a particular element on an element-wide basis. XSL style sheets can rearrange and reorder elements; they can hide some elements and display others. Furthermore, XSL style sheets can choose the style to use not only based on the tag, but also on the contents and attributes of the tag, the position of the tag in the document and relative to other elements, and a variety of other criteria. You can even include JavaScript in XSL style sheets that reformats the data or evaluates expressions.

Although CSS has the advantage of broader browser support, XSL is far more flexible and powerful, and better suited to XML documents. Because XML documents with XSL style sheets can be easily converted to HTML documents with CSS style sheets, this book focuses its attention on XSL. XSL style sheets are introduced in Chapter 2 and explored in great detail in Chapter 4.

URLs and URIs

XML documents can live on the Web just like HTML and other documents. On the Web, XML documents are referred to by URLs, just like HTML files (for example, `http://sunsite.unc.edu/xml/books.xml`).

Most of the XML specifications refer to URIs rather than the more familiar URLs. URI stands for Uniform Resource Identifier. URIs are a slightly more general scheme for locating resources on the Internet that focuses a little more on the resource and a little less on the location. In theory, a URI could find the closest copy of a mirrored document or locate a document moved from one site to another. In practice, URIs are still an area of active research – the only kinds of URIs actually supported by current software are URLs.

Linking

As long as XML documents are posted on the Internet, you're going to want to be able to address them and link between them. Although XML permits standard HTML link tags, XML lets you go further with XLL, the eXtensible Linking Language. XLL is divided into two parts: XLinks for linking and XPointers for addressing individual parts of a document.

XLinks allow any element to become a link, not just a single tag. Furthermore, links can be bidirectional, multidirectional, or even point to multiple mirror sites from which the closest is selected. XLinks use normal URLs to identify the site they're linking to.

XPointers are a means of linking not just to a particular document at a particular location, but to a particular part of a particular document. An XPointer can refer to a particular element of a document; to the first, the second, or the seventeenth such element; to the first element that's a child of a given element; and so forth. XPointers provide extremely powerful connections between documents without requiring the targeted document to contain additional markup just so its individual pieces can be linked.

Furthermore, unlike HTML anchors, XPointers don't just refer to a point in a document. They can point to ranges or spans. Thus, an XPointer may be used to select a particular part of a document, so that it can be copied or loaded into a program, for example.

Chapter 9 discusses XLinks and XPointers.

Unicode

Although the Web is international, most of its text is English. XML is starting to change that. XML provides full support for the two-byte Unicode character set, as well as its more compact representations. This character set supports almost every character commonly used in every modern script on Earth.

Unfortunately, XML alone is not enough. You need three things to read a script:

1. A character set for the script

2. A font for the character set

3. An operating system and application software that understands the character set

If you want to write in the script as well as read it, you also need an input method for the script. For limited use, however, XML defines character references that enable you to use pure ASCII to encode characters not available in your native character set.

Chapter 8 explores how international text is represented in computers, how XML understands text, and how you can take advantage of the available software to read and write in languages other than English.

XML Applications

As discussed in the preceding section, XML is designed to enable the creation of markup languages in a variety of disciplines that can be read and understood by standard tools. These markup languages are called *XML applications.*

 You'd probably expect an XML application to be a piece of software like Netscape, MSXML, or JUMBO that edits, validates, browses, or somehow works with XML documents — but the convention is that the words *XML application* do mean a markup language for a specific domain written according to the constraints of XML. Think of "XML application" as shorthand for "an application of XML to a particular domain."

Each XML application has its own syntax and vocabulary that adheres to the fundamental rules of XML. This situation mirrors human language, where many different languages each have their own vocabularies and grammar, but nonetheless all languages adhere to certain rules imposed by human anatomy and the structure of the brain. This book examines the underlying rules that all XML-based languages follow and a few specific examples of XML applications.

To this end, it's inspiring to look at some of the uses of XML, even in the early stage of its development. These examples give you some idea of the wide applicability of XML. Many more applications are being created or ported from other formats during the writing of this book.

Chemical Markup Language

Peter Murray-Rust's Chemical Markup Language (CML) may be the first XML application. CML was originally developed as an SGML application, and gradually transitioned to XML as the XML standard developed.

CML is an approach to managing chemical information with XML/SGML tools and Java. Molecular documents often contain thousands of different objects in a very detailed fashion. CML handles these objects in a straightforward manner that can be easily indexed and searched by a computer. CML can be used to describe complex molecular structures and sequences, spectrographic analysis, crystallography, publishing, chemical databases, and so forth. Its vocabulary includes molecules, atoms, bonds, crystals, formulas, sequences, symmetries, reactions, and other items from chemistry. CML is also intended to send complex data over the Web. Since the underlying XML is platform-independent, the problem of platform dependency that plagues common binary formats used in the molecular sciences is avoided.

Professor Murray-Rust also created JUMBO, the first general-purpose XML browser. Figure 1-1 shows Version 1 of JUMBO displaying a CML file.

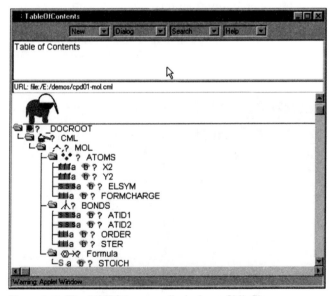

Figure 1-1: The JUMBO browser displaying a CML file

Mathematical Markup Language

Legend claims that Tim Berners-Lee invented the World Wide Web and HTML at CERN so high-energy physicists could exchange papers and preprints. Personally, I've never believed that story. I grew up in physics; while I've wandered back and forth between physics, applied math, astronomy, and computer science over the years, papers in all these disciplines contained lots of equations. Until now, seven years after the Web was invented, there hasn't been any good way to include equations in Web pages.

There have been a few hacks — Java applets that parse a custom syntax, converters that turn LaTeX equations into GIF images, custom browsers that read TeX files — but none of these attempts have produced high-quality results or caught on with Web authors, even in scientific fields. With MathML, however, this predicament is starting to change.

MathML, the Mathematical Markup Language, is an XML application for including equations in Web pages. MathML is sufficiently expressive to handle almost all math from grammar school arithmetic through calculus and differential equations. It can handle more advanced topics as well, though there are definite gaps in some of the more advanced and obscure notations used by certain subfields of mathematics. While MathML has limitations on the high end of pure mathematics and theoretical physics, it is sufficiently expressive to handle almost all educational, scientific, engineering, business, economics, and statistics needs. In addition, MathML is likely to be expanded in the future, so even the purest of the pure mathematicians and the most theoretical of the theoretical physicists can publish their research on the Web. MathML finishes the evolution of the Web into a serious tool for scientific research and communication (despite its long digression as a new medium for advertising brochures). Figure 1-2 shows Maxwell's equations in the W3C's test-bed Web browser, Amaya. You can find out more about MathML and download Amaya from the W3C Web site at http://www.w3.org/.

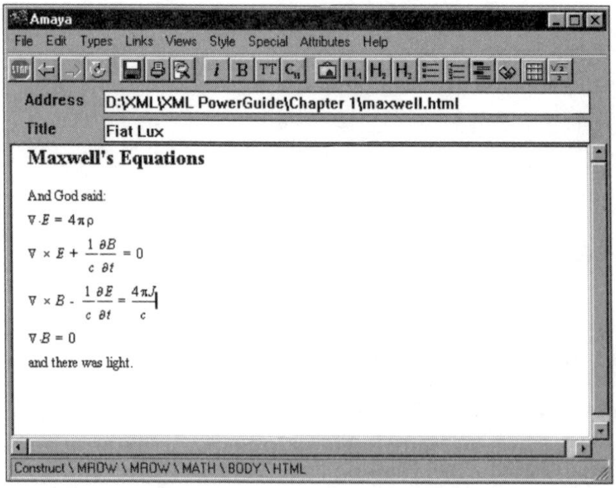

Figure 1-2: The AMAYA browser displaying Maxwell's equations written in MathML

Microsoft's Channel Definition Format

Microsoft's Channel Definition Format (CDF) is an XML-based markup language for defining channels. Channels allow Web sites to notify readers of changes to critical information automatically. Similar to subscription services, this method is alternately called Webcasting or push. CDF was first introduced in Internet Explorer 4.0.

A CDF file is an XML document separate from (but linked to) the HTML documents in a site. The channel defined in the CDF document establishes the parameters for a connection between the readers and the content on the site. The data can be transferred through push (sending notifications or whole Web sites to registered readers) or through pull (readers choose to load the page in their Web browser and get the update information).

Because the CDF file is simply an addition to the site, you don't need to rewrite your site to take advantage of CDF. A link to a CDF file on your Web page downloads a copy of the channel index to the reader's machine. This link enables the reader to access the current data, as defined in the channel, with a click on an icon. Figure 1-3 shows the IDG Active Channel in Internet Explorer 4.0. Chapter 10 explores channels and CDF in depth.

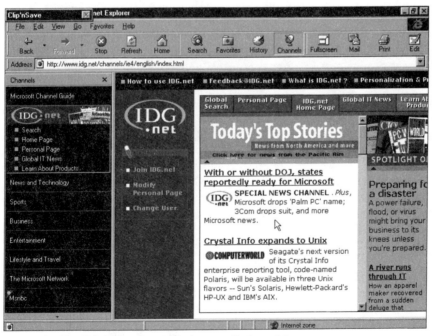

Figure 1-3: The IDG Active Channel in Internet Explorer 4.0

Classic Literature

Jon Bosak has translated the complete plays of Shakespeare into XML. The complete text of the plays is included, but XML markup distinguishes between titles, subtitles, stage directions, speeches, lines, speakers, and so forth.

What does this system offer over a book or even a plain text file? To a human reader, the answer is not much. To a computer doing textual analysis, however, it offers the opportunity to easily distinguish between the different elements into which the plays have been divided. For instance, this system makes it simple to extract all lines spoken by Romeo in *Romeo and Juliet.*

Furthermore, by altering the style sheet with which the document is formatted, actors can easily print a version of the script with their lines in bold face and the preceding and following lines in italics. Other tasks requiring the separation of plays into the lines uttered by different speakers are more easily accomplished with the XML-formatted versions than with the raw text.

Bosak also marked up English translations of the Old and New Testaments, the Koran, and the Book of Mormon. The markup in these texts is a little different. For instance, the markup doesn't distinguish between speakers. Thus, you couldn't use these particular XML documents to create a red letter Bible, for example, though a different set of tags could help in that project. (A red letter Bible prints words spoken by Jesus in red.) Because these files are in English, rather than the original languages, they're not as useful for scholarly textual analysis. Still, time and resources permitting, these projects show the breadth of capabilities with XML. You simply need to invent a different vocabulary and syntax than the Bosak configuration to describe the same data. You can retrieve these documents from `http://sunsite.unc.edu/pub/sun-info/standards/xml/eg/`.

Synchronized Multimedia Integration Language (SMIL)

SMIL (pronounced smile) is a W3C-standard XML application for writing TV-like multimedia presentations for the World Wide Web. SMIL documents don't describe the actual multimedia content (that is, the videos and sound files played) but instead describe when and where the content is played.

For instance, a typical SMIL document may say that the browser should simultaneously play the sound file `beethoven9.mid`, show the video file `corange.mov`, and display the HTML file `clockwork.htm`. Then, when the browser is done, it should play the video file `2001.mov`, the audio file `zarathustra.mid`, and display the HTML file `aclarke.htm`. The SMIL document eliminates the need to embed low bandwidth data (like text) in high bandwidth data (like video) just to combine the two forms.

Furthermore, in addition to specifying the time sequencing of data, the editor can position the individual graphics elements on the display and attach links to media objects. Concurrently, the text of the respective novels could be subtitling the presentation. You can find out more about SMIL at `http://www.w3.org/AudioVideo/`.

Open Software Description (OSD)

Marimba and Microsoft codeveloped the Open Software Description (OSD) format. Like other XML applications, OSD is a vocabulary and syntax that describes a particular domain. In this case, the domain is software updates.

OSD defines XML tags that describe software components, including their versions, underlying structure, relationships to other components, and dependencies. These descriptions provides enough information for software updates to be pushed to users over CDF channels, rather than requiring them to manually download and install each update. Only information about the update is kept in the CDF file. The actual update files are stored in a separate archive and downloaded when needed.

There is considerable controversy about whether or not this is actually a good approach. Many software companies, including Microsoft, have a long history of releasing updates that cause more problems than they fix. Many users prefer to stay away from new software until more adventurous souls have given it a shakedown.

One Note of Caution

I've outlined a lot of exciting developments in this chapter. Unfortunately, not all of these features are not available yet. In fact, much of this chapter relies on the promise of XML, rather than the current reality.

XML excited lots of people in the software industry, and many programmers are working hard to turn these dreams into reality. New software brings the dream closer to reality every day, but some of the software isn't fully cooked yet. Developing real applications with XML can be like eating raw oysters: tasty, but if you aren't careful, you can catch a nasty case of flesh-eating bacteria.

Throughout the rest of this book, I point out not only what is supposed to happen, but what actually does happen. Depressingly these are all too often not the same. Nonetheless, with a little caution you can do real work right now with XML.

Summary

In this chapter, you learned some of the things XML can do for you. In particular, you learned the following concepts:

- XML is a metamarkup language that allows the creation of markup languages for particular documents and domains.

- XML tags describe the structure and semantics of a document's content, not the format of the content. The format is described by a separate style sheet.

- XML is built on the foundations provided by HTML, Cascading Style Sheets, and URLs.

- XML also introduces XSL style sheets and XLL linking to accomplish more than you can with just CSS and URLs.

- XML grew out of user frustration with the complexity of SGML and the inadequacies of HTML.

- Specific applications of XML have already been developed for chemistry, math, multimedia, and more.

- Be careful. XML isn't completely finished. XML will change and expand, and you will encounter bugs in current XML software.

In the next chapter, you are introduced to the basics of XML. You learn how to write an XML document. You also learn how to add a style sheet to the XML file so that it can be converted to HTML and viewed in any standard Web browser.

Chapter 2

Beginning XML

IN THIS CHAPTER

◆ Creating a simple XML document

◆ Preparing a style sheet for your document

◆ Browsing HTML

◆ Serving straight XML

◆ Working through an XML example

THIS CHAPTER TEACHES you how to create simple XML documents with tags you define that make sense for your document. You learn how to write a style sheet for a document that describes how the content of those tags should be displayed. Finally, you learn how to convert XML documents plus the XSL style sheet into HTML so standard Web browsers can view them.

Because this chapter teaches you by example, not from first principals, it does not cross all the *t*'s and dot all the *i*'s. Experienced readers may notice a few exceptions and special cases that aren't discussed here. Don't worry about these; you'll get to them over the next several chapters. For the most part, you don't need to worry about the technical rules right up front. As with HTML, you can learn and do a lot by copying simple examples that others have prepared and modifying them to fit your needs.

Toward that end, I encourage you to follow along by typing in this chapter's examples and loading them into the different programs I discuss (all of which are included on the CD-ROM). These specific examples give you a basic feel for XML that makes the technical details in future chapters easier to grasp.

Hello XML

This section follows an old programmer's tradition of introducing a new language with a program that prints "Hello World" on the console. XML is a markup language, not a programming language, but the basic principle still applies. It's easiest to get started if you begin with a complete, working example upon which you can expand rather than starting with more fundamental pieces that do not work by themselves.

Thus, in this section you type an actual XML document and save it in a file, write a style sheet for the document, and convert the document to HTML so you can load it into a Web browser. When you finish this section, you'll have correctly installed and run all the basic tools you need for XML development. If you do encounter problems with the basic tools, those problems are easier to debug and fix in the context of the short, simple documents used here rather than in the context of the more complex documents developed in the rest of the book.

Creating a Simple XML Document

Let's start with the simplest XML document I can imagine:

```
<?xml version="1.0" standalone="yes"?>
<foo>
Hello XML!
</foo>
```

The preceding document is not very complicated, but it is a good XML document. To be more precise, it's a well-formed XML document. This document can be typed in any convenient text editor like Notepad, BBEdit, or emacs.

 XML has special terms for documents that it considers *good* depending on the exact set of rules they satisfy. *Well-formed* is one of those terms, but we'll get to that in Chapter 3.

Saving Your XML File

Once you've typed it, save your document in a file called foo.xml, hello.xml, HelloWorld.xml, MyFirstDocument.xml, or some other name. The three letter extension .xml is fairly standard. Make sure you save it in plain text format, however, and not in the native format of a word processor like WordPerfect or Microsoft Word.

 If you're using Notepad on Windows to edit your files, be sure to enclose the filename in double quotes — for example, "hello.xml", not merely hello.xml — when saving the document. (See Figure 2-1.) Without the double quotes, Notepad appends the .txt extension to your filename, naming it hello.xml.txt, not what you want at all.

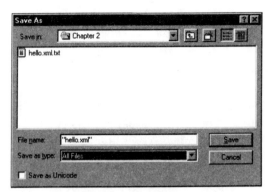

Figure 2-1: When saving a file in Notepad, be sure to place the filename in quotes.

The Windows NT version of Notepad gives you the option to save the file in Unicode. Surprisingly, Unicode works too, though for now you should stick to basic ASCII. XML files may be either Unicode or a compressed version of Unicode called UTF-8. UTF-8 is a strict superset of ASCII, so pure ASCII files are also valid XML files. Chapter 8 discusses this subject in more detail.

Examining Your Simple XML Document

Let's look closely at the simple XML document discussed in the preceding section. The first line is the XML declaration:

```
<?xml version="1.0" standalone="yes"?>
```

The preceding line is an example of an XML processing instruction. Processing instructions begin with <? and end with ?>. The first word after the <? is the name of the processing instruction, which is xml in this example.

The XML declaration has version and standalone attributes. An *attribute* is a name-value pair separated by an equals (=) sign. The name is on the left-hand side of the equals sign and the value is on the right-hand side with its value given between double quote marks. In this example, the version attribute has the value 1.0 and the standalone attribute has the value yes.

Every XML document begins with an XML declaration that specifies the version of XML in use. The version attribute says this document conforms to XML 1.0. The XML declaration may also have a standalone attribute that tells you whether or not the document is complete in this one file or whether it needs to import other files. In this example, and for the next several chapters, all documents are complete unto themselves so the standalone attribute is set to "yes".

```
<foo>
Hello XML!
</foo>
```

Collectively, the preceding three lines form a `foo` element. Separately, `<foo>` is a start tag; `</foo>` is an end tag; and `Hello XML!` is the content of the `foo` element.

What does the `<foo>` tag mean? The short answer is "whatever you want it to mean." Rather than relying on a few hundred predefined tags, XML lets you create the tags you need. The `<foo>` tag, therefore, has whatever meaning you assign it. The same XML document could have been written in the three following ways:

```
<?xml version="1.0" standalone="yes"?>
<greeting>
Hello XML!
</greeting>
```

Or:

```
<?xml version="1.0" standalone="yes"?>
<P>
Hello XML!
</P>
```

Or:

```
<?xml version="1.0" standalone="yes"?>
<document>
Hello XML!
</document>
```

Although the tags have different names, at this point these documents are equivalent because they have the same structure and content.

Assigning Semantic and Style Meaning to XML Tags

Meaning can be imparted to tags in two ways. *Semantic meaning* is the first manner. This sort of meaning exists outside the document — in the mind of the author or in another computer program that generates or reads these files.

For instance, a Web browser that understands HTML but not XML assigns the meaning "paragraph" to the tags `<P>` and `</P>` but not to the tags `<greeting>` and `</greeting>`, `<foo>` and `</foo>`, or `<document>` and `</document>`. An English-speaking human is more likely to understand `<greeting>` and `</greeting>` or `<document>` and `</document>` than `<foo>` and `</foo>` or `<P>` and `</P>`. Meaning, like beauty, is in the mind of the beholder.

As relatively dumb machines, computers can't really understand the meaning of anything. They simply process bits and bytes according to predetermined formulas (albeit very quickly). A computer is just as happy to use `<foo>` or `<P>` as it is to use the more meaningful `<greeting>` or `<document>` tag. Even a Web browser can't really understand the meaning of a paragraph. All the browser knows is that when a paragraph is encountered, a blank line should be placed before the next element.

Naturally, it's better to pick tags that closely reflect the purpose of the information they contain. Many disciplines like math and chemistry are working on creating industry standard tag sets. These sets should be used when appropriate. Most tags are made up as you need them.

A list of other possible tags follows:

`<MOLECULE>`

`<INTEGRAL>`

`<PERSON>`

`<SALARY>`

`<author>`

`<email>`

`<planet>`

`<sign>`

Style meaning is the second kind of meaning associated with a tag. This specifies how the content of a tag is to be presented on a computer screen or other output device. Style meaning says whether a particular element is bold, italic, green, 24 points, and so forth. Computers are better at understanding style than semantic meaning. In XML, style meaning is applied through style sheets, which are the subject of the next section and Chapter 4.

Preparing a Style Sheet for Your Document

The beauty of XML is that you can create any tags you need. Of course, because you have almost complete freedom in creating tags, there's no way for a generic browser to anticipate your tags and provide rules for displaying them. Therefore, you also need to write a style sheet for your document that tells browsers how to display particular tags. Like tag sets, style sheets can be shared between different documents and different people, and your style sheets can be integrated with style sheets others have written.

More than one style sheet language is available. The one used in this book is called XSL, the eXtensible Style Language. XSL is currently the most powerful and flexible style sheet language, and the only one designed specifically for use with XML.

For example, refer to the preceding XML document:

```
<?xml version="1.0" standalone="yes"?>
<greeting>
Hello XML!
</greeting>
```

This document was saved in a file called greeting.xml. As you'll note, it only contains one tag, <greeting>, so you only need to define the style for the greeting tag. The outermost tag in a document is called the *root*. Listing 2-1 is a simple style sheet specifying that the root is to be rendered as an <H1> header:

Listing 2-1: greeting.xsl

```
<xsl>
  <rule>
    <root/>
      <H1>
        <children/>
      </H1>
  </rule>
</xsl>
```

The <xsl></xsl> tags delimit the style sheet itself much as <html></html> delimits a Web page. The style sheet contains one rule (everything between <rule> and </rule>). Every rule has a target and an action. The target is the elements in the XML document to which this rule applies. The action is the output produced when the rule is triggered. A style sheet processor reads both an XML document and its associated style sheet. It matches the elements found in the document with the targets in the style sheet. For each target that's found, it takes the action given in that target's rule.

The empty <root/> tag means the target of this rule is the root element of the XML document. The root element of the greeting.xml file is the greeting element. This rule says all children of the root of the XML document — that is, everything in the document between <greeting> and </greeting> — should be wrapped in a single <H1> header.

Indents and line breaks are used here purely to make the style sheet easier to understand. This formatting has no effect on the rendered output.

Listing 2-1 should be typed in a text editor and saved in a new file called greeting.xsl in the same directory as greeting.xml. The .xsl extension stands for eXtensible Style Sheet. Chapter 4 discusses XSL style sheets in more detail.

Once again, the extension — .xsl — is important, although the exact filename is not important. If a style sheet is applied only to a single XML document, however, it's often convenient to use the document's name with the extension .xsl instead of .xml.

You may notice that the tags used by the extensible style sheets look a lot like XML tags. That's because they are XML tags. An XSL style sheet is an XML document. XSL is an XML application used to describe style data. In this example, `<xsl>` is the root element. It contains a single `<rule>` element. The `<rule>` element contains an empty `<root/>` element and an `<H1>` element. The `<H1>` element contains a single empty `<children/>` element. The `<children/>` element is shorthand for everything that the `<H1>` element contains – that is, everything that comes between `<H1>` and `</H1>`. With all these elements together, this rule says that the rendered output should surround the complete contents of the root element with an `<H1></H1>` pair.

The `<root/>` tag is not the root element of the style sheet. Rather, it targets the root element of the XML document to which this style sheet is applied.

Browsing XML

Now that you've created your first XML document and style sheet, you're going to want to look at it. As of this writing, there's no general purpose XML browser available. Instead, you need to convert the document into HTML first. You can convert statically by running a program that converts your .xml and .xsl files into .html files and then serve the .html files. You can also convert dynamically by using an ActiveX control or JavaScript program that makes the necessary conversions on the fly. This section discusses how to convert statically with the MSXSL processor and dynamically with ActiveX.

Statically Converting XML to HTML

Use the following instructions to convert your XML files to HTML statically. You need Windows 95 or NT and Internet Explorer 4.0 or later installed. Similar tools for other platforms and browsers that don't require conversion to HTML are both under development.

The following conversions are performed with early alphas of these tools. You may want to check Microsoft's Web site at `http://www.microsoft.com/xml/xsl/` to see if more recent versions are available and if any instructions have changed.

Assuming you have already installed Internet Explorer 4.0 (included on the CD-ROM), you must next install the free Microsoft XSL Command-line Utility. This utility is available from Microsoft's Web site at `http://www.microsoft.com/xml/xsl/msxsl.htm` in a file called `MSXSL.EXE`. This file should be copied somewhere convenient in your path, such as `C:\WINNT\system32`.

Next, open a DOS command prompt window and `cd` into the directory that contains the `greeting.xml` and `greeting.xsl` files from the preceding two sections. Then type the following command:

```
C:\XML> msxsl -i greeting.xml -s greeting.xsl -o greeting.htm
```

This command tells DOS to run the MSXSL program on the XML file `greeting.xml`, format the output according to the instructions found in `greeting.xsl`, and place the output in the file `greeting.htm`. The file `greeting.htm` should now contain the following text:

```
<H1>
 Hello XML!
</H1>
```

You can now load the rendered file `greeting.html` into any standard Web browser as shown in Figure 2-2.

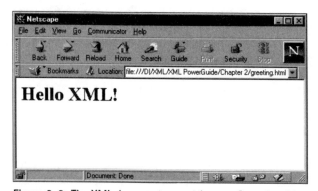

Figure 2-2: The XML document `greeting.xml` rendered in the Netscape browser

Technically, the `-s` and `-o` flags are only necessary when the style sheet and output filenames do not match the input filename. You can get the same result in this case by typing the following:

```
C:\XML> msxsl -i greeting.xml
```

In general, however, a single style sheet is used for many different XML documents, so the -s flag is necessary at a minimum.

If you get an error message like

```
The name specified is not recognized as an
internal or external command, program, or batch file
```

when you try to run MSXSL, make sure the directory where MSXSL.EXE is installed is included in your path. You can set the path in your AUTOEXEC. BAT file (Windows 95) or in the System control panel environment tab (Windows NT). Also, make sure you spelled the command properly.

Dynamically Converting XML to HTML

A Web server primarily receives requests for files and serves the requested files as quickly as possible. In that respect, an XML file is just like any other file. Unfortunately, current Web browsers don't understand XML: if you want to serve raw XML files without converting them to HTML first, you also need to provide users with a program they can use to view the files. You can use a number of programs, including JavaScript programs, Java applets, and ActiveX controls, for this purpose.

For now, however, I focus on introducing the most complete program that handles the broadest range of XML: the Microsoft XSL ActiveX Control. This program derives from the same code base as the MSXSL command-line utility introduced in the last section. Like that utility, it has the severe disadvantage of working only with Internet Explorer 4.0 on Windows 95 or NT (and not reliably even on these platforms). At the time of this writing, however, it's the only tool that doesn't require the XML author to be a Java or JavaScript programmer. Instead, you can merely crib a few lines of code that Microsoft provides to invoke the ActiveX control.

You need to write an HTML page that serves as a wrapper around the XML data. The XSL ActiveX control embedded in the HTML page downloads both the XML file and its associated style sheet and renders the XML as HTML inside the page. A JavaScript embeds the rendered XML. Listing 2-2 shows a simple HTML wrapper for the greeting program.

Listing 2-2: An HTML file that uses ActiveX to embed XML dynamically

```
<HTML>
<HEAD>
<TITLE>Dynamically Rendered XML</TITLE>
</HEAD>
<BODY>
```

```
<OBJECT ID="XSLControl"
  CLASSID="CLSID:2BD0D2F2-52EC-11D1-8C69-0E16BC000000"
  codebase="http://www.microsoft.com/xml/xsl/msxsl.cab"
  style="display:none">
<PARAM NAME="documentURL" VALUE="greeting.xml">
<PARAM NAME="styleURL" VALUE="greeting.xsl">
</OBJECT>

<SCRIPT FOR=window EVENT=onload>
  var xslHTML = XSLControl.htmlText;
  document.all.item("xslTarget").innerHTML = xslHTML;
</SCRIPT>

<DIV id=xslTarget></DIV>

</BODY>
</HTML>
```

The preceding HTML document has three main parts:

◆ The <OBJECT> tag that downloads the ActiveX control

◆ The script that runs the ActiveX control

◆ The <DIV> element that embeds the output of the control in the
  HTML page

The <OBJECT> element refers to a particular ActiveX control downloaded from
Microsoft's Web site. Because the security model of ActiveX relies on code signing
supported by a digital signature, this tag must be used verbatim. All four attribute
values — ID, CLASSID, codebase, and style — must match Listing 2-2. You can
copy these values out of the sample file on the CD-ROM.

Note that you do not (at least not yet) include the ActiveX control on your own
Web site and point the URL in the codebase at that file. You must point to this
exact file on Microsoft's Web site.

 As this example is based on an early alpha, these characteristics are likely to
change in future versions. Therefore, make sure to check Microsoft's Web
site at http://www.microsoft.com/xml/xsl/ for the latest version.

To render other documents or use a different style sheet, change the value of the
documentURL and styleURL <PARAM> tags, respectively.

The <SCRIPT> tag contains a simple JavaScript that invokes the XSL ActiveX
control to parse the XML document and style sheet given in the <PARAM> tags and

store the result in the item named `xslTarget`. This sequence happens for the window in which the document is displayed and every time the page is loaded or reloaded.

```
<SCRIPT FOR=window EVENT=onload>
  var xslHTML = XSLControl.htmlText;
  document.all.item("xslTarget").innerHTML = xslHTML;
</SCRIPT>
```

This preceding script allows the `<DIV>` tag to refer to `xslTarget` to insert the rendered document into the Web page.

```
<DIV id=xslTarget></DIV>
```

In addition to changing the XML document and style sheet, you can add additional HTML markup and text to the document. Aside from delivery methods (standalone converter vs dynamic ActiveX control), the major difference between the Microsoft ActiveX control and the MSXML application is the former embeds the rendered XML inside a preexisting HTML document, while the latter generates a completely new document from scratch. The MSXSL program requires all formatting information to be included in the style sheets while the ActiveX control is more suited for use with HTML templates into which XML data is poured.

Converting a Web Page to XML

On my Cafe au Lait Web site, I maintain a list of books about Java, written in HTML. The entire page is too long to reprint here, but you can view the most current version at `http://sunsite.unc.edu/javafaq/books.html`. You should probably take a look at this page and view the source before continuing. Figure 2-3 shows this page in a Web browser.

In the example, I walk you through the process of converting this page to XML. Essentially, you can use the same technique if you were designing the page from scratch, which would actually be easier than going through the following conversion. Along the way, you learn how and why XML tags are chosen and discover more details of XML tags and XSL style sheets.

The book lists on this page are concrete examples of exactly the sort of content for which XML works extremely well. It is a large list of highly structured data with precise meanings. XML enables you to treat each of these things as exactly what it is – no more, no less. A publisher is a publisher, an ISBN number is an ISBN number, and so forth.

HTML, by contrast, provides no means of distinguishing between publishers, ISBN numbers, page counts, prices, and so forth. They're all simply list items. XML provides much more granularity.

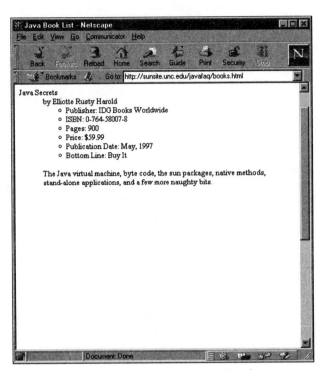

Figure 2-3: My Cafe au Lait Web site in HTML before conversion to XML

Defining Tags for the Books

The page in Figure 2-3 can mostly be divided into books. Each book has a title, a name, a publisher, an ISBN number, a number of pages, a price, a publication date, and a recommendation. Each of these elements can be represented as a string of text.

The page shown in Figure 2-3 consists of a lot of HTML entries like the one shown in Listing 2-3.

Listing 2-3: The sample book list's HTML listing

```
<dt>Java Secrets
<dd> by Elliotte Rusty Harold
<ul>
<li>Publisher: IDG Books Worldwide
<li>ISBN: 0-764-58007-8
<li>Pages: 900
<li>Price: $59.99
<li>Publication Date: May, 1997
<li>Bottom Line: Buy It
```

```
</ul><P>
The Java virtual machine, byte code, the sun packages, native
 methods, standalone applications, and a few more naughty bits.<P>
```

This HTML produces a reasonably attractive page, but it doesn't say much regarding the content of the tags. For example, the ISBN number is not distinguished from the price, which is not distinguished from the page count, which is not distinguished from the publisher, and so forth. Among other problems, this makes it difficult for a program to parse the page and find entries that meet certain criteria, such as books with multiple authors.

XML enables you to define different tags for each of these items, as shown in Listing 2-4:

Listing 2-4: The Java Secrets listing in XML

```
<book>
<title>Java Secrets</title>
<author>Elliotte Rusty Harold</author>
<publisher>IDG Books Worldwide</publisher>
<isbn>0-764-58007-8</isbn>
<pagecount>900</pagecount>
<price>$59.99</price>
<pubdate>May, 1997</pubdate>
<recommendation>Buy It</recommendation>
<blurb>
The Java virtual machine, byte code, the sun packages, native
 methods, standalone applications, and a few more naughty bits.
</blurb>
</book>
```

Notice that now only the data is included between the tags. The generic field labels like "ISBN" and "Bottom Line" can be filled in when the page is rendered. Also notice that only the meaning is specified. Indents and bullets can be filled in when the page is rendered. Instructions for rendering are provided by style sheets.

This format extends easily to special cases. For instance, consider a book with multiple authors but no blurb in the following example:

Discover Java
by Ed Tittel, Bill Brogden
Publisher: IDG Books Worldwide
ISBN: 0-7645-8024-8
Pages: 352
Price: $24.99
Publication Date: 1997
Bottom Line: ????

This example can easily be encoded, as shown in Listing 2-5:

Listing 2-5: An XML listing for a book with multiple authors

```
<book>
<title>Discover Java </title>
<author>Ed Tittel</author>
<author>Bill Brogden</author>
<publisher>IDG Books Worldwide</publisher>
<ISBN>0-7645-8024-8</ISBN>
<pagecount>352</pagecount>
<price>$24.99</price>
<pubdate>1997</pubdate>
<recommendation>????</recommendation>
</book>
```

A DTD can impose restrictions on the contents of an element – for instance, requiring every book to have a blurb or an ISBN number. You'll learn how to impose these restrictions in Chapter 5. Unless a requirement is specifically imposed, however, tags may contain arbitrary data and elements.

You may want to impose restrictions on the format of an element's content, such as making sure that all date elements contain dates and not arbitrary strings of text. Regrettably, XML does not go this far. You cannot require a format for an element's character content, though you can restrict which other elements are allowed inside of a given element.

The books themselves are divided into different categories: top-ten, in-print, out-of-print, and not yet published. I could make different tags for each of these categories. The categories are just different versions of the same element, however, and other categories may be added or deleted. Therefore, let's classify them as `<bookcategory>`. Listing 2-6 illustrates a simple example:

Listing 2-6: The sample book list with a `<bookcategory>` tag

```
<bookcategory>
<categoryname>In Print</categoryname>
<book>
<title>Java Secrets</title>
<author>Elliotte Rusty Harold</author>
<publisher>IDG Books Worldwide</publisher>
<ISBN>0-764-58007-8</ISBN>
<pagecount>900</pagecount>
<price>59.99</price>
<pubdate>May, 1997</pubdate>
<recommendation>Buy It</recommendation>
<blurb>
The Java virtual machine, byte code, the sun packages, native
  methods, standalone applications, and a few more naughty bits.
```

```
</blurb>
</book>
<book>
<title>Discover Java </title>
<author>Ed Tittel</author>
<author>Bill Brogden</author>
<publisher>IDG Books Worldwide</publisher>
<ISBN>0-7645-8024-8</ISBN>
<pagecount>316</pagecount>
<price>$24.99</price>
<pubdate>1997</pubdate>
<recommendation>????</recommendation>
</book>
</bookcategory>
```

Of course, the full listing would contain many more books.

I've added a `categoryname` element inside the `bookcategory` element. In this case, the value of that element is "In Print". This element is used to provide a heading for the list.

These tags are sufficient to handle the books. Although the books are the primary content of the page, they are not the only elements on the page. The page also contains some header information, other front matter, and a standard signature block.

You can approach this information in several ways. You can simply leave it as HTML and embed the XML in the HTML document using the Microsoft XSL ActiveX Control. If you have a lot of nonstandard data that doesn't lend itself to semantic markup, this method is the simplest route.

The second approach uses modified XML tags that mirror their HTML counterparts. For example, <P> and </P> work as XML tags as well as HTML tags. With this method, you'll need to quote all your attribute values, use one case for the HTML tags (HTML tags are not case-sensitive but XML tags are), and finish empty tags with /> instead of just >. The next chapter discusses the exact details. Aside from limited backward compatibility, however, this approach doesn't help a great deal right now. Primarily, this approach is useful if you already have an HTML-compatible DTD and style sheet upon which to fall back. Because you don't have these elements yet, let's use the following method.

This third approach defines new XML tags. Some of these tags resemble semantic HTML tags like <TITLE> and <P>, but others are quite different. I use this approach in the following sections. Since much of what we develop (such as a general signature block) is not specific to books, you can reuse it in many other contexts.

Choosing Tags for the Front Matter

The next step is to choose tags for the front matter. The top of the HTML page, shown in Figure 2-4, is more free-form text. You can assign a precise meaning to the individual paragraphs aside from the meanings HTML provides, but most of the tags would seem forced and would not be applicable to more than one or two paragraphs. Therefore, I use XML tags that closely mirror their HTML counterparts to describe data in this section.

Figure 2-4: The beginning of the sample book list page

To convert this page to XML, several important elements need to be included as XML tags. The first element is the document header, the second is a simple paragraph of text, and the third is a definition list and its elements. Listing 2-7 illustrates the appearance of these elements in HTML:

Listing 2-7: The sample book list in HTML

```
<h1>Java Book List</h1>

Here are some books currently in print and soon anticipated about
  Java. All books that are in print and which I've had an opportunity
  to review get one of three ratings:
<dl>
<dt>Buy It
<dd>
An essential book for any Java programmer.

<dt>Browse It
```

```
<dd>
This book may be useful for some people. Skim through it in
your local bookstore to see if you like it before laying out your
  cash.

<dt>Recycle It
<dd>
Toss it in the recycling bin. ("Burn it" would have been more
  alliterative here, but I have a general aversion to advocating book
  burning, even in jest. I also considered "bag it" and "barf on it"
  at which I point I decided alliteration wasn't that important.).

</dl>
```

Note that these ratings are mutable depending on the competition and
the comparison between the book and the current release of Java.
Generally a book's rating will go down over time except when a new
edition is released.

Because there's no point in redefining everything, you can use tags similar to their
HTML counterparts. Thus, Listing 2-8 illustrates the XML version of the document:

Listing 2–8: The sample book list in XML

```
<h1>Java Book List</h1>
<p>
Here are some books currently in print and soon anticipated about
  Java. All books that are in print and which I've had an opportunity
  to review get one of three ratings:
</p>
<dl>
<dt>Buy It</dt>
<dd>
An essential book for any Java programmer.
</dd>

<dt>Browse It</dt>
<dd>
<p>
This book may be useful for some people. Skim through it in your
  local bookstore to see if you like it before laying out your cash.
</p>
</dd>

<dt>Recycle It</dt>
<dd>
<p>
Toss it in the recycling bin. ("Burn it" would have been more
  alliterative here, but I have a general aversion to advocating book
  burning, even in jest. I also considered "bag it" and "barf on it"
  at which I point I decided alliteration wasn't that important.).
</p>
```

```
</dd>
</dl>
<p>
Note that these ratings are mutable depending on the competition and
    the comparison between the book and the current release of Java.
    Generally a book's rating will go down over time except when a new
    edition is released.
</p>
```

Notice the changes made in the XML version. First, all open tags were closed. You cannot say `<dt>Recycle It` and rely on the nearest `<dd>` to close the `<dt>`. Instead, each `<dt>` must be explicitly closed with a `</dt>`, just as each `<p>` must be matched with a closing `</p>`. Otherwise, this example is the usual collection of HTML tags.

Choosing Tags for the Header

HTML documents contain headers with titles and possibly other items like metatags. Most of this header information is not directly shown to the browser. The header for the Java books page follows:

```
<html>
<head>
<title>Java Book List</title>
</head>
<body bgcolor="#ffffff" text="#000000">
```

In XML, some of this information can be encoded via a style sheet that applies to the root tag. In the preceding example, the root tag is `<html>`; in XML, the most common choice of root tag is simply `<document>`. The `<head>` tag can be brought into the document unchanged.

The `<title>` tag could be brought into the document unchanged except that I've already defined `<title>` as referring to a book title. I shouldn't use the same tag to refer to two different elements in the same page, even in different contexts. Therefore, I'll call this tag `<pagetitle>` instead of simply `<title>`.

 A future version of XML may add namespaces to allow similarly named tags to be used in different contexts.

Finally, the attributes should be removed from the body tag because they are styles rather than semantic information. Also, don't forget that the document must begin with an XML declaration. Thus, in XML the beginning of the file looks like this:

```
<?xml version="1.0" standalone="yes"?>
<document>
<head>
<pagetitle>Java Book List</pagetitle>
</head>
<body>
```

Both `<body>` and `<document>` are closed at the end of the file as follows:

```
</body>
</document>
```

Choosing Tags for the Signature

The final part of the page is my standard signature block at the bottom of the page as shown in Figure 2-5. The signature block contains links to other pages on the site, the e-mail address of the page's author, a copyright notice, and the last-modified date. Although this information isn't used elsewhere on the page, it is used on other pages in the same site. Therefore, it's worth the time to define XML tags for these items rather than merely using a set of generic HTML-like tags. In this chapter, however, I omit the links. Chapter 7 revisits this example while discussing linking in XML.

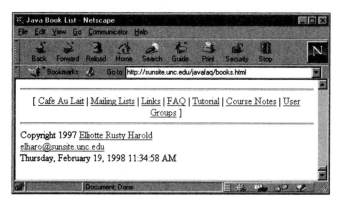

Figure 2-5: The signature block from the books page

The signature has four parts: a horizontal rule, the copyright, the e-mail address, and the last-modified date. The horizontal rule is formatting information that can be embedded via a style sheet. For the other items, create new XML elements like the following:

```
<signature>
  <copyright>1997 Elliotte Rusty Harold</copyright>
  <email>elharo@sunsite.unc.edu</email>
  <lastModified>
    Monday, December 22, 1997 10:09:54 AM
  </lastModified>
</signature>
```

This defines both the signature block itself and its individual pieces.

Examining and Viewing Your XML Document

Listing 2-9 is a small version of the books.xml file that shows all the tags and the overall structure of the document though several hundred books have been omitted in the interests of space.

Listing 2-9: books.xml

```
<document>
<head>
<pagetitle>Java Book List</pagetitle>
</head>
<body>

<h1>Java Book List</h1>

<p>
Here are some books currently in print and soon anticipated about
  Java.  All books that are in print and which I've had an
  opportunity to review get one of three ratings:
</p>
<dl>
<dt>Buy It</dt>
<dd>
An essential book for any Java programmer.
</dd>
<dt>Browse It</dt>
<dd>
This book may be useful for some people. Skim through it in your
  local bookstore to see if you like it before laying out your cash.
</dd>
<dt>Recycle It</dt>
<dd>
Toss it in the recycling bin.  ("Burn it" would have been more
  alliterative here, but I have a general aversion to advocating book
  burning, even in jest. I also considered "bag it" and "barf on it"
  at which I point I decided alliteration wasn't that important.).
</dd>
</dl>
```

```
<p>
Note that these ratings are mutable depending on the competition and
 the comparison between the book and the current release of Java.
 Generally a book's rating will go down over time except when a new
 edition is released.
</p>

<bookcategory>
<categoryname>In Print</categoryname>
<book>
<title>Java Secrets</title>
<author>Elliotte Rusty Harold</author>
<publisher>IDG Books Worldwide</publisher>
<isbn>0-764-58007-8</isbn>
<pagecount>900</pagecount>
<price>$59.99</price>
<pubdate>May, 1997</pubdate>
<recommendation>Buy It</recommendation>
<blurb>
The Java virtual machine, byte code, the sun packages, native
 methods, standalone applications, and a few more naughty bits.
</blurb>
</book>
</bookcategory>
<signature>
<copyright> 1997 Elliotte Rusty Harold</copyright>
<email>elharo@sunsite.unc.edu</email>
<lastmodified>
  Thursday, February 19, 1998 11:34:58 AM
</lastmodified>
</signature>
</body>
</document>
```

At this point, you should probably run the document through the MSXSL processor or another syntax checker to verify that the document is well-formed. Since XML is not as forgiving as HTML, it's important to make sure you don't forget to close any tags or quote any attributes. For MSXSL, you'll need at least a simple style sheet to view the document and check for errors. A sample style sheet in Listing 2-10 follows:

Listing 2-10: A minimal style sheet

```
<xsl>
  <rule>
    <root/>
    <HTML>
      <HEAD>
        <TITLE>An XML Document</TITLE>
```

```
      </HEAD>
      <BODY>
        <children/>
      </BODY>
    </HTML>
  </rule>
</xsl>
```

This rule merely wraps the document's entire character data in standard HTML document tags. The XML markup tags are not passed through into the finished document. The document won't produce particularly pretty output – in fact, all the data tends to run together as shown in Figure 2-6 – but it warns you of errors in the file such as unclosed or overlapping tags. For example, the following error message is reported if you delete the closing </pagetitle> tag from Listing 2-9:

```
C:\XML>msxsl -i books.xml
Error parsing document 'books.xml'
ParseException: End tag 'head' does not match start tag 'pagetitle'
Location: file:///C:/XML/books.xml (10,8)
Context: <document><head><pagetitle>
```

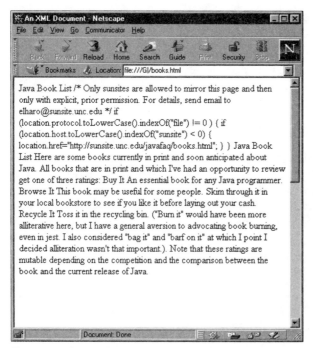

Figure 2-6: The books page with a minimal style sheet

Writing a Style Sheet for the Final Document

The style sheet in Listing 2-10 checks a document's syntax, but it certainly doesn't produce attractive output. The final step in preparing an XML page for the Web is to write a real style sheet that produces attractive output.

For the most part, a style sheet defines one rule for each tag. Therefore, first list the tags. These following tags are used:

`<document>`	`<head>`	`<pagetitle>`	`<categoryname>`
`<body>`	`<h1>`	`<p>`	`<dl>`
`<dt>`	`<dd>`	`<bookcategory>`	`<book>`
`<title>`	`<author>`	`<publisher>`	`<isbn>`
`<pagecount>`	`<price>`	`<recommendation>`	`<blurb>`
`<pubdate>`	`<signature>`	`<copyright>`	`<email>`
`<lastmodified>`			

The `document` element is the root of the document. Therefore, `document` alone has a rule that uses a tag other than `<target-element>`. Let's give it a very simple rule, as follows:

```
<rule>
  <root/>
    <html>
      <children/>
    </html>
</rule>
```

In the midst of numerous tags, it's easy to miss one. Before proceeding, let's create a default rule that applies to all elements for which no specific rule exists. This rule colors those elements red, so they stand out and also includes the name of the unstyled tag in the HTML source. The `<SPAN>` tag, introduced in HTML 4.0 and supported by Netscape and Internet Explorer 4.0 and later, is useful for this purpose.

```
<rule>
   <target-element/>
   <SPAN color="red" unstyledTag="=tagName">
      <children/>
   </SPAN>
   </rule>
```

This rule acts on any tag not defined elsewhere and formats that text as red using `<SPAN color="red">`. Furthermore, the unusual construct

```
unstyledTag="=tagName"
```

inserts the name of the tag to which this rule was applied into the output. This insertion makes the tag name appear in the HTML as the `unstyledTag` attribute value of the `<SPAN>` tag, as follows:

```
<SPAN color="red" unstyledTag="pagecount">
```

The HTML produced by this style sheet still isn't pretty, but it warns of omissions in the style sheet, which are then easily corrected.

Put this rule together with the root rule to make the following style sheet, as shown in Listing 2-11:

Listing 2-11: A preliminary style sheet

```
<xsl>
  <rule>
    <root/>
      <html>
        <children/>
      </html>

  </rule>
  <rule>
    <target-element/>
    <SPAN color="red" unstyledTag="=tagName">
        <children/>
   </SPAN>
  </rule>

</xsl>
```

At this point, it's useful to run the document and its style sheet through the XSL processor and make sure it doesn't report any error messages. Figure 2-7 shows the results of this process. Since essentially all tags are undefined, all content appears in red. (If nothing looks particularly red to you, imagine you're looking at this picture on a color monitor instead of a printed page. I considered using boldface instead, but boldface often appears in actual text and is not an obvious indicator of a problem.) As the style sheet grows to encompass more of the tags, successive renderings show fewer red elements. You can view source and look for `unstyledTag` attributes to identify unstyled tags.

Now let's start looking at the individual tags that must be styled, in the approximate order of appearance in the sample document. The first such tag is `<head>`. It merely needs to be passed on unchanged. This tag's rule follows:

```
  <rule>
    <target-element type="head"/>
      <head>
        <children/>
      </head>
  </rule>
```

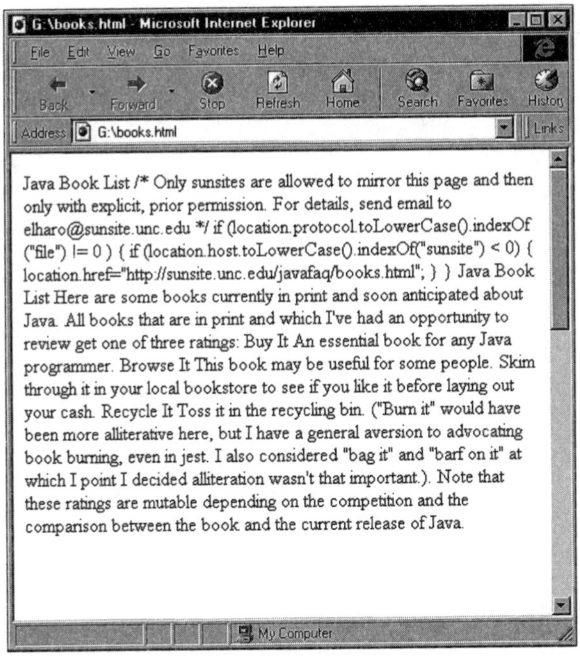

Figure 2-7: The books page with the preliminary style sheet

The `type` attribute of the `<target-element/>` tag selects the elements to which this rule applies. This attribute is used for all nonroot rules. Similar rules are used for all XML tags to be processed by converting them to XML basically unchanged. This tag's general pattern follows:

```
<rule>
  <target-element type="X"/>
    <X>
      <children/>
    </X>
</rule>
```

In this general pattern, *X* is the name of both the XML and the HTML tag. For instance, the paragraph tag is defined by the following rule:

```
<rule>
  <target-element type="p"/>
    <p>
      <children/>
    </p>
</rule>
```

The `<h1>` and `<dl>` tags can also be handled in this manner:

```
<rule>
  <target-element type="h1"/>
  <h1>
    <children/>
  </h1>
</rule>

<rule>
  <target-element type="dl"/>
  <dl>
    <children/>
  </dl>
</rule>
```

A rule that merely changes the name of the tag is not much harder. Its general pattern follows:

```
<rule>
  <target-element type="oldname"/>
    <newname>
      <children/>
    </newname>
</rule>
```

For instance, the rule to change `<pagetitle>` to `<title>` follows:

```
<rule>
  <target-element type="pagetitle"/>
    <title>
      <children/>
    </title>
</rule>
```

Tags can easily add style information or other attributes. For instance, the following rule says that the body of the HTML should have a background color of white and a text color of black:

```
<rule>
  <target-element type="body"/>
  <body bgcolor="#FFFFFF" text="#000000">
    <children/>
  </body>
</rule>
```

Empty HTML tags like `<dt>` and `<dd>` must be closed with `/>` when used as an action in a style sheet. This condition is redundant in HTML but required for the XSL style sheet, which must itself conform to XML specs. The XSL processor should strip off these extra forward slashes when converting to HTML, however. Thus, the rule for the `<dt>` XML element looks like the following:

```
<rule>
  <target-element type="dt"/>
  <dt/>
    <children/>
</rule>
```

Style sheets can specify additional text to be included in the document as well as style information. For instance, the following rule says that the word `"copyright"` should be placed before the copyright information:

```
<rule>
  <target-element type="copyright"/>
  Copyright
    <children/><br/>
</rule>
```

Tags that do not have clear HTML counterparts are still formatted in the same fashion. For instance, consider our reoccurring book example. It must map the `<book>`, `<title>`, `<author>`, `<publisher>`, `<isbn>`, `<pagecount>`, `<price>`, `<recommendation>`, `<blurb>`, and `<pubdate>` tags. None of these tags are HTML tags.

The title rule merely includes the content of the tag. No special formatting needs to be applied.

```
<rule>
   <target-element type="title"/>
     <children/>
</rule>
```

The author tag is easy to deal with as long as there's a single author. Just associate it with the `<dd>` tag as follows:

```
<rule>
   <target-element type="author"/>
     <dd/>
     <children/>
</rule>
```

However, multiple authors are trickier. The first author should have a `<dd>` and subsequent authors should merely have a comma and a space. This task will be addressed in Chapter 4.

The `<pagecount>` tag can be associated with the `<li>` HTML tag as follows:

```
<rule>
  <target-element type="pages"/>
```

```
<li/>Pages:
   <children/>
</rule>
```

The `<publisher>`, `<isbn>`, `<pagecount>`, `<price>`, and `<recommendation>` tags are set in a similar manner.

Adding the appropriate `<ul>` and `</ul>` tags at the beginning and end of the list, respectively, is not a trivial process. The simplest way adds one more XML tag that groups this information and to which a rule can be applied, as in the following example:

```
<book>
<title>Java Secrets</title>
<author>Elliotte Rusty Harold</author>
<publisher>IDG Books Worldwide</publisher>
<bookinfo>
<isbn>0-764-58007-8</isbn>
<pagecount>900</pagecount>
<price>$59.99</price>
<pubdate>May, 1997</pubdate>
<recommendation>Buy It</recommendation>
</bookinfo>
<blurb>
The Java virtual machine, byte code, the sun packages, native
 methods, standalone applications, and a few more naughty bits.
</blurb>
</book>
```

Then you can apply a rule that converts `<bookinfo>` to `<ul>` as follows:

```
<rule>
  <target-element type="bookinfo"/>
  <ul>
    <children/>
  </ul>
</rule>
```

What you really want, however, is just the indent that the unordered list provides. In fact, even using a list item is bad form because the example uses semantic markup to indicate style information. Chapter 4 discusses how to apply precise indenting and style sheets that don't misuse semantic markup. If you're familiar with cascading style sheets and HTML 4.0, you may be able to guess how to do it already. (Hint: consider the `<SPAN>` tag introduced earlier in this section.)

You may prefer not to prefix price, ISBN, publisher, page count, and recommendation with words because the information is self-explanatory and the extra words are redundant. If so, you can change the appearance of the page merely by changing the style sheet to remove the offending text. The document itself does not have to change. In this case, because you want to repeat the same procedure for all these elements, you can use a single rule with multiple `<target-element>` tags that match all the parts. For example:

```
<rule>
  <target-element type="pages"/>
  <target-element type="isbn"/>
  <target-element type="publisher"/>
  <target-element type="price"/>
  <target-element type="recommendation"/>
  <li/>
    <children/>
</rule>
```

The `<blurb>` is merely a paragraph of text, so it's easy to handle:

```
<rule>
  <target-element type="blurb"/>
    <p>
      <children/>
    </p>
</rule>
```

The remaining part of the book list is the category. The category contains both a category name element (which we'll place in an `<h2>` header) and book elements (which have already been defined):

```
<rule>
    <target-element type="bookcategory"/>
    <dl>
      <children/>
    </dl>
</rule>

<rule>
  <target-element type="categoryname"/>
  <h2><children/></h2>
</rule>
```

All the remaining styles are simple modifications of these basic patterns. Listing 2-12 shows the style sheet for the finished document.

Listing 2-12: The books.xsl style sheet

```
<xsl>

  <rule>
    <root/>
      <html>
        <children/>
      </html>
  </rule>
```

```
<rule>
  <target-element/>
  <SPAN color="red" unstyledTag="=tagName">
  <children/>
 </SPAN>
</rule>

<rule>
  <target-element type="head"/>
    <head>
      <children/>
    </head>
</rule>

<rule>
  <target-element type="p"/>
    <p>
      <children/>
    </p>
</rule>

<rule>
  <target-element type="pagetitle"/>
    <title>
      <children/>
    </title>
</rule>


<rule>
  <target-element type="body"/>
  <body bgcolor="#FFFFFF" text="#000000">
    <children/>
  </body>
</rule>

<rule>
  <target-element type="h1"/>
  <h1>
    <children/>
  </h1>
</rule>

<rule>
  <target-element type="dl"/>
  <dl>
    <children/>
  </dl>
</rule>

<rule>
  <target-element type="dt"/>
  <dt/>
```

```
      <children/>
  </rule>

  <rule>
    <target-element type="dd"/>
    <dd/>
      <children/>
  </rule>

  <rule>
    <target-element type="bookcategory"/>
    <dl>
      <children/>
    </dl>
  </rule>

  <rule>
    <target-element type="categoryname"/>
    <h2><children/></h2>
  </rule>

  <rule>
    <target-element type="book"/>
    <dt/>
      <children/>
  </rule>

  <rule>
    <target-element type="title"/>
      <children/>
  </rule>

  <rule>
    <target-element type="author"/>
      <dd/>
      <children/>
  </rule>

  <rule>
    <target-element type="blurb"/>
      <p>
        <children/>
      </p>
  </rule>

<rule>
    <target-element type="publisher"/>
    <li/> Publisher:
      <children/>
  </rule>

  <rule>
    <target-element type="isbn"/>
```

```
    <li/> ISBN:
      <children/>
  </rule>

  <rule>
    <target-element type="pages"/>
    <li/> Pages:
      <children/>
  </rule>

  <rule>
    <target-element type="price"/>
    <li/> Price:
      <children/>
  </rule>

  <rule>
    <target-element type="recommendation"/>
    <li/> Bottom Line:
      <children/>
  </rule>


  <rule>
    <target-element type="signature"/>
    <hr/>
      <children/>
  </rule>

  <rule>
    <target-element type="copyright"/>
    Copyright
      <children/><br/>
  </rule>

  <rule>
    <target-element type="email"/>
      <children/><br/>
  </rule>

  <rule>
    <target-element type="lastmodified"/>
    Last modified:
      <children/><p/>
  </rule>

</xsl>
```

You have a solid page at this point. You can still improve the page, however. The example leaves out reordering elements and relies too heavily on the exact order in which elements appear. Ideally, a book category should have no more than one category name and that name should appear before all the category's children in the output – even if it doesn't in the input. XSL can provide this capability, but it requires some more advanced tricks (Chapter 4 returns to this example).

The example also omits element attributes. The real page has <META> and <SCRIPT> tags in the header that aren't included here. You may want to consider how to include scripts, keywords, descriptions, and other metainformation. These attributes are not particularly hard to include if you don't hew too closely to the HTML model. In particular, keep in mind that just because a piece of data is only an attribute in HTML doesn't mean it can't be a full-fledged element in XML.

As you may have noticed, this example is essentially a database report. XML is particularly well-suited for formatting database reports since every field and record can be an XML element – in fact, the data from this page is stored in a FileMaker database. The element can even have the same name as the database field.

Overall, this example may strike you as an awful lot of work to produce something that could have been written in HTML in the first place. The benefits of XML will become apparent when browsers support it natively and make conversion unnecessary. Then Web spiders and other automated programs will be able to gauge the contents of the page in a more accurate fashion.

Furthermore, you won't need to write a new style sheet or tag set from scratch for every document. In many cases, you'll be able to reuse preexisting style sheets – either your own previous style sheets or standard style sheets across a profession. With industry standard style sheets and tag sets, search engines can become even more powerful and useful.

Summary

In this chapter, you created simple XML documents. You also learned the following skills:

◆ How to invent tags that fit your document, rather than trying to fit your document into a limited, predefined set of tags.

◆ How to write a style sheet that specifies how the contents of each element are formatted and presented.

◆ How to use MSXSL and style sheets to convert XML documents into regular HTML so they can be viewed in standard Web browsers.

In the next chapter, we begin crossing the *t*'s and dotting the *i*'s as you explore the detailed rules of a well-formed document. In later chapters, you learn how to do even more with style sheets.

Chapter 3

Formalizing XML

IN THIS CHAPTER

- ◆ XML documents

- ◆ Text in XML

- ◆ Comments

- ◆ Entity references

- ◆ CDATA

- ◆ Tags

- ◆ Attributes

- ◆ Well-formedness rules

HTML 4.0 HAS about three hundred different tags. Most of these tags have half a dozen possible attributes for several thousand possible variations. Because XML is more powerful than HTML, you may think XML would have even more tags, but you'd be wrong. XML gets its power through simplicity and extensibility – not a plethora of tags.

Actually, XML predefines almost no tags at all. Instead, XML enables you to define your own tags as needed. These tags and the documents built from them are not completely arbitrary, however. They have to follow a specific set of rules elaborated in this chapter. A document that follows these rules is *well-formed*. Well-formedness is the minimum criteria necessary for XML parsers, processors, and browsers to read your files. In this chapter, you'll examine the rules for well-formed documents and focus on how XML differs from HTML.

Defining XML Documents

An XML document contains XML markup and text. The document is a sequential set of bytes of fixed length which adheres to certain constraints and may or may not be a file. For instance, an XML document may:

♦ Be stored in a database.

♦ Be read from a network stream.

♦ Be created on the fly in memory by a CGI program.

♦ Be a combination of several different files, each of which is embedded in another.

♦ Never exist in a file of its own.

Nothing essential is lost if you think of an XML document as a file, as long as you remember that it may not be a file on a hard drive.

XML documents are made up of storage units called *entities*. Each entity contains either text or binary data, but never both types of data. Text data is comprised of characters. Binary data is used for images, applets, and so forth.

For example, a raw HTML file that includes <IMG> tags is an entity but not a document. An HTML file plus all the pictures embedded in it through the <IMG> tag is a complete document.

In this chapter, I discuss only simple XML documents that have a single entity — the document itself. Furthermore, these documents will only contain text data, not binary data like images or applets. In later chapters, however, I demonstrate how external entities and entity references can combine multiple files and other data sources to create a single XML document.

Text in XML

Text consists of characters. A character is a letter, a digit, a punctuation mark, a space, a tab, and so forth. XML uses the Unicode character set which not only includes the usual letters and symbols from English and other Western European alphabets, but also includes the Cyrillic, Greek, Hebrew, Arabic, and Devanagari alphabets as well as the most common Han ideographs for Chinese and Japanese and the Hangul syllables from Korean. This chapter sticks to English text; Chapter 8 introduces these different scripts.

A document's text is divided into character data and markup. To a first approximation, markup describes a document's logical structure while character data is the basic information of the document. For example, recall Listing 2-2, greeting.xml, from the preceding chapter:

```
<?xml version="1.0" standalone="yes"?>
<greeting>
Hello XML!
</greeting>
```

In this example, `<?xml version="1.0" standalone="yes"?>`, `<greeting>`, and `</greeting>` are markup. `Hello XML!` is the character data. One of the big advantages of XML over other formats is that XML clearly separates the actual data of a document from its markup.

Markup includes all tags, processing instructions, DTDs, entity references, character references, comments, and CDATA section delimiters. Everything else is character data. This distinction is tricky, however, because some markup turns into character data when a document is processed. For example, the markup `&gt;` is turned into the greater than sign character (>). The character data left after the document is processed and all markup that refers to character data is replaced by the actual character data is called *parsed character data* (PCDATA).

Comments

XML comments are almost exactly like HTML comments. They begin with `<!--` and end with `-->`. All data between the `<!--` and `-->` is ignored by the XML processor. Use comments to make notes to yourself or comment out sections of text, as in the following example:

```
<?xml version="1.0" standalone="yes"?>
<!--This is the second example from XML: eXtensible Markup Language-->
<greeting>
Hello XML!
<!--Goodbye XML-->
</greeting>
```

Comments may not come before the XML declaration, which absolutely must be the first item in the document. For example, the following example is not acceptable:

```
<!--This is the second example from XML: eXtensible Markup Language-->
<?xml version="1.0" standalone="yes"?>
<greeting>
Hello XML!
<!--Goodbye XML-->
</greeting>
```

Comments may not be placed inside a tag. For example, the following usage is illegal:

```
<?xml version="1.0" standalone="yes"?>
<greeting>
Hello XML!
</greeting> <!--Goodbye--> >
```

Comments may be used to surround and hide tags, however. In the following example, the `<antigreeting>` tag and all its children are commented out. These tags are not shown when the document is rendered.

```
<?xml version="1.0" standalone="yes"?>
<document>
<greeting>
Hello XML!
</greeting>
<!--
<antigreeting>
Goodbye XML!
</antigreeting>
-->
</document>
```

Because comments effectively delete sections of text, make sure the remaining text is still a well-formed XML document. Be careful not to comment out essential tags, such as in the following document:

```
<?xml version="1.0" standalone="yes"?>
<greeting>
Hello XML!
<!--
</greeting>
-->
```

After the commented text is removed, the following remains:

```
<?xml version="1.0" standalone="yes"?>
<greeting>
Hello XML!
```

Because the `<greeting>` tag is not matched by a closing `</greeting>` tag, this document is no longer a well-formed XML document.

One final constraint exists on comments. The two-hyphen string `--` may not occur inside a comment except as part of its opening or closing tag. For example, the following is an illegal comment:

```
<!--The red door--that is, the second one--was left open-->
```

This constraint means you cannot nest comments as in the following example:

```
<?xml version="1.0" standalone="yes"?>
<document>
  <greeting>
    Hello XML!
  </greeting>
<!--
  <antigreeting>
    <!--Goodbye XML!-->
  </antigreeting>
-->
</document>
```

You also may run into trouble if you're commenting out a lot of C, Java, or JavaScript source code that's full of expressions like `i--` or `numberLeft--`. Generally, it's not hard to work around this problem once you recognize it.

Entity References

XML predefines the five entity references listed in Table 3-1. Entity references are used in XML documents in place of specific characters that would otherwise be interpreted as part of markup. For instance, the entity reference `&lt;` stands for the less than sign <, which would otherwise be interpreted as the start of a tag.

TABLE 3-1 XML PREDEFINED ENTITY REFERENCES

Entity Reference	Character
&amp;	&
&lt;	<
&gt;	>
&quot;	"
&apos;	'

Raw less than signs and ampersands in normal XML text are always interpreted as starting tags and entity references, respectively. (The abnormal text is CDATA sections, which are described in the following section.) Therefore, less than signs and ampersands must always be encoded as `&lt;` and `&amp;`, respectively. For example, you would write the phrase `Ben & Jerry's New York Super Fudge Chunk Ice Cream` as `Ben &amp; Jerry's New York Super Fudge Chunk Ice Cream`.

Greater than signs, double quotes, and apostrophes must be encoded when they would otherwise be interpreted as part of markup. It's easier to encode all of these characters rather than determine whether a particular usage would be interpreted as markup, however.

Entity references may also be used inside tags, as in the following example;

```
<PARAM name="joke" value="The diner said,
  &quot;Waiter, There&apos;s a fly in my soup!&quot;">
</param>
```

CDATA

Generally, anything inside a pair of <> angle brackets is markup and anything that is not inside these brackets is character data. In CDATA sections, however, all text is pure character data. Anything that looks like a tag or an entity reference is really just the text of the tag or the entity reference. The XML processor does not try to interpret it in any way.

Use CDATA sections when you want all text to be interpreted as pure character data rather than markup. CDATA sections are primarily useful when you have a large block of text that contains a lot of <, >, &, or " characters but no markup — such as C and Java source code, for example.

CDATA sections are also extremely useful if you're trying to write about XML in XML. For example, this book contains many small blocks of XML code. If I converted the book to XML, I'd have to painstakingly replace all the less than signs with < and all the ampersands with & as follows:

```
&lt;?xml version="1.0" standalone="yes"?&gt;
&lt;greeting&gt;
Hello XML!
&lt;/greeting&gt;
```

To avoid these conversions, I can instead use a CDATA section to indicate that a block of text is to be presented as is with no translation. CDATA sections begin with <![CDATA[and end with]]>, as in the following example:

```
<![CDATA[
<?xml version="1.0" standalone="yes"?>
<greeting>
Hello XML!
</greeting>
 ]]>
```

The only disallowed text within a CDATA section is the closing CDATA tag]]>. Comments may appear in CDATA sections but do not act as comments. Both the comment tags and all the text they contain will be rendered.

Since a CDATA section may not contain]]>, CDATA sections cannot nest. If you need to write about CDATA sections in XML, you have to use the < and & escapes.

You don't need CDATA sections too often, but when you do need them, you need them badly.

Tags

Markup distinguishes XML files from plain text files. Tags constitute the largest part of markup (Chapter 2 shows you how to use tags). This section more precisely defines tags and the details of their usage.

In brief, a *tag* is anything in an XML document that begins with < and ends with > and is not inside a comment or a CDATA section. Thus, an XML tag has the same form as an HTML tag. Start (or opening) tags begin with a < followed by the name of the tag. End (or closing) tags begin with a </ followed by the name of the tag. The first > encountered closes the tag. Empty tags are closed with a />.

Names

Every tag has a name. Tag names must begin with a letter or an underscore (_). Subsequent characters in the name may include letters, digits, underscores, hyphens, and periods. The names cannot include white space. (The underscore often substitutes for white space.) The following are legal XML tags:

```
<HELP>
<Book>
<volume>
<heading1>
<section.paragraph>
<Mary_Smith>
<_8ball>
```

Colons are also technically legal in tag names, but this character will probably be used in the future to introduce namespaces into XML. (*Namespaces* enable you to mix and match tag sets that may use the same tag names.) Until then, you should not use colons in your tag names.

The following are illegal XML tags:

```
<Book%7>
<volume control>
<1heading>
<Mary Smith>
<.employee.salary>
```

 The rules for tag names actually apply to names of many other things as well. The same rules are used for attribute names, entity names, and a number of other constructs you encounter over the next several chapters.

Closing tags have the same name as their opening tag but are prefixed with a / after the initial angle bracket. For example, if the opening tag is `<FOO>`, the closing tag is `</FOO>`. The following are the end tags for the previous set of legal start tags:

```
</HELP>
</Book>
</volume>
</heading1>
</section.paragraph>
</Mary_Smith>
</_8ball>
```

Unlike HTML, where `<P>` and `<p>` are the same tag and a `</p>` can close a `<P>` tag, XML names are case-sensitive. The following are not proper end tags for the preceding set of legal start tags.

```
</help>
</book>
</Volume>
</HEADING1>
</Section.Paragraph>
</MARY_SMITH>
</_8BALL>
```

When using a tag set developed by someone else, you must adopt their case convention.

Empty Tags

Many HTML tags do not have closing tags. For example, there are no `</LI>`, `</IMG>`, `</HR>`, or `</BR>` tags. Some Web designers and HTML tools include `</LI>` tags after their list items, but the HTML 4.0 standard specifically denies that this tag is required. Like all unrecognized tags in HTML, the presence of an unnecessary `</LI>` has no effect on the rendered output.

In XML, however, these tags may not simply be ignored. The whole point of XML is to allow new tags to be discovered as a document is parsed. Furthermore, an XML processor must be able to determine on the fly whether an unknown tag has an end tag.

XML distinguishes between tags with or without closing tags. *Empty tags*, tags without closing tags, are closed with a slash and a closing angle bracket /`>`, such as `<BR/>` or `<HR/>`.

Current Web browsers deal inconsistently with these tags. If you're trying to maintain backwards compatibility, however, use closing tags without including text as follows:

```
<BR></BR>
<HR></HR>
<IMG></IMG>
```

When you learn about DTDs and style sheets in the following chapters, you'll see a couple more ways to maintain backward and forward compatibility with HTML in documents that must be parsed by legacy browsers.

Attributes

Start tags and empty tags may optionally contain attributes. *Attributes* are name-value pairs separated by an equals sign (=), as shown in the following example:

```
<greeting language="English">
Hello XML!
<movie src="WavingHand.mov"/>
</greeting>
```

In the preceding example, the `<greeting>` tag has a language attribute, which has the value `English`. The `<movie>` tag has a `src` attribute, which has the value `WavingHand.mov`.

Attribute names are strings that follow the same rules as tag names. That is, attribute names must begin with a letter or an underscore (_). Subsequent letters in the name may include letters, digits, underscores, hyphens, and periods. The names cannot include white space. (The underscore often substitutes for white space.)

Attributes values are also strings. Even when the string shows a number, as in the following `LENGTH` attribute, that number is the two characters 7 and 2 — not the number 72.

```
<RULE LENGTH="72"/>
```

If you're writing code to process XML, you'll need to convert the string to a number before performing arithmetic on it.

Unlike attribute names, there are few limits on the content of an attribute value. Attribute values may contain white space, begin with a number, or contain any punctuation characters (except, sometimes, for single and double quotes).

XML attribute values are delimited by quote marks. Unlike HTML attributes, XML attributes must be enclosed in quotes. Double quotes are commonly used. If the attribute value itself contains a double quote, single quotes may be used, as in the following example:

```
<RECT LENGTH='7"' WIDTH='8.5"'/>
```

If the attribute value contains both single and double quotes, both quotes must be replaced with the entity references ' (apostrophe) and " (double quote), as in the following example:

```
<RECT LENGTH='8&apos;7&quot;' WIDTH="10&apos;6&quot;"/>
```

The same tag cannot have two attributes with the same name. The following example is illegal:

```
<RECT SIDE="8" SIDE="10"/>
```

Attribute names are case-sensitive. The SIDE attribute is not the same as the side or the Side attribute. Therefore, the following example is legal:

```
<BOX SIDE="8" side="10" Side="31"/>
```

The preceding example is extremely confusing, however, and I strongly urge you not to write markup in this manner.

Well-Formed XML

Although you can make up as many tags as you need, your XML documents need to follow certain rules to be well-formed. If a document is not well-formed, most attempts to read or render it will fail.

To be well-formed, all markup, character data, and comments must adhere to the rules given in the preceding sections. Furthermore, the tags and character data must relate to each other in accordance with the following list of rules:

1. The document must start with an XML declaration.

2. Elements that contain character data or other elements must have matching start and end tags.

3. Tags denoting empty elements must end with />.

4. The document must contain exactly one element that completely contains all other elements.

5. Elements may nest but may not overlap.

6. The characters < and & may only be used to start tags and entities, respectively.

7. The only entity references that appear are &, <, >, ', and ".

The preceding rules must be adjusted slightly for documents that have a DTD, and there are additional rules for well-formedness that define the relationship between the document and its DTD, but we'll explore these complications in following chapters. For now, let's look at each of these simple rules in more detail.

1. Start with an XML Declaration

The XML declaration for XML 1.0 follows:

```
<?xml version="1.0" standalone="yes"?>
```

This declaration must be the first item in the file. XML processors read the first several bytes of the file and compare those bytes against various encodings of the string <?xml to determine which character set is being used (UTF-8, big-endian Unicode, or little-endian Unicode). Nothing (except perhaps for an invisible byte order mark – refer to Chapter 8 for more information on this subject) should come before this declaration, including white space. For instance, a blank line is not an acceptable way to start an XML file.

2. Match Start Tags and End Tags

Web browsers are relatively forgiving if you forget to close an HTML tag. For instance, if you include a <B> tag in your document but no corresponding </B> tag, the entire document after the <B> tag will be formatted bold. The document will still be displayed, however.

XML is not so forgiving. Every nonempty tag (that is, tags that do not end with />), must be closed with the corresponding end tag. If a document fails to close a tag, the browser or renderer simply reports an error message and does not display any of the document's content in any form.

3. End Empty Tags with />

Tags that do not contain data, such as HTML's <BR>, <HR>, and <IMG>, do not require closing tags. However, empty XML tags must be identified by closing with a /> rather than just a >. For example, the XML equivalent of <BR>, <HR>, and <IMG> are <BR/>, <HR/>, and <IMG/>, respectively.

Current Web browsers deal inconsistently with these tags. If you're trying to maintain backwards compatibility, however, use closing tags without including text as follows:

```
<BR></BR>
<HR></HR>
<IMG></IMG>
```

4. One Element Completely Contains All Other Elements

An XML document begins with a prolog. The prolog is an XML declaration, optionally followed by DTD (discussed starting in Chapter 5). The root start tag, also known as the document tag, must follow the prolog. This tag is a nonempty tag that encloses the entire document. It may have, but does not have to have, the name *root* or *document*. For instance, the root element is `<greeting>` in the following document:

```
<?xml version="1.0" standalone="yes"?>
<greeting>
Hello XML!
</greeting>
```

5. Tags May Nest but May Not Overlap

Tag pairs may contain other tag pairs, but they may not contain a start tag without its corresponding end tag or an end tag without its matching start tag. For example, the following code is legal XML:

```
<pre><code>int n = n + 1;</code></pre>
```

The following code is not legal XML, however, because the closing `</pre>` tag comes before the closing `</code>` tag:

```
<pre><code>int n = n + 1; </pre></code>
```

Most HTML browsers can handle this case with ease. XML browsers are required to report an error for this construct, however.

Empty tags may appear anywhere, of course, as in the following example:

```
<people>Isaac Newton<hr/>William Shakespeare</people>
```

In combination with rule 4 – the document must contain exactly one element which completely contains all other elements – this rule implies that for all nonroot elements, there is exactly one other element that contains the nonroot element but does not contain any other element that contains the nonroot element. This immediate container is called the *parent* of the nonroot element. The nonroot element is called the *child* of the parent element. Thus, each nonroot element always has exactly one parent, but a single element may have an indefinite number of children or no children at all.

Consider Listing 3-1. The root element is the document element. This element contains a single child — a bookcategory element. The bookcategory element contains some character data (In Print) as well as two book children. The first book element contains eight children: title, author, publisher, isbn, pages, price, recommendation, and blurb. The second book element contains seven children: title, author, publisher, isbn, pages, recommendation, and blurb. Each of these elements contains only character data — not more children.

Listing 3-1: Parents and Children

```
<?xml version="1.0" standalone="yes"?>
<document>
  <bookcategory>
    In Print
    <book>
      <title>Java Secrets</title>
      <author>Elliotte Rusty Harold</author>
      <publisher>IDG Books Worldwide</publisher>
      <isbn>0-764-58007-8</isbn>
      <pages>900</pages>
      <price>$59.99</price>
      <recommendation>Buy It</recommendation>
      <blurb>
        The Java virtual machine, byte code, the sun
        packages, native methods, stand-alone applications,
        and a few more naughty bits.
      </blurb>
    </book>

    <book>
      <title>JavaBeans</title>
      <author>Elliotte Rusty Harold</author>
      <publisher>IDG Books Worldwide</publisher>
      <isbn>0-7645-8052-3</isbn>
      <pagecount>355</pagecount>
      <price>39.99</price>
      <recommendation>Buy It</recommendation>
      <blurb>An excellent introduction to JavaBeans</blurb>
    </book>
</book>
```

In programmer terms, this means that an XML document forms a *tree*. Figure 3-1 shows why this structure is called a tree. The structure starts from the root and gradually bushes out to the leaves on the end of the tree. Trees have a number of nice properties that are convenient for people writing programs that read XML documents. However, the tree structure in and of itself isn't of great importance to people who simply edit XML documents by hand.

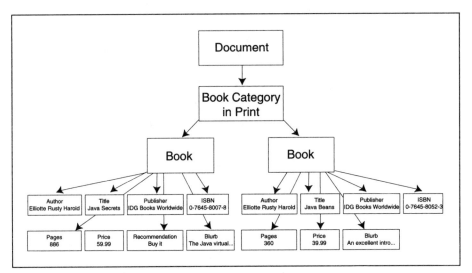

Figure 3-1: Listing 3-1's tree structure

6. Attribute Values Must Be Quoted

In XML, all attribute values must be enclosed by quote marks. This isn't true in HTML. For instance, HTML allows tags with unquoted attributes like the following:

```
<a href=http://sunsite.unc.edu/xml/>
```

The only restriction is that the attribute value must not contain embedded spaces itself.

XML requires all attribute values to be enclosed in quote marks, whether or not the attribute value includes spaces:

```
<a href="http://sunsite.unc.edu/xml/">
```

If an attribute value itself includes double quotes, you may use single quotes to surround the value instead:

```
<IMG ALT='And God said, "Let there be light,"
    and there was light'/>
```

If an attribute value includes both single and double quotes, you may use the entity reference ' for a single quote (an apostrophe) and " for a double quote:

```
<PARAM name="joke" value="The diner said,
    &quot;Waiter, There&apos;s a fly in my soup!&quot;">
```

7. Use Only < and & to Start Tags and Entities, Respectively

XML assumes an opening angle bracket always starts a tag and an ampersand always starts an entity reference. (HTML technically makes these assumptions as well, but most browsers are more forgiving.) For example, consider the following line:

```
<h1>A Homage to Ben & Jerry's
    New York Super Fudge Chunk Ice Cream</h1>
```

Web browsers will probably display it correctly, but for maximum safety you should escape the ampersand with & as in the following line:

```
<h1>A Homage to Ben &amp; Jerry's New York Super Fudge Chunk Ice
    Cream</h1>
```

The open angle bracket (<) is similar. Consider the following common line of Java code:

```
<code>    for (int i = 0; i <= n; i++ ) { </code>
```

Both XML and HTML consider the less than sign in <= to be the start of a tag. The tag continues until the next >. Thus, this line gets rendered as

```
for (int i = 0; i
```

rather than

```
for (int i = 0; i <= n; i++ ) {
```

The =n; i++) { is interpreted as part of an unrecognized tag.

The less than sign can be included in text in both XML and HTML by writing it as < as in the following example:

```
<code>    for (int i = 0; i &lt;= n; i++ ) { </code>
```

Well-formed XML requires & to be written as & and < to be written as < whenever they're used as themselves rather than as part of a tag or entity.

8. Use Only &, <, >, ', and " as Entity References

You're probably familiar with a number of entity references from HTML. For example, © inserts the copyright symbol © and ® inserts the registered trademark symbol ®. Other than the five entity references already discussed, however, entity references can only be used in XML unless they're defined in a DTD first.

Because you don't know about DTDs yet, if the ampersand character & appears anywhere in your document, it must be immediately followed by amp;, lt;, gt;, apos;, or quot;. All other uses violate well-formedness. In the next chapter, you'll learn how DTDs make it possible to define new entity references that insert particular symbols or chunks of boiler plate text.

Summary

In this chapter, you learned the rules that an XML document must follow to be well-formed. In particular, you learned the following skills:

◆ In an XML document, text is divided into markup and character data.

◆ Character data is the document's basic information.

◆ Markup describes this basic information.

◆ In CDATA sections, delimited by <[CDATA[and]]>, characters which would normally be interpreted as markup are instead treated as character data.

◆ Authors may use comments, delimited by <!-- and -->, to insert notes to themselves or collaborators not intended to be seen by the end reader.

◆ Entity references enable authors to insert characters like &, <, >, and quotation marks that would otherwise be interpreted as markup.

◆ Tags begin with < and end with >. Each tag has a name and perhaps some attributes.

◆ Each start tag must be matched by an end tag of the form </tagname>.

◆ Empty tags must be closed with />.

◆ Attributes are contained in start or empty tags. They have a name and a quoted string value.

After combining these rules, it is not particularly difficult to write well-formed XML documents. XML browsers are less forgiving of poor syntax than HTML browsers, however, so you need to be careful.

If you violate any of the well-formedness constraints described in this chapter, the MSXSL processor and other XML parsers report a syntax error. Thus, the process of writing XML resembles the process of writing code in a real programming language. You write it, then you compile it, and when the compilation fails you note the errors reported and fix them.

Generally, this iterative process contains several edit-compile cycles before you get to look at the finished document. Despite this sequence, there's no question that writing XML is much easier than writing C or Java source code. With a little practice, you'll build up to a point where you have relatively few errors and can write XML almost as quickly as you can type.

Chapter 4

XSL

ONE OF THE fundamental principals of XML is the separation of data from the presentation of the data. The last several chapters have focused on how you describe data. This chapter focuses on how you present data.

Each XML document can be associated with an XSL style sheet that describes how individual elements should be formatted. XSL style sheets provide far more detailed control over appearance than possible with standard or nonstandard HTML. This chapter shows how to use style sheets to provide custom appearances that give a Web site with a unified look and feel.

What Is XSL?

XSL is based on the Document Style Semantics and Specification Language (DSSSL) and Cascading Style Sheets (CSS). Although it's simpler than DSSSL and more powerful than CSS, the basic format should seem familiar to anyone acquainted with either DSSSL or CSS. Furthermore, XSL uses JavaScript to provide more complex, dynamic behaviors.

An XSL style sheet is itself an XML document. The elements of this document are a series of rules that describe how particular XML tags are to be converted to flow objects as the XML document is read. The flow objects are marked up text.

The markup language of the output flow objects can be either HTML or DSSSL. This chapter focuses on HTML because it is simpler, more widely understood, and better supported by current tools.

The XML document and its associated style sheet are combined by an XSL processor to produce an HTML document. In the basic procedure, an XML document and an XSL style sheet are both fed into an XSL processor. The processor applies the style sheet to the document and outputs an HTML file. This HTML file can then be placed on a Web server for the world to view. You can even automate the process with CGI scripts, Java servlets, or ActiveX controls – while you write and save XML documents, these XML documents are converted to HTML on the fly and served to browsers.

Using the XSL Processor

The XSL processor can be a standalone program like MSXSL (discussed in a following section) or part of a larger XML browser. You can think of the XSL processor as a black box into which XML elements are fed. For every element that goes into the box, the processor consults the style sheet to find the rule that matches the element. When it finds the rule, the processor takes whatever action the rule says to take; generally, to output the element's content plus assorted markup. On occasion, however, the rule may ask the processor to perform more complicated operations such as sorting the data before outputting it, running a particular JavaScript program on the data, or adding missing content to the data.

Rather than being one long conversion process, the XSL processor formats each element upon receipt. Most of the time, the XSL processor processes elements recursively, though this behavior can be changed.

In essence, an XSL processor receives input from the XML processor and – depending on the elements it receives – outputs formatted data. For example, every time the XSL processor receives a `<strong>` element from the XML processor, it may output the same content as bold text. If the XSL processor is an audio renderer, it may simply pump up the volume a notch as it reads the `<strong>` element. Other styles are certainly possible.

DSSSL

DSSSL, the Document Style Semantics and Specification Language, (pronounced *dissal*, rhymes with *thistle* or *missal*) is an extremely powerful, extensible, and precise means of specifying exactly what you want to see on the page. Furthermore, DSSSL is an ISO standard (10179:1996).

Regrettably, DSSSL, like SGML, is quite complex and not widely understood. Furthermore, a DSSSL file requires an additional level of translation before it becomes something you can read or print. Because this book's primary focus is on the use of XML on Web pages, this chapter will instead focus on output as HTML. DSSSL could easily be a book in its own right.

The exact format of the processor output depends on the style sheet used by the processor. If the style sheet changes, inputting the same XML document to the XSL processor produces different output.

In this book, the XSL processor of choice is Microsoft's MSXSL, which was introduced in Chapter 2. To summarize briefly, you convert .xml and .xsl files into a single .html file by feeding the .xml and .xsl files as input to MSXSL in a DOS window. For example,

```
C:\XML> msxsl -i books.xml -s books.xsl -o books.html
```

This example tells DOS to run the `msxsl` program on the XML file `books.xml`, format the output according to the instructions found in `books.xsl`, and place the output in the file `books.html`.

Technically, the `-s` and `-o` flags are only necessary when the style sheet and output file names do not match the input file name. You can get the same result in this case by typing the following:

```
C:\XML> msxml -i books.xml
```

In general, a single style sheet is used for many different XML documents, so the -s flag is necessary at a minimum.

Understanding How XSL Works

As previously mentioned, an XSL style sheet is itself an XML document. The root element of the style sheet is `<xsl>`. Each `<xsl>` element contains one or more rule elements. Each rule has a target and an action. The *target* is a sort of regular expression defining to which XML elements the rule applies. The *action* is the list of flow objects generated when the rule is applied.

An XSL processor reads an XML document looking for elements that match its targets. Each time it encounters a matching element, the processor takes the action specified in the rule. Generally, each action is just a series of HTML or DSSSL tags to be output in some combination with the content of the element. Actions may also output nonmarkup text or even run simple scripts or programs.

The root element of an XSL style sheet is `<xsl>`. The xsl element contains rule elements. The rule elements contain one or more targets followed by the action. In other words, a typical style sheet has the following basic form:

```
<xsl>

  <rule>
    <target-element type="tagname"/>
    action
  </rule>

  <rule>
    <target-element type="tagname"/>
    action
  </rule>

</xsl>
```

The action is the combination of HTML tags, new text, and XML element content to be output. For example, suppose you want to replace XML book elements with HTML paragraphs. In other words, when the XSL processor reads the XML element `<book>Principia Discordia</book>`, it should write the text `<p>Principia Discordia</p>`. The following rule accomplishes this:

```
  <rule>
    <target-element type="book"/>
    <p><children/></p>
  </rule>
```

The `<children/>` tag refers to the contents of the target. When this rule is applied to a particular book element, the string `<p>` is written on the output, followed by the contents of that book element, followed by the string `</p>`. Character data in the book element is simply written on the output. If the book element contains child elements, however, then those child elements are also compared against the rules in the style sheet before they're written. In general, processing is recursive.

On occasion, the XSL style sheet won't specify a rule that matches every element in the document. The XSL processor provides a default rule if no other rule applies. The default rule looks like this:

```
<rule>
  <target-element/>
  <children/>
</rule>
```

This rule says that the children of any matched element should be output. If the children include other elements, they are output recursively. If the matched element contains character data, it is simply written onto the output. By default, all output takes place in the order in which the input appears in the XML document. In following sections, you'll learn ways to reorder elements in the output.

Occasionally, you need to make slight adjustments to standard HTML tags to make the XSL style sheet a well-formed XML document. For example, empty tags like `<br>` must be written as `<br/>` in the XSL style sheet. The XSL processor is responsible for converting this tag to the HTML standard tag `<br>` when it processes a document.

The rest of this chapter mostly consists of elaborating various ways to specify targets and take actions.

HTML in XSL

Although XSL does not support arbitrary HTML tags as output, it does support most of the important semantic tags. XSL tends to omit formatting tags like `<B>` and `<I>`, and even relatively semantic formatting tags like `<CODE>`, `<STRONG>`, and `<EM>`. Instead, the effects of these tags should be achieved through style attributes as described in a following section. In particular, XSL supports the following tags. Tags listed in parentheses should only appear as children of their parent element.

- SCRIPT
- PRE
- HTML (TITLE; META; BASE)
- BODY
- DIV
- BR
- SPAN
- TABLE (CAPTION; COL; COLGROUP; THEAD; TBODY; TFOOT; TR; TD)
- A
- FORM (INPUT; SELECT; TEXTAREA)
- HR
- IMG (MAP; AREA)
- OBJECT (PARAM; FRAMESET)

The 1-7-1998 technology preview release of MSXSL on which this chapter is based does not implement these restrictions. The release allows arbitrary HTML tags, including formatting tags like <B>, <I>, <CODE>, <STRONG>, and <EM>.

Most of these tags are straightforward. If you are not familiar with these tags, consult any decent HTML reference, such as the Web Design Group's Web authoring reference at http://www.htmlhelp.com/reference/ or Ed Tittel's *Hip Pocket Guide to HTML 4* (IDG Books Worldwide, Inc., 1998, ISBN 0-7645-3196-4). However, I will pull out two tags that are going to be especially useful in the context of XSL for special treatment. These are <SPAN> and <DIV>.

The <SPAN> and <DIV> tags are used to apply formatting to particular regions of text. The <SPAN> tag merely applies the formatting. The <DIV> tag also blocks off the text from what precedes and follows it, much like enclosing the text in <P></P> would do. <SPAN> is used for inline elements (tags that apply to only part of a sentence or a paragraph). <DIV> works for block level elements that should not be run together with word wrapping.

Listing 4-1 is a simple XSL style sheet with a single rule that puts each element in its own <DIV> block. Figure 4-1 shows the result of processing the books.xml page, Listing 2-9 from Chapter 2, with this style sheet.

Listing 4-1: The div.xsl style sheet

```
<xsl>
  <rule>
    <target-element/>
    <DIV><children/></DIV>
  </rule>
</xsl>
```

Listing 4-2 is a similar style sheet that puts each and every element in its own <SPAN> block. Figure 4-2 shows the result of processing the books.xml **page,** Listing 2-9 from Chapter 2, with this style sheet.

Listing 4-2: The span.xsl style sheet

```
<xsl>
  <rule>
    <target-element/>
    <SPAN><children/></SPAN>
  </rule>
</xsl>
```

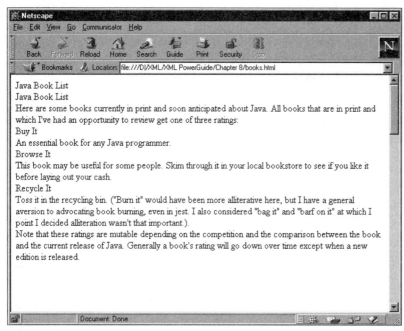

Figure 4-1: Elements separated with <DIV>

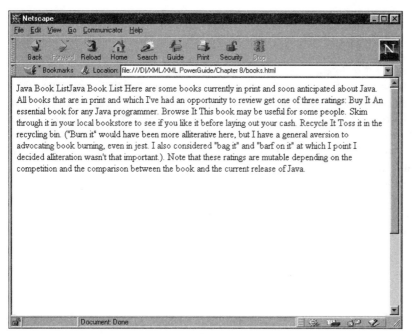

Figure 4-2: Elements separated with <SPAN>

Figures 4-1 and 4-2 show the results after Listing 2-9 has been formatted with the style sheets in Listings 4-1 and 4-2 – these figures illustrate the basic difference between <SPAN> and <DIV>. Note, however, that Figure 4-1 and Figure 4-2 are both produced by the same XML file. Changing the style sheet alone, without even touching the XML file, radically changes what the reader sees.

In fact, back in Chapter 2 when Listing 2-9 was first introduced, the style sheet wasn't even in the back of my head! That's how separate style sheets and data files are in XML. This clean division between data and formatting, in which one can be developed almost independently of the other, is extremely useful. It's one of the key ideas HTML is missing, which has led to much needless bickering between so-called HTML purists and graphic designers transitioning to the Web. Separating the information design from the graphic design enables writers and designers to each do what they do best without stepping on each other's toes.

The <DIV>-based style sheet in Listing 4-1 is more appropriate for general use. Most of the time, however, you'll develop a more focused style sheet that uses both <SPAN> and <DIV> as well as other tags to apply more attractive formatting. By themselves, <DIV> and <SPAN> aren't very useful: <SPAN> does exactly nothing while <DIV> acts mostly like a redundant <P>. However, you can apply a style attribute to a <DIV> or <SPAN> tag to work some real magic.

Style Attributes

HTML 4.0 adds a style attribute to most tags (all tags except <BASE>, <BASEFONT>, <HEAD>, <HTML>, <META>, <PARAM>, <SCRIPT>, <STYLE>, and <TITLE>), though it's most common in <SPAN> and <DIV> tags. In fact, <SPAN> elements primarily exist to possess style attributes.

The attribute specifies how the content inside the element will be formatted with a syntax based on Cascading Style Sheets. Cascading Style Sheets, introduced in HTML 4.0, are an alternative to XSL. CSS enables you to set font properties, box properties, colors, text spacing, and more for the standard HTML tags. For example, to specify that a level 2 heading is to be formatted in 16 point Universe bold italic, you could write the following:

```
<H2 style="font-size: 16pt; font-weight: bold;
   font-style: italic; font-family: Universe;">
   Style Atributes
</H2>
```

HTML purists may object at this point that this approach of including style information in HTML files mixes content and presentation, which is exactly what XML and style sheets intend to avoid. This objection is misguided, however.

In all the following listings, HTML is used purely as an output format. The original data resides only in the XML files. This HTML may not be ideal, but as long as the HTML is not edited directly (only automatically generated from the XML document and the XSL style sheet), the data and the presentation can remain separate until they're seen by the end reader.

In theory, HTML style attributes specify formatting for the element in one of many different style languages. In practice, everyone uses Cascading Style Sheets. Technically, an HTML document that uses style attributes in any of its tags should specify the language of those attributes in a `<META>` header like the following:

```
<META http-equiv="Content-Style-Type" content="text/css">
```

In practice, most Web browsers still do the right thing with the formatting if you leave this header out. Nonetheless, it certainly doesn't hurt to include this tag in the HTML `<HEAD>` element.

Listing 4-3 is a variation on Listing 4-1, using style attributes to say that each element should be formatted in 20 point bold Courier. Figures 4-3 and 4-4 show the resulting output in Navigator 4.0 and Internet Explorer 4.0, respectively.

Listing 4-3: A style sheet for a page in 20 point bold Courier

```
<xsl>
  <rule>
    <target-element/>
    <DIV style="font-size: 20pt;
      font-weight: bold; font-family: Courier;">
      <children/>
    </DIV>
  </rule>
</xsl>
```

Figures 4-3 and 4-4 demonstrate several problems. Most importantly, just because you can specify a font does not mean it will actually be available, as you can tell from the bitmappy type. While Courier is easily available on Macs, it isn't very reliable on Windows, where these ugly screen shots were taken. The reverse is true for some popular Windows fonts like Arial or Times New Roman. One problem that's not so obvious here is that Windows fonts tend to appear larger than the same point size on a Mac. Too much precision regarding a page's appearance can lead to illegibility for much of your audience. It's better not to overspecify.

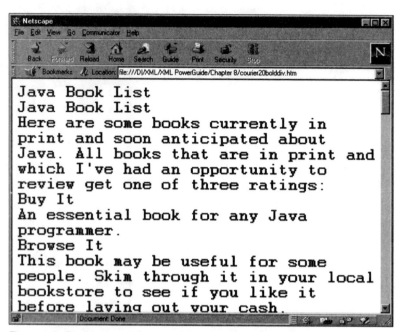

Figure 4-3: The books.xml page with styled elements in Navigator 4.0

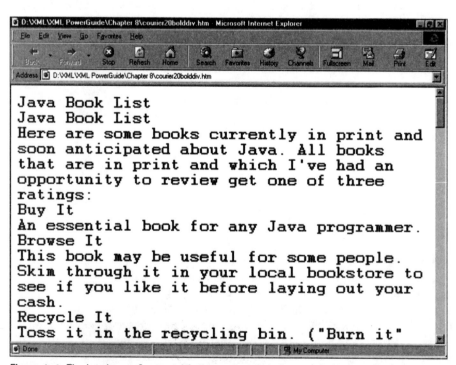

Figure 4-4: The books.xml page with the same styled elements in Internet Explorer 4.0

XSL allows one shortcut for applying styles to elements. Rather than using the style tag directly, you can simply include each style as an attribute. For example, Listing 4-3 could have been written as follows:

```
<xsl>
  <rule>
    <target-element/>
    <DIV font-size="20pt" font-weight="bold"
       font-family="Courier">
      <children/>
    </DIV>
  </rule>
</xsl>
```

While the preceding <DIV> tag is not valid HTML, the XSL processor automatically converts this tag to the valid form given in Listing 4-3. The end result is the same. You are welcome to use either syntax for including style attributes in the HTML tags, though this may become confusing if you're working with both HTML and XML/XSL documents.

Style Inheritance

Many (though not all) styles applied to an HTML element also apply to the element's children. This approach can be used to apply default styles to the entire document or parts of the document. For example, Listing 4-3 provides a style attribute for each <DIV> tag used on each element. You could more efficiently apply the style to the root element and let all the other elements inherit it. Listing 4-4 demonstrates.

Listing 4-4: A style sheet for a page in 20 point bold Courier applied to the entire document

```
<xsl>
  <rule>
    <root/>
    <DIV style="font-size: 20pt;
      font-weight: bold; font-family: Courier;">
      <children/>
    </DIV>
  </rule>
  <rule>
    <target-element/>
    <DIV>
      <children/>
    </DIV>
  </rule>
</xsl>
```

The Web page produced by this rule still looks the same, but is quite a bit smaller and somewhat quicker to download.

Styles to Choose From

Cascading style sheet properties are divided into five general kinds of properties: font properties, color properties, text properties, box properties, and classification properties. As a general rule, you'll only set a few of these for any given element.

Most of the properties are inherited by child elements unless specifically overridden. For example, if you're happy with the font you've chosen for the body of the document, you don't need to respecify that same font for each element appearing in the body — just for those that use something different. Furthermore, all of these properties have reasonable defaults if no element specifies a value.

FONT PROPERTIES

Font properties enable you to determine, within the limits of the browser's available fonts and capabilities, font family (Helvetica, Times, Zapf Chancery, and so forth), font style (normal, italic, or oblique), font variant (normal or small caps), font weight (normal or bold), and font size (small, large, 12 point, and so forth).

Table 4-1 lists the available font properties along with their possible values. In this and subsequent tables, the default value of each property is given in bold face type (where a default exists). Property values with an indefinite number of possible values are given in italics.

TABLE 4-1 CSS FONT PROPERTIES

Property	Values	Comments
font-family	*name*, serif, sans-serif, monospace, fantasy, cursive	More than one value may be given, in which case the first font is used. For example, font-name: Helvetica, Arial, sans-serif
font-style	**normal**, italic, oblique	Not all fonts have italic or oblique representations.
font-variant	**normal**, small-caps	Normal and SMALL-CAPS.
font-weight	normal, bold, 100, 200, 300, **400**, 500, 600, 700, 800, 900, lighter, bolder	Not all fonts possess the full range of 100 – 900 of weights given here. Intermediate values (for example, 450) are not allowed.

Continued

Property	Values	Comments
font-size	xx-small, x-small, small, medium, large, x-large, xx-large, larger, smaller, *length, percentage*	The constants are relative to the font size of the parent element or the browser's default font. Exact lengths like 12pt or 0.5in are almost certain to cause problems for some readers.

For example, the *name* value for the font-family property indicates that any string name may be used (for example, Helvetica, Courier, Arial, and so forth) as in the following:

```
<SPAN style="font-family: Courier;">
  <children/>
</SPAN>
```

On the other hand, the nonitalic values like serif, sans-serif, and monospace are keywords that should be used exactly as given. For example:

```
<SPAN style="font-family: monospace;">
  <children/>
</SPAN>
```

The font-family property is unusual in that it allows multiple values to be specified, separated by commas. For example:

```
<SPAN style="font-family: Courier New, Courier, monospace;">
  <children/>
</SPAN>
```

The first font is used if available. Otherwise, the second font is used if available, and so forth down to the last font in the list. The last one in the list should always be one of the generic names serif, sans-serif, monospace, fantasy, or cursive. Each Web browser should be able to provide a reasonable implementation of each of these font styles.

A number of properties such as font-size may be specified as lengths or percentages. A length is a number followed by the units, such as 36px or 0.5in (36 pixels and half an inch, respectively). For example:

```
<SPAN style="font-size: 14pt">
  <children/>
</SPAN>
```

Table 4-2 lists the available units and their abbreviations. Ems and exs are relative to the current font. Pixels are relative to the screen resolution. Relative units are generally preferred to absolute units like inches or centimeters.

TABLE 4-2 STYLE UNITS FOR LENGTHS

Unit	Meaning
em	the width of the letter *m* in the current font
ex	the height of the letter *x* in the current font
px	pixels, approximately 90 to the inch
pt	points, approximately 72 to the inch
in	inches
cm	centimeters
mm	millimeters
pc	pica

Sizes are also often specified as a percentage. In the context of font sizes, this is generally a percentage of the font size of the parent element. For example, in the following chunk of HTML, the word jumped is 18 points while the rest of the text is 12 points.

```
<P STYLE="font-size:12pt">The quick brown fox
<SPAN STYLE="font-size:150%;">jumped</span>
over the lazy dog.</P>
```

COLOR AND BACKGROUND PROPERTIES

Color properties specify the color of the element as well as details of the element's background, such as a background color or image. Table 4-3 lists the color and background properties that can be applied to an element. Generally, color is specified as an RGB (Red, Green, Blue) hexadecimal triple like #000000 (black) or #00FF00 (bright green). Many colors can also be specified by name. The acceptable names follow:

aqua	black	blue	fuchsia
gray	green	lime	maroon
navy	olive	purple	red
silver	teal	white	yellow

TABLE 4-3 COLOR AND BACKGROUND PROPERTIES

Property	Value
color	*color name*, *#RRGGBB*
background-color	**transparent**, *color name*, *#RRGGBB*
background-image	**none**, *URL*
background-repeat	repeat, repeat-x, repeat-y, **no-repeat**
background-attachment	**scroll**, fixed
background-position	top, center, bottom, *length*, *percentage*

TEXT PROPERTIES

Text properties affect spacing, alignment, indentation, and so forth. Table 4-4 lists the text properties that can be applied to an element. Most of these properties are specified with specific predefined keywords.

TABLE 4-4 TEXT PROPERTIES

Property	Values
text-align	left, right, center, justify
text-indent	*length*, *percentage*
word-spacing	**normal**, *length*
letter-spacing	**normal**, *length*
text-decoration	**none**, underline, line-through, overline, blink
vertical-align	**baseline**, sub, super, top, text-top, middle, bottom, text-bottom, percentage
text-transform	capitalize, uppercase, lowercase, **none**

BOX PROPERTIES

Table 4-5 lists the CSS box properties. Box properties allow extremely precise positioning of elements on a page in both absolute and relative coordinates. To position elements, each element is placed in a normally invisible, rectangular box. Then the box is placed on the page in either relative or absolute coordinates. The box's properties specify both how the elements are positioned relative to the box and how the box is positioned relative to the page. Each box is enclosed in a border (which by default has zero width and is invisible). Extra white space outside the border is the box's *margin*. Extra white space inside the border is the box's *padding*.

TABLE 4-5 BOX PROPERTIES

Property	Value	Comments
margin-top	*length, percentage*, auto	Extra white space outside the top border of the box. Percentages are a fraction of the box's height.
margin-right	*length, percentage*, auto	Extra white space outside the right border of the box. Percentages are a fraction of the box's width.
margin-bottom	*length, percentage*, auto	Extra white space below the bottom border of the box. Percentages are a fraction of the box's height.
margin-left	*length, percentage*, auto	Extra white space to the left of the box's border. Percentages are a fraction of the box's width.
margin	*length, percentage*, auto	Repeated four times — this sets the values for top, right, bottom, and left margins, respectively.
padding-top	*length, percentage*	Extra white space between the top border of the box and the box's contents. Percentages are a fraction of the box's height.
padding-right	*length, percentage*	Extra white space between the right border of the box and the box's contents. Percentages are a fraction of the box's width.
padding-bottom	*length, percentage*	Extra white space between the bottom border of the box and the box's contents. Percentages are a fraction of the box's height.

Continued

Property	Value	Comments
padding-left	*length, percentage*	Extra white space between the left border of the box and the box's contents. Percentages are a fraction of the box's width.
padding	*length, percentage*	Repeated four times — this sets the padding for top, right, bottom, and left, respectively.
border-top-width	*length*, thin, **medium**, thick	Width of the box's top border.
border-right-width	*length*, thin, **medium**, thick	Width of the box's right border.
border-bottom-width	*length*, thin, **medium**, thick	Width of the box's bottom border.
border-left-width	*length*, thin, **medium**, thick	Width of the box's left border.
border-width	*length*, thin, **medium**, thick	Repeated four times — this sets the width of the top, right, bottom, and left borders, respectively.
border-color	*color, #RRGGBB*	Color of the border.
border-style	**none**, dotted, dashed, solid, double, groove, ridge, inset, outset	
width	*length, percentage*, **auto**	Width of the box. Percentages are of the width of the parent element.
height	*length, percentage*, **auto**	Height of the box. Percentages are of the height of the parent element.
float	left, right, **none**	By default, a box is inlined. If float is set to left, however, the element moves to the left of the screen and text flows around on the right, or vice versa with a value of right.
clear	left, right, **none**, both	The clear property specifies where floating elements may not appear. For instance, if an element's clear property is set to left, an element will be moved below any floating element on its left.

CLASSIFICATION PROPERTIES

Table 4-6 lists the CSS classification properties. Classification properties mostly affect list items. Among other things, these properties determine the characteristics of list bullets and the display of individual list items.

TABLE 4-6 CLASSIFICATION PROPERTIES

Property	Value	Comments
display	**block**, inline, list-item, **none**	Are line breaks inserted before and after the element? Is a list bullet used?
white-space	**normal**, pre, nowrap	Are multiple spaces compressed to a single space? Do lines wrap without an explicit \<br\>?
list-style-type	**disc**, circle, square, decimal, lower-roman, upper-roman, lower-alpha, upper-alpha, none	Which list bullet is used?
list-style-image	URL	An image to be used as a list bullet.
list-style-position	inside, **outside**	Inside list items wrap lines under the list bullet.

Choosing Targets

Each XSL rule has one or more *targets*; that is, patterns for elements to which the rule applies. Most commonly, targets are set with the type attribute of the target-element tag. For example, the following specifies that a rule applies to publisher elements:

```
<target-element type="publisher"/>
```

If no type is specified, then the rule applies to all elements. No more than one rule is applied to one element, however. If more than one rule matches a particular element, the most specific match is chosen. If no rules match a particular element, the default rule is applied.

You often need to specify more than just the name of the tag to which the rule applies. Targets can be chosen based on position in the document, position relative to other elements, attribute values, elements that contain the elements, elements the element contains, and more.

For example, the Microsoft Word style sheet used to write this book has styles called "Code" and "Code Last". Given a ten line listing, the Code style applies to the first nine lines of code. The Code Last style applies only to the last line of code. The Code style uses no extra space before and after each paragraph, while the Code Last style provides 12 points of space after the paragraph. This space helps separate the code from the normal, noncode text. This scheme is useful for the layout team producing this book, but it's painful for an author to manually adjust the style of the last line of every listing, particularly when the last line may change several times as the manuscript is edited. The code style should be smart enough to tell whether a particular line is the last line and adjust the space after accordingly. Microsoft Word isn't this smart yet, but XSL is.

The Root Rule

Most documents need special handling for the root or document element, which is generally selected by something other than a `target-element` tag. Instead, this element is selected with the `<root/>` tag. You commonly use this tag to wrap the normal HTML header and body around a document's content.

Listing 4-5 demonstrates with a style sheet that places most elements between `<DIV>` tags but places the root element between `<html><body>` and `</body></html>`. The second rule matches all elements including the root element, but because the first rule more specifically matches the root element, only this first rule is used on the root element.

Listing 4-5: A style sheet with a root rule

```
<xsl>
  <rule>
    <root/>
    <html>
    <body>
      <children/>
    </body>
    </html>
  </rule>
  <rule>
    <target-element/>
    <DIV>
      <children/>
    </DIV>
  </rule>
</xsl>
```

Children and Parents

You often want to format elements differently depending on the contexts in which they appear. For example, you might want a title element inside a header element to become an HTML `<title>`. On the other hand, you may want a title element inside a body element to be formatted as an `<H1>` header.

On the other hand, you may want to base styling on the children of the element. For example, if a book element contains only a name, you may want it inline with the text. If it contains lots of detailed information like the publisher, price, page count, summary, and so forth, you may want to separate it from the rest of the text. In other words, you'd like to be able to include a citation for *Java Secrets* (IDG Books Worldwide, 1997) in a sentence without starting a new paragraph. If the book element contains multiple paragraphs of text itself, you want to separate it out.

Although you could define two separate elements – one for an inline book and one for an out-of-line book – using the same element enables both people and automated tools to more easily identify all the places where books are found. This is a formatting decision, not a decision about what kind of book the element represents.

To match targets based on the parents of the target or the children the target contains, you use ⟨element⟩ tags. Each ⟨element⟩ tag has a type attribute whose value is the name of the element the tag represents. The hierarchy of the ⟨element⟩ tags matches the hierarchy of the actual tags you're trying to match.

For example, the following rule says that the content of an XML title element should be placed between HTML ⟨title⟩ and ⟨/title⟩ tags, but only if the XML title element appears inside a header element.

```
<rule>
  <element type="header">
    <target-element type="title"/>
  </element>

  <title>
    <children/>
  </title>
</rule>
```

On the other hand, the following rule says that the content of an XML title element should be italicized, but only if the XML title element appears inside a book element.

```
<rule>
  <element type="book">
    <target-element type="title"/>
  </element>
  <SPAN style="font-style: italic;">
    <children/>
  </SPAN>
</rule>
```

The ⟨element⟩ tag can also be used to specify the children that must be present before the rule takes effect. For example, this rule says that a book element is to be formatted with a ⟨DIV⟩ tag, but only if it contains a blurb element:

```
<rule>
  <target-element type="book">
    <element type="blurb"/>
  </target-element>
  <DIV>
    <children/>
  </DIV>
</rule>
```

The same style sheet can also contain a rule that applies to book elements without blurbs. This rule may simply output the content of the element without adding any special formatting.

```
<rule>
  <target-element type="book"/>
  <children/>
</rule>
```

When both these rules are present, the most specific rule takes precedence. Thus, the second rule only applies if the book doesn't contain a blurb. If the first rule is not present, the second rule applies both to elements with or without blurbs.

You can use fairly complicated, multiple, nested `<element>` tags within a single rule to specify precisely when you want the rule to apply. However, only the presence or absence — not the order — of child tags is significant.

Wild Cards

The `<element>` tag only works when you know the exact sequence of ancestors and children you're mirroring. If you aren't sure what may come between the element you're targeting and the ancestor or child you're matching against, you can use the `<any>` tag. This tag matches zero or more of any element.

For example, suppose you want to specify that a person's name is formatted in bold if the person element appears in a contacts element. However, the contacts element need not be the immediate parent of the person. You could use the following rule:

```
<rule>
  <element type="contacts">
    <any>
      <element type="person"/>
        <target-element type="name"/>
      </element>
    </any>
  </element>
  <SPAN style="font-weight: bold">
    <children/>
  </SPAN>
</rule>
```

If you want to match exactly one element in the hierarchy, but you don't know what that element is, you can use the `<element>` tag without a type attribute. For example:

```
<rule>
  <element type="contacts">
    <element>
      <element type="person"/>
        <target-element type="name"/>
      </element>
    </element>
  </element>
  <SPAN style="font-weight: bold">
    <children/>
  </SPAN>
</rule>
```

Attributes

The attribute element targets elements by attribute. It's quite flexible. Among other things it can target all elements that have a certain attribute, all elements that have a certain attribute with a certain value, a particular element that has a particular value for a particular attribute, an element one of whose ancestors has a particular attribute with a particular value, and more.

The syntax of the attribute tag follows:

```
<attribute name="attribute_name" value="attribute_value"/>
```

In the XSL style sheet, the attribute element is a child of the element whose attribute you're trying to match. For example, suppose a book contains a publisher attribute as in the following:

```
<book publisher="IDG Books Worldwide, Inc.">
```

The following rule makes all books whose publisher is IDG Books bold:

```
<rule>
  <target-element type="book">
    <attribute name="publisher" value="IDG Books"/>
  </target-element>
  <SPAN style="font-weight: bold">
    <children/>
  </SPAN>
</rule>
```

Once again, the target-element element is nonempty. In this case, it contains an attribute element. Attributes always belong to some element, perhaps in the target or the target's parents or children, but they do belong to some element.

You can also test the attributes of a parent. For example, suppose the book element has various children and only the title child element should be bold if the parent's publisher attribute is IDG Books. In this case, you simply include the `<attribute>` tag as a child of the parent element tag, as this rule demonstrates:

```
<rule>
  <element name="book">
    <attribute name="publisher" value="IDG Books"/>
    <target-element type="title"/>
    <SPAN style="font-weight: bold">
      <children/>
    </SPAN>
  </element>
</rule>
```

Attributes of children may also be tested. For example, suppose you want to include book elements that contain a blurb element and exclude books that don't contain a blurb element. The following two rules accomplish that:

```
<rule>
  <target-element type="book">
    <element name="blurb">
  </target-element>
  <DIV>
    <children/>
  </DIV>
</rule>
<rule>
  <target-element type="book"/>
</rule>
```

The second rule matches any book but only applies to those that don't match the first, more specific rule. Because it does not specify any action, book elements without blurbs are quietly dropped from the document when it's rendered.

You can test for multiple attribute values by simply including more attribute tags. For example, suppose you want to apply bold face to books whose publisher is IDG Books and whose price is $39.95. That is, you want to find books that look like the following:

```
<book publisher="IDG Books" price="$39.95">
```

Simply include attribute tags for both publisher and price in the rule as follows:

```
<rule>
  <element name="book">
    <attribute name="publisher" value="IDG Books"/>
    <attribute name="price" value="$39.95"/>
    <target-element type="title"/>
    <SPAN style="font-weight: bold">
```

```
        <children/>
      </SPAN>
    </element>
  </rule>
```

Sometimes you only want to know that an element has an attribute without knowing precisely what the value of the attribute is. For example, if you want to highlight books with a price attribute, you can set the has-value attribute in the <attribute> tag to yes, as in the following:

```
<rule>
  <element name="book">
    <attribute name="price" has-value="yes"/>
    <target-element type="title"/>
    <SPAN style="font-weight: bold">
      <children/>
    </SPAN>
  </element>
</rule>
```

Although somewhat less common, you can also set has-value to no, which doesn't do quite what you expect. Instead of matching attributes with no value assigned, it matches attributes with a default value assigned.

ID ATTRIBUTES

Elements may possess an ID attribute. If an element has an ID attribute, the value of this attribute must be globally unique; that is, two elements in the same XML document are not allowed to have the same ID.

Chapter 7 discusses how to use a DTD to specify that a particular attribute of a particular element is an ID type attribute. In the meantime, you can use the style sheet to identify particular attributes as IDs. This is accomplished through an <id> element with the following syntax:

```
<id attribute="attribute_name"/>
```

Here, attribute_name is the attribute which must act as an ID. The <id> element generally appears inside an element or target-element element that names the element with the ID attribute.

The person or program that creates the XML file must ensure they do not inadvertently give the same ID to two different elements. If an ID is duplicated, the XSL processor should produce an error.

Uniqueness is the key to IDs. By adding an <id> attribute to a <target-element> tag, you can specify exactly which element you want the rule to match. You don't want to do this too often – the power of XML derives from applying the same rules to many different elements, after all – but this is an indispensable technique for many special cases.

You can also add an ID attribute to an <element> tag – generally one that represents the parent or child of an element you're trying to match. In this case, the rule may still apply to more than one child of the ID'd element, but it only applies to siblings, not to arbitrary elements of the type.

The 1-7-1998 technology preview release of MSXSL on which this chapter is based does not yet support ID attributes.

CLASS ATTRIBUTES

Elements may possess a class attribute. Elements with the same value of the same class attribute are (in some sense) grouped together. These elements do not have to have the same type. You can use the style sheet to identify particular attributes as class attributes, which is accomplished through a <class> element with the following syntax:

```
<class attribute="class_name"/>
```

Here *class_name* is the attribute that must act as a class ID. The <class> element generally appears inside an element or target-element element that names the element that can belong to the class.

The 1-7-1998 technology preview release of MSXSL on which this chapter is based does not yet support class attributes.

Position

You can also specify formatting rules that apply to elements based on their position in the parent element. To use these rules, add only and position attributes to the element or target-element tags. The only attribute can have the following two values:

- ◆ of-type
- ◆ of-any

The of-type value requires that the target be the only element of its type that's a child of its parent. The of-any value requires that the target be the only child of any type of its parent.

For example, suppose you want to indent list elements half an inch if the list contains more than one element. If there is only one element in the list, you just want to treat it as a normal paragraph. Assuming list items are bracketed with <list-item> tags, the following two rules accomplish that goal:

```
<rule>
  <target-element type="list-item" only="of-type"/>
  <DIV>
    <children/>
  </DIV>
</rule>
<rule>
  <target-element type="list-item"/>
  <DIV style="text-indent: 0.5in">
    <children/>
  </DIV>
</rule>
```

The first rule applies only to a list-item that is the single list item contained in its parent. The second applies to all other list items.

If you want to specify that a target-element must be the only child of its parent, regardless of type, then you can use of-any as the value of the only attribute instead. For example:

```
<rule>
  <target-element type="list-item" only="of-any"/>
  <DIV>
    <children/>
  </DIV>
</rule>
```

The only attribute may be applied to element tags as well.

It's also common to want to apply special formatting to the first and last elements in a group. The position attribute of the element and target-element tags allows this. The position attribute has four valid values:

- first-of-type
- last-of-type
- first-of-any
- last-of-any

Suppose you want to make the first element of a document bold, regardless of the element. The following rule does this:

```
<rule>
  <element type="document">
    <target-element position="first-of-any"/>
    <DIV style="font-weight: bold">
      <children/>
    </DIV>
  </element>
</rule>
```

Notice that the customary type attribute of the <target-element> tag has been omitted. This rule applies to the first elements found inside a document element regardless of type.

You can also use the position attribute with element tags. For example, suppose you want to make the title of the first book in a book list larger than the titles of the following books. This rule accomplishes that:

```
<rule>
  <element type="title" position="first-of-type">
    <target-element type="title"/>
  </element>
  <DIV style="font-size: larger">
    <children/>
  </DIV>
</rule>
```

This rule does not say that the title is the first title, but rather that this title belongs to the first book. If there is more than one title of the first book, this rule applies to both titles.

Recall the book element of Chapter 2. Most books had a single author while some books had multiple authors. Suppose you want to separate the authors with commas so you get something like "Ed Tittel, Mary Madden, Earl Follis" rather than "Ed Tittel Mary MaddenEarl Follis". While it's easy to place a comma and a space after every author, it's a little harder to place a comma and a space after every author except the last. The trick is to use the last-of-type position. You define one rule that applies to all authors and includes a comma and a space, then a second rule that applies only to the last author without a comma and space. The two rules follow:

```
<rule>
  <target-element type="author"/>
  <children/>,
</rule>

<rule>
  <target-element type="author" position="last-of-type"/>
  <children/>
</rule>
```

Resolving Conflicts

So far you've seen mostly small, simple examples. In practice, style sheets commonly have dozens, even hundreds of rules, especially once you start merging style sheets that cover different domains. A single element is often the target of more than one rule. In these cases, the rule that most closely matches the element is applied, while the other rules are not applied. Multiple rules are never applied to a single element.

The obvious question is how one defines "most closely matches". When there are multiple rules whose patterns match an element, the right rule is selected in order according to the following ten criteria:

1. the rule with the highest importance as specified by the rule's importance attribute

2. the rule with the most ID attributes

3. the rule with the most class attributes

4. the rule with the most element or target-element elements that have a type attribute

5. the rule with the fewest *wildcards* – where a wildcard is an any element, or an element or target-element element that does not have a type attribute

6. the rule with the highest priority as specified by the priority attribute of the rule

7. the rule with the most only attributes in element and target-element tags

8. the rule with the most position attributes in element and target-element tags

9. the rule with the most attribute tags

10. the rule that comes last in the style sheet

The last rule is the absolute tiebreaker that can always decide between two rules if all other criteria fail.

The importance and priority attributes are special attributes of the rule element that can specify the rule takes precedence, regardless of the usual order. For example:

```
<rule importance="10">
  <target-element type="author" position="last-of-type"/>
  <children/>
</rule>
```

The 1-7-1998 technology preview release of MSXSL on which this chapter is based does not yet support importance or priority attributes. Although you can include these attributes in a rule, they have no actual effect on the final output.

Taking Action

The previous section concentrated on matching patterns; that is, choosing the elements with which you wanted to take action. This section expands on the actions you can take. You'll see how to add content and markup to the output, how to select the elements that are output, and how to reorder those elements.

Adding Content

The basic action is outputting a series of well-formed HTML tags along with the contents of the original XML element that was matched. As well as tags, you can also include additional text not present in the XML document. For example, the following inserts the word "Copyright" in front of a `<copyright>` element:

```
<rule>
  <target-element type="copyright"/>
  Copyright <children/>
</rule>
```

By changing the style sheet, you can produce the © symbol instead. The following relies on HTML's `&copy;` entity.

```
<rule>
  <target-element type="copyright"/>
  &copy; <children/>
</rule>
```

You are not required to include the contents of the element either. For example, the following rule simply omits `<private>` elements from the final output:

```
<rule>
  <target-element type="private"/>
</rule>
```

This example may be a useful trick for an XML editor that wants to maintain some data internally that's not relevant to the end user.

Action does not have to be this simple, however. You can choose from several ways to include children of the element in the output; in particular, you can replace the catch-all `<children/>` tag with more specific requests via `<select-elements>`.

Select

When a target is matched, an action that includes a `<children/>` tag simply outputs all the children of the element that matched the target – possibly while recursively applying other rules to the children. The children are generally output in the order they appear in the XML document, possibly with a little extra content inserted by the style sheet.

Sometimes, though, you don't want to simply output the children. Often, you want to include some children but exclude others. You may also want to output all the children but always in a particular order, regardless of the order they appear in the XML document. The `<target-elements>` tag applies patterns to the input. The `<select-elements>` tag applies patterns to the output so you can organize, reorder, and select the exact elements that appear in the rendered output.

Recall the book element from Chapter 2. A typical entry looks like the following:

```
<book>
  <title>Java Secrets</title>
  <author>Elliotte Rusty Harold</author>
  <publisher>IDG Books Worldwide</publisher>
  <ISBN>0-764-58007-8</ISBN>
  <pages>900</pages>
  <price>59.99</price>
  <pubdate>May, 1997</pubdate>
  <recommendation>Buy It</recommendation>
  <blurb>
    The Java virtual machine, byte code, the sun packages,
    native methods, stand-alone applications, and a few more
    naughty bits.
  </blurb>
</book>
```

Suppose you want to format this as a citation like the following:

Java Secrets (IDG Books Worldwide, 1997)

In particular, you want to omit many of the book's children. To proceed, you need to select the individual children you want to include rather than simply including them all with the `<children/>` tag.

The `<select-elements>` tag accomplishes this task. Each select-elements element contains a pattern that matches particular children of the element the rule matches. This pattern is similar to the pattern used as a target. It can contain target-element, element, and any elements. Those elements matched by the pattern in the select-elements element are output. Unmatched elements are not output.

The draft XSL proposal actually specifies using a `<select>` tag for this purpose, instead of `<select-elements>`. This `<select>` tag has a potential conflict with the HTML form tag of the same name, however. Therefore, the 1-7-1998 technology preview release of MSXSL uses `<select-elements>` instead. At this point, it is unclear whether the standard will be changed to use `<select-elements>`, or MSXSL will be changed to use `<select>` or something completely new will be devised. This chapter uses `<select-elements>`, but check the Microsoft and W3C Web sites for the latest word.

For example, the following rule selects only the title, publisher, and pubdate children from each book element:

```
<rule>
  <target-element type="book"/>
  <span font-style="italic">
  <select-elements>
    <target-element type="title"/>
  </select-elements>
  </span>
  (
  <select-elements>
    <target-element type="publisher"/>
  </select-elements>,
  <select-elements>
    <target-element type="pubdate"/>
  </select-elements>
  )
</rule>
```

`<select-elements>` can reorder entries too. For example, if the XML is hand-crafted, some book elements may mix up the order of the ISBN number, the page count, the price, and so forth. If you simply use `<children/>` to select the output, the order of the elements in the XML input is maintained in the HTML output. By using `<select-elements>` instead, you can guarantee a particular order in the output regardless of the order in the input, as shown by the rule in Listing 4-6:

Listing 4-6: A rule that guarantees a particular order for book children

```
<rule>
    <target-element type="book"/>

    <dt/>
    <select-elements>
      <target-element type="title"/>
```

```
    </select-elements>
    <dd/>
    <select-elements>
       <target-element type="author"/>
    </select-elements>
    <ul>
      <li/>Publisher:
      <select-elements>
       <target-element type="publisher"/></select-elements>
      <li/>ISBN:
      <select-elements>
       <target-element type="isbn"/>
      </select-elements>
      <li/>Pages:
        <select-elements>
          <target-element type="pagecount"/>
        </select-elements>
        <li/>Price: $
        <select-elements>
          <target-element type="price"/>
        </select-elements>
        <li/>Publication date:
        <select-elements>
          <target-element type="pubdate"/>
        </select-elements>
        <li/>Bottom Line:
        <select-elements>
          <target-element type="recommendation"/>
        </select-elements>
    </ul>
    <P>
      <select-elements>
        <target-element type="blurb"/>
      </select-elements>
    </P>
  </rule>
```

Previously, a book listing was created by recursively processing rules for each of the individual child elements. Among other problems, this approach made it extremely difficult to insert HTML markup that depended on a subset of an element's children; for instance, putting the publisher, date, ISBN number, recommendation, price, and page count — but not author — in an unordered list. By using `<select-elements>` instead of `<children/>`, this task almost becomes easy.

This rule does not, however, check to see if each element is present. Thus, you can end up with empty listings as shown in Figure 4-5. Notice in several of the listings, pages is blank, publication date is blank, and so forth.

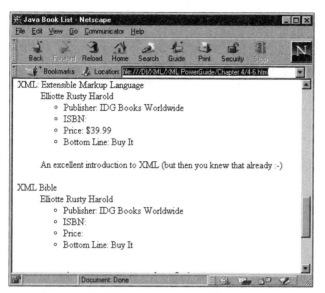

Figure 4-5: The books page after the rule in Listing 4-6
is applied

If you'd simply like to omit the unavailable children, you need to move the extra formatting of each item into a separate rule that applies just to that element. Then, if the element isn't present, the rule won't fire. Listing 4-7 demonstrates, and Figure 4-6 shows the results of using this rule. You can still wrap `<ul></ul>` around the entire list. By combining `<children/>` rules with `<select-elements>` rules, you achieve results impossible with either rule alone.

Listing 4-7: Omitting elements from output that aren't present in the XML document

```
<rule>
  <target-element type="book"/>

  <dt/>
  <select-elements>
    <target-element type="title"/>
  </select-elements>
  <dd/>
  <select-elements>
    <target-element type="author"/>
  </select-elements>
  <ul>
    <select-elements>
      <target-element type="publisher"/>
    </select-elements>
```

```
      <select-elements>
        <target-element type="isbn"/>
      </select-elements>
      <select-elements>
        <target-element type="pagecount"/>
      </select-elements>
      <select-elements>
        <target-element type="price"/>
      </select-elements>
      <select-elements>
        <target-element type="pubdate"/>
      </select-elements>
      <select-elements>
        <target-element type="recommendation"/>
      </select-elements>
    </ul>
    <P>
      <select-elements>
        <target-element type="blurb"/>
      </select-elements>
    </P>
  </rule>

<rule>
    <target-element type="publisher"/>
    <li/> Publisher:
      <children/>
  </rule>

<rule>
    <target-element type="isbn"/>
    <li/> ISBN:
      <children/>
  </rule>

<rule>
    <target-element type="pages"/>
    <li/> Pages:
      <children/>
  </rule>

<rule>
    <target-element type="price"/>
    <li/> Price:
      <children/>
  </rule>

<rule>
    <target-element type="recommendation"/>
    <li/> Bottom Line:
      <children/>
  </rule>
```

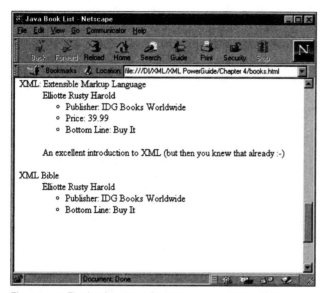

Figure 4-6: The books page after the rules in Listing 4-7
are applied

One thing you cannot do, however, though it seems quite natural, is include extra text between `<select-elements>` and `</select-elements>`. For example, consider the following fragment of a rule:

```
<select-elements>
  <li/>Price: $<target-element type="price"/>
</select-elements>
```

While the preceding example seems the simplest way to place a `<li>Price: $` in front of the price element content, the extra text is summarily dropped from the output – only the price element content appears. You can do this sort of thing by using JavaScript, which will be discussed in a following section.

The possibility of reordering elements, and selecting elements according to certain patterns, is extremely powerful. This capability makes document formats and orders much less rigid. For example, in the books page from Chapter 2, the books are divided up into separate book category elements. Categories are available for in print, out of print, not yet published, top-ten, and non-Java. To simplify, think instead of the information about a book's category as a part of the book. Furthermore, different books can have many different categories. For example, one book may be part of both a top ten category and an in print category:

```
<book>
<topten/>
<inprint/>
<title>JavaBeans</title>
```

```
<author>Elliotte Rusty Harold</author>
<publisher>IDG Books Worldwide, Inc.</publisher>
<isbn>0-7645-8052-3</isbn>
<pagecount>355</pagecount>
<price>39.99</price>
<recommendation>Buy It</recommendation>
<blurb>An excellent introduction to JavaBeans</blurb>
</book>
```

The XSL rule in Listing 4-8 selects all the book elements that appear inside a document element. Those books with a `<topten/>` child are placed in one list while those with an `<inprint/>` child are placed in another list. Some books may appear in both lists.

Listing 4-8: Selecting those elements that contain `<topten/>` or `<inprint/>` elements

```
<rule>
  <target-element type="document"/>

  <dl>
    <select from="descendants">
      <element type="book">
        <target-element type="topten"/>
      </element>
    </select>
  </dl>
  <dl>
    <select from="descendants">
      <element type="book">
        <target-element type="inprint"/>
      </element>
    </select>
  </dl>
</rule>
```

You may imagine other ways to define categories. For example, you can make a book's category the content of a category element, as follows:

```
<category>Top ten</category>
<category>In Print</category>
```

Alternately, you can make the category an attribute of an empty category tag:

```
<category type="top ten"/>
<category type="inprint"/>
```

You can work with these sorts of categories. However, the patterns that match them will have to wait until JavaScript functions are discussed below.

By default, the `<select-elements>` tag only allows you to select immediate children of the parent element. You can also select any descendant simply by setting the source attribute of the select-elements tag to descendants. For example:

```
<select-elements source="descendants">
```

For example, imagine you need a style sheet that makes a table of contents for a document by selecting all part, chapter, section, and subsection elements in a book document. In general, parts contain chapters, which contain sections, which contain subsections.

```
<rule>
  <target-element type="book"/>
  <select from="descendants">
    <target-element type="part"/>
    <target-element type="chapter"/>
    <target-element type="section"/>
    <target-element type="subsection"/>
  </select>
</rule>
```

Without setting the from attribute of `<select-elements>` to descendants, only the outermost elements (probably the parts) would be selected.

Macros

You may want to perform the same action on multiple elements. For instance, you may define different elements for salesperson, manager, janitor, programmer, secretary, receptionist, and thirty other different job titles. You may still want to format each title in a similar manner for a list of employees working for the company, though.

XSL enables you to define macros that apply the same set of potentially complex rules to different objects.

A macro is enclosed in `<define-macro>` tags. The opening `<define-macro>` tag contains a name attribute that serves as the name of the macro. In the body of the macro element, you'll find the macro's replacement text, generally along with one or more `<contents/>` tags specifying where the element contents belong. Thus, the general format of a macro is something like the following:

```
<define-macro name="macro-name">
  HTML markup
    <contents/>
  More HTML markup
</define-macro>
```

Note that macros are the first element you've encountered that can appear in an XSL style sheet outside of a rule.

For example, the following simple macro places a blue box with one-pixel borders, margin, and padding around its contents.

```
<define-macro name="box">
  <div style="margin: 1px 1px 1px 1px;
  padding: 1px 1px 1px 1px;
  border-width: 1px 1px 1px 1px;
  border-style: solid;
  border-color: blue">
    <contents/>
  </div>
</define-macro>
```

Now rather than retyping the rule for every element you want to box in, you can merely use a <box> tag like the following:

```
<rule>
  <target-element type="note"/>
  <box>
    <children/>
  </box>
</rule>
```

The entire box element is replaced by the box macro's body. In the box macro's body, however, the <contents/> element is replaced by the actual contents of the box element. The preceding case is a simple example, but in general both the macro text and the contents of the macro can be quite complex – including both elements, extra text, patterns, and more. For example:

```
<rule>
  <target-element type="note"/>
  <box>
    <h2>Note</h2><children/>
  </box>
</rule>
```

 The 1-7-1998 technology preview release of MSXSL on which this chapter is based does not yet support macros.

Sometimes, it is useful to allow arguments to be passed to a macro. For instance, you may want the box color to be adjusted for each element, but still have a default of blue. You can allow this capability by including an arg element in the define-macro element. The syntax of the arg element follows:

```
<arg name="argument_name" default="argument_default"/>
```

For example:

```
<define-macro name="box">
  <arg name="boxcolor" default="blue"/>
  <div style="margin: 1px 1px 1px 1px;
  padding: 1px 1px 1px 1px;
  border-width: 1px 1px 1px 1px;
  border-style: solid;
  border-color: =boxcolor">
    <contents/>
  </div>
</define-macro>
```

The string =boxcolor in the <div> tag is replaced by whatever value the rule assigns to boxcolor, or blue if no such color is assigned.

To assign colors, simply include boxcolor as an attribute of the <box> element in the rule. For example:

```
<rule>
  <target-element type="note"/>
  <box boxcolor="red">
    <children/>
  </box>
</rule>
```

A single macro may have an indefinite number of rules. This capability can be useful for providing a lot of default values while allowing any to be overridden.

Importing Style Sheets

MathML is an application of XML that allows equations to be formatted. Among hundreds of others, typical MathML tags include the following:

<msup>	<mfenced>	<mrow>	<mi>
<mo>	<mn>	<apply>	<power/>
<plus/>	<ci>	<cn>	<cos>
<minus/>	<reln>	<eq/>	<over/>

When you combine the positioning aspects of CSS with the mathematical symbols available in Unicode, it's theoretically possible to write mathematical equations that can be displayed in an XML browser. In practice, this task is anything but easy. In the not too distant future, someone will probably develop an XSL style sheet for MathML, thereby saving you from having to create this style sheet yourself.

Other specialized notations like ChemML for chemistry, MusicML for music, and many others have equally complex formatting requirements. Thus, it's fortunate that you can build a single style sheet out of other style sheets in a fairly simple fashion. The style sheets are referred to by (possibly relative) URLs so they can reside anywhere on the Internet.

To import a style sheet into your own style sheet, use an import tag as follows:

```
<import href="stylesheet_url"/>
```

For example:

```
<import href="http://www.w3.org/Math/mathml.xsl"/>
```

You can also use relative URLs, which are filled in with the missing pieces from the style sheet's own URL (just as a relative URL in HTML's `<A>` element is filled in). For example, the following import element imports a style sheet called `musicml.xsl` in the same directory as the current file:

```
<import href="musicml.xsl"/>
```

The complete text of the imported style sheet replaces the import tag in the main document. Imported style sheets may import still other style sheets as long as there aren't any cycles. (That is, style sheet A may not import style sheet B if style sheet B imports style sheet A.)

When importing style sheets, two different rules may be defined for the same element. In this case, the usual rules for deciding between two rules apply. That is, the most specific rule applies. If all else fails, whichever rule appears first in the final style sheet after the completion of all imports takes control. No preference is given to a rule merely because it appears in the main style sheet, rather than an imported one.

The 1-7-1998 technology preview release of MSXSL on which this chapter is based does not yet import style sheets.

Style Rules

So far, only one rule has been applied to each element. When multiple rules match an element, the one with the target that most specifically matches the element is chosen. This order makes the behavior of XSL style sheets relatively easy to analyze, because you only need to find the single rule that applies to each element.

You may occasionally find it useful to merge many different rules, however. For example, you may want to make any element with a draft attribute red without changing the other formatting assigned to the many different elements with a draft attribute. You can perform this task with style rules.

Style rules add styles to elements in a similar way to how CSS style sheets cascade. Multiple style rules may apply to a single element, with each one adding its own bit of formatting to the element.

The basic syntax of a style rule follows:

```
<style-rule>
  <!-- target -->
  <target-element type="tag-name"/>
  <!-- style -->
  <apply style_name1="style_value1" style_name2="style_value2".../>
</style-rule>
```

Here, the target exactly matches a rule element. The target can contain attribute tags, wild cards, or other parts of a pattern. A style-rule's target acts exactly like a rule's target, selecting a particular subset of elements to apply the rule to. Instead of an action, however, the target is followed by a single `<apply/>` tag. The `<apply/>` tag contains one or more attributes. Each attribute name is the name of a CSS property, and each attribute value is the value of the CSS property.

For example, the following style rule says that any element with a draft attribute with the value "1" should be colored red:

```
<style-rule>
  <target-element>
    <attribute name="draft" value="1">
  </target-element>
  <apply color="red"/>
</style-rule>
```

The key difference between the preceding example and a rule is that the example applies in addition to any other rule or style rule defined for elements.

Named Styles

Named styles are similar to macros for applying style properties. They enable you to associate a series of CSS-style values with a particular name. The general syntax for naming styles follows:

```
<define-style name="style_name"
    style_name1="style_value1" style_name2="style_value2".../>
```

This syntax is located in the XSL style sheet as a direct child of the <xsl> root element. Here, style_name is the name you give to this combination of CSS properties. style_name1, style_name2, and so forth are names of CSS properties like font-weight, color, or padding. Style_value1, style_value2, and so forth are values of the CSS properties.

For example, the following tag defines a style named box that places a blue box with 1 pixel borders, margin, and padding around its contents.

```
<define-style name="box" margin="1px 1px 1px 1px"
    padding="1px 1px 1px 1px"
    border-width="1px 1px 1px 1px";
    border-style="solid"
    border-color="blue"/>
```

Rather than retyping these attributes for every element you want to box in, you can merely use a box attribute like the following:

```
<rule>
  <target-element type="note"/>
  <h2>Note</h2>
  <div use="box">
    <children/>
  </div>
</rule>
```

You can also use a named style in a style-rule instead of an apply element. For example:

```
<define-style name="first_draft" color="blue"/>

<style-rule>
  <target-element>
    <attribute name="draft" value="1">
  </target-element>
  <first_draft/>
</style-rule>
```

Including Styles in XML Tags

In theory, XML completely separates the actual data of a document from the formatting of that data. The data, and only the data, appears in the XML document. The formatting, and only the formatting, appears in the XSL style sheet. Unfortunately, real life and real problems are often messier than theory allows for. Therefore, XSL allows formatting information to be embedded in the XML document if absolutely necessary.

The first way to embed XSL formatting directly in an XML document adds an xsl attribute to an XML tag. An XSL attribute looks like the following:

```
<xml_tag_name xsl::CSS_property_name="CSS_property_value">
```

The XSL attribute begins with the string `xsl::`, followed by the CSS property that's being set, an equals sign, and the quoted value of that property. For example:

```
<book xsl::font-style="italic">
```

The most common use of this technique applies a particular style to a particular element quickly without inventing new tags, attributes, or XSL rules. Keep in mind, this is almost never necessary, but it is sometimes quicker than the alternatives.

You can also define more complex rules by including them at the beginning of the XML document. These rules' target-elements may have an ID attribute that matches the ID of a particular element somewhere in the document. For example:

```
<rule>
  <target-element id="specialcasebold"/>
    <DIV font-weight="bold">
      <children/>
    </DIV>
</rule>
```

Later in the document, you may find elements like the following:

```
<book id="specialcasebold">
```

You can create rules with this approach that apply only to this document. This capability is most useful when you're using a company or industry-standard style sheet that you can't change but would like to augment.

Modes

Occasionally, you may want to display the same data in more than one part of the document. For example, a Web page's <TITLE> is customarily repeated in an <H1> header at the top of the page. In XML terms, the same title element must be placed in both the header and the body of the document. Modes accomplish this task, which happens completely inside the XSL style sheet. No cooperation from the XML author or change to the XML document is required.

A mode attribute is added to the <children/> or <select-elements> tags used to choose elements for an XSL rule and to the rule tag itself. For example, consider the three rules in Listing 4-9. The pagetitle element is now placed in a title element in the header where the second rule applies and in an <H1> header in the document where the third rule applies. The second and third rules are distinguished only by the modes. The select-elements tag in the header uses the header-mode mode and associated rule while the body of the document uses the default mode and rule.

Listing 4-9: Modes to distinguish between header and body

```
<rule>
  <root/>
  <HTML>
  <HEAD>
    <select-elements>
       <target-element mode="header-mode" type="pagetitle"/>
    </select-elements>
  </HEAD>
  <BODY>
    <children/>
  </BODY>
 </HTML>
</rule>

<rule>
  <target-element type="pagetitle"/>
  <H1>
    <children/>
  </H1>
</rule>

<rule>
  <target-element type="pagetitle" mode="header-mode"/>
  <title>
    <children/>
  </title>
</rule>
```

JavaScript

XSL style sheets can contain embedded scripts written in the JavaScript language. These scripts may be executed when the processor processes a document, or may be passed into the output HTML file from whence they are run by the reader's Web browser.

These scripts can be quite complex, but most of the time they're fairly simple. In fact, they're usually one line of code or less. The non-JavaScript savvy reader can merely use a few of the lines given here as cookbook formulas for certain tasks. Readers who know JavaScript can easily expand on these simple examples.

Scripts as Attribute Values

The most common place to encounter scripts in XSL files is as the value of attributes. Any attribute value that begins with an equals sign is a script. For example:

```
<rule>
  <target-element type="note"/>
  <SPAN font-size="=10 + 2 +'pt'">
    <children/>
  </SPAN>
</rule>
```

This script sets the font size to 12 points by adding 10 + 2 and concatenating the result (12) with the string pt. The first tag output from this rule follows:

```
<SPAN style="font-size:12pt">
```

Of course, this example is a little forced, because you could have simply set the attribute value to 12pt in the first place. You can do more, however, when you add built-in functions, global variables, and function declarations.

Eval

While JavaScript is most commonly used for attribute values, it can also insert content into the output document with the eval element. You can include an `<eval></eval>` block almost anywhere in a style sheet. The contents of the eval element are run as a simple program and the output of the program or function is inserted into the document in place of the eval element.

For example, the following rule inserts the string 2 + 2 = 4 into the output document in place of a `<formula/>` tag:

```
<rule>
  <target-element type="formula"/>
  <DIV>
    <eval>
      "2 + 2 = " + (2+2)
    </eval>
  </DIV>
</rule>
```

An eval element almost always contains a reference to a function – either a built-in function or a user-defined function. Therefore, let's examine function declarations next.

Function Declarations

Sometimes a single line of JavaScript isn't sufficient. More complicated operations are generally encapsulated as functions. A function may take arguments and return values. You can use the define-script element to prepare one or more functions accessible from all subsequent rules. A single define-script element in the top of the XSL file customarily includes all the necessary functions.

For example, the following define-script element defines a JavaScript function called factorial that takes a single int as an argument and returns an int:

```
<define-script><![CDATA[

  function factorial(n) {

    var result = 1;
    for (i=1; i <= n; i++) {
      result = result * i;
    }

    return result;

  }]]>

</define-script>
```

Notice that the actual JavaScript code appears in a CDATA block to prevent accidental misinterpretation of the < sign.

A rule that uses this function has to provide a value for the argument. For example:

```
<rule>
  <target-element type="formula"/>
  <DIV>
    <eval>
      factorial(10);
    </eval>
  </DIV>
</rule>
```

In the output, the preceding example is replaced with the HTML code that uses the value of the function:

```
<DIV>
3628800
</DIV>
```

(3,628,800 is the value of 10!.)

XML Object Model

XSL provides an element class that contains a number of extremely useful built-in JavaScript methods that enable you to access otherwise inaccessible parts of the XML file. These methods include the values of attributes and the contents of elements. Sometimes, these functions alone can accomplish your desired results. Other times, you may need to combine them with custom JavaScript code.

To format dates in winter differently than dates in spring, for example, use these built-in functions to check the contents of a date element to see what month it is. If you want to make bold any books whose price is less than $40.00, you can use the item() and children() functions to retrieve the contents of a book's price element, and then use standard JavaScript to convert the price string to a number and compare it against 40.

Programmers accustomed to procedural languages like C and Perl should remember that JavaScript is an object-based language. Therefore, functions are generally invoked on a particular element. Most often, this is the element the rule that contains the script has matched. It can also be the element matched by the tag that contains the script. This particular element is referred to as this.

Thus, you may say this.getAttribute("draft") or this.children(). The this variable is optional and can be implied, if omitted when used inside a target-element, select-elements, or element. In these cases, the function implicitly refers to the targeted, selected, or matched element.

GETATTRIBUTE(ATTRIBUTENAME)

This useful function returns the value of the named attribute and is used inside a target-element, element, or select-elements element. The element being targeted or selected is the one whose attribute value is returned. Once you have the value, you can use standard JavaScript operators and functions to match the value against various conditions.

For example, in HTML an <APPLET> element that embeds a Java applet looks something like this:

```
<APPLET code="MyApplet" width=100 height=100
   alt=" This text is supposed to be shown if the browser knows about
   the applet tag but can't play the applet; e.g. if the user has
   turned off Java in the browser. ">
This text is shown if the browser doesn't know about the applet tag.
</APPLET>
```

Assuming applets are embedded into XML files in the same way they're embedded into HTML, the following rule replaces the applet tag with the contents of its alt attribute.

```
<rule>
  <target-element type="APPLET">
  <DIV>
```

```
    <eval> this.getAttribute("alt");</eval>
  </DIV>
</rule>
```

The same technique works for images and other elements with alt attributes.

CHILDREN()

The children() function returns an enumeration of the immediate children of the element. For example, the style sheet in Listing 4-10 prints the name of each element, followed by the names of its children. Figure 4-7 shows the results. Although these results aren't very pretty, you generally don't use this function in isolation. Instead, you use item() to select particular elements for special processing.

Listing 4-10: Enumerating the children

```
<xsl>
  <rule>
    <target-element/>
    <DIV>
      <div color="red">
        <eval> this.tagName;</eval>:
        <eval> this.children;</eval>:
      </div>
      <children/>
    </DIV>
  </rule>
</xsl>
```

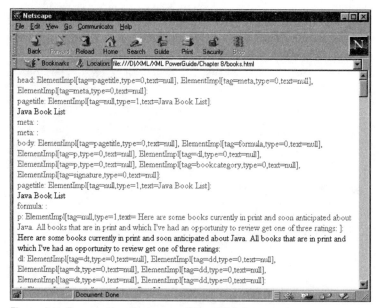

Figure 4-7: Enumerating the names of the child elements

TEXT()

The text() method returns the contents of the element as text with any markup removed. This method is incredibly useful when you want to base the formatting of an element on the contents of that element. For example, the following rule replaces a book's price with either the word cheap or expensive, depending on whether the price is less than $40.00.

```
<rule>
   <target-element type="price"/>
   <li/> Price:
      <eval>
        lessthan(parseFloat(text), 40, "cheap", "expensive");
      </eval>
</rule>
```

The parseFloat() function is a JavaScript library function that converts the string of text returned by text into a floating point number. lessthan is the following user-defined function:

```
function lessthan(n1, n2, trueresult, falseresult) {

  if (n1 < n2) return trueresult
  else return falseresult;

}
```

If you're going to use more than a single line of JavaScript code, you should write the code as one or more user-defined functions in a define-script element.

LENGTH()

The length() method returns the number of components of an enumeration, which are similar to the one returned by children(). It can be used in conjunction with children() and item() to loop through all the children of an element.

Listing 4-11 is a simple style sheet that prints the name of each element along with the number of its children. Figure 4-8 shows the results of using this style sheet.

Listing 4-11: The length() element

```
<xsl>
  <rule>
    <target-element/>
    <DIV>
      <div color="red;">
        The
        <eval> this.tagName;</eval> element has
```

```
      <eval> this.children.length;</eval> children.
      </div>
      <children/>
    </DIV>
  </rule>
</xsl>
```

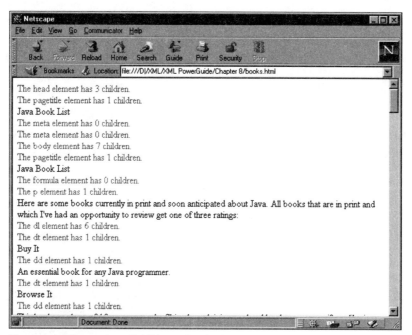

Figure 4–8: The number of children of each element as returned by the length function

ITEM(INDEX) / ITEM(ELEMENTTYPE) / ITEM(ELEMENTTYPE, INDEX)

The overloaded item() function retrieves the requested items from an enumeration. If the argument is an elementType, an array of elements is returned. If the argument is an integer, then the element at that position is returned. If both a type and an integer are provided, then the nth element of that type is returned.

For example, Listing 4-12 is a simple style sheet that prints the name of each element followed by the names of that element's children. The children() function returns each element's children. The item() function returns along with the number of its children.

Listing 4-12: The indexed item() function

```
<xsl>

  <define-script><![CDATA[

    function listchildren() {

      var result = children.item(0).tagName;
      for (i = 1; i < children.length; i++) {
        result += ", " + children.item(i).tagName;
      }

      return result;

    }

  ]]>

  </define-script>

  <rule>
    <target-element/>
    <DIV>
      <eval> tagName;</eval>:
      <eval> listchildren();</eval>
    </DIV>
    <children/>
  </rule>
</xsl>
```

TAGNAME

The tagName() function returns the XML name of the element. For example, the style sheet in Listing 4-13 uses tagName() to output each element, prefixed with its tag name. Figure 4-9 shows the result of using this style sheet to format `books.xml`.

Listing 4-13: Using `tagnames.xsl` to output each element

```
<xsl>
  <rule>
    <target-element/>
    <DIV>
      <SPAN color="red">
        <eval>this.tagName</eval>:
      </SPAN>
      <children/>
    </DIV>
  </rule>
</xsl>
```

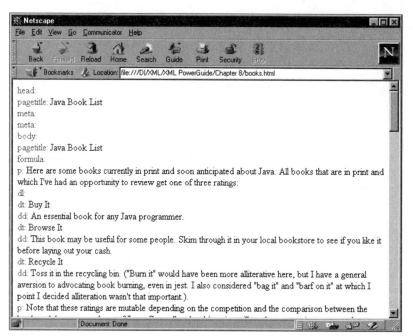

Figure 4-9: The tag names included in the output

PARENT()

The parent() function returns the parent element of the current element. This function can be used in conjunction with children() and item() to navigate around the hierarchy of the document.

Built-in Functions

XSL also provides several useful standalone functions. Unlike the object-based methods of the last section, these functions do not have a reference they can use implicitly. Instead, all data must be passed to these functions as arguments:

- ◆ ancestor(elementType, element) – The ancestor() function returns the string contents of the closest ancestor of the element argument with the specified type. It returns null if no such ancestor exists or the ancestor exists but is empty.

- ◆ childNumber(element) – The childNumber() function returns the position of an element relative to its siblings of the same type. It's often used to number elements.

◆ ancestorChildNumber(elementType, element) – The ancestorChild
Number() function returns the number of the nearest ancestor that has
type elementType relative to its siblings of the same type, or null if there
is no such ancestor.

◆ path(element) – The path() function returns an array, which includes
the position of the element with respect to its siblings of the same type,
the number of the parent of the element with respect to its siblings of the
same type, and so forth up the tree to the root element. The length of this
array is the depth of the element in the tree.

◆ hierarchicalNumberRecursive(elementType, element) – The hierarchical
NumberRecursive() function acts like the path() function, but only returns
child numbers of elements of the requested elementType. This function is
most often used for calculating subsection numbers like Section 3.1.4
when all sections share the same tag, and only their nesting level
distinguishes them.

◆ formatNumber(n, format) – The formatNumber() function formats a
number as a string for use in lists and returns the formatted string. The
first argument n is the number to format. The second argument format
is a string that tells how the number should be formatted. The possible
format strings and their meanings are listed in Table 4-7.

◆ formatNumberList(list, format, separator) – Given an array of numbers,
the formatNumberList() function returns a string containing formatted
numbers, separated from each other by the separator string. The format
strings are the same ones used with format() and given in Table 4-7.
The formatNumberList() is often used in conjunction with path() or
hierarchicalNumberRecursive().

TABLE 4-7 FORMAT STRINGS

String	Meaning
"1"	0, 1, 2, and so forth.
"01"	pad with leading zeroes to the given width; for example: 00, 01, 02, 10, 11, 100, 101
"a"	0, a - z, aa - zz
"A"	0, A - Z, AA - ZZ
"i"	small Roman numerals: for example: 0, i, ii, iii, iv, ...
"I"	Roman numerals; for example: 0, I, II, III, IV, ...

The 1-7-1998 technology preview release of MSXSL on which this chapter is based does not yet implement padding with leading zeroes or Roman numerals.

SCRIPT Tags

You may also want to embed scripts in the output file without having them processed by the XSL processor. To accomplish this task, simply include the relevant script in the action between `<SCRIPT>` and `</SCRIPT>` tags as you would normally write it in XML. The only trick is that you should also enclose the script code in a CDATA block to prevent accidental misinterpretation of: less than signs (<) as the start of a tag; and HTML comment blocks that often enclose scripts to hide them from non-JavaScript aware browsers.

For example, the following code embeds a simple script in the header used on many of my pages to keep them from being mirrored on other Web servers. If someone copies the page onto another server and then browses it, they'll be redirected to the original site. This code doesn't stop someone who knows you don't allow mirroring, but it may warn an unaware person that you don't allow mirroring.

```
<rule>
  <target-element type="head"/>
    <head>
      <children/>
      <script language="javascript"><![CDATA[ <!--
      /* Only sunsites are allowed to mirror this
         page and then only with explicit, prior
         permission. For details, send email to
         elharo@sunsite.unc.edu */
    if (location.protocol.toLowerCase().indexOf("file") != 0 ) {
      if (location.host.toLowerCase().indexOf("sunsite") < 0) {
        location.href="http://sunsite.unc.edu/javafaq/ ";
      }
    }
    ]]> // --> </script>
    </head>
</rule>
```

Linking to Style Sheets

As of early 1998, the only way to show your carefully crafted XML files reliably to the world in anything approximating their full glory is by converting them to HTML, as shown in this chapter. In the not too distant future, however, both

Netscape and Microsoft are expected to release more full-featured XML browsers that can read and display XML files directly. At that point, the Web browser must be able to locate the right style sheet for the right document.

The current suggestion (which is subject to change) for specifying a style sheet from within an XML document places an xml-stylesheet processing instruction in the document:

```
<?xml-stylesheet href="stylesheet_URL" type="text/xsl" ?>
```

Here stylesheet_URL is a relative or absolute URL to the style sheet.

Generally, this processing instruction is placed in the prolog, after the XML declaration and perhaps before or after the DTD. For example:

```
<?xml version="1.0" standalone="no"?>
<?xml-stylesheet href="professional.xsl" type="text/xsl" ?>
<!DOCTYPE document SYSTEM "professional.dtd" [
]>
<document>
```

DTDs are introduced in the next chapter. As before, this processing instruction may not come before the XML declaration.

Summary

In this chapter, you learned that XSL style sheets describe how individual elements are displayed in HTML. You also learned the following concepts:

♦ An XSL processor like MSXSL converts an XML document and its associated style sheet into an HTML document that can be read by current Web browsers.

♦ Style instructions are stored in rule elements.

♦ Each rule has a pattern and an action. The pattern defines the elements to which the rule applies. The action specifies the flow objects the XSL processor outputs when the rule fires.

♦ When multiple rules apply to one element, only the most specific rule is applied.

♦ Flow objects are generally the contents of the element, along with some combination of HTML markup.

♦ <SPAN> and <DIV> allow CSS rules to be applied to individual elements.

♦ Multiple XSL style sheets can be combined with the import tag.

- ◆ Macros and named styles enable you to create a sort of glossary for commonly used formatting rules.

- ◆ Style rules apply formatting to flow objects on top of formatting applied by the rule. Multiple style rules may act on a single element.

- ◆ JavaScript functions can be used in attribute values and in eval elements. The define-script element holds user-defined functions. The fundamental object is the element.

- ◆ XML documents can specify their preferred style sheet with an `<?xml-stylesheet>` processing instruction.

Part II

Advanced XML

Chapter 5

Using DTDs in XML Documents

IN THIS CHAPTER

◆ Using DTDs

◆ Exploring a document's structure

◆ Building a DTD

◆ Understanding element type declarations

◆ Exercising discipline over children

◆ Combining elements

◆ Using empty tags

XML HAS BEEN described as a metamarkup language; that is, a language for describing markup languages. This chapter explores its use as such a metalanguage and discusses how to design and create new markup languages for use in specialized domains such as music, mathematics, astronomy, electronics, genealogy, and any other field you can imagine.

Such markup languages (otherwise known as tag sets) are defined via a document type definition, which is the subject of this chapter.

Working with DTDs

The acronym DTD stands for document type definition. A *document type definition* provides a list of the elements, tags, attributes, and entities contained in the document, and their relationship to each other. DTDs specify a set of rules for the structure of a document. For example, a DTD may say that a `<document>` contains a title and one or more `<book>`s, and that every `<book>` must have exactly one `<isbn>`, exactly one `<title>`, one or more `<author>`s, and may or may not contain a single `<subtitle>`.

DTDs may be included in the file that contains the document they describe, or they may be linked to from an external URL. Such *external DTDs* can be shared by different documents and Web sites. DTDs provide a means for applications, organizations, and interest groups to agree on, document, and enforce adherence to markup standards.

For example, publishers want authors to adhere to particular formats for easier book layout and production. Authors like to write words in a row without worrying about whether they remembered to match up each bullet point in the front of the chapter with a subhead inside the chapter. If the author writes in XML, the publisher can easily check whether the author adhered to the predetermined format, and even find out exactly where and how the author deviated from the format. XML makes it much easier to correct deviations than if fallible humans have to read through the document and hope to spot all the minor format deviations based on style alone.

DTDs also help ensure that different people and programs can read each other's files. For instance, if chemists can agree on a single DTD for basic chemical notation, possibly via the intermediary of an appropriate professional organization like the American Chemical Society, then they can be assured that they can all read and understand the papers they're all writing. Two chemists can trade papers and preprints electronically over the Internet without worrying about whether the person on the other end owns the same word processor with which the document was written. Even if proprietary software creates the document, the document can still be read and displayed by any other program that understands DTDs. If the recipient doesn't have the same DTD, it can be included with the document. Thus, XML is a self-describing format.

Furthermore, a DTD can act as a template into which data is poured by showing how the different elements of a page are arranged without actually providing the data for those elements. A DTD enables you to see the structure of your document separate from the actual data. As a result, you can slap a lot of fancy styles and formatting onto the underlying structure without destroying the structure, much as a house can be painted without changing its basic architectural plan. The reader of your page may not even see or be aware of the underlying structure, but both human authors and JavaScripts, CGIs, servlets, databases and other programs can use this structure.

DTDs can be used for other tasks as well. You can define glossary entities that insert boilerplate text like a signature block or an address. You can ascertain that data entry clerks are adhering to the necessary format. You can migrate data to and from relational and object databases. You can even use XML as an intermediate format to convert between different formats with suitable DTDs. Let's get started and see what DTDs really look like.

Including DTDs in Documents

A DTD is included in a document's prolog after the XML declaration and before the actual document data begins. It consists of a series of markup declarations declaring particular elements, entities, and attributes. This chapter focuses on element declarations. Chapters 6 and 7 introduce entity and attribute declarations, respectively.

Recall the first example from Chapter 2:

```
<?xml version="1.0" standalone="yes"?>
<foo>
Hello XML!
</foo>
```

This document contains a single foo element that is delimited by `<foo>` and `</foo>` tags. (Remember, `<?xml?>` is a processing instruction, not a tag.) Listing 5-1 shows this document with a DTD that declares the document contains a single element named foo and the foo element contains text:

Listing 5-1: Hello XML with DTD

```
<?xml version="1.0" standalone="yes"?>
<!DOCTYPE foo [
  <!ELEMENT foo (#PCDATA)>
]>
<foo>
Hello XML!
</foo>
```

The DTD comes between the XML declaration and the document itself. The XML declaration and the DTD together are called the *prolog* of the document. In the preceding example, `<?xml version="1.0" standalone="yes"?>` is the XML declaration; `<!DOCTYPE foo [ <!ELEMENT foo (#PCDATA)> ]>` is the DTD; and `<foo>` `Hello XML!` `</foo>` is the document.

This document can be combined with a style sheet and rendered in HTML, just as in Chapter 2 using MSXSL. In fact, you can use the same style sheet:

```
C:XML\>msxsl -i 5.1.xml -s greeting.xsl -o 5.1.html
```

The results are the same as before. The MSXSL tool does not concern itself with the DTD — it only cares that the document is well-formed. To understand and use the DTD, you need to use a tool that checks that the document is not only well-formed but also valid.

Exploring the DTD

To see how a document with a DTD differs from the same document without a DTD, compare Chapter 2's Hello XML code with Listing 5-1.

The three new lines added to Listing 5-1 constitute the only difference between these two sets of code:

```
<!DOCTYPE foo [
  <!ELEMENT foo (#PCDATA)>
]>
```

These lines are this document's DTD. A DTD begins with `<!DOCTYPE` and ends with `]>`. The beginning and end are customarily placed on separate lines; but line breaks and extra white space aren't significant. The same DTD could be written on a single line like the following:

```
<!DOCTYPE foo [ <!ELEMENT foo (#PCDATA)> ]>
```

The name of the root element – foo in this example – follows `<!DOCTYPE`. This is not just a name but a requirement. Any valid document with this DTD must have the root element `<foo>`.

The DTD is closed with `]>`. In between, you find the list of element and attribute declarations and entity references in the document, including the root element. In this simple example, the root element is the only element. This chapter focuses on element declarations. Chapters 6 and 7 introduce entity and attribute declarations, respectively.

The `<!ELEMENT>` tag (case-sensitive like all XML tags) is an element type declaration. In this case, the name of the declared element is `foo`. This element may contain parsed character data (#PCDATA). *Parsed character data* is essentially any nonmarkup text, including entity references like `&amp;`.

This DTD says that a valid document must look like the following:

```
<foo>
various random text but no markup
</foo>
```

A valid document may not look like the following two examples:

```
<foo>
<sometag>various random text<sometag>
<someEmptyTag/>
</foo>
```

Or

```
<foo>
<foo>various random text</foo>
</foo>
```

This document must consist of nothing more and nothing less than nonmarkup text between an opening `<foo>` and a closing `</foo>`. Unlike a merely well-formed document, a valid document does not allow arbitrary tags. Any tags used must be declared in the document's DTD. Furthermore, they must only be used in a way permitted by the DTD. In Listing 5-1, the `<foo>` tag can only be used as the root element, and may not be nested.

Java Runtimes and CLASSPATHs

I should warn you that installing MSXML (or any other pure Java program) on Windows is far from trivial. In particular, you need to adjust your CLASSPATH environment variable to make sure it includes all the classes MSXML needs to run. The self-extracting installer is supposed to do this for you, but failed to do so in my tests. If you're only running MSXML from the MSXML directory, you don't need to do this, but it's much more convenient to be able to run from the directory where your files are rather than the one where the program is located.

The MSXML directory contains a file called `msxml.class` and a folder called `classes`. You should be able to add these two directories to your CLASSPATH, and run MSXML; but even that process failed in my tests. I recommend you create a directory called `classes` at the top of your C drive (for example, C:\classes) and move both the `msxml.class` file and the `com` directory inside the `msxml\classes` directory to C:\classes. Then add C:\classes to your CLASSPATH in a DOS prompt window as follows:

```
C:\> set CLASSPATH=C:\classes;%CLASSPATH%
```

In Windows 95, you can place this line in your `autoexec.bat` file to avoid typing it in every session. In Windows NT, you can set this in the System control panel's environment tab.

Validating the Document

A *validating parser* reads a DTD and checks whether a document adheres to the rules specified by the DTD. If it does, the parser passes the data along to the XML application (such as a Web browser or a database). If the parser finds a mistake, such as a book without an ISBN number, then it reports the error. If you're writing XML by hand, you'll want to validate your documents with a tool like MSXML before posting them, so you can be confident that readers won't encounter errors. Some authoring tools also provide validation on the fly during tagging, and thus prevent you from making markup errors in the first place.

At the time of this writing, only a few validating parsers exist for XML. Microsoft's MSXML tool is used in this book's examples (not to be confused with the nonvalidating MSXSL tool of Chapter 2). MSXML is available from Microsoft's Web site at `http://www.microsoft.com/xml`. Several others are discussed in Appendix C.

Unlike MSXSL, MSXML is written in Java and should run on any system with a Java 1.1 or later compliant virtual machine such as Sun's JDK or Microsoft's Java SDK. If you installed Internet Explorer 4.0, Microsoft's virtual machine and the accompanying jview program for running standalone Java applications were also installed. Jview is used in the following examples because it has better support for

Windows file names than the interpreter in Sun's JDK. The difference, however, is not really important as long as the file you're validating is in the same directory as the XML file.

You run the validator by passing both its name and the name of the file you want to validate to the java or jview program from a command-line window as follows:

```
C:\XML\> jview msxml 5.1.xml
```

By default, no output is produced if the file is valid. However, if an error is encountered, it will be reported. For example, suppose you change foo to foo2 as follows:

```
<?xml version="1.0"?>
<!DOCTYPE foo2 [
  <!ELEMENT foo (#PCDATA)>
]>
<foo>
Hello XML!
</foo>
```

The preceding example is no longer a valid document. Running MSXML tells you why:

```
C:\XML>jview msxml 5.1.xml
Root element name must match the DOCTYPE name
Location: file:/C:/ 5.1.xml(5,2)
Context: <null>
```

This warning says that the name between <!DOCTYPE and [must match the name of the root element. You'll encounter many different errors throughout this chapter.

You can use the -d flag to MSXML to request that the XML be output in a "pretty printed" fashion as follows:

```
C:\XML>jview msxml -d 5.1.xml
<?XML version="1.0" standalone="yes"?>
<!DOCTYPE foo [
  <!ELEMENT foo (#PCDATA)*>]>
<foo> Hello XML! </foo>
```

You can also use the -d1 flag to show a tree structure form of the document as follows:

```
C:\XML>jview msxml -d1 5.1.xml
DOCUMENT
|---XMLDECL
|    +---CDATA " version="1.0" standalone="yes"""
|---WHITESPACE 0xa
```

```
|---DOCTYPE  NAME="foo"
|   |---WHITESPACE 0xa 0x20 0x20
|   +---ELEMENTDECL foo (#PCDATA)*
|---WHITESPACE 0xa
|---ELEMENT foo
|   +---PCDATA " Hello XML! "
+---WHITESPACE 0xa 0xa
```

This tree shows how elements relate to each other, and may be useful for debugging. You have several other command-line options of no great importance. If you're curious, run the MSXML program without arguments or consult the online documentation.

None of these examples produce especially attractive output, but a validating parser like MSXML isn't designed to display XML files. Instead, the parser divides the document into a tree structure, and passes the nodes of the tree to the program displaying the data. This program may be a Web browser like Navigator or Internet Explorer, a database, or a custom program you've written yourself. You only use the MSXML parser to verify that you've written good XML that other programs will not have trouble with. In essence, this is a proofreading or quality assurance phase, not your finished output.

Exploring a Document's Structure

The first step to creating a DTD appropriate for a particular document is to understand the structure of the information. Sometimes information is quite structured, as in a contact list. Other times, it may be relatively free-form, as in an illustrated short story or a magazine article.

Let's use a relatively structured site as an example. The New York Women Composers Web site, which I maintain at `http://sunsite.unc.edu/nywc`, is mostly a catalog of the organization's membership, works, and publishers. Figure 5-1 shows the site's publishers page.

 New York Women Composers, Inc. is a New York not-for-profit corporation controlled by its members: women composers of serious concert music or women in musical occupations who support the composers in their efforts to be recognized. The mission of New York Women Composers, Inc. is the improvement of conditions for all women composers. This in turn depends on the climate of acceptance for women composers in general, rather than for a few notables, whose successes are often used to dismiss the claims of other women. The goal of New York Women Composers, Inc. is the success of music by women because of merit, regardless of a composer's gender.

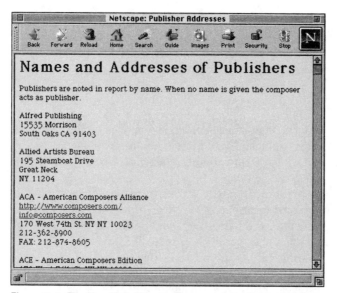

Figure 5-1: The New York Women Composers' Publishers Catalog

Like the book catalog in Chapter 2, the list in Figure 5-1 is an extremely common item to put on a Web site, and an excellent use of XML. The fundamental unit of this page is the publisher. Each publisher has the following information:

- Name
- Web site URL
- E-mail address
- Snail mail address
- Voice phone
- Fax phone

A typical listing looks like the following:

```
ACA - American Composers Alliance
info@composers.com
http://www.composers.com/
170 West 74th St. NY NY 10023
212-362-8900
FAX: 212-874-8605
```

This listing lends itself well to encoding in XML. One possible way to encode a publisher follows:

```
<publisher>
  <name> ACA - American Composers Alliance</name>
  <homepage>http://www.composers.com/</homepage>
  <email>info@composers.com</email>
  <address>170 West 74th St. NY NY 10023</address>
  <voice>212-362-8900</voice>
  <fax>212-874-8605</fax>
</publisher>
```

The address element can and probably should be broken up into more granular pieces. For example:

```
<address>
  <street>170 West 74th St.</street>
  <city>NY</city>
  <state>NY</state>
  <zip>10023</zip>
</address>
```

The preceding example gives you the following:

```
<publisher>
  <name> ACA - American Composers Alliance</name>
  <homepage>http://www.composers.com/</homepage>
  <email>info@composers.com</email>
  <address>
    <street>170 West 74th St.</street>
    <city>NY</city>
    <state>NY</state>
    <zip>10023</zip>
  </address>
  <voice>212-362-8900</voice>
  <fax>212-874-8605</fax>
</publisher>
```

The page has a few other pieces like a heading and some navigational links at the bottom, but for now let's assume it only consists of a list of publishers. Of course not all listings are complete. Music publishing is a fairly staid business and many publishers don't have fax machines, much less e-mail addresses and home pages. and even when they do that information hasn't necessarily been communicated to the maintainers of the catalog. For instance, consider the listing for Alfred Publishing:

```
Alfred Publishing
15535 Morrison
South Oaks CA 91403
```

Overall this information is easy to categorize. A list contains publishers. A publisher has a name, a home page, an e-mail address, a voice number, a fax number, and a snail mail address. A snail mail address has a street, a city, a state, a zip, and perhaps a country. These can all be elements, and thus should all be included in the DTD for the page.

A DTD goes beyond merely listing the elements on the page, however. It lists the relationships between the elements. For instance, a DTD can require that a publisher has exactly one name. It can also require that the name element should be inside (and never outside) a publisher element, and note that a publisher may but does not have to have a home page. It can allow (but not require) the publisher to have an indefinite number of voice phone numbers and e-mail addresses.

A DTD can require that an address have exactly one street, city, state, and zip code, but make it optional whether an address has a suite or apartment number. Furthermore, it can require that the street, city, state, and zip elements be used in a particular order. A DTD can also require that elements occur in a particular context. For instance, the street, city, state, and zip elements may only be used inside an address element.

Table 5-1 lists the different elements for this particular list and their conditions. Each element has a list of the other elements it must contain, the other elements it may contain, and the element (if any) in which it must be contained. In some cases, an element may contain more than one child element of the same type. For example, a publisher could have an 800 phone number and a regular phone number. In the table, the possibility of multiple children is indicated by suffixing (s) onto the end of the element's name.

TABLE 5-1 THE ELEMENTS IN THE NEW YORK WOMEN COMPOSERS'
PUBLISHER LIST

Element	Must Contain	May Contain	Must Be Contained In
document	title	anything	nothing (this is the root element)
publisher list		publisher(s)	
publisher	name	home page(s), e-mail(s), address(s), voice(s), fax(s)	
name	parsed character data		publisher
address	street, city, state, zip	suite, country	publisher
email	parsed character data		publisher
homepage	parsed character data		publisher
voice	parsed character data		publisher

Continued

Element	Must Contain	May Contain	Must Be Contained In
fax	parsed character data		publisher
street	parsed character data		address
suite	parsed character data		address
city	parsed character data		address
state	parsed character data		address
zip	parsed character data		address
country	parsed character data		address

You can often cut and paste from one DTD to another. Many of these elements can be reused in other contexts. For instance, the description of a publisher works for essentially any directory, whether that directory contains publishers, plumbers, government agencies, or any other sort of organization.

You can also include one DTD in another so that a document draws tags from both. You might, for example, use a DTD that describes the different possible formats of addresses in great detail; then nest that DTD inside the broader DTD for many different contact lists. You'll learn how to do this in Chapter 6.

Furthermore, work is underway to define a namespace mechanism for XML that allows for inheritance from DTD elements, though this feature isn't yet part of the XML 1.0 standard described in this book.

Now that you've identified the information you're storing as well as the optional and required relationships between these elements, you're ready to build a DTD for the document that concisely — if a bit opaquely — summarizes those relationships.

Building a DTD

DTDs use a simple regular expression grammar to precisely specify what is and isn't allowed in a document. This sounds complicated, but it simply means you add a punctuation mark like * or + to an element to indicate that it may occur more than once; may or may not occur; or must occur at least once.

DTDs are conservative. Everything not explicitly permitted is forbidden, but DTD syntax does enable you to specify relationships compactly that are cumbersome to specify in sentences. For instance, DTDs make it easy to say that a street must come before a suite, which must come before the city, which must come before the state, which must come before the zip, which must come before the country, and all of this information may only appear inside an address.

In this section, you'll see the gradual development of a DTD that describes the publishers Web page as shown in Figure 5-1. This example isn't exactly how this would be done in the so-called real world, because I'm going to stop along the way to introduce various new constructs. Furthermore, I'm going to have to be careful that at each stage I don't use techniques you haven't seen yet. Thus, the example doesn't always proceed in the simplest or most elegant fashion. In Chapter 11, after you've seen the many different things you can do with DTDs, you'll encounter another example that uses the full power of DTDs as they're really meant to be used, and focuses more on elegance than on covering each piece of DTD syntax.

Element Type Declarations

It's easiest to build DTDs hierarchically, working from the outside in. This approach enables you to build a sample document while you're building the DTD to verify that the DTD is itself correct and describes the proper format.

The first thing you need in a DTD is the root tag. A popular (though not required) choice for this tag is <document>. The following example is the basic beginning of every DTD:

```
<!DOCTYPE document [

]>
```

This example merely says that the root tag is <document>, but does not say anything about what a document element may or may not contain. Therefore, you must next declare your tags.

Every tag used in a valid XML document must be declared exactly once in the DTD with an element type declaration. An *element type declaration* specifies the name of a tag, the allowed children of the tag, and whether the tag is empty. (By default, tags are nonempty.)

The first tag you have to declare is the root tag, which is <document> in this example. <!DOCTYPE document [only says that the root tag is <document>; it does not actually declare the document tag. That's done with this line of code:

```
<!ELEMENT document ANY>
```

All element type declarations begin with <!ELEMENT (case-sensitive) and end with >. They include the name of the tag being declared (document in this example) and the allowed contents of that tag. The ANY keyword (again, case-sensitive) says that all possible elements as well as parsed character data are allowed in a document element. Using ANY is common for root elements — especially of unstructured documents — but should be avoided in most other cases. Generally, you should be as precise as possible about the content of each tag. You will find that your DTD will be refined throughout the process of your initial attempts to define it, and will likely become less strict over time – to reflect uses and contexts you did not imagine during the first cut – so it's best to start out strict and loosen things up later.

Although any element may appear inside the document, elements that appear must also be declared. The first element you need is a title. The element declaration for the title follows:

```
<!ELEMENT title (#PCDATA)>
```

This declaration says that a title may only contain parsed character data – that is, text that's not markup. It may not contain children of its own.

The document and title element declarations are included in the DTD as follows:

```
<!DOCTYPE document [
  <!ELEMENT document ANY>
  <!ELEMENT title (#PCDATA)>
]>
```

As usual, spacing and indentation are not significant. The order in which the element declarations appear isn't relevant either. The following DTD means exactly the same thing as the preceding DTD:

```
<!DOCTYPE
   document
   [
     <!ELEMENT title (#PCDATA)>
     <!ELEMENT document ANY>
   ]>
```

Both of these DTDs say that a document element may contain parsed character data and any number of any other declared elements in any order. The only other such declared element is title, which may only contain parsed character data. For instance, consider the file in Listing 5-2.

Listing 5-2: A valid file

```
<?xml version="1.0" standalone="yes"?>
<!DOCTYPE document [
  <!ELEMENT document ANY>
  <!ELEMENT title (#PCDATA)>
]>
<document>
  <title>Publishers of New York Women Composers</title>
</document>
```

MSXML parses the file into the following tree:

```
C:\XML>jview msxml -d1 5.2.xml
DOCUMENT
|---XMLDECL
|   +---CDATA " version="1.0" standalone="yes""
|---WHITESPACE 0xa
|---DOCTYPE  NAME="document"
|   |---WHITESPACE 0xa 0x20 0x20
|   |---ELEMENTDECL document ANY
|   |---WHITESPACE 0xa 0x20 0x20
|   +---ELEMENTDECL title (#PCDATA)*
|---WHITESPACE 0xa
|---ELEMENT document
|   |---WHITESPACE 0xa 0x20 0x20
|   |---ELEMENT title
|   |   +---PCDATA "Publishers of New York Women Composers"
|   +---WHITESPACE 0xa
+---WHITESPACE 0xa
```

Because the document tag may also contain parsed character data, you can add additional text outside of the title, as Listing 5-3 demonstrates.

Listing 5-3: A document that contains a title and normal text

```
<?XML version="1.0" standalone="yes"?>
<!DOCTYPE document [
    <!ELEMENT document ANY>
    <!ELEMENT title (#PCDATA)>
]>
<document>
 <title>
    Publishers of the Music of New York Women Composers
 </title>
Publishers are noted in report by name.
When no name is given the composer acts as publisher.

Alfred Publishing
15535 Morrison
South Oaks CA 91403

</document>
```

MSXML parses this file into the following tree:

```
C:\XML>jview msxml -d1 5.3.xml
DOCUMENT
|---XMLDECL
|   +---CDATA " version="1.0" standalone="yes""
|---WHITESPACE 0xa
|---DOCTYPE  NAME="document"
|   |---WHITESPACE 0xa 0x20 0x20 0x20
|   |---ELEMENTDECL document ANY
|   |---WHITESPACE 0xa 0x20 0x20 0x20
```

```
|    +---ELEMENTDECL title (#PCDATA)*
|---WHITESPACE 0xa
|---ELEMENT document
|    |---WHITESPACE 0xa 0x20
|    |---ELEMENT title
|    |    +---PCDATA " Publishers of the Music of New York Women
Composers "
|    +---PCDATA " Publishers are noted in report by name. When no
name is given the composer acts as publisher. Alfred Publishing
15535 Morrison South Oaks CA 91403 " +---WHITESPACE 0xa
```

Parsers like MSXML are supposed to pass along white space in the document's text unchanged. This feature was a relatively late change in the XML specification that is not implemented in MSXML. As a result, all the source text runs together in the output. Chapter 7 discusses how to use the `xml:space` attribute to force MSXML to behave properly in this case. Microsoft may have fixed this bug by the time you read this section. Check their Web site at `http://www.microsoft.com/xml/` for the most recent information.

If you attach a simple style sheet to the document like the one in Listing 5-4, you can render it into HTML and load it into a Web browser as before. Figure 5-2 shows the results of using this simple style sheet.

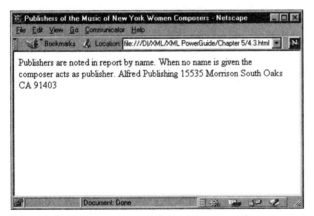

Figure 5-2: The beginnings of the publishers catalog

Listing 5-4: A style sheet for valid documents

```
<xsl>

  <rule>
    <root/>
    <html>
      <children/>
    </html>
  </rule>
```

```
<rule>
  <target-element type="title"/>
  <head>
    <title>text</title>
  </head>
</rule>

</xsl>
```

This style sheet only defines two rules: one for the root element, document; and the other for the title element. The document and title elements are the only two elements defined so far. Because MSXSL is a nonvalidating processor (one that doesn't check the DTD), other rules could have been defined. Provided you can safely assume that the document is valid (verified by MSXML), the style sheet can be simpler than otherwise necessary. For instance, you don't need to worry about there being more than one title element — the validator tells you that's not the case. Similarly, you don't have to worry that the title element may contain child elements. The DTD says that a title may only contain #PCDATA (that is, text). Without relying on these facts, the title rule would have to take on the complexity of Listing 5-5.

Listing 5-5: A style sheet that does not assume the restrictions imposed by the DTD

```
<xsl>

  <rule>
    <root/>
    <html>
      <head>
        <select-elements mode="header">
         <target-element type="title" position="last-of-type"/>
         <children/>
        </select-elements>
      </head>
      <body>
        <children/>
      </body>
    </html>
  </rule>

  <rule>
    <target-element type="title"/>

    <!-- no action -->
  </rule>

  <rule mode="header">
    <target-element type="title"/>
    <title><eval>text</eval></title>
  </rule>

</xsl>
```

The moral of this story: it's much simpler to put your restrictions in the DTD rather than in the style sheet. Style sheets are simpler when they can make reasonable assumptions about what does and doesn't appear in the document in what contexts – precisely what DTDs specify.

On the other hand, the formatting is restricted by the presence of only two elements: title and document. To do a better job of formatting, you also need to do a better job of identifying and tagging the data.

Of course, one of the main purposes of a DTD is to limit the tags used in a document. For instance, Listing 5-6 attempts to use the as yet undeclared tag `<publisher>`.

Listing 5-6: A document with an undeclared element

```
<?xml version="1.0" standalone="yes"?>
<!DOCTYPE document [
   <!ELEMENT document ANY>
   <!ELEMENT title (#PCDATA)>
]>
<document>
 <title>
    Publishers of the Music of New York Women Composers
 </title>
Publishers are noted in report by name.
When no name is given the composer acts as publisher.

<publisher>
Alfred Publishing
15535 Morrison
South Oaks CA 91403
</publisher>

</document>
```

Parsing should fail because a publisher element has not been declared. In fact, MSXML 1.8 incorrectly accepts this file as valid. Microsoft may have fixed this bug by the time you're reading this. Check their Web site at http://www.microsoft.com/xml/ for the most recent information.

Listing 5-7 shows the corrected file that declares a publisher element.

Listing 5-7: A valid file that declares the publisher element

```
<?xml version="1.0" standalone="yes"?>
<!DOCTYPE document [
   <!ELEMENT document ANY>
   <!ELEMENT title (#PCDATA)>
   <!ELEMENT publisher (#PCDATA)>
]>
<document>
 <title>
```

```
        Publishers of the Music of New York Women Composers
   </title>
   Publishers are noted in report by name.
   When no name is given the composer acts as publisher.

   <publisher>
   Alfred Publishing
   15535 Morrison
   South Oaks CA 91403
   </publisher>

   </document>
```

Now, MSXML successfully parses the file and generates the expected tree:

```
C:\ >jview msxml -d1 5.5.xml
DOCUMENT
|---XMLDECL
|    +---CDATA " version="1.0" standalone="yes""
|---WHITESPACE 0xa
|---DOCTYPE   NAME="document"
|    |---WHITESPACE 0xa 0x20 0x20 0x20
|    |---ELEMENTDECL document ANY
|    |---WHITESPACE 0xa 0x20 0x20 0x20
|    |---ELEMENTDECL title (#PCDATA)*
|    |---WHITESPACE 0xa 0x20 0x20 0x20
|    +---ELEMENTDECL publisher (#PCDATA)*
|---WHITESPACE 0xa
|---ELEMENT document
|    |---WHITESPACE 0xa 0x20
|    |---ELEMENT title
|    |    +---PCDATA " Publishers of the Music of New York
Women Composers "
|    |---PCDATA " Publishers are noted in report by name. When no
name is given the composer acts as publisher. "
|    |---ELEMENT publisher
|    |    +---PCDATA " Alfred Publishing 15535 Morrison South Oaks
CA 91403 "
|    +---WHITESPACE 0xa 0xa
+---WHITESPACE 0xa
```

If you add this simple rule to handle the publisher tag to the style sheet in Listing 5-4, a slightly improved result appears, as shown by Figure 5-3.

```
<rule>
  <target-element type="publisher"/>
  <P>
    <children/>
  </P>
</rule>
```

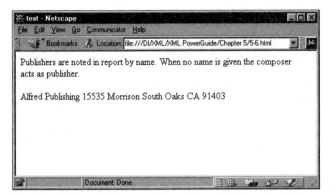

Figure 5-3: The publishers catalog with a defined and styled
publishers element

A document can be invalid for many other reasons. For now, let's look at one
more common problem. The `<title>` tag is declared to have parsed character data
content only. Adding a child element to a title, even a declared child like publisher,
is invalid. Listing 5-8 shows a document that's invalid because it has a title element
that contains a publisher element and another title element (a subtitle perhaps).

Listing 5-8: A document that's invalid because the title element has children

```
<?xml version="1.0" standalone="yes"?>
<!DOCTYPE document [
   <!ELEMENT document ANY>
   <!ELEMENT title (#PCDATA)>
   <!ELEMENT publisher (#PCDATA)>
]>
<document>
 <title>
    Publishers of the Music of New York Women Composers
    <title>The Publishers</title>

   <publisher>
   Alfred Publishing
   15535 Morrison
   South Oaks CA 91403
   </publisher>

</title>

Publishers are noted in report by name.
When no name is given the composer acts as publisher.

</document>
```

The error message from MSXML follows:

```
C:\XML>jview msxml -d1 5.6.xml
Invalid element 'title' in content of 'title'.  Expected [PCDATA]
Location: file:/D:/XML/XML PowerGuide/Chapter 5/5.6.xml(11,4)
Context: <document><title>
```

Notice that MSXML only catches the first error in the file. The presence of a publisher element inside the title element is an equally bad problem, but before MSXML can get far enough to see that problem, it's already given up and reported the file invalid. Some other validating processors can actually get past the first error, and identify multiple errors in the document.

Disciplining Children

Because the document element was declared to accept any element as a child, elements could be tossed in willy-nilly. This situation is useful when you have more or less unstructured text like a magazine article where paragraphs, sidebars, bulleted lists, numbered lists, graphs, photographs, and subheads may appear anywhere in the document.

Sometimes you want to exercise a little more discipline and control over the placement of your data, however. For instance, you can require that every publisher have exactly one name; every address have a street, city, state, and zip; and the publisher's name come before its address. This may be useful if you're using this document to print mailing labels, for example, because you'd only like to print labels for the addresses to which the post office can actually deliver.

For instance, to declare that a publisher must have a name you simply declare a name element, and then include name in parentheses at the end of the publisher declaration as follows:

```
<!ELEMENT publisher (name)>
<!ELEMENT name (#PCDATA)>
```

Each attribute used should be declared in its own <!ELEMENT> tag exactly once, even if it may appear as a child in other <!ELEMENT> tags. In the preceding example, the declaration of name occurs after the declaration of publisher that refers to it, but that doesn't matter. XML allows these sorts of forward references. The order in which the element tags appear is irrelevant as long as their declarations are all contained inside the DTD.

The DTD in Listing 5-9 says that a publisher has exactly one name, and nothing else. A name contains parsed character data (that is, raw text), and nothing else.

Listing 5-9: Publishers have names

```
<?xml version="1.0" standalone="yes"?>
<!DOCTYPE document [
  <!ELEMENT document ANY>
  <!ELEMENT title (#PCDATA)>
  <!ELEMENT publisher (name)>
```

```
  <!ELEMENT name (#PCDATA)>
]>
<document>
 <title>
    Publishers of the Music of New York Women Composers
</title>

  <publisher>
    <name>Alfred Publishing</name>
  </publisher>

Publishers are noted in report by name.
When no name is given the composer acts as publisher.

</document>
```

The declaration `<!ELEMENT publisher (name)>` no longer allows publishers to have anything except a name. For instance, a publisher element may no longer contain parsed character data like the following:

```
  <publisher>
    <name> ACA - American Composers Alliance</name>
    info@composers.com
    http://www.composers.com/
    170 West 74th St. NY NY 10023
    212-362-8900
    Fax: 212-874-8605
  </publisher>
```

Of course, you don't really want a publisher to contain parsed character data. Instead, you want it to contain other elements, as follows:

```
  <publisher>
    <name> ACA - American Composers Alliance</name>
    <email>info@composers.com</email>
    <homepage>http://www.composers.com/</homepage>
    <address>170 West 74th St. NY NY 10023</address>
    <voice>212-362-8900</voice>
    <fax>212-874-8605</fax>
  </publisher>
```

You can declare that each publisher has exactly one name, e-mail, homepage, address, voice, and fax element by including those names in the declaration of the publisher element, separated by commas, and declaring each of those elements in its own element tag as containing PCDATA (or other elements). For example:

```
<!DOCTYPE document [
   <!ELEMENT document ANY>
   <!ELEMENT title (#PCDATA)>
   <!ELEMENT publisher (name, email, homepage, address,
     voice, fax)>
```

```
   <!ELEMENT name (#PCDATA)>
   <!ELEMENT email (#PCDATA)>
   <!ELEMENT homepage (#PCDATA)>
   <!ELEMENT address (#PCDATA)>
   <!ELEMENT voice (#PCDATA)>
   <!ELEMENT fax (#PCDATA)>
]>
```

Listing 5-10 shows a valid document that follows this DTD.

Listing 5-10: A more granular publisher list

```
<?xml version="1.0" standalone="yes"?>
<!DOCTYPE document [
   <!ELEMENT document ANY>
   <!ELEMENT title (#PCDATA)>
   <!ELEMENT publisher (name, email, homepage, address, voice, fax)>
   <!ELEMENT name (#PCDATA)>
   <!ELEMENT email (#PCDATA)>
   <!ELEMENT homepage (#PCDATA)>
   <!ELEMENT address (#PCDATA)>
   <!ELEMENT voice (#PCDATA)>
   <!ELEMENT fax (#PCDATA)>
]>
<document>
 <title>
    Publishers of the Music of New York Women Composers
 </title>
 <publisher>
    <name> ACA - American Composers Alliance</name>
    <email>info@composers.com</email>
    <homepage>http://www.composers.com/</homepage>
    <address>170 West 74th St. NY NY 10023</address>
    <voice>212-362-8900</voice>
    <fax>212-874-8605</fax>
 </publisher>
 <publisher>
    <name>Alfred Publishing</name>
    <email></email>
    <homepage></homepage>
    <address>15535 Morrison South Oaks CA 91403</address>
    <voice></voice>
    <fax></fax>
 </publisher>
</document>
```

In some applications, you may want to allow a single publisher to have multiple phone numbers, fax numbers, e-mail addresses, home pages, or even snail mail addresses. The next sections show you how to implement this information.

Because the publication of new classical music is a relatively small operation, however, most publishers have only a single address or phone number. Furthermore, a reader is likely to prefer a single point of contact — unless additional information is provided indicating one of several phone numbers they should use (for example, the first phone number is for sales and the second is for inquiries from prospective composers). Finally, for various technical reasons, restricting these elements to no more than one apiece makes the information much easier to store in a relational database.

Listing 5-11 is a style sheet with rules for all these new elements. The publisher element is formatted as a definition list item. `<select-elements>` is used extensively to distinguish between what goes in the `<dt>` and `<dd>` parts of each list item. The name is selected out as the logical choice for the `<dt>`. The remaining elements are placed in an unordered list inside the `<dd>`. The URL is hot-linked. The other elements are covered by a single rule that turns them into list items.

Listing 5-11: A style sheet that organizes the publisher children

```
<xsl>

  <rule>
    <root/>
    <html>
      <children/>
    </html>
  </rule>

  <rule>
    <target-element type="title"/>
    <head>
      <title><children/></title>
    </head>
  </rule>

  <rule>
    <target-element type="publisher"/>

    <dt/>
    <select-elements>
      <target-element type="name"/>
    </select-elements>
    <dd/><ul>
      <select-elements>
        <target-element type="email"/>
      </select-elements>
      <select-elements>
        <target-element type="homepage"/>
      </select-elements>
      <select-elements>
        <target-element type="address"/>
      </select-elements>
      <select-elements>
        <target-element type="voice"/>
      </select-elements>
      <select-elements>
```

```
          <target-element type="fax"/>
        </select-elements>
    </ul>
</rule>


<rule>
  <target-element type="address"/>
  <target-element type="email"/>
  <target-element type="voice"/>
  <target-element type="fax"/>

  <li><children/></li>
</rule>

<rule>
  <target-element type="homepage"/>
  <li><a href="=text"><children/></a></li>
</rule>

</xsl>
```

Figure 5-4 shows the rendered output. The same visual effects could have been achieved with Cascading Style Sheets and style attributes, but this approach works satisfactorily and is more compatible with older browsers. This approach also helps clarify exactly what's going on in the style sheet.

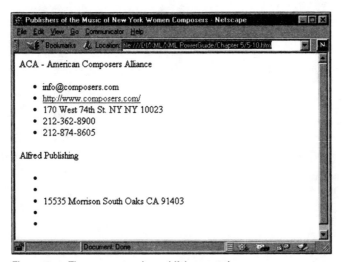

Figure 5-4: The more granular publishers catalog

If you look closely at the style sheet in Listing 5-11, or if you run it on Listing 5-10 and inspect the output HTML file, you may notice a few problems. In particular, the body and dl elements you expect to find are missing. This could be fixed with some fancy footwork in the style sheet, but what's really required is the ability to specify in the DTD that an element may have zero or more children of a particular type. Then, the solution becomes almost trivial. You'll see exactly how this is accomplished in the following section, "Designating Zero or More Children."

Making Child Elements Optional

The Alfred Publishing element in Listing 5-8 contains several effectively empty elements because no e-mail address, phone numbers, or home page were known. Nonetheless, these children had to be included (though they were empty), because the DTD required it. The final result would be more attractive if you could simply omit child elements that a particular parent doesn't have.

You can indicate that a child element is optional by appending a question mark (?) to its name in the parent element's declaration. For example, the following element declaration says that a publisher must have a name, but may or may not have a single e-mail address, home page, snail mail address, voice number, or fax number.

```
<!ELEMENT publisher (name, email?, homepage?, address?,
    voice?, fax?)>
```

Listing 5-12 is the same as Listing 5-10 except for the declaration of the publisher element. This new declaration allows publishers to omit information that doesn't apply to them. In this case, all the elements are present in the first publisher, ACA, but not in the second publisher, Alfred Publishing.

Listing 5-12: A contact list with optional elements

```
<?xml version="1.0" standalone="yes"?>
<!DOCTYPE document [
  <!ELEMENT document ANY>
  <!ELEMENT title (#PCDATA)>
  <!ELEMENT publisher (name, email?, homepage?,
      address?, voice?, fax?)>
  <!ELEMENT name (#PCDATA)>
  <!ELEMENT email (#PCDATA)>
  <!ELEMENT homepage (#PCDATA)>
  <!ELEMENT address (#PCDATA)>
  <!ELEMENT voice (#PCDATA)>
  <!ELEMENT fax (#PCDATA)>
]>
<document>
```

```
<title>
   Publishers of the Music of New York Women Composers
</title>
 <publisher>
    <name> ACA - American Composers Alliance</name>
    <email>info@composers.com</email>
    <homepage>http://www.composers.com/</homepage>
    <address>170 West 74th St. NY NY 10023</address>
    <voice>212-362-8900</voice>
    <fax>212-874-8605</fax>
 </publisher>
 <publisher>
    <name>Alfred Publishing</name>
    <address>15535 Morrison South Oaks CA 91403</address>
 </publisher>
</document>
```

Listing 5-12 simply allows different arrangements of the same elements present in Listing 5-10. No new elements have been added. Therefore, you don't need a new style sheet to render this document – Listing 5-11 still works perfectly well. Figure 5-5 shows the results.

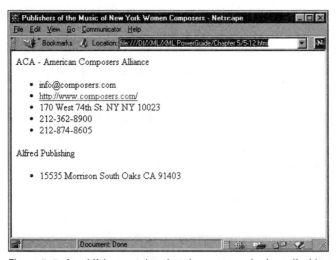

Figure 5-5: A publishers catalog that does not require inapplicable or unavailable elements to be included

Although child elements of publisher other than name may now be omitted, they may not be reordered. With this DTD, for instance, the home page may not come before the e-mail address. The following publisher element is invalid because the voice and fax numbers appear at the beginning of the element rather than the end:

```
<publisher>
  <name> ACA - American Composers Alliance</name>
  <voice>212-362-8900</voice>
  <fax>212-874-8605</fax>
  <email>info@composers.com</email>
  <homepage>http://www.composers.com/</homepage>
  <address>170 West 74th St. NY NY 10023</address>
</publisher>
```

This may seem inflexible – and indeed there are ways around it as you'll see soon. You should keep in mind that although the source document cannot be reordered, this isn't necessarily true of the output document. In the last chapter, you saw how to use style sheets to display information to the user in different orders than it appears in the source document. Only the source needs to conform to the DTD, not the output.

Designating Zero or More Children

The complete list of publishers itself forms an obvious element, which can be unimaginatively called <publisher_list>. Grouping all the publishers together into a single element enables you to apply group-wide formatting (such as indenting the whole group) and allows programs reading your data to enumerate all the publishers in a document more easily.

A publisher list contains publishers. In general, the list contains more than one publisher, with two in the preceding examples. Thus, you could declare the publisher list as follows:

```
<!ELEMENT publisher_list (publisher, publisher)>
```

This example specifies that a publisher list must have exactly two publishers. Suppose you want more flexibility to allow publishers to be added to or deleted from the document without having to change the DTD. To specify that a parent may contain zero or more child elements of a particular type, attach an asterisk to the end of the child's name in the parent's element declaration. For example:

```
<!ELEMENT publisher_list (publisher*)>
```

Listing 5-13 shows one valid document according to this definition.

Listing 5-13: Zero or more publishers

```
<?xml version="1.0" standalone="yes"?>
 <! DOCTYPE document [
   <!ELEMENT document (title, publisher_list)>

   <!-- document children -->
   <!ELEMENT title (#PCDATA)>
   <!ELEMENT publisher_list (publisher*)>
```

```
  <!-- publisher children -->
  <!ELEMENT publisher (name, email?, homepage?, address?, voice?,
fax?)>
  <!ELEMENT name (#PCDATA)>
  <!ELEMENT email (#PCDATA)>
  <!ELEMENT homepage (#PCDATA)>
  <!ELEMENT address (#PCDATA)>
  <!ELEMENT voice (#PCDATA)>
  <!ELEMENT fax (#PCDATA)>
]>
<document>
 <title>
   Publishers of the Music of New York Women Composers
 </title>
  <publisher_list>
    <publisher>
      <name> ACA - American Composers Alliance</name>
      <email>info@composers.com</email>
      <homepage>http://www.composers.com/</homepage>
      <address>170 West 74th St. NY NY 10023</address>
      <voice>212-362-8900</voice>
      <fax>212-874-8605</fax>
    </publisher>
    <publisher>
      <name>Alfred Publishing</name>
      <address>15535 Morrison South Oaks CA 91403</address>
    </publisher>
  </publisher_list>
</document>
```

This DTD contains one more change. It now specifies that the document element contains a single title, followed by a single publisher_list. Enclosing the publishers in a publisher list element also allows a few improvements to be made in the style sheet, as Listing 5-14 shows. In particular, you can insert <body> and </body> tags in the appropriate places, and also include the title in an <h1> header at the beginning of the document. Figure 5-6 shows the rendered results.

Listing 5-14: A style sheet that uses an <h1> header and <body> and <dl> elements

```
<xsl>

  <rule>
    <root/>
    <html>
      <head>
        <title>
          <select-elements>
            <target-element type="title"/>
          </select-elements>
        </title>
      </head>
      <body>
```

```
      <h1>
        <select-elements>
          <target-element type="title"/>
        </select-elements>
      </h1>
      <select-elements>
        <target-element type="publisher_list"/>
      </select-elements>
    </body>
  </html>
</rule>

<rule>
  <target-element type="title"/>
  <children/>
</rule>

<rule>
  <target-element type="publisher_list"/>
  <dl>
    <children/>
  </dl>
</rule>

<rule>
  <target-element type="publisher"/>

  <dt/>
  <select-elements>
    <target-element type="name"/>
  </select-elements>
  <dd/><ul>
    <select-elements>
      <target-element type="email"/>
    </select-elements>
    <select-elements>
      <target-element type="homepage"/>
    </select-elements>
    <select-elements>
      <target-element type="address"/>
    </select-elements>
    <select-elements>
      <target-element type="voice"/>
    </select-elements>
    <select-elements>
      <target-element type="fax"/>
    </select-elements>
  </ul>
</rule>

<rule>
  <target-element type="address"/>
  <target-element type="email"/>
```

```
<target-element type="voice"/>
<target-element type="fax"/>

<li><children/></li>
</rule>

<rule>
<target-element type="homepage"/>
<li><a href="=text"><children/></a></li>
</rule>

</xsl>
```

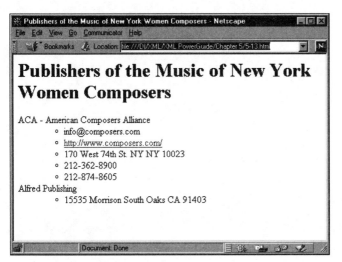

Figure 5-6: The publishers catalog with an <h1> header and
<body> and <dl> elements

Listing 5-13 is not the only possible document that matches this DTD, however. The following document is also a valid document, because it contains all required elements in their required order and does not contain any undeclared elements.

```
<document>
 <title>
    Publishers of the Music of New York Women Composers
 </title>
 <publisher_list>
   <publisher>  <name> Publisher A</name> </publisher>
 </publisher_list>
</document>
```

In fact, even the following document without any publishers at all is valid, because the DTD allows a publisher list to contain zero publishers.

```
<document>
 <title>
    Publishers of the Music of New York Women Composers
 </title>
 <publisher_list>

 </publisher_list>
</document>
```

One or More Children

So far, you've seen markers that specify a parent must have exactly one child of a particular type, zero or one children of a particular type (?), and any number of children of a particular type (*). The final marker you need is one that requires a parent to possess one or more occurrences of a particular child. This marker is the plus sign (+).

Among other things, plus signs are useful when describing addresses. For example, consider the following addresses:

Bill Clinton
1600 Pennsylvania Ave.
Washington DC 20500

IDG Books Worldwide, Inc.
919 E. Hillsdale Blvd.
Suite 400
Foster City CA 94405-2112

IDG Sweden AB
Sturegatan 11
S-106 78 Stockholm
Sweden

Elliotte Rusty Harold
Dept. of Mathematics
Cullimore Hall
Room 611
New Jersey Institute of Technology
University Heights
Newark NJ 07102

The last address is particularly nasty. It not only has a name, a city, a state, and a zip code, but also has a department, a building, a room, an organization, and a neighborhood in the city! A few years ago, that address was my real address (but no longer – please don't send me mail there). You could make all of the items possible attributes of an address element, but even so, someone else would come along with a rural route, drawer, or some other part of an address you hadn't considered. You can make tags for the basic parts of most addresses – street, city, state, zip, country, and so forth – but you also need one catchall tag that allows you to insert arbitrary extra information. Zero or more of these tags should be allowed in an address element.

The simplest method treats the tags as parts of the street but allows multiple streets. This method requires every address to have a street, a city, a state, and a zip, but occasionally allows the street to be a building, a university, or another identifying factor. The following element declaration describes such an address:

```
<!ELEMENT address (street+, city, state, zip, country?)>
```

The + after street signifies that each address must contain one or more street elements, all of which must come before the city, state, and zip. Exactly one city, state, and zip must appear in that order; optionally, a single country can appear at the end. Given the liberal definition of "street" adopted previously and also allowing "state" to include provinces and "zip" to include almost any foreign postal code, this approach should be sufficient for almost every address. This definition may occasionally encounter problems with a few international addresses without postal codes or states. In these cases, however, the tags can still be included, but with empty content.

Listing 5-15 shows the latest sample of a publisher page using the new address tags and the complete DTD.

Listing 5-15: One or more streets in an address

```
<?xml version="1.0" standalone="yes"?>
<!DOCTYPE document [
    <!ELEMENT document (title, publisher_list)>

    <!-- document children -->
    <!ELEMENT title (#PCDATA)>
    <!ELEMENT publisher_list (publisher*)>

    <!-- publisher elements -->
    <!ELEMENT publisher (name, email?, homepage?,
        address?, voice?, fax?)>
    <!ELEMENT name (#PCDATA)>
    <!ELEMENT email (#PCDATA)>
    <!ELEMENT homepage (#PCDATA)>

    <!-- address elements-->
    <!ELEMENT address (street+, city, state, zip, country?)>
    <!ELEMENT street (#PCDATA)>
    <!ELEMENT city (#PCDATA)>
    <!ELEMENT state (#PCDATA)>
    <!ELEMENT zip (#PCDATA)>
    <!ELEMENT country (#PCDATA)>
```

```
   <!ELEMENT voice (#PCDATA)>
   <!ELEMENT fax (#PCDATA)>
]>
<document>
 <title>
    Publishers of the Music of New York Women Composers
 </title>

 <publisher_list>
    <publisher>
      <name> ACA - American Composers Alliance</name>
      <email>info@composers.com</email>
      <homepage>http://www.composers.com/</homepage>
      <address>
        <street>170 West 74th St.</street>
        <city>NY</city>
        <state>NY</state>
        <zip>10023</zip>
      </address>
      <voice>212-362-8900</voice>
      <fax>212-874-8605</fax>
    </publisher>
    <publisher>
      <name>Alfred Publishing</name>
      <address>
        <street>15535 Morrison</street>
        <city>South Oaks</city>
        <state>CA</state>
        <zip>91403</zip>
      </address>
    </publisher>
    <publisher>
      <name>Music 70</name>
      <address>
        <street>250 West 57th Street</street>
        <street># 232</street>
        <city>NY</city> <state>NY</state>
        <zip>10107</zip>
      </address>
    </publisher>
  </publisher_list>

</document>
```

You could almost use the style sheet in Listing 5-14 here. You would simply allow the default rule to control the new street, city, state, zip and country elements. MSXSL doesn't place space between elements by default, however, leaving you with addresses like "170 West 74th St.NYNY10023" instead of "170 West 74th St. NY NY 10023."

You can fix this problem in several ways. The simplest approach adds the two rules shown in Listing 5-16 to the style sheet. These rules wrap the child elements and the extra spaces in <SPAN> tags. MSXML respects white space inside <SPAN>,

\<DIV\>, and other HTML tags. Figure 5-7 shows Listing 5-15 after it's been rendered with this style sheet. (Although this figure may seem similar to Figure 5-6, you should note that Figure 5-6 shows an address element, while Figure 5-7 shows street, state, and zip elements.)

Listing 5-16: Rules for the address children

```
<rule>
  <target-element type="street"/>

  <SPAN><children/> </SPAN>
</rule>

<rule>
  <target-element type="city"/>
  <target-element type="state"/>
  <target-element type="zip"/>
  <target-element type="country"/>

  <SPAN> <children/> </SPAN>
</rule>
```

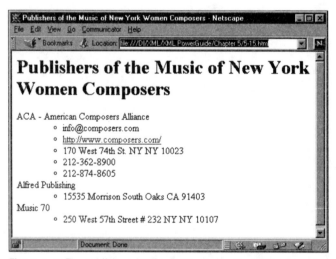

Figure 5-7: The publishers catalog with street, city, state, zip, and country elements

Combining Elements

As you just learned, a single parent element generally has many children. The children are separated by commas to indicate they must occur in sequence. Each such child element may be suffixed with either a question mark, a plus sign, or an asterisk to adjust the number of times it appears in that place in the sequence. For example, suppose you want to say that a document element, rather than having any children at all, must have exactly one title, followed by any number of paragraphs of text, followed by one or more publisher lists, followed by any number of paragraphs of text, followed by an optional signature block; you can write its element declaration as follows:

```
<!ELEMENT document (title, p*, publisher_list+, p*, signature?)>
```

You can also use the vertical bar to combine elements to indicate that one or the other is required. You can also group combinations of elements in parentheses, then suffix asterisks, question marks, and plus signs to the parentheses to indicate that particular combinations of elements must occur zero or more, zero or one, or one or more times. You can group these parenthesized combinations into still larger parenthesized groups to produce complex structures. Some following examples will clarify this approach.

Allowing Authors to Choose among Elements

So far, the assumption has been made that the tags appear or do not appear in a specific order. You may, however, wish to give your document more options, like choosing between different elements in a given place. For example, it may be important for a U.S. political cartography program to distinguish between states and territories, because only the former have senators and congressmen. By distinguishing such details, lobbying organizations can more easily target mailings to people with a higher chance of influencing legislation.

You can indicate the user needs to input either one or another element (for example, a state or a territory) by separating child elements with a vertical bar (|), rather than a comma (,), in the parent's element declaration. For example:

```
<!ELEMENT location (state | territory)>
<!ELEMENT address (street+, city, location, zip, country?)>
<!ELEMENT state (#PCDATA)>
<!ELEMENT territory (#PCDATA)>
```

The vertical bar is even more useful and less cumbersome when you group elements with parentheses.

Nesting Parentheses

The final thing you need to know about arranging child elements in parent element declarations is how to group elements with parentheses. Parentheses combine elements so they appear as a single element at some level. For example, consider the following element declaration:

```
<!ELEMENT address (street+, city, location, zip, country?)>
```

In some sense, this declaration says that an address element contains a single element, which itself is made up of one or more street elements, a city, a state, a zip, and an optional country element.

Each set of parentheses combines several elements as a single element. This parenthesized element can then be nested inside other parentheses in place of a single element. Furthermore, it may then have a plus sign, a comma, or a question mark affixed. This technique is very powerful. For example, rather than creating a somewhat artificial location element that always contains exactly one state or territory child, you can use parentheses to specify that an address element must contain either a state or a territory – but not both.

```
<!ELEMENT address (street+, city, (state | territory),
   zip, country?)>
```

As another example, consider a list composed of two elements that must alternate with each other (which is essentially how HTML's definition list works). Each <dt> tag should be matched with exactly one <dd> tag. If you replicate this structure in XML, the declaration of the dl element looks as follows:

```
<!ELEMENT dl  ((dt, dd)*)>
```

The extra parentheses are necessary to indicate that the matched <dt><dd> pair is repeated, not just <dd> alone.

Often, elements appear in more or less random orders. News magazine articles generally have a title, followed by mostly paragraphs of text with graphs, photos, sidebars, subheads, and pull quotes interspersed throughout, and perhaps a byline at the end. You can indicate this sort of arrangement by listing all the possible child elements in the parent's element declaration separated by vertical bars and grouped inside parentheses; then place an asterisk outside the closing parenthesis to indicate that zero or more occurrences of any element in the parentheses are allowed. For example:

```
<!ELEMENT article (title, (p | photo | graph | sidebar
   | pullquote | subhead)*, byline?)>
```

As another example, suppose you want to say that a document element, rather than having any children at all, must have exactly one title, followed by any number of freely mingled paragraphs of text and publisher lists, followed by an optional signature block. You can write its element declaration as follows:

```
<!ELEMENT document (title, (p | publisher_list)*, signature?)>
```

This example is not the only way to describe this structure. In fact, it may not even be the best approach. An alternative method declares a body element that contains paragraphs and publishers and nests that element between the title and the signature. For example:

```
<!ELEMENT document (title, body, signature?)>
<!ELEMENT body ((p | publisher_list)*)>
```

The difference between these two approaches is that the second requires an additional <body> element to be placed in the document. This element provides an additional level of organization that may (or may not) be useful to the application reading the document. Ask yourself whether the reader of this document (who may be another computer program) may ever want to consider the body material as a single item in its own right, separate from the title and the signature, and distinguished from the sum of its elements.

For another example, consider international addresses. Addresses outside the United States don't always follow U.S. conventions. In particular, postal codes sometimes precede the state or follow the country, as in the two following examples:

Doberman-YPPAN
Box 2021
St. Nicholas QUEBEC
CAN GOS-3LO

Editions Sybex
10/12 villa Coeur-de-Vey
75685 Paris Cedex 14
France

While your mail will probably arrive, even if the individual pieces of the address are out of order, you should allow an address to be more flexible. The following address element declaration that permits such flexibility:

```
<!ELEMENT address (street+, (city | state | zip | country)*)>
```

This example says that an address must have one or more streets followed by any number of cities, states, postal codes, or countries. Even this approach is less than ideal if you want to allow for no more than one of each item. Unfortunately, this method is beyond the power of a DTD to enforce. By allowing more flexible ordering of elements, you give up some ability to control the maximum number of each element.

On the other hand, you may have a list composed of different kinds of elements, which may appear in an arbitrary order (for example, a list of recordings which may contain CDs, albums, and tapes). An element declaration to differentiate between the different categories for this list could look as follows:

```
<!ELEMENT music_list ((cd | album | tape)*)>
```

For another example, suppose you're maintaining an inventory list at a used bookstore. Modern books can be identified by ISBN number, but older books may not have such a number. For older books, you must specify the author, title, edition, publisher, and binding. (It was exactly this sort of confusion that led to ISBN numbers in the first place.) The following book element uses nested parentheses to specify that each book must have either an ISBN number or an author-title-edition-publisher-binding sequence, or may have both items.

```
<!ELEMENT book ((isbn | ( author, title, edition,
publisher, binding))+)>
```

A few things are still difficult to handle in element declarations. For example, there's no good way to say that a document must begin with a title element and end with a signature element, but may contain any other elements between those two. Difficulty arises because ANY may not be combined with other child elements.

In general, the less precise you are about where items appear, the less control you have over how many of items exist. For example, you can't say that a document can have no more than one title but that the title may appear anywhere in the document.

Still, using parentheses to create blocks of elements, either in sequence with a comma or in parallel with a vertical bar, enables you to create quite complicated structures with detailed rules for how different elements may follow each other. Try not to go overboard with this, though. Simpler solutions are better. The more complicated your DTD becomes, the harder it is to write valid files that satisfy the DTD, to say nothing of the complexity in maintaining the DTD itself. Just ask Dave Raggett, one of the maintainers of the HTML DTD during the free-for-all days of the Great Netscape Tag Expansion.

Using Mixed Content

You may have noticed that in most of the examples shown so far, most parents contained either child elements or parsed character data – not both. The only exceptions are the document elements in early examples where the full list of tags was not yet developed. In these cases, because <document> could contain ANY data, it was allowed to contain both child elements and raw text.

You can declare tags that contain both child elements and parsed character data. These tags are called *mixed content*. You might use mixed content to allow an arbitrary block of text to be suffixed to each publisher listing. For example:

```
<!ELEMENT publisher (#PCDATA | name | email | homepage
  | address | voice | fax)* >
```

Listing 5-17 shows a valid document that uses mixed content in the publisher element.

Listing 5-17: A publisher listing with mixed content

```
<?xml version="1.0" standalone="yes"?>
<!DOCTYPE document [
  <!ELEMENT document ANY>
  <!ELEMENT title (#PCDATA)>
  <!ELEMENT publisher_list (publisher*)>
  <!ELEMENT publisher (#PCDATA | name | email | homepage
    | address | voice | fax)* >
  <!ELEMENT name (#PCDATA)>
  <!ELEMENT email (#PCDATA)>
  <!ELEMENT homepage (#PCDATA)>
  <!ELEMENT address (street+, city, state, zip, country?)>
  <!ELEMENT street (#PCDATA)>
  <!ELEMENT city (#PCDATA)>
  <!ELEMENT state (#PCDATA)>
  <!ELEMENT zip (#PCDATA)>
  <!ELEMENT country (#PCDATA)>
  <!ELEMENT voice (#PCDATA)>
  <!ELEMENT fax (#PCDATA)>
]>
<document>
 <title>
    Publishers of the Music of New York Women Composers
 </title>

 <publisher_list>
    <publisher>
      <name> ACA - American Composers Alliance</name>
      <email>info@composers.com</email>
      <homepage>http://www.composers.com/</homepage>
      <address>
        <street>170 West 74th St.</street>
        <city>NY</city>
        <state>NY</state>
        <zip>10023</zip>
      </address>
      <voice>212-362-8900</voice>
      <fax>212-874-8605</fax>
       The web site provides access to ACA's complete catalog
       and allows you to rent or purchase scores.
    </publisher>
    </publisher_list>

</document>
```

Mixing child elements with parsed character data severely restricts the structure you can impose on your documents. In particular, you can only specify the names of the child elements that can appear. You cannot constrain the order in which they appear, the number of each that appears, or whether they appear at all.

In terms of DTDs, you can think of this as meaning that the child part of the DTD must look like the following:

```
<!ELEMENT parent (#PCDATA | child1 | child2 | child3)* >
```

Other than changing the number of children, almost anything else is invalid. You cannot use commas, question marks, or plus signs in an element declaration that includes #PCDATA. A list of elements and #PCDATA separated by vertical bars is valid – any other use is invalid. For example, the following is illegal:

```
<!ELEMENT publisher (name, email, homepage, address, #PCDATA >
```

The primary reason to mix content is during the process of converting old text data to XML, and are testing your DTD by validating as you add new tags – rather than finishing the entire conversion and then trying to find the bugs. This is a good technique, and I recommend you use it. After all, it is much easier to recognize a bug in your code immediately rather than several hours later. However, this technique should only be used as a crutch while developing, and should not be visible to the end user. When your DTD is finished, it should not mix element children with parsed character data. You can always create a new tag that holds parsed character data.

For example, you can include a block of text at the end of each publisher listing by declaring a new <blurb> tag that only holds #PCDATA and adding it as the last child element of publisher, as follows:

```
<!ELEMENT publisher (name, email?, homepage?,
    address?, voice?, fax?, blurb?)>
  <!ELEMENT blurb (#PCDATA)>
```

This example does not significantly change the actual text of the document. It only adds one more optional element with its opening and closing tags to each publisher element, as shown in Listing 5-18. It does make the document much more robust, however. Furthermore, XML applications that receive the tree from the XML processor have a much easier time handling the data when it's in the more structured format allowed by nonmixed content.

Listing 5-18: A revised publisher list – now without mixed content

```
<?xml version="1.0" standalone="yes"?>
<!DOCTYPE document [
  <!ELEMENT document ANY>
  <!ELEMENT title (#PCDATA)>
  <!ELEMENT publisher_list (publisher*)>
  <!ELEMENT publisher (name, email?, homepage?,
    address?, voice?, fax?, blurb?)>
  <!ELEMENT name (#PCDATA)>
  <!ELEMENT email (#PCDATA)>
```

```
    <!ELEMENT homepage (#PCDATA)>
    <!ELEMENT address (street+, city, state, zip, country?)>
    <!ELEMENT street (#PCDATA)>
    <!ELEMENT city (#PCDATA)>
    <!ELEMENT state (#PCDATA)>
    <!ELEMENT zip (#PCDATA)>
    <!ELEMENT country (#PCDATA)>
    <!ELEMENT voice (#PCDATA)>
    <!ELEMENT fax (#PCDATA)>
    <!ELEMENT blurb (#PCDATA)>
]>
<document>
 <title>
    Publishers of the Music of New York Women Composers
 </title>

 <publisher_list>
    <publisher>
      <name> ACA - American Composers Alliance</name>
      <email>info@composers.com</email>
      <homepage>http://www.composers.com/</homepage>
      <address>
        <street>170 West 74th St.</street>
        <city>NY</city>
        <state>NY</state>
        <zip>10023</zip>
      </address>
      <voice>212-362-8900</voice>
      <fax>212-874-8605</fax>
      <blurb>
       The web site provides access to ACA's complete catalog
       and allows you to rent or purchase scores.
      </blurb>
    </publisher>
    </publisher_list>

</document>
```

The style sheet for this example is a simple revision of Listing 5-16. You only need one additional select-elements element in the publisher action to insert the blurb text into the output, as demonstrated in Listing 5-19. Figure 5-8 shows the rendered output.

Listing 5-19: A publisher rule that includes blurbs

```
<rule>
    <target-element type="publisher"/>

    <dt/>
    <select-elements>
      <target-element type="name"/>
```

```
    </select-elements>
    <dd/><ul>
      <select-elements>
        <target-element type="email"/>
      </select-elements>
      <select-elements>
        <target-element type="homepage"/>
      </select-elements>
      <select-elements>
        <target-element type="address"/>
      </select-elements>
      <select-elements>
        <target-element type="voice"/>
      </select-elements>
      <select-elements>
        <target-element type="fax"/>
      </select-elements>
    </ul>
    <select-elements>
      <target-element type="blurb"/>
    </select-elements>
  </rule>
```

Figure 5-8: The publishers catalog with blurbs

Mixed content also presents problems for style sheets. Generally, you want to define one format for the character data of the parent and another format for the child elements. In practice, however, this is extremely difficult, and requires extensive manipulation of select-elements tags and JavaScript. It is much easier not to mix character data and element content.

Empty Tags

Occasionally, it's useful to define a tag that has no content, which is called an *empty* tag. Examples in HTML include the image, horizontal rule, and break tags (`<img>`, `<hr>`, and `<br>`). In XML, these tags become `<img/>`, `<hr/>`, and `<br/>`.

Valid documents must declare both the empty and nonempty tags used. Because empty tags by definition don't have children, they're quite easy to declare. You merely use an `<!ELEMENT>` tag containing the name of the empty element as normal, but use the keyword EMPTY (case-sensitive like all XML keywords) instead of a list of children. For example:

```
<!ELEMENT br EMPTY>
<!ELEMENT img EMPTY>
<!ELEMENT hr EMPTY>
```

 MSXML 1.8 does not require empty tags to be declared in the DTD. This is incorrect. Microsoft may have fixed this bug by the time you read this section. Check their Web site at `http://www.microsoft.com/xml/` for the most recent information.

Listing 5-20 is a valid document that uses both empty and nonempty tags.

Listing 5-20: A valid document that uses empty tags

```
<?xml version="1.0" standalone="yes"?>
<!DOCTYPE document [
    <!ELEMENT document (title, signature)>
    <!ELEMENT title (#PCDATA)>
    <!ELEMENT copyright (#PCDATA)>
    <!ELEMENT email (#PCDATA)>
    <!ELEMENT br EMPTY>
    <!ELEMENT hr EMPTY>
    <!ELEMENT lastmodified (#PCDATA)>
    <!ELEMENT signature (hr, copyright, br, email,
        br, lastmodified)>
]>
<document>
  <title>Empty Tags</title>
  <signature>
    <hr/>
    <copyright>1998 Elliotte Rusty Harold</copyright><br/>
    <email>elharo@sunsite.unc.edu</email><br/>
    <lastmodified>Thursday, March 10, 1998</lastmodified>
  </signature>
</document>
```

This EMPTY keyword is not used for tags with opening and closing tags, but no content. For example, consider the following tags:

```
<br></br>
<hr></hr>
<img></img>
```

These tags are declared as follows:

```
<!ELEMENT br (#PCDATA)>
<!ELEMENT hr (#PCDATA)>
<!ELEMENT img (#PCDATA)>
```

Empty tags are treated just like normal tags inside style sheets. The only stipulation is that because these are empty tags, there's no point to including a `<children/>` element inside the action for an empty tag.

Listing 5-21 is a simple style sheet that works with Listing 5-20. Figure 5-9 shows the rendered output.

Listing 5-21: A style sheet for empty tags

```
<xsl>

  <rule>
    <root/>
    <html>
      <head>
        <title>
          <select-elements>
            <target-element type="title"/>
          </select-elements>
        </title>
      </head>
      <body>
        <h1>
          <select-elements>
            <target-element type="title"/>
          </select-elements>
        </h1>
        <select-elements>
          <target-element type="signature"/>
        </select-elements>
      </body>
    </html>
  </rule>

  <rule>
    <target-element type="hr"/>
```

```
    <hr/>
  </rule>

  <rule>
    <target-element type="br"/>
    <br/>
  </rule>

  <rule>
    <target-element type="signature"/>
      <children/>
  </rule>

  <rule>
    <target-element type="copyright"/>
    Copyright <children/>
  </rule>

  <rule>
    <target-element type="email"/>
    <children/>
  </rule>

  <rule>
    <target-element type="lastmodified"/>
    Last Modified <children/>
  </rule>

</xsl>
```

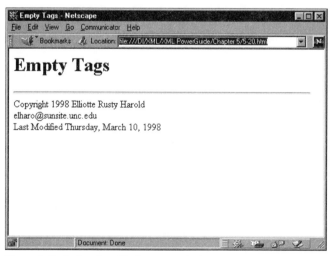

Figure 5-9: A signature that uses empty tags

Summary

In this chapter, you learned how to use a DTD to describe the structure of a document; that is, both its required and optional elements, and how those elements relate to each other. In particular, you learned the following concepts:

- A document type definition (DTD) provides a list of the elements, tags, attributes, and entities contained in the document, and their relationship to each other.

- A DTD is included in a document's prolog, after the XML declaration and before the actual document data begins. It consists of a series of markup declarations declaring particular elements, entities, and attributes contained between `<!DOCTYPE` *rootname* `[` and `]>` where *rootname* is understood to be the name of the root element.

- DTDs lay out the permissible tags and the structure of a document. A document that adheres to the rules of its DTD is said to be valid.

- Element type declarations declare the name and children of an element.

- Children separated by commas in an element type declaration must appear in the same order in that element inside the document.

- A question mark (?) means the child may or may not appear (it's optional, in other words).

- An asterisk (*) means zero or more instances of the element may appear.

- A plus sign (+) means one or more instances of the element may appear.

- A vertical bar (|) allows one element or another to be used.

- Parentheses group child elements to allow more detailed element declarations.

- Mixed content contains both elements and parsed character data, but limits the structure you can impose on the parent element.

- Empty elements are declared with the EMPTY keyword.

In the next chapter, you learn more about DTDs, including how entity references provide replacement text, how to mark sections as optional or ignored, how to separate DTDs from the documents they describe so they can be easily shared between documents, and how to use multiple DTDs to describe a single document.

Chapter 6

Assembling Documents from Multiple Data Sources

IN THIS CHAPTER

◆ Understanding entities

◆ Separating DTDs from documents

◆ Merging DTDs

◆ Exploring internal and external DTDs

◆ Processing instructions

◆ Understanding notations and unparsed entities

◆ Evaluating conditional sections

A TYPICAL XML file is divided into two parts: the prolog and the data. The prolog includes the XML declaration and the DTD. The data is the actual marked-up text. In the preceding examples, the prolog and the data have been part of the same file. In this chapter, however, you discover that a single XML document may draw both data and declarations from many different sources, which may be in different files. In fact, some of the data may draw directly from databases, CGI scripts, or other nonfile sources.

Entities

An XML document is composed of a prolog followed by one or more entities. An *entity* may be a file, a database record, or another item that contains data. For example, all the complete XML files and style sheets in the this book's examples are entities.

The primary purpose of an entity is to hold content. Generally, this *content* is text, but in special cases it may be binary data (like the bits of a GIF image).

Furthermore, most entities have names by which they can be identified. Note that neither the prolog, the XML declaration, nor the DTD are entities. Entities are for content – not for structure, rules, or grammar. An XSL style sheet is an entity, but only because it itself is a well-formed XML document. The entity that makes up the style sheet is not one of the entities that composes the XML document to which the style sheet applies.

The root element of the document is one entity, though it does not have a name. The root element is the outermost element of the document that contains all other elements and is not itself contained in any element. Because every well-formed XML document has a root element, every well-formed XML document has at least one entity.

There are two kinds of entities: internal and external. *Internal entities* are defined completely within the document. The root element is one such entity. *External entities* draw their content from another source located via a URL. The main document only includes a reference to the URL where the actual content resides. In HTML, an <IMG> tag represents an external entity (the actual image data) while the document itself contained between the <html> and </html> tags is an internal entity.

Entities may be either parsed or unparsed. The content of parsed entities is text that follows XML's rules. The content of unparsed entities is binary data or text that does not adhere to XML's rules. Instead, unparsed entities follow a notation declared in the DTD. Currently, unparsed entities aren't well supported (if at all) by most XML processors.

Entity references allow data from multiple entities to be merged together to form a single document. *General entity references* merge data into the document content. *Parameter entity references* merge declarations into the document's DTD. The <, >, ', &quote;, and & entity references in Chapter 3 are predefined entity references that refer to the text entities <, >, ', ", and &, respectively.

General Entity References

Think of a general entity reference as an abbreviation for either commonly used text or text that's hard to type. Instead of typing the same footer at the bottom of every page, you can simply define that text as the footer entity in the DTD and then type &footer; at the bottom of each page. Furthermore, if you decide to change the footer block (perhaps because your e-mail address changes), simply make the change once in the DTD instead of on every page that shares the footer.

General entity references begin with an ampersand (&) and end with a semicolon (;), with the entity's name in between these two characters. For instance, < stands for the less than sign (<) while & stands for the ampersand (&). The name of the entity is composed of any set of alphanumeric characters and the underscore. No white space or other punctuation characters are permitted. Like most everything else in XML, entity references are case-sensitive.

Although the colon (:) is technically permitted, this character is being saved for use with namespaces in a future version of XML.

DEFINING A GENERAL ENTITY REFERENCE

You can define your own general entity references in the DTD. Entity references are defined in a document's DTD via the `<!ENTITY>` tag, which has the following format:

```
<!ENTITY name "replacement text">
```

The *name* is the abbreviation for the entity. The reader views the *replacement text*, which must appear in quotes.

For example, my name is the somewhat excessive "Elliotte Rusty Harold" (blame my parents for that one). Even with years of practice I still make typos with that phrase. I can define an entity reference for my name so that every time I type &erh;, the reader will see "Elliotte Rusty Harold". The declaration for this reference follows:

```
<!ENTITY erh "Elliotte Rusty Harold">
```

Listing 6-1, a slight modification of Listing 5-20 from Chapter 5, uses the &erh; entity reference:

Listing 6-1: The erh entity reference

```
<?xml version="1.0" standalone="yes"?>
<!DOCTYPE document [

    <!ENTITY erh "Elliotte Rusty Harold">

    <!ELEMENT document (title, sig)>
    <!ELEMENT title (#PCDATA)>
    <!ELEMENT copyright (#PCDATA)>
    <!ELEMENT email (#PCDATA)>
    <!ELEMENT hr EMPTY>
    <!ELEMENT lastmodified (#PCDATA)>
    <!ELEMENT signature (hr, copyright, email, lastmodified)>
]>
<document>
  <title>&erh;</title>
  <signature>
    <hr/>
```

```
   <copyright>1998 &erh;</copyright>
   <email>elharo@sunsite.unc.edu</email>
   <lastmodified>Thursday, March 10, 1998</lastmodified>
  </signature>
</document>
```

Notice in particular that the entity reference &erh; appears inside both the signature and title elements even though these are declared to accept only #PCDATA as children. This arrangement is legal because entity references qualify as parsed character data. As long as the entity reference itself is declared in the DTD, you do not need to declare it separately as a child of the elements in which it appears.

Furthermore, entity references do not require any special support in the style sheet. Style sheet processors should make the appropriate substitutions from entity references to their replacement text as necessary. The 1-7-1998 technology preview release of MSXSL does not expand entity references into their replacement text, but future tools will offer this capability.

Follow the same model to declare the entity references for the copyright, the e-mail address, or the last modified date:

```
<!ENTITY copy98 "Copyright 1998">
<!ENTITY email "elharo@sunsite.unc.edu">
<!ENTITY lm "last modified: ">
```

The date was not included in the &lm; entity because it's likely to change from document to document; there is no advantage to making it an entity reference.

Now the document part of Listing 6-1 can be rewritten even more compactly like this:

```
<document>
  <title>&erh;</title>
  <signature>
    <hr/>
    &copy98; &erh;
    &email;
    &lm; Thursday, March 12, 1998
  </signature>
</document>
```

One of the advantages of using entity references instead of the full text is that these references make it easy to change the text. This is especially useful when a single DTD is shared between multiple documents. (You'll learn this skill in the following "Sharing Common DTDs Among Documents" section.) For example, suppose I decide to use the e-mail address eharold@solar.stanford.edu instead of elharo@sunsite.unc.edu. Instead of searching and replacing through multiple files, I simply change one line of the DTD as follows:

```
<!ENTITY email "eharold@solar.stanford.edu">
```

This example brings up several points. First, you might want to combine the &copy98; and &erh; entities into the single entity: "Copyright 1998 Elliotte Rusty Harold". Certainly, you can redefine the copy98 entity like this:

```
<!ENTITY copy98 "Copyright 1998 Elliotte Rusty Harold">
```

USING ENTITY REFERENCES IN THE DTD
You may wonder whether it's possible to go further and include one entity inside another as follows:

```
<!ENTITY copy98 "Copyright 1998 &erh;">
```

This example is in fact valid, because the entity appears as part of something that will be part of the document content. You can also use general entity references in other places in the DTD that ultimately become part of the document content (such as a default attribute value), although there are restrictions. The first restriction – the statement cannot use a circular reference as follows:

```
<!ENTITY erh "&copy98 Elliotte Rusty Harold">
<!ENTITY copy98 "Copyright 1998 &erh;">
```

The second restriction – the declaration of the reference must come before any use of the reference. For example, the following statement is invalid because the &erh; reference is used before it's declared.

```
<!ENTITY copy98 "Copyright 1998 &erh;">
<!ENTITY erh "&copy98 Elliotte Rusty Harold">
```

Unlike element declarations, general entity declarations cannot use forward references.

The third restriction – general entity references may not insert text that is only part of the DTD and will not be used as part of the document content. For example, the following attempted shortcut fails:

```
<!ENTITY pcd "(#PCDATA)">
<!ELEMENT animal &pcd;>
<!ELEMENT food &pcd;>
```

MSXML produces this error message:

```
C:\XML>jview msxml -d1 invisible.xml
Unexpected token '&' inside tag <animal>
Location: file:/C:/XML/invisible.xml(9,12)
Context: <DOCTYPE><animal>
```

It's often useful, however, to have entity references in a DTD. For this purpose, XML uses the parameter entity reference, which will be discussed in the following section.

The only restriction on general entity values is that they may not contain the three characters %, &, and ". The lack of restrictions means that an entity may contain tags and span multiple lines. For example, the following address entity is valid:

```
<!ENTITY address "Dept. of Computer Science<br/>
                  Polytechnic University<br/>
                  5 Metrotech Plaza<br/>
                  Brooklyn NY 11201 ">
```

Although this example is valid, MSXML 1.8 again does not quite follow the standard. MSXML will therefore report this entity as illegal.

The next obvious question is whether it's possible for entities to have parameters. For instance, is there some way you can include a date in each separate &lm; on each page? The answer is no; entities are only for static replacement text. If you need to pass data to an entity, you should really use a tag instead along with the appropriate rendering instructions in the style sheet.

PREDEFINED GENERAL ENTITY REFERENCES

XML predefines five general entity references, as listed in Table 6-1. These five entity references are used in XML documents in place of specific characters that would otherwise be interpreted as part of markup. For instance, the entity reference < stands for the less than sign (<), which would otherwise be interpreted as the beginning of a tag.

TABLE 6-1 XML PREDEFINED ENTITY REFERENCES

Entity Reference	Character
&amp;	&
&lt;	<
&gt;	>
&quot;	"
&apos;	'

For maximum compatibility, it is recommended (but not strictly required) that you declare these references in your DTD if you're going to use them. Declaration is actually quite tricky because you must also escape the characters in the DTD without using recursion. To declare these references, use character references containing the hexadecimal ASCII value of each character. Listing 6-2 is a DTD for these five entity references.

Listing 6-2: A DTD for the predefined entity references

```
<!ENTITY lt    "&#38;#60;">
<!ENTITY gt    "&#62;">
<!ENTITY amp   "&#38;#38;">
<!ENTITY apos  "&#39;">
<!ENTITY quot  "&#34;">
```

Parameter Entity References

General entity references may only be used in a DTD in places where they will become part of the document body. General entity references may not insert text that is only part of the DTD and will not be used as part of the document content. It's often useful, however, to have entity references in a DTD. For this purpose, XML uses the parameter entity reference.

Parameter entity references are very similar to general entity references – with the following two key differences:

♦ Parameter entity references begin with a percent sign (%) rather than an ampersand.

♦ Parameter entities can only appear in the DTD, not the document content.

Parameter entities are declared in the DTD like general entities with the addition of a percent sign before the name. The syntax follows:

```
<!ENTITY % name "replacement text">
```

The *name* is the abbreviation for the entity. The reader views the *replacement text*, which must appear in quotes.

An example follows:

```
<!ENTITY % erh "Elliotte Rusty Harold">
<!ENTITY copy "Copyright 1998 %erh;">
```

The preceding failed attempt to abbreviate (#PCDATA) works when a parameter entity reference replaces the general entity reference:

```
<!ENTITY % pcd "(#PCDATA)">
<!ELEMENT animal %pcd;>
<!ELEMENT food %pcd;>
```

More than in these simple examples, the real value of parameter entity references appears in sharing common attributes between tags and merging in external DTDs, as you'll see in the next several sections.

Parameter entity references must be declared before they're used. The following example is invalid because the %pcd; reference is only declared after it's been used twice:

```
<!ELEMENT food %pcd;>
<!ELEMENT animal %pcd;>
<!ENTITY % pcd "(#PCDATA)">
```

The larger the block of text you're replacing and the more times you use it, the more useful parameter entity references become. For instance, suppose your DTD declares a number of block level container elements like paragraph, cell, and heading. Each of these container elements may contain an indefinite number of inline elements like person, degree, model, product, animal, ingredient, and so forth. The element declarations for the container elements could appear as the following:

```
<!ELEMENT paragraph
    (person | degree | model | product | animal | ingredient)*>
<!ELEMENT cell
(person | degree | model | product | animal | ingredient)*>
<!ELEMENT heading
    (person | degree | model | product | animal | ingredient)*>
```

The container elements all have the same contents. If you invent a new element like equation, cd, or account, this tag has to be declared as a possible child of all three container elements. Adding it to two but forgetting to add it to the third element may cause trouble. This problem is even worse when you have thirty or three hundred container elements instead of three.

The DTD is much easier to maintain if you don't give each container a separate child list. Instead, make the child list a parameter entity reference; then use that parameter entity reference in each of the container element declarations. An example follows:

```
<!ENTITY % inlines
    "(person | degree | model | product | animal | ingredient)*">

<!ELEMENT paragraph %inlines;>
<!ELEMENT cell %inlines;>
<!ELEMENT heading %inlines;>
```

To add a new element, you only have to change a single parameter entity declaration, rather than three, thirty, or three hundred element declarations.

External Entity References

Until now, all the XML documents you've seen have been standalone with internal entities. Each file has been complete unto itself, containing both its content and its

DTD. No other files, either local or remote, have been required to parse the document. External entity references, however, enable you to create more diverse documents.

Before you examine external entity references, however, let's further explore internal entities. Documents using internal entities are very close to the HTML model. The complete text of the document is available in a single file. Images, applets, sounds, and other non-HTML data may be linked in, but at least all the text is present. Of course, the HTML model has some problems. In particular, it's quite difficult to embed dynamic information in the file. You can embed dynamic information by using CGI, applets, fancy database software, server side includes, and various other means, but HTML alone only provides a static document. You have to go outside HTML to build a document from multiple pieces. Frames are perhaps the simplest HTML solution to this problem, but they are a user interface disaster that consistently confuse and annoy users.

Part of the problem is that one HTML document does not naturally fit inside another. Every HTML document should have exactly one <body>, but no document should have more than one body. Server side includes only enable you to embed fragments of HTML – never an entire valid document – inside a document. In addition, server side includes are server dependent and not truly part of HTML.

XML, however, is more flexible. One document's root tag is not necessarily the same as another document's root tag. Even if two documents share the same root tag, the DTD may declare that the tag is allowed to contain itself. The XML standard does not prevent XML documents from being embedded in XML documents when convenient.

XML goes further, however, by defining a mechanism whereby an XML document can be built out of multiple smaller XML documents found either on local or remote systems. The parser is responsible for merging all the different documents together in a fixed order. Documents may contain other documents, which may contain other documents. As long as there's no *recursion* (an error reported by the processor), the application only sees a single complete document; in essence, a client side include.

Use an external general entity reference to embed one document in another. In the DTD, you can declare the external reference with this following syntax:

```
<!ENTITY name SYSTEM "URI">
```

URI stands for *Uniform Resource Identifier*. URIs are similar to URLs but allow for more precise specification of the linked resource. Furthermore, URIs separate the resource from the location so a Web browser can select the nearest or least congested of several mirrors without requiring an explicit link to that mirror (at least that's the theory). URIs are an area of active research and heated debate. Therefore, in practice and certainly in this book, URIs are exactly like URLs for all intents and purposes.

You may want to put the same signature block on almost every page of a site. Let's assume the signature block is the XML code shown in Listing 6-3. Furthermore, let's assume that this code is in a file that can be retrieved from the URL `http://sunsite.unc.edu/xml/signature.xml`.

Listing 6-3: An XML signature file

```
<signature>
  <copyright>1998 Elliotte Rusty Harold</copyright>
  <email>elharo@sunsite.unc.edu</email>
</signature>
```

Associate this file with the entity reference `&sig;` by adding the following declaration to the DTD:

```
<!ENTITY sig SYSTEM "http://sunsite.unc.edu/xml/signature.xml">
```

Now, you can include the contents of that file in a document at any point merely by using `&sig;`, as illustrated with a simple document in Listing 6-4. Aside from the addition of the external entity reference, note that the standalone attribute of the XML declaration now has the value "no" because this file is no longer complete. The file requires the additional data from `signature.xml`.

Listing 6-4: An external entity reference

```
<?xml version="1.0" standalone="no"?>
<!DOCTYPE document [
   <!ELEMENT document (title, signature)>
   <!ELEMENT title (#PCDATA)>
   <!ELEMENT copyright (#PCDATA)>
   <!ELEMENT email (#PCDATA)>
   <!ELEMENT signature (copyright, email)>
   <!ENTITY sig SYSTEM
      "http://sunsite.unc.edu/xml/signature.xml">
]>
<document>
  <title> Entity references</title>
  &sig;
</document>
```

Once again, MSXML 1.8 doesn't do a perfect job of following the spec here. While it can handle external entities, it has trouble when those entities contain required markup as in Listing 6-4, where the required signature element comes from the `&sig;` external entity. MSXML 1.8 does a much better job when the external entities only contain optional elements. It also runs into trouble if the included document contains an XML declaration or a DTD.

Sharing Common DTDs among Documents

All preceding examples have included the DTD in the document's prolog. The real power of XML, however, comes from creating common DTDs that can be shared between many documents written by different people. If the DTD is not directly included in the document, but rather linked in from an external source, changes made to the DTD automatically propagate to all documents that use that DTD. On the other hand, changes made to a DTD do not necessarily guarantee backward compatibility. Incompatible changes can break documents that depend on them.

When an external DTD is used, the <!DOCTYPE> tag changes. Instead of including the DTD in square brackets, the SYSTEM keyword is followed by an absolute or relative URL where the DTD can be found. The syntax follows:

```
<!DOCTYPE root_element_name SYSTEM "DTD_URL">
```

Here root_element_name is simply the name of the root element as before; SYSTEM is an XML keyword; and DTD_URL is a relative or absolute URL where the DTD can be found. An example follows:

```
<!DOCTYPE document SYSTEM "publishers.dtd">
```

Let's convert a familiar listing to demonstrate this process. Listing 5-15 in Chapter 5 creates the publisher page using new address tags and a complete DTD. We'll convert this listing to use an external DTD. You may want to refer back to Chapter 5 to see the listing with an internal DTD.

First, strip out the DTD and put it in a file of its own. The DTD constitutes everything between the opening <!DOCTYPE document [and the closing]> exclusive. <!DOCTYPE document [and]> are not included. This can be saved in a file called publishers.dtd as shown in Listing 6-5. The file name is not important, though the extension .dtd is conventional.

Listing 6-5: The publisher DTD

```
<!ELEMENT document (title, publisher_list)>

    <!-- document children -->
    <!ELEMENT title (#PCDATA)>
    <!ELEMENT publisher_list (publisher*)>

    <!-- publisher elements -->
    <!ELEMENT publisher (name, email?, homepage?,
      address?, voice?, fax?)>
    <!ELEMENT name (#PCDATA)>
    <!ELEMENT email (#PCDATA)>
    <!ELEMENT homepage (#PCDATA)>
```

```
<!-- address elements-->
<!ELEMENT address (street+, city, state, zip, country?)>
<!ELEMENT street (#PCDATA)>
<!ELEMENT city (#PCDATA)>
<!ELEMENT state (#PCDATA)>
<!ELEMENT zip (#PCDATA)>
<!ELEMENT country (#PCDATA)>
<!ELEMENT voice (#PCDATA)>
<!ELEMENT fax (#PCDATA)>
```

Next, you need to modify the document itself. The XML declaration is no longer a standalone document because it depends on a DTD in another file. Therefore, the standalone attribute must be changed to "no", as follows:

```
<?xml version="1.0" standalone="no"?>
```

Then you must change the `<!DOCTYPE>` tag so it points to the DTD, as follows:

```
<!DOCTYPE document SYSTEM "publishers.dtd">
```

The top of the `publishers.xml` file now looks like the following:

```
<?xml version="1.0" standalone="no"?>
<!DOCTYPE document SYSTEM "publishers.dtd">
<document>
 <title>
    Publishers of the Music of New York Women Composers
 </title>

<publisher_list>
```

The rest of the document remains exactly the same as in Listing 5-15.

Make sure that both `publishers.xml` and `publishers.dtd` are in the same directory and then run MSXML on the `publishers.xml` file normally. If all is well, this sequence should produce identical output to running MSXML on Listing 5-15. With this process, you simply separate the DTD from the document it describes. You can now use this same DTD to describe other documents.

If you add a style sheet, you'll then have the three essential parts of the document stored in three different files. The data is in the document file, the structure and semantics applied to the data is in the DTD file, and the formatting is in the style sheet. This structure enables you to inspect or change any or all of these relatively independently.

The DTD and the document are more closely linked than the document and the style sheet. Changing the DTD generally requires revalidating the document and may require edits to the document to bring it back into conformance with the DTD. The necessity of this sequence depends on your edits; adding tags is rarely an issue, though removing tags may be problematic.

Remote DTDs

If a DTD is applied to multiple documents, you cannot always put the DTD in the same directory as each document for which it is used. You can use URIs to specify precisely where the document may be found.

For example, let's suppose the publisher DTD is found at `http://sunsite.unc.edu/xml/dtds/publishers.dtd`. You could locate it by using the following `<!DOCTYPE>` tag in the prolog:

```
<!DOCTYPE document SYSTEM
    "http://sunsite.unc.edu/xml/dtds/publishers.dtd">
```

This example uses a full URL valid from anywhere. You may also wish to locate DTDs relative to the Web server's document root or the current directory. In general, any reference that forms a valid URL relative to the location of the document is acceptable. An example follows:

```
<!DOCTYPE document SYSTEM "/xml/dtds/publishers.dtd">
<!DOCTYPE document SYSTEM "dtds/publishers.dtd">
<!DOCTYPE document SYSTEM "../ publishers.dtd">
```

Public DTDs

The `SYSTEM` keyword is intended for private DTDs used by a single author or group. Part of the promise of XML, however, is that broader organizations covering an entire industry like the ISO or the IEEE will standardize public DTDs to cover their fields. This standardization saves individuals from having to reinvent tag sets for the same items and makes it easier to exchange interoperable documents.

DTDs designed for writers outside the creating organization use the `PUBLIC` keyword instead of the `SYSTEM` keyword. Furthermore, the DTD gets a name. The syntax follows:

```
<!DOCTYPE root_element_name PUBLIC "DTD_name" "DTD_URL">
```

Once again, *root_element_name* is simply the name of the root element. `PUBLIC` is an XML keyword that indicates this DTD is intended for broad use and has a name. `DTD_name` is the name associated with this DTD. Some XML processors may attempt to use this name to retrieve the DTD from a central repository. Finally, `DTD_URL` is a relative or absolute URL where the DTD can be found if it cannot be retrieved by name from a well-known repository.

DTD names are slightly different from XML names. They may contain only the ASCII alphanumeric characters, the space, carriage return, line feed characters, and the following punctuation marks: -'()+,/:=?;!*#@$_%. Furthermore, the names of public DTDs follow a few conventions.

If a DTD is an ISO standard, its name begins with the string "ISO". If a non-ISO standards body has approved the DTD, its name begins with a plus sign (+). If no standards body has approved the DTD, its name begins with a hyphen (-). These initial strings are followed by a double slash (//) and the name of the DTD's owner, which is then followed by another double slash and the type of the document the DTD describes. Then there's another double slash followed by an ISO 639 language identifier, such as EN for English. These codes are listed in Table A-11 of Appendix A.

For example, the publisher DTD can be named as follows:

```
-//Elliotte Rusty Harold//DTD music publishers//EN
```

This example says that this DTD is not standards body approved (-), belongs to Elliotte Rusty Harold, describes music publishers, and is written in English. A full <!DOCTYPE> tag pointing to this DTD with this name follows:

```
<!DOCTYPE document PUBLIC
    "-//Elliotte Rusty Harold//DTD music publishers//EN"
    "http://sunsite.unc.edu/xml/dtds/publishers.dtd">
```

You may have noticed that many HTML editors like BBEdit automatically place the following string at the beginning of every HTML file they create:

```
<!DOCTYPE HTML PUBLIC "-//W3C//DTD HTML//EN">
```

Now you know what this string means! It says the document follows a non-standards-body-approved (-) DTD for HTML produced by the W3C in the English language.

Merging DTDs

The preceding examples have used monolithic DTDs that include all the tags used in the document. This technique becomes unwieldy with longer documents, however. Furthermore, you will often want to use part of a DTD in many different places.

In Chapter 5, for example, the publisher element is defined to contain an address element. This definition of address is quite general, however, and could easily be used in other contexts. Although the list of predefined entity references in Listing 6-2 would be useful in most XML files, you don't want to copy and paste it all the time.

External DTDs enable you to build large DTDs from smaller ones. That is, one DTD may link to another and in so doing pull in the elements and entities declared in the first. Although cycles are prohibited — DTD 1 may not refer to DTD 2 if DTD 2 refers to DTD 1 — such nested DTDs can become large and complex.

At the same time, breaking a DTD into smaller, more manageable chunks makes the DTD easier to analyze. Many of the examples in the preceding chapter are perhaps unnecessarily large because an entire document is stored and described in a single file. Indeed, some elements of the actual Web page are omitted to make the examples more manageable (such as the signature block). The document is much easier to understand when split into separately defined DTDs, however.

Furthermore, using smaller, modular DTDs that only describe one set of tags makes it easier to mix and match DTDs created by different people or organizations. For instance, if you're writing a science fiction screenplay in which the characters sometimes discuss chemistry, you can use a DTD that's designed for screenplays and a DTD that's designed for chemistry. If you're writing about the design of a building, you may need DTDs for architecture, plumbing, landscaping, and electrical wiring.

You can probably think of more examples where you need to mix and match concepts (and therefore tags) from different fields. Human thought doesn't restrict itself to narrowly defined categories. It tends to wander all over the map, using inappropriate but useful analogies from one field to suggest directions in other fields. The discovery of the ring structure of benzene came from a dream of a snake eating its tail. Benzene doesn't have much to do with snakes, but such unrelated connections are common in human writing. XML needs to support such connections.

CREATING SEPARATE DTDS FOR ONE DOCUMENT

Let's look one more time at the publisher document at `http://sunsite.unc.edu/nywc/publishers.html` to examine how the data is structured. This time let's look at the unexpurgated document in its entirety, but pay more attention to what is and isn't unique about the file. In particular, you want to see which sections are unique to this document and which aren't. Those sections that might be used in other documents can be separated out into separate DTDs.

As previously stated, the `address` element can be separated out. Listing 6-6 is a DTD solely for an address.

Listing 6-6: An address DTD for the publisher's Web page

```
<!ELEMENT address (street+, city, state, zip, country?)>
<!ELEMENT street (#PCDATA)>
<!ELEMENT city (#PCDATA)>
<!ELEMENT state (#PCDATA)>
<!ELEMENT zip (#PCDATA)>
<!ELEMENT country (#PCDATA)>
```

By itself, this DTD doesn't enable you to create interesting documents. The DTD doesn't even declare a root element — that declaration always has to be made in the document itself. Listing 6-7 shows a simple valid file that only uses the DTD in Listing 6-6. By itself, this simple file is not important; however, other, more complicated files can be built out of these small parts.

Listing 6-7: A file using the address DTD

```
<?xml version="1.0" standalone="no"?>
<!DOCTYPE address SYSTEM "address.dtd">
<address>
  <street>170 West 74th St.</street>
  <city>NY</city>
  <state>NY</state>
  <zip>10023</zip>
</address>
```

What are the other parts of the document that could have their own DTDs? Obviously, a publisher is a big part. You could write its DTD as follows:

```
<!ELEMENT publisher (name, email?, homepage?, address?,
   voice?, fax?)>
<!ELEMENT name (#PCDATA)>
<!ELEMENT email (#PCDATA)>
<!ELEMENT homepage (#PCDATA)>
<!ELEMENT voice (#PCDATA)>
<!ELEMENT fax (#PCDATA)>
```

On closer inspection, however, you should notice that something is missing: the definition of the address element. The definition is in a separate file called address.dtd and needs to be connected to this DTD.

Once again, MSXML 1.8 is a little more forgiving of bad XML than it ought to be. In this context, MSXML simply accepts the address element and all its children (provided they're well-formed) without actually checking them against a DTD.

CONNECTING DTDS WITH EXTERNAL PARAMETER ENTITY REFERENCES

You connect DTDs with external parameter entity references. For a private DTD, this connection takes the following form:

```
<!ENTITY % name SYSTEM "URI">
%name;
```

An example follows:

```
<!ENTITY % address SYSTEM "address.dtd">
%address;
```

In the preceding example, a relative URL is used. This technique assumes that the file `address.dtd` will be found in the same place as the linked DTD. If that's not the case, you can use a full URL as follows:

```
<!ENTITY % address SYSTEM
  "http://sunsite.unc.edu/xml/dtds/address.dtd">
%address;
```

Listing 6-8 shows a completed publisher DTD that includes a reference to the address DTD:

Listing 6-8: The publisher DTD

```
<!ELEMENT publisher (name, email?, homepage?, address?,
  voice?, fax?)>
<!ELEMENT name (#PCDATA)>
<!ELEMENT email (#PCDATA)>
<!ELEMENT homepage (#PCDATA)>
<!ELEMENT voice (#PCDATA)>
<!ELEMENT fax (#PCDATA)>
<!ENTITY % address SYSTEM "address.dtd">
%address;
```

ORGANIZING THE STRUCTURE OF YOUR DOCUMENT

Once you've defined the basic elements of the document, you need to organize the structure of the document that includes these and possibly other elements. It's generally useful to divide a document into the following categories:

◆ A header, which includes titles, keywords, author tags, and other metainformation.

◆ A footer, which includes copyright information, signatures, an e-mail address for the author of the page, last modified dates, and so forth.

◆ The main body of the document.

Most documents fit this tripartite structure reasonably well, though it can be changed if necessary. Certainly, this structure is designed for Web pages. Other applications of XML like books, invoices, database records, serialized objects, and so forth will likely have different structures.

You must then decide how to make trade-offs between flexibility and structure. For example, do you require that a footer contain exactly one copyright, exactly one e-mail address, and exactly one last modified date in that order? Or do you merely list the available elements and allow any number of them to be placed in any order? In terms of DTDs, does your footer look like this:

```
<!ELEMENT footer (copyright, email, lastmodified)>
```

Or like this:

```
<!ELEMENT footer (copyright | email | lastmodified)*>
```

Of course, you can mix and match to your taste, making the e-mail address optional but not allowing more than one, as follows:

```
<!ELEMENT footer (copyright, email?, lastmodified)>
```

The real dichotomy is between highly structured documents with a precise set of elements that occur in a precise order and loosely structured documents that only list the possible elements in an unspecified order. Structured documents are easier for computer programs to manage. Flexible documents are easier for human beings to write. Although I prefer to structure the header and footer tightly and allow more freedom in the body of the page, you may choose to proceed differently.

A header probably contains a title, some keywords, a description, and perhaps the author, creation date, and modification date of the page. Listing 6-9 illustrates a typical DTD for these elements.

Listing 6-9: A typical header DTD

```
<!ELEMENT header (title, author, created, modified,
    keyword*, description?)>
<!ELEMENT title (#PCDATA)>
<!ELEMENT author (#PCDATA)>
<!ELEMENT created (#PCDATA)>
<!ELEMENT modified (#PCDATA)>
<!ELEMENT keyword (#PCDATA)>
<!ELEMENT description (#PCDATA)>
```

Listing 6-10 shows a simple header that obeys this DTD.

Listing 6-10: The header element

```
<?xml version="1.0" standalone="no"?>
<!DOCTYPE header SYSTEM "header.dtd" >
  <header>
    <title>Music Publishers</title>
    <author>Elliotte Rusty Harold</author>
    <created>3/10/1998</created>
    <modified>3/10/1998</modified>
    <keyword>women composers</keyword>
    <keyword>classical music</keyword>
    <keyword>new music</keyword>
    <description>
     This page contains basic contact
     information for publishers who publish
     the works of NYWC members.
    </description>
  </header>
```

Inheritance of XML Element Types

One thing this may bring to mind is that XML doesn't really have a strong data typing mechanism. For instance, there's no way to specify that a modified element contains a date. You could go further with a double level as follows:

```
<!ELEMENT modified (date)>
<!ELEMENT date (#PCDATA)>
```

Honestly, however, this approach doesn't add much because there's no way to require the content of a <date> element to be any data type reasonably or programmatically recognized as a date.

Alternately, you can use the more generic type without providing information about the data type's representation, as follows:

```
<!ELEMENT header (title, person, date, date,
    keyword*, description?)>
<!ELEMENT title (#PCDATA)>
<!ELEMENT person (#PCDATA)>
<!ELEMENT date (#PCDATA)>
<!ELEMENT description (#PCDATA)>
```

This approach is easier on Web robots and other automated programs that understand a finite number of data types. It provides fewer cues to the page author about the expectations in each element, however. You can give some cues with comments, but a real solution to this problem needs some sort of inheritance mechanism so that an author can be specified as a type of person. Some preliminary proposals have been made for inheritance mechanism in XML, but it's unclear at this writing whether any of these proposals will ultimately be adopted.

A footer typically contains a signature block with basic contact and copyright information and perhaps a navigation bar. A navigation bar contains a list of URLs and names. The signature block contains copyright information as well as an e-mail address where the page maintainer can be contacted and the date on which the page was last modified. Although the navbar and the signature can be placed in separate DTDs, you don't gain much functionality with this separation. Both elements are combined in the complete footer DTD in Listing 6-11.

Listing 6-11: The footer DTD containing both the navbar and signature

```
<!ELEMENT footer (navbar?, signature)>
<!ELEMENT navbar (link)*>
<!ELEMENT link (url, name)>
<!ELEMENT url (#PCDATA)>
<!ELEMENT name (#PCDATA)>
<!ELEMENT copyright (#PCDATA)>
```

```
<!ELEMENT email (#PCDATA)>
<!ELEMENT lastmodified (#PCDATA)>
<!ELEMENT signature (copyright, email, lastmodified)>
```

Listing 6-12 is a footer solely built with this DTD.

Listing 6-12: A typical footer element

```
<?xml version="1.0" standalone="no"?>
<!DOCTYPE footer SYSTEM "footer.dtd" >
  <footer>
    <navbar>
      <link>
        <url>/nywc/</url>
        <name>Home</name>
      </link>
      <link>
        <url>bios.html</url>
        <name>Biographies</name>
      </link>
      <link>
        <url>updates.html</url>
        <name>Updates</name>
      </link>
    </navbar>
    <signature>
      <copyright>1998 New York Women Composers</copyright>
      <email>elharo@sunsite.unc.edu</email>
      <lastmodified>3/10/1998</lastmodified>
    </signature>

  </footer>
```

Next comes the body. The body often pulls in different elements – paragraphs, images, applets, lists, publishers, records, and almost anything else you can imagine. For this example, however, let's keep the body simple. Let's say only that it may contain an indefinite number of paragraphs of text, followed by an indefinite number of publishers, followed by an indefinite number of paragraphs of text. These specifications should be sufficient provided the headline is taken from the title in the header. Listing 6-13 shows a possible body DTD.

Listing 6-13: The body DTD

```
<!ELEMENT body (p*, publisher*, p*)>
<!ELEMENT p (#PCDATA)>
<!ENTITY % publisher SYSTEM "publisher.dtd">
%publisher;
```

The p and body elements are declared while the publisher element is linked in from the publisher.dtd file. Listing 6-14 is a valid body document.

Listing 6-14: The `body.xml` file

```
<?xml version="1.0" standalone="no"?>
<!DOCTYPE body SYSTEM "body.dtd">
<body>
  <p>
    Publishers are noted in report by name.
    When no name is given the composer acts as publisher.
  </p>
    <publisher>
      <name> ACA - American Composers Alliance</name>
      <email>info@composers.com</email>
      <homepage>http://www.composers.com/</homepage>
      <address>
        <street>170 West 74th St.</street>
        <city>NY</city>
        <state>NY</state>
        <zip>10023</zip>
      </address>
      <voice>212-362-8900</voice>
      <fax>212-874-8605</fax>
    </publisher>
    <publisher>
      <name>Alfred Publishing</name>
      <address>
        <street>15535 Morrison</street>
        <city>South Oaks</city>
        <state>CA</state>
        <zip>91403</zip>
      </address>
    </publisher>
    <publisher>
      <name>Music 70</name>
      <address>
        <street>250 West 57th Street</street>
        <street># 232</street>
        <city>NY</city> <state>NY</state>
        <zip>10107</zip>
      </address>
    </publisher>

  <p>
    If a publisher does not respond, please write or
    call the composer or NYWC. Addresses are the latest we have.
  </p>

</body>
```

CREATING A DTD TO TIE THE PAGE TOGETHER

Finally, you have to put together the DTD that describes the page itself. This process is easy because a document is just a header, followed by the body, followed by the footer. Thus, the document's DTD just needs to declare a root element built from a header, a body, and a footer, and reference those three DTDs. Listing 6-15 demonstrates this process.

Listing 6-15: The document DTD

```
<!ENTITY % header SYSTEM "header.dtd">
%header;
<!ENTITY % body SYSTEM "body.dtd">
%body;
<!ENTITY % footer SYSTEM "footer.dtd">
%footer;
<!ELEMENT document (header, body, footer)>
```

You don't need to explicitly refer to the address and publisher DTDs – they're included via the body DTD. Listing 6-16 shows a valid document that uses the document DTD.

Listing 6-16: The completed `publishers.xml` file with a body, a header, and a footer

```
<?xml version="1.0" standalone="no"?>
<!DOCTYPE document SYSTEM "document.dtd">
<document>
  <header>
    <title>Music Publishers</title>
    <author>Elliotte Rusty Harold</author>
    <created>3/10/1998</created>
    <modified>3/10/1998</modified>
    <keyword>women composers</keyword>
    <keyword>classical music</keyword>
    <keyword>new music</keyword>
    <description>
     This page contains basic contact
     information for publishers who publish
     the works of NYWC members.
    </description>
  </header>

 <body>
 <p>
   Publishers are noted in report by name.
   When no name is given the composer acts as publisher.
 </p>
   <publisher>
     <name> ACA - American Composers Alliance</name>
     <email>info@composers.com</email>
     <homepage>http://www.composers.com/</homepage>
     <address>
       <street>170 West 74th St.</street>
       <city>NY</city>
       <state>NY</state>
       <zip>10023</zip>
     </address>
```

```
      <voice>212-362-8900</voice>
      <fax>212-874-8605</fax>
    </publisher>
  <publisher>
    <name>Alfred Publishing</name>
    <address>
      <street>15535 Morrison</street>
      <city>South Oaks</city>
      <state>CA</state>
      <zip>91403</zip>
    </address>
  </publisher>
  <publisher>
    <name>Music 70</name>
    <address>
      <street>250 West 57th Street</street>
      <street># 232</street>
      <city>NY</city> <state>NY</state>
      <zip>10107</zip>
    </address>
  </publisher>

  <p>
    If a publisher does not respond, please write or
    call the composer or NYWC. Addresses are the latest we have.
  </p>

</body>

<footer>
  <navbar>
    <link>
      <url>/nywc/</url>
      <name>Home</name>
    </link>
    <link>
      <url>bios.html</url>
      <name>Biographies</name>
    </link>
    <link>
      <url>updates.html</url>
      <name>Updates</name>
    </link>
  </navbar>
  <signature>
    <copyright>1998 New York Women Composers</copyright>
    <email>elharo@sunsite.unc.edu</email>
    <lastmodified>3/10/1998</lastmodified>
  </signature>

</footer>

</document>
```

You may have noticed that Listing 6-16 could have been built by combining the bodies of the three files `header.xml`, `body.xml`, and `footer.xml`. You can use external general entity references for this approach. The resulting file could look like Listing 6-17:

Listing 6-17: The completed `publishers.xml` file with an external body, an external header, and an external footer

```
<?xml version="1.0" standalone="no"?>
<!DOCTYPE document SYSTEM "document.dtd" [
  <!ENTITY head SYSTEM "header.xml">
  <!ENTITY foot SYSTEM "footer.xml">
  <!ENTITY torso SYSTEM "body.xml">
]>
<document>
  &head; &torso; &foot;
</document>
```

The preceding listing is easier to understand than Listing 6-16 because it's broken cleanly into well-separated pieces. While excessive subdivision can leave one wondering exactly where or how particular elements and entities are defined (especially if you use parameter entities that depend on other parameter entities), it's not generally difficult to find clean separations between the different parts of the document.

The preceding example actually combines declarations in both external and internal DTDs, which is the subject of the next section.

Internal and External DTDs

Although most documents consist of easily defined pieces, not all documents follow a common template. In particular, the body parts of documents change from one page to the next, even within the same Web site. If a particular document has a different structure than other pages on the site, it can be useful to define its structure in the document itself rather in a separate DTD. This approach also makes the document easier to edit.

Until Listing 6-17, preceding documents used either internal or external element declarations. A document can use both declarations, however. The internal declarations are placed inside square brackets at the end of the `<!DOCTYPE>` tag. For example, if you want to use the default header and footer DTDs, but define the body to match the page, you can use the following prolog:

```
<?xml version="1.0" standalone="no"?>
<!DOCTYPE document SYSTEM "document.dtd" [
  <!ELEMENT body (p*, publisher*, p*)>
  <!ELEMENT p (#PCDATA)>
```

```
<!ENTITY % publisher SYSTEM "publisher.dtd">
%publisher;
]>
```

This DTD states that the overall structure is specified by the document DTD. Instead of using the definitions of body, p, and publisher found in that document, however, you use the definitions given between the square brackets.

In the event of a conflict with elements of the same name in external DTDs, the elements declared internally take precedence. This precedence provides a crude, partial inheritance mechanism. For example, suppose you have a page of specifically international publishers and you want to require a country on this page. You could use most of the same declarations used in preceding examples, but change the address element to require a country as follows:

```
<!DOCTYPE publisher SYSTEM "publisher.dtd" [
  <!ELEMENT address (street+, city, state, zip, country)>
]>
```

Processing Instructions

In HTML, comments are often abused to support proprietary extensions to HTML like server side includes, browser-specific scripting languages, database templates, and several dozen other items outside the purview of the HTML standard. The advantage of using comments is that other systems simply ignore the extraneous data they don't understand. The disadvantage of this approach is that a document stripped of its comments may no longer be the same document, and that comments intended as mere documentation may sometimes be unintentionally processed as input to these proprietary extensions.

XML provides an explicit mechanism for embedding information in a file intended for proprietary applications rather than the XML parser or browser. This mechanism is the processing instruction.

A *processing instruction* is a string of text included almost anywhere in an XML document's character data between <? and ?> marks. The processing instruction begins with the name of the application for which the processing instruction is intended, followed by the data for the instruction. You've already seen one such instruction – the XML declaration that begins every valid XML file:

```
<?xml version="1.0" standalone="yes" ?>
```

Processing instructions that begin with the string xml are reserved for uses defined in the XML standard. Otherwise, you are free to use any name and any string of text inside a processing instruction other than the closing string ?>. For instance, the following examples are all valid processing instructions:

```
<?gcc HelloWorld.c ?>
<?acrobat document="passport.pdf"?>
<?Dave remember to replace this one?>
```

An XML parser won't necessarily do anything with these instructions. It merely passes them along to the application. The application is responsible for deciding what to do with the instructions. Most applications simply ignore processing instructions they don't understand.

Notations and Unparsed Entities

Embedding XML in XML is useful, but many documents require other kinds of data. A typical Web page can include GIF and JPEG images, Java applets, ActiveX controls, various kinds of sounds, and so forth. In XML, any block of non-XML data is called an *unparsed entity* because the XML processor won't attempt to understand it. At most, it informs the application of the entity's existence and provides the application with the entity's name and possibly (though not necessarily) its content.

You link to an unparsed entity through an external general entity reference as you link to an external XML file. In addition, you include the NDATA keyword and the type of the data in the entity declaration. For example, to associate the entity reference &logo; with the GIF image http://sunsite.unc.edu/javafaq/logo.gif, place the following declaration in your DTD:

```
<!ENTITY logo SYSTEM "http://www.w3.org/xml/logo.gif" NDATA gif>
```

The XML standard is quite vague on what qualifies as a valid data type to follow an NDATA statement. In fact, the standard only requires that the type be a valid XML name. It would seem more useful to require a MIME type and subtype like image/gif or text/html. Unfortunately, because a forward slash (/) is not a valid character in an XML, MIME types are specifically prohibited! In most cases, however, the MIME subtype alone is sufficient to identify the data.

As usual, you can use URLs relative to the current document if it's more convenient. An example follows:

```
<!ENTITY logo SYSTEM "logo.gif" NDATA gif>
<!ENTITY logo SYSTEM "/xml/logo.gif" NDATA gif>
<!ENTITY logo SYSTEM "../logo.gif" NDATA gif>
```

Unlike general entity references, you cannot simply include an unparsed entity reference at an arbitrary location in the document. Unparsed entity references may only appear as an attribute value of an element with the type ENTITY or ENTITIES (this will be discussed in the following chapter).

Each unparsed entity is associated with a notation. In theory, the *notation* is the format of the non-XML data. A notation is a set of rules that the data follows, which are generally quite different from the rules that XML data follows. In practice, these rules are merely the name of a program that understands the data format involved.

Notations are declared in the DTD at the same level as elements, attributes, and entities. Each notation declaration contains a name and an external identifier according to the following syntax:

```
<!NOTATION name SYSTEM "externalID">
```

An example follows:

```
<!NOTATION hqx SYSTEM "StuffIt Expander">
```

The parser simply passes that data along to the application (which is free to ignore it). This declaration says that data notated with the notation hqx may be passed to the StuffIt Expander application for processing.

Notations are also sometimes used in concert with processing instructions. Because processing instructions can contain fairly arbitrary data, it's relatively easy for them to contain instructions determining what the action of external program listed in the notation. The application must determine which processing instructions belong with which notations.

Conditional Sections

When developing DTDs or documents, it's often necessary to comment out parts of the DTD that aren't yet reflected in the documents. In addition to using comments directly, you can omit a particular group of declarations in the DTD by wrapping it in an IGNORE directive. The syntax follows:

```
<![ IGNORE
  declarations that are ignored
]]>
```

As usual, white space doesn't really affect the syntax, but you should keep the opening <![IGNORE and the closing]]> on separate lines for easy viewing.

You can ignore any declaration or combination of declarations – elements, entities, attributes, or even other IGNORE blocks – but you must ignore entire declarations. The IGNORE construct must completely enclose the entire declarations it removes from the DTD. You cannot ignore a piece of a declaration (such as the NDATA gif in an unparsed entity declaration).

You can also specify to include a particular section of declarations – that is, not ignored. The syntax for the INCLUDE directive is just like the IGNORE directive with a different keyword:

```
<![ INCLUDE
  declarations that are included
]]>
```

When an INCLUDE is inside an IGNORE, the INCLUDE and its declarations are ignored. When an IGNORE is inside an INCLUDE, the declarations inside the IGNORE are still ignored. In other words, an INCLUDE never overrides an IGNORE.

Given these conditions, you may wonder why INCLUDE even exists. No DTD would be changed if all INCLUDE blocks were simply removed, leaving only their contents. INCLUDE appears to be completely extraneous.

There is one neat trick with parameter entity references and both IGNORE and INCLUDE that you can't do with IGNORE alone, however. First define a parameter entity reference as follows:

```
<!ENTITY % fulldtd "IGNORE">
```

You can ignore elements by wrapping them in the following construct:

```
<![ %fulldtd;
  declarations
]]>
```

%fulldtd; evaluates to IGNORE, so the declarations are ignored. Now, suppose you make the one word edit to change fulldtd from IGNORE to INCLUDE as follows:

```
<!ENTITY % fulldtd "INCLUDE">
```

Immediately, all the IGNORE blocks are converted to INCLUDE blocks. In effect, you have a one-line switch to turn blocks on or off.

In this example, I've only used one switch, fulldtd. This switch can be used in multiple IGNORE/INCLUDE blocks in the DTD. You can also have different groups of IGNORE/INCLUDE blocks that you switch on or off based on different conditions.

This capability is particularly useful when designing DTDs to be included in other DTDs. The ultimate DTD can change the behavior of the DTDs it embeds by changing the value of the parameter entity switch.

Summary

In this chapter, you learned that XML documents are built from both internal and external entities. Entity references declared in the DTD form a blueprint of how the document fits together. In particular, you learned the following concepts:

◆ XML documents are built from entities.

◆ General entity references have the form &name; and are used in a document's content.

◆ Parameter entity references have the form %name; and are used exclusively in the DTD.

◆ Internal entity references are replaced by an entity value given in the entity declaration.

◆ External entity references are replaced by the data at a URL specified in the entity declaration after the SYSTEM keyword.

◆ You can use the SYSTEM keyword in a <!DOCTYPE> tag to apply a DTD in another file to the document.

◆ You can merge different DTDs with external parameter entity references.

◆ Public DTDs follow set naming conventions and can be searched for in a central repository if one is available. Otherwise, a URL is used.

◆ Processing instructions contain instructions passed along unchanged for the processor. These instructions are intended to be used by another application.

◆ Unparsed entities allow XML documents to contain non-XML text or binary data as attributes. Notations describe the program used to process such data.

◆ INCLUDE and IGNORE blocks specify that the enclosed declarations of the DTD are or are not (respectively) to be considered when parsing the document.

In the next chapter, you learn how to declare attributes for elements in the DTD. You also learn how to finish embedding unparsed and binary data in XML documents by making such data an attribute of an XML tag.

Chapter 7

Describing Elements with Attributes

IN THIS CHAPTER

♦ Defining attributes

♦ Declaring attributes in DTDs

♦ Using multiple attributes

♦ Understanding default values for attributes

♦ Examining attribute types

♦ Using predefined attributes

SOME XML TAGS include attributes. Attributes contain information intended for the application that's reading the XML data – not for the human that's reading the document. All the basic information on the page should be available as plain text even when all the tags are completely stripped out of the page. Attributes are intended for extra information associated with an element (like an ID number) used only by programs that read and write the file, and not for the content of the element that's read and written by humans.

Defining Attributes

As discussed in Chapter 3, start tags and empty tags may optionally contain attributes. *Attributes* are name-value pairs separated by an equals sign (=). An example follows:

```
<greeting language="English">
Hello XML!
</greeting>
<movie src="WavingHand.mov"/>
```

In the preceding example, the `<greeting>` tag has a language attribute, which has the value English. The `<movie>` tag has an src attribute, which has the value

WavingHand.mov. The greeting's content is Hello XML!. The language in which the content is written is useful information about the content. The language itself, however, is not part of the content.

Similarly, the movie element's content is the binary data stored in the file WavingHand.mov. The name of the file is not the content, though the name tells you where the content can be found. Once again, the attribute contains information about the content of the element, rather than the content itself.

Elements can possess more than one attribute. An example follows:

```
<rect width="30" height="45"/>
<script language="javascript" encoding="8859_1">...</script>
```

In the preceding example, the language attribute of the script element has the value javascript. The encoding attribute of the script element has the value 8859_1. The width attribute of the rect element has the value 30. The height attribute of the rect element has the value 45. These values are strings, not numbers.

End tags cannot possess attributes. The following example is illegal:

```
<script>...</script language="javascript" encoding="8859_1">
```

Declaring Attributes in DTDs

Like elements and entities, the attributes used in a document must be declared in the DTD for the document to be valid. The <!ATTLIST> tag declares these attributes. <!ATTLIST> has the following form:

```
<!ATTLIST Element_name Attribute_name Type Default_value>
```

Element_name is the name of the element possessing this attribute. *Attribute_name* is the name of the attribute. *Type* is the kind of attribute (discussed in a following section) that will be one of the ten valid types listed in Table 7-1. The most general type is CDATA. Finally, *Default_value* is the value the attribute takes on if no value is specified for the attribute.

TABLE 7-1 ATTRIBUTE TYPES

Type	Meaning
CDATA	Character data — text that is not markup
Enumerated	A list of possible values, exactly one of which must be used

Continued

Type	Meaning
ID	A unique name not shared by any other ID type attribute in the document
IDREF	The value of an ID type attribute of an element in the document
IDREFS	Multiple IDs of elements separated by white space
ENTITY	The name of an entity declared in the DTD
ENTITIES	The names of multiple entities declared in the DTD, separated by white space
NMTOKEN	An XML name
NOTATION	The name of a notation declared in the DTD
NMTOKENS	Multiple XML names separated by white space

For example, consider the following simple tag:

```
<greeting language="Spanish">
```

The preceding tag is declared as follows in the DTD:

```
<!ELEMENT greeting #PCDATA>
<!ATTLIST greeting language CDATA "English">
```

The `<!ELEMENT>` tag simply says that a greeting element contains parsed character data. That's nothing new. The `<!ATTLIST>` tag says that greeting tags have an attribute with the name language whose value has the type CDATA — a string of text. If a greeting tag without a language attribute is encountered, the value English is used by default.

The attribute list is declared separately from the tag itself. The name of the element to which the attribute belongs is included in the `<!ATTLIST>` tag. This attribute declaration applies only to that element, which is greeting in the preceding example. If other elements also have language attributes, they require separate `<!ATTLIST>` declarations.

As with most tags in XML declarations, the exact order in which attribute declarations appear is not important. These declarations can come before or after the element declaration with which they're associated. In fact, you can even declare an attribute more than once (though I don't recommend this practice), in which case the first such declaration takes precedence.

You even can declare attributes for tags that don't exist, although this is uncommon. Perhaps you could declare these nonexistent attributes as part of the initial editing of the DTD, with a plan to come back later and declare the elements.

Multiple Attributes

Tags often have multiple attributes. HTML's IMG tag can possess height, width, alt, border, align, and several other attributes. In fact, most HTML tags can have multiple attributes. XML tags can also have multiple attributes. For instance, a rect tag naturally needs both a length and a width.

```
<rect length="70px" width="85px"/>
```

These attributes can be declared in several attribute declarations, with one declaration for each attribute. An example follows:

```
<!ELEMENT rect EMPTY>
<!ATTLIST   rect length CDATA "0px">
<!ATTLIST   rect width CDATA "0px">
```

The preceding example says that <rect> elements possess length and width attributes, each of which has the default value 0px.

You can combine the two <!ATTLIST> tags into a single declaration as follows:

```
<!ATTLIST rect length CDATA "0px"
                width CDATA "0px">
```

This single declaration includes the meaning of the two separate tags: the rect tag has two attributes called length and width, each with type CDATA and each with a default value of 0px. This notation can also be used when the attributes have different types or defaults. An example follows:

```
<!ATTLIST rect length CDATA "15px"
                width CDATA "34pt">
```

I'm not very fond of this style. To me, this style is excessively confusing and relies too much on proper placement of extra white space for legibility (though the white space is insignificant to the actual meaning of the tag). You will certainly encounter this style in DTDs written by other people, however, so you need to understand it.

Default Values for Attributes

Instead of specifying an explicit default attribute value like 0px, you can require that the author provide a value, allow the value to be omitted completely, or even use the default value. These requirements are specified with the three following keywords: #REQUIRED, #IMPLIED, and #FIXED, respectively.

Required

You may not always have a good option for a default value. For example, when writing a DTD for use on your intranet, you may want to require that all documents have at least one empty <author/> tag. This tag is not normally rendered, but it can identify the person who created the document. This tag can have name, email, and extension attributes so the author may be contacted for further information or if changes to the document are required. An example follows:

```
<author name="Elliotte Rusty Harold"
  email="elharo@sunsite.unc.edu" extension="3459"/>
```

Instead of providing default values for these tags, suppose you want to force anyone posting a document on the intranet to identify themselves. While XML can't prevent someone from attributing authorship to "Mickey Mouse", it can at least require that authorship is attributed to someone by using #REQUIRED as the default value. An example follows:

```
<!ELEMENT author EMPTY>
<!ATTLIST author name CDATA #REQUIRED>
<!ATTLIST author email CDATA #REQUIRED>
<!ATTLIST author extension CDATA #REQUIRED>
```

If the parser encounters an <author/> tag that does not include one or more of these attributes, it returns an error. An example follows:

```
C:\XML>jview msxml -d1 5.3.xml
Attribute 'name' is required.
Location: file:/C:/XML/5.3.xml(20,-1)
Context: <document><author>
```

You may also want to use #REQUIRED to force people to give their images width, height, and alt attributes. An example follows:

```
<!ELEMENT image EMPTY>
<!ATTLIST image alt CDATA #REQUIRED>
<!ATTLIST image width CDATA #REQUIRED>
<!ATTLIST image height CDATA #REQUIRED>
```

Any attempt to omit these attributes (as all too many Web pages do) produces an invalid document. The XML processor notices the error and informs the author of the missing attributes.

Implied

Sometimes you may not have a good option for a default value, but you do not want to require the author of the document to include a value, either. For example, suppose some of the people posting documents to your intranet are offsite free-lancers who have e-mail addresses but lack phone extensions. Therefore, you don't want to require them to include an extension attribute in their <author/> tags. An example follows:

```
<author name="Elliotte Rusty Harold"
        email="elharo@sunsite.unc.edu"/>
```

You still don't want to provide a default value for the extension, but you do want to enable authors to include such an attribute. In this case, use #IMPLIED as the default value as follows:

```
<!ELEMENT author EMPTY>
<!ATTLIST author name CDATA #REQUIRED>
<!ATTLIST author email CDATA #REQUIRED>
<!ATTLIST author extension CDATA #IMPLIED>
```

If the XML parser encounters an <author/> tag without an extension attribute, it informs the XML application that no value is available. The application is free to act on this notification as it chooses. For example, if the application is feeding elements into an SQL database where the attributes are mapped to fields, the application would probably insert a null into the corresponding database field.

Fixed

Finally, you may want to provide a default value for the attribute without enabling the author to change it. For example, you may wish to specify an identical company attribute of the author tag for anyone posting documents to your intranet. An example follows:

```
<author name="Elliotte Rusty Harold" company="TIC"
        email="elharo@sunsite.unc.edu" extension="3459"/>
```

You can require that everyone use this value of the company by specifying the default value as #FIXED, followed by the actual default. An example follows:

```
<!ELEMENT author EMPTY>
<!ATTLIST author name      CDATA #REQUIRED>
<!ATTLIST author email     CDATA #REQUIRED>
```

```
<!ATTLIST author extension  CDATA #IMPLIED>
<!ATTLIST author company    CDATA #FIXED "TIC">
```

After this specification, document authors are no longer required to include the fixed attribute in their tags. If they don't include the fixed attribute, the default value will be used. If they do include the fixed attribute, however, they must use an identical value – otherwise, the parser will return an error. An example follows:

```
C:\XML>jview msxml -dl 6.3.xml
Attribute company should have the fixed value "TIC"
Location: file:/C:/XML/6.3.xml(22,15)
Context: <document><author>
```

As usual, this example relies on the page author to check whether their document is valid. If you cannot make this assumption, you can always install a program that periodically validates all XML files on your intranet server and e-mails errors to the author or Webmaster.

Attribute Types

All preceding example attributes have CDATA type attributes. This is the most general type, but there are nine other types permitted for attributes. The ten permitted types are:

- ◆ CDATA
- ◆ **Enumerated**
- ◆ NMTOKEN
- ◆ NMTOKENS
- ◆ ID
- ◆ IDREF
- ◆ ENTITY
- ◆ ENTITIES
- ◆ NOTATION
- ◆ **Enumerated** NOTATION

Eight of the preceding attributes are constants used in the type field, while enumerated and enumerated NOTATION are special enumerated types that indicate the attribute must take its value from a list of possible values. Let's investigate each attribute in depth.

CDATA

CDATA is the most general attribute type. It means the value may be any string of text that does not contain a less than sign (<), an ampersand (&), or quotation marks ("). These characters may be inserted using the usual entity references (<, &, and ") or by their ASCII values using character references.

In fact, even if the value itself contains double quotes, they do not have to be escaped. Instead, single quotes may be used to delimit the attributes, as in the following example:

```
<RECT LENGTH='7"' WIDTH='8.5"'/>
```

If the attribute value contains single and double quotes, they must be replaced with the entity references ' (apostrophe) and " (double quote). An example follows:

```
<RECT LENGTH='8&apos;7&quot;' WIDTH="10&apos;6&quot;"/>
```

Enumerated

The enumerated type is not an XML keyword. Instead, it is a list of possible values for the attribute, separated by vertical bars. The document author can set any one member of the list as the value of the attribute. The default value must be one of the values in the list.

For example, suppose you want an element to be visible or invisible. You may want the element to have a visible attribute, which could only have the values true or false. If that element is the simple p element, then the <!ATTLIST> declaration would look as follows:

```
<!ATTLIST p visible (true | false) "true">
```

The preceding declaration says that the <p> tag may or may not have a visible attribute. If it does have a visible attribute, the value of that attribute must be either true or false. If it does not have such an attribute, the value true is assumed. An example follows:

```
<p visible="false">You can't see me! Nyah! Nyah!</p>
```

By itself, this declaration is not a magic incantation that enables you to hide document text. It still relies on the application to understand that it shouldn't display invisible elements. Whether the element is shown or hidden, it would probably be set through a style sheet rule applied to elements with visible attributes.

The XML parser returns an error if a value is not in the list, as follows:

```
C:\XML>jview msxml -d1 invisible.xml
Attribute value 'no' is  not in the allowed set.
```

```
Location: file:/C:/XML/invisible.xml(10,17)
Context: <document><p>
```

NMTOKEN

The NMTOKEN attribute type restricts the value of the attribute to be a valid XML name. As discussed in Chapter 3, XML names must begin with a letter or an underscore (_). Subsequent letters in the name may include letters, digits, underscores, hyphens, and periods. They may not include white space. (The underscore often substitutes for white space.) Technically, they may include a colon, but you shouldn't use this character because it's intended to be part of a future name space mechanism.

The NMTOKEN attribute type is primarily useful when you're using a programming language to manipulate the XML data. It's not a coincidence that – except for allowing colons – the preceding rules match the rules for identifiers in Java, JavaScript, and many other programming languages.

For example, you could use NMTOKEN to associate a particular Java class with an element. Then you could use Java's reflection API to pass the data to a particular method in a particular class.

The NMTOKEN type is also useful when you need to pick from any large group of names that aren't specifically part of XML but meet XML's name requirements. The most significant of these requirements is no white space. For example, it could be used for an attribute whose value had to map to an 8.3 DOS file name. On the other hand, it wouldn't work well for UNIX, Macintosh, or Windows NT file name attributes because those names often contain white space.

For example, suppose you want to require a state attribute in an <address/> tag to be a two-letter abbreviation. There's no way you can force this characteristic with a DTD, but you can prevent people from entering "New York" or "Puerto Rico" with the following <!ATTLIST> declaration:

```
<!ATTLIST address state NMTOKEN #REQUIRED>
```

On the other hand, "California", "Nevada", and other single word states are still legal values. Of course, you could simply use an enumerated list with several dozen two-letter codes, but that approach is more work than most people want to expend. For that matter, do you even know the two-letter codes for all fifty U.S. states, all the territories and possessions, and all Canadian provinces? On the other hand, if you define this list once in a parameter entity reference in a DTD file, you can reuse the file many times over.

NMTOKENS

The NMTOKENS attribute type is an rare plural form of NMTOKEN. It allows the value of the attribute to be composed of multiple XML names, separated from each other by white space. NMTOKENS is mostly used for the same reasons as NMTOKEN, but only when multiple names are required.

For example, if you want to require multiple two-letter state codes for a states attribute, you can use the following example:

```
<!ATTLIST address states NMTOKENS #REQUIRED>
```

Then you could have an address tag as follows:

```
<address states="MI NY LA CA">
```

ID

The ID type uniquely identifies the element in the document. Authoring tools and other applications commonly use ID to help enumerate the elements of a document without concern for their exact meaning or relationship to each other.

An attribute value of type ID must be a valid XML name – that is, it begins with a letter and is composed of alphanumeric characters and the underscore without white space. A particular name may not be used as an ID attribute of more than one tag. Furthermore, each element may not have more than one attribute of type ID.

Typically, IDs exist solely for the convenience of programs that manipulate the data. In many cases, multiple elements can be effectively identical except for the value of an ID attribute. If IDs are chosen in some predictable fashion, a program can enumerate all the different elements or all the different elements of one type in the document.

The ID type is incompatible with #FIXED. An attribute cannot be both fixed and have ID type because a #FIXED attribute can only have a single value while each ID type attribute must have a different value. Most ID attributes use #REQUIRED, as Listing 7-1 demonstrates.

Listing 7-1: A required ID attribute

```
<?xml version="1.0" standalone="yes"?>
<!DOCTYPE document [
   <!ELEMENT document (p*)>
   <!ELEMENT p (#PCDATA)>
   <!ATTLIST p pnumber ID #REQUIRED>
]>

<document>
   <p pnumber="p1">The quick brown fox</p>
   <p pnumber="p2"> The quick brown fox </p>
</document>
```

Using the same ID twice in one document causes the parser to return an error, as in the following example:

```
C:\XML>jview msxml -d1 id.xml
ID null is already used on element p
```

```
Location: file:/C:/XML/id.xml(11,32)
Context: <document><p>
```

IDREF

The IDREF type allows the value of one attribute to be an element found elsewhere in the document. The value of the IDREF attribute must be the ID of an element elsewhere in the document; that is, the IDREF attribute value must be identical to the value of an ID attribute in another element. For example, Listing 7-2 shows the IDREF and ID attributes used to connect children to their parents.

Listing 7-2: family.xml

```
<?xml version="1.0" standalone="yes"?>
<!DOCTYPE document [
    <!ELEMENT document (person*)>
    <!ELEMENT person (#PCDATA)>
    <!ATTLIST person pnumber ID #REQUIRED>
    <!ATTLIST person father IDREF #IMPLIED>
    <!ATTLIST person mother IDREF #IMPLIED>
]>

<document>
    <person pnumber="a1">Susan</person>
    <person pnumber="a2">Jack</person>
    <person pnumber="a3" mother="a1" father="a2">Chelsea</person>
    <person pnumber="a4" mother="a1" father="a2">David</person>
</document>
```

You generally use this uncommon but crucial type when you need to establish connections between elements (as in Listing 7-2) that use IDs and IDREFs to associate children with their parents. Each child is given father and mother attributes containing the IDs of its father and mother.

You cannot easily and directly use an IDREF to link parents to their children because each parent has an indefinite number of children. As a workaround, you can group all the children of the same parents into a family and link to the family. Even this approach falters in the face of half-siblings where only one parent is shared. In short, IDREF works for many-to-one relationships but not for one-to-many relationships.

ENTITY

An ENTITY type attribute enables you to link external binary data – that is, an unparsed entity – into the document. The value of the entity attribute is the name of an external parameter entity declared in the DTD that links to the external binary data.

The classic example of an ENTITY attribute is an image. The image is binary data available from another URL. Provided the XML browser is prepared to support it, you can include an image in an XML document with the following declarations in your DTD:

```
<!ELEMENT image EMPTY>
<!ATTLIST image source ENTITY #REQUIRED>
<!ENTITY logo SYSTEM "logo.gif">
```

Then, at the desired image location in the document, insert the following image tag:

```
<image source="&logo;">
```

Once again, this approach is not a magic formula that all XML browsers automatically understand, but browsers can include such external data in this manner. To that extent, it works for applets, sounds, and other embeddable binary data.

ENTITIES

ENTITIES is a relatively rare plural form of ENTITY. An ENTITIES type attribute has a value part that consists of multiple entity names separated by white space. Each entity name refers to an external binary data source. You can use this approach for a slide show that rotates different pictures, as in the following example:

```
<!ELEMENT slideshow EMPTY>
<!ATTLIST slideshow sources ENTITIES #REQUIRED>
<!ENTITY pic1 SYSTEM "cat.gif">
<!ENTITY pic2 SYSTEM "dog.gif">
<!ENTITY pic3 SYSTEM "cow.gif">
```

Then, at the point in the document where you want the slide show to appear, insert the following tag:

```
<slideshow sources="pic1 pic2 pic3">
```

NOTATION

The NOTATION attribute type allows an attribute to have a value specified by a notation declared in the DTD. You can use this type to specify the preferred helper application for an unparsed entity. For example, you could include the following declarations in the DTD:

```
<!ELEMENT sound EMPTY>
<!ATTLIST sound source ENTITY #REQUIRED>
<!ATTLIST sound player NOTATION #REQUIRED>
<!ENTITY spacemusic SYSTEM "/sounds/space.wav">
<!NOTATION sm SYSTEM "mplay32.exe">
```

Then, you write the following tag in the document:

```
<sound src="&spacemusic;" player="sm">
```

Enumerated NOTATION

The NOTATION attribute type also has an enumerated form. In this type, the NOTATION keyword is followed by a set of parentheses containing the list of allowed notation names separated by vertical bars.

You can use this approach to specify different helper applications for different platforms. The browser can pick the available helper application, as in the following example:

```
<!ELEMENT sound EMPTY>
<!ATTLIST sound source ENTITY #REQUIRED>
<!ENTITY spacemusic SYSTEM "/sounds/space.wav">
<!NOTATION mp SYSTEM "mplay32.exe">
<!NOTATION st SYSTEM "soundtool">
<!NOTATION sm SYSTEM "Sound Machine">
<!NOTATION gs SYSTEM "GhostScript">
<!NOTATION pdf SYSTEM "acrobat.exe">
<!ATTLIST sound player NOTATIONS (mp | sm | st) #REQUIRED>
```

This example says that the player attribute of the sound tag may be set to mp, st, or sm, but not gs or pdf.

At first glance, this approach may appear to be inconsistent with the handling of other list attributes like ENTITIES and NMTOKENS, but these two approaches are quite different. ENTITIES and NMTOKENS have a list of attributes in the actual element in the document but only one value in the attribute declaration in the DTD. NOTATION only has a single value in the attribute of the actual element in the document, however. The list of possible values occurs in the attribute declaration in the DTD.

Predefined Attributes

In a way, two attributes are predefined in XML. You must declare these attributes in your DTD for each element to which they apply, but you should only use these declared attributes for their intended purposes. Such attributes are identified by a name that begins with xml:. Therefore, you should not begin your own attributes with the string xml.

These two attributes are `xml:space` and `xml:lang`. The `xml:space` attribute describes how white space is handled in the element. The `xml:lang` attribute describes the language (and optionally, dialect and country) in which the element is written.

xml:space

In HTML, white space is relatively insignificant. Although the difference between one space and no space is significant, the difference between one space and two spaces, one space and a carriage return, or one space and three carriage returns is not important.

For text in which white space is significant — computer source code, certain mainframe database reports, or the poetry of e. e. cummings, for example — you can use a `<pre>` element to specify a monospaced font and preservation of white space.

XML, however, preserves white space by default. The XML processor passes all white space characters to the application unchanged. The application usually ignores the extra white space. However, the XML processor can tell the application that certain elements contain significant white space to be preserved. The page author uses the `xml:space` attribute to indicate these elements to the application.

If an element contains significant white space, the DTD should have an `<!ATTLIST>` for the `xml:space` attribute. This attribute will have an enumerated type with the two values, `default` and `preserve`, as shown in Listing 7-3.

Listing 7-3: Java source code with significant white space

```
<?xml version="1.0" standalone="yes"?>
<!DOCTYPE program [
  <!ELEMENT program (#PCDATA)>
  <!ATTLIST program xml:space (default|preserve) 'preserve'>
]>
<program xml:space="preserve">public class AsciiTable {

  public static void main (String[] args) {

    for (int i = 0; i &lt; 128; i++) {
      System.out.println(i + "    " + (char) i);
    }


  }

}
</program>
```

All white space is passed to the application, regardless of whether `default` or `preserve` is selected as `xml:space`'s value. With a value of `default`, however, the application does what it would normally do with extra white space. With a value of `preserve`, the application treats the extra white space as significant.

Significance depends somewhat on the eventual destination of the data. For example, extra white space in Java source code is relevant to a source code editor but not to a compiler.

Children of an element for which xml:space is defined are assumed to behave similarly as their parent (either preserving or not preserving space), unless they possess an xml:space attribute with a conflicting value.

xml:lang

The xml:lang attribute identifies the language in which the element's content is written. The value of this attribute can have type CDATA, NMTOKEN, or an enumerated list. Specifically, each of these attributes values should ideally be one of the two-letter language codes defined by the original ISO-639 standard, as listed in Table A-11 in Appendix A.

For instance, consider the two examples of the following sentence from Petronius's *Satiricon* in both Latin and English. Both sentences are enclosed in a sentence tag, but the first sentence tag has an xml:lang attribute for Latin while the second has an xml:lang attribute for English.

Latin:

```
<sentence xml:lang="la">
Veniebamus in forum deficiente now die, in quo notavimus frequentiam
  rerum venalium, non quidem pretiosarum sed tamen quarum fidem male
  ambulantem obscuritas temporis facillime tegeret.</sentence>
```

English:

```
<sentence xml:lang="en">
We have come to the marketplace now when the day is failing, where
  we have seen many things for sale, not for the valuable goods but
  rather that the darkness of the time may most easily conceal their
  shoddiness. </sentence>
```

While an English-speaking reader can easily tell which is the original text and which is the translation, a computer can use the hint provided by the xml:lang attribute. This distinction allows a spell checker to determine whether to check a particular element and designate which dictionary to use. Search engines can inspect these language attributes to determine whether to index a page and return matches based on the user's preferences.

The language applies to the element and all its children until one of its children declares a different language.

The declaration of the `<sentence>` tag can appear as follows:

```
<!ELEMENT sentence (#PCDATA)>
<!ATTLIST sentence xml:lang NMTOKEN "en">
```

 MSXML 1.8 allows the `xml:lang` attribute to be added to a tag, even if it was not specifically declared.

If no appropriate ISO code is available, you can use one of the codes registered with the IANA, though currently IANA only adds four additional codes as listed in Table 7-2. The most current list can be found at `http://www.isi.edu/in-notes/iana/assignments/languages/tags`.

TABLE 7-2 THE IANA LANGUAGE CODES

Code	Language
no-bok	Norwegian "Book language"
no-nyn	Norwegian "New Norwegian"
i-navajo	Navajo
i-mingo	Mingo

An example follows:

```
<p xml:lang="no-nyn">
```

If neither the ISO nor the IANA has a code for the language you need (Klingon perhaps?), you may define new language codes. These "x-codes" must begin with the string x- or X- so they may be identified as user-defined, private use codes. An example follows:

```
<p xml:lang="x-klingon">
```

How many languages are there?

XML is a little behind the times in this area. The original ISO-639 standard language codes were formed from two case-insensitive ASCII alphabetic characters. This standard allows no more than 26 × 26 or 676 different codes. More than 676 different languages are spoken on Earth today (not even counting dead languages like Etruscan). In practice, the reasonable codes are somewhat less than 676 because you'd like the language abbreviations to have some relation to the name of the language.

ISO-639, part two, uses three-letter language codes, which should handle all languages spoken on Earth. The XML standard specifically requires two-letter codes, however.

The value of the language attribute may include additional subcode segments, which are separated from the primary language code by a hyphen. Most often, the first subcode segment is a two-letter country code specified by ISO 3166, as listed in Appendix C. You can retrieve the most current list from `http://www.isi.edu/in-notes/iana/assignments/country-codes`.

An example follows:

```
<p xml:lang="en-US">Put the body in the trunk of the car.</p>
<p xml:lang="en-GB">Put the body in the boot of the car.</p>
```

If the first subcode segment is not a two-letter ISO country code, it should be a character set subcode for the language registered with the IANA, such as `csDECMCS`, `roman8`, `mac`, `cp037`, or `ebcdic-cp-ca`. The current list is available from `ftp://ftp.isi.edu/in-notes/iana/assignments/character-sets`. An example follows:

```
<p xml:lang="en-mac">
```

The final possibility is that the first subcode is another x-code that begins with `x-` or `X-`. An example follows:

```
<p xml:lang="en-x-tic">
```

By convention, language codes are written in lowercase and country codes are written in uppercase. However, this is merely a convention. This is one of the few parts of XML that is case-insensitive, because of its heritage in the case-insensitive ISO standard.

Like all attributes used in valid documents, the xml:lang attribute must be specifically declared for those elements to which it directly applies. (The xml:lang attribute indirectly applies to children of elements that have specified xml:lang attributes, but these children do not require separate declaration.)

You may not want to permit arbitrary values for xml:lang. The permissible values are also valid XML names, so the attribute is commonly given as having NMTOKEN type. An example follows:

```
<!ELEMENT p (#PCDATA)>
<!ATTLIST p xml:lang NMTOKEN #IMPLIED "en">
```

Alternately, if only a few languages or dialects are permitted, an enumerated type may be used. For example, the following DTD says that the <P> element may be either English or Latin.

```
<!ELEMENT p (#PCDATA)>
<!ATTLIST p xml:lang (en | la) "en">
```

Summary

In this chapter, you learned how to declare attributes for elements. In particular, you learned the following concepts:

◆ Attributes are declared in an <!ATTLIST> tag in the DTD.

◆ One <!ATTLIST> tag can declare an indefinite number of attributes for only one element.

◆ Attributes normally have default values, but this condition can be changed by using the keywords #REQUIRED, #IMPLIED, or #FIXED.

◆ There are ten attribute types: CDATA, enumerated, NMTOKEN, NMTOKENS, ID, IDREF, ENTITY, ENTITIES, NOTATION, and enumerated NOTATION.

◆ The xml:space attribute determines whether the white space in an element is significant.

◆ The xml:lang attribute specifies the language in which an element's content appears.

In the next chapter, you learn about Unicode and how XML supports text written in languages other than English as well as non-Roman scripts like Greek, Cyrillic, Hebrew, Chinese, and Arabic.

Chapter 8

International Character Sets

IN THIS CHAPTER

◆ Speaking like a native

◆ Using scripts, character sets, fonts, and glyphs

◆ Understanding the major character sets

◆ Writing in Unicode

◆ Writing XML in other character sets

THE WEB IS international, yet most of its text is written in English. By providing full support for the double-byte Unicode character set and its more compact representations, XML is starting to change this trend. Unicode supports almost every character commonly used in all modern languages on Earth.

In this chapter, you explore how to write XML documents in languages other than English, how international text is represented in computer applications, how XML understands text, and what software you need to read and write languages other than English.

Speaking like a Native

Although over 80 percent of the Web's text is English (see `http://www.isoc.org:8080/palmares.html`), there are still many pages in German, French, Spanish, Chinese, Arabic, Hebrew, Russian, Hindi, and more. Most of the time, unfortunately, these pages come out looking less than ideal.

The quality of Web pages deteriorates when they use more complicated, less Western scripts like Chinese and Japanese. Figure 8-1 shows the home page for IDG Japan viewed in an English browser. The bitmapped image of the magazine cover shows the proper Japanese (and English) text, but the text around the image looks like a few English words intermixed with absolute gibberish. This text is obviously not the Kanji characters you're supposed to see.

Figure 8-1: The home page of IDG Japan viewed in an English browser

When viewed with the proper encoding and application software and the correct installed font, these pages can appear as originally conceived. You can select the encoding for a Web page from the View/Encoding menu in Netscape Navigator or from the View/Fonts menu in Internet Explorer. In an ideal world, the Web server would tell the Web browser what encoding to use and the Web browser would listen. Furthermore, the Web server would send the Web browser any necessary fonts it needed to display the page. In practice, however, the Web server either doesn't tell the Web browser which encoding to use, or the Web browser doesn't listen. In addition, the Web server almost never sends the Web browser the right fonts if the Web browser doesn't already have them. Therefore, you often need to install the fonts and select the encoding manually, even trying several options when more than one encoding is available for a script. For instance, a Cyrillic page might be encoded in Windows 1251, ISO-8859-5, or KOI8-R.

Remember that even when you can identify the encoding, there's no guarantee you have fonts available to display it. Figure 8-2 shows the IDG Japan home page with a Japanese encoding, but without an installed Japanese font on the computer. Most of the characters in the text are shown as the missing character glyph, which is a box (▓).

Figure 8-2: The home page of IDG Japan in Kanji without the necessary fonts installed

If you have a Japanese localized edition of your operating system with the necessary fonts or additional software like Apple's Japanese Language Kit or NJStar's NJWin (http://www.njstar.com/) that adds Japanese language support to your existing system, you can view the text as (more or less) conceived. Figure 8-3 demonstrates.

Of course, the higher quality the fonts you use, the better the text will look. Chinese and Japanese fonts tend to be quite large (there are over 80,000 characters in Chinese alone) and distinctions between individual ideographs can be quite subtle. Japanese publishing generally requires higher quality paper and printing than Western publishing to maintain the fine detail necessary for Japanese letters. Regrettably, a 72 dpi computer monitor can't do justice to most Japanese and Chinese characters, except at almost obscenely large point sizes.

Figure 8-3: The home page of IDG Japan in Kanji with the necessary fonts installed

Because each page can only have one encoding, it is difficult to write a single Web page integrating multiple scripts, such as a French commentary on a Chinese text. For this reason, the Web community needs a single, universal character set to display all characters for all computers and Web browsers. Although such a set doesn't quite exist yet, XML and Unicode get as close as currently possible to this ideal set.

XML files are written in Unicode, a double-byte character set that can represent most characters in most of the world's languages. If a Web page is written in Unicode (as XML pages are) and the browser understands Unicode (as XML browsers should), then characters from different languages can easily be included on the same page.

Furthermore, the browser doesn't need to distinguish between different encodings like Windows 1251, ISO-8859-5, or KOI8-R. The browser can just presume everything's written in Unicode. As long as the double-byte set has the space to hold all the different characters, there's no need to use more than one character set. As a result, browsers don't need to detect which character set is in use.

Scripts, Character Sets, Fonts, and Glyphs

Unfortunately, XML alone is not enough to allow you to read a script. You will also need the following:

1. A character set for the script

2. A font for the character set

3. An operating system and application software that understands the character set

If you also want to write in the script, you'll need an input method – although for limited use, XML defines character references that enable you to use pure ASCII to encode characters not available in your native character set.

Most human languages have written forms. The set of characters used to write a language is called a *script*. A script may (or may not) be a phonetic alphabet. For instance, Chinese, Japanese, and Korean (CJK for short) are written with ideographic characters that represent whole words.

Different languages often share scripts, albeit with slight variations. For instance, the modern Turkish alphabet is essentially the familiar English alphabet minus the letters *q*, *w*, and *x* and with six extra letters ğ, ş, ı, ç, ö, and ü. Chinese, Japanese, and Korean, on the other hand, share essentially the same 80,000 Han ideographs, though many characters have different meanings in the respective languages.

 Of course, the word *script* is also used to refer to programs written in weakly typed, interpreted languages like JavaScript, Perl, and AppleScript. In this chapter, the word *script* refers to the characters used to write a language, not to any sort of program.

Even the same language can use different scripts. In Romania, Romanian is written with the Roman alphabet. In Moldova, one of the Confederation of Independent States in the former Soviet Union, Romanian is written in the Cyrillic alphabet. However, the Roman alphabet is making a comeback in Moldova since the breakup of the Soviet Union. Cyrillic itself replaced the Glagolitic script a millennium ago.

As long as a computer doesn't attempt to grasp the meaning of the words it processes, working with a script is equivalent to working with any language that can be written in that script.

Four elements are required for each script a computer program processes:

1. A character set for the script

2. A font for the character set

3. An input method for the character set

4. An operating system and application software that understands the character set

If any of these elements are missing, you won't be able to write easily in the script, though XML does provide a work-around adequate for occasional use. If your application is only missing an input method, you'll be able to read text written in the script, but you won't be able to write in it.

Character Sets

Computers only understand numbers. Before they can work with text, that text has to be encoded as numbers in a specified character set. For example, the popular ASCII character set encodes the capital letter A as 64. The capital letter B is encoded as 65. C is 66, and so forth.

These semantic encodings provide no style or font information. 66 is **C**, C, or even **C**. Information about how the character is drawn is stored elsewhere.

Fonts Provide Glyphs for Characters

A font is a collection of glyphs for a character set, generally in a specific size, face, and style. **C**, C, and **C** are all the same character, but they are drawn with different glyphs. Nonetheless, their essential meaning is identical.

The storage of glyphs varies from system to system. They may be bitmaps or vector drawings; they may even be hot lead on a printing press. The form of storage is unimportant – just remember that a font tells the computer how to draw each character in the character set.

Input Methods Let You Enter Text

English speakers don't think much about input methods for scripts. We just type on our keyboards and everything's hunky-dory. The same scenario exists in most of Europe, where a slightly modified keyboard handles input with a few extra umlauts, cedillas, or thorns (depending on the country).

Radically different character sets like Cyrillic, Hebrew, Arabic, and Greek are more troublesome. A keyboard contains a finite number of keys, generally not enough for both Arabic and Roman letters, or both Arabic and Greek letters. If two of these sets are needed, however, you can have a Greek lock key that shifts the keyboard from Roman to Greek and back. You can even print both Greek and Roman letters on the keys in different colors. The same scheme works for Hebrew, Arabic, Cyrillic, and other non-Roman alphabetic character sets.

This scheme breaks down when faced with ideographic scripts like Chinese and Japanese, however. True Japanese keyboards can have 5,000 different keys; that's still less than 10 percent of the language! Although syllabic, phonetic, and radical representations can reduce the number of keys, a keyboard is probably not an appropriate means of entering text in these languages. Reliable speech and handwriting recognition have even greater potential in Asia than in the West.

Because speech and handwriting recognition still haven't reached the reliability of even a mediocre typist like myself, most current input methods map multiple sequences of keys on the keyboard to a single character. For example, you might hit Alt + ~ (tilde), then type HASHI, then the Enter key to enter the Japanese character 橋, which means bridge.

Application and Operating System Software

As of this writing, the major Web browsers (Navigator and Internet Explorer) display non-Roman scripts surprisingly well. If the underlying OS supports a given script and has the right fonts installed, a Web browser can probably display it.

MacOS 7.1 and later versions can handle all common scripts in the world today. The base operating system sold in the Americas and Europe only supports western European languages, however. Chinese, Japanese, Korean, Arabic, Hebrew, and Cyrillic are available as language kits that cost about $100 a piece. Each kit provides fonts and input methods for languages written in those scripts. An Indian language kit handles the Devanagari, Gujarati, and Gurmukhu scripts common on the Indian subcontinent.

Windows NT 4.0 uses Unicode as its native character set (for more information on this character set, please refer to the Unicode section later in this chapter). As such, the operating system does a fairly good job with Roman languages, Cyrillic, Greek, Hebrew, and a few others. The Lucida Sans Unicode font covers about 1,300 of the most common 40,000 Unicode characters. Microsoft Office 97 includes Chinese, Japanese, and Korean fonts you can install to read text in these languages. (Look in the Fareast folder in the Valupack folder on your Office CD-ROM.) You can also download a variety of international language packs and input method editors that work in Internet Explorer 4.0 for Windows from `http://www.microsoft.com/ie/ie40/`.

Microsoft claims Windows NT 5.0 will also include fonts covering most of the Chinese-Japanese-Korean ideographs, as well as input methods for these scripts.

They also promised that Windows 95 would include Unicode support, however, which was dropped before shipment. Consequently, don't hold your breath. Ideally, Microsoft would provide full international support in all NT versions rather than relying on localized systems.

Microsoft's consumer operating systems, Windows 3.1, 95, and 98, do not fully support Unicode. Instead, they rely on localized systems that can only handle basic English characters plus the localized script.

The major UNIX variants have varying levels of support for Unicode. Solaris 2.6 supports European languages, Greek, and Cyrillic. Chinese, Japanese, and Korean are supported via localized versions of the OS using non-Unicode encodings. Linux only has embryonic support for Unicode, but this support may improve to a useful level in the near future.

The Major Character Sets

Different computers in different locales use different default character sets. Most modern computers use a superset of the ASCII character set, which encodes the English alphabet and the most common punctuation and white space characters. In the United States, Macs use the MacRoman character set, Windows PCs use a character set called Windows ANSI, and most UNIX workstations use ISO Latin-1. These sets are extensions of ASCII that support additional characters like ç and ¿ needed for western European languages like French and Spanish. In other locales, such as Japan, Greece, and Israel, computers use a still more confusing hodgepodge of character sets that usually support ASCII plus the local language.

This approach doesn't work on the Internet. When reading the *San Jose Mercury News*, you probably won't turn the page and be confronted with columns written in German or Chinese. On the Web, however, a user could easily follow a link and find themselves staring at a page full of Japanese. Even if the surfer can't read Japanese, it would still be nice if they saw a correct version of the language, as seen in Figure 8-3, instead of a random collection of characters like in Figure 8-1.

XML addresses this problem by moving beyond small, local character sets to one large set that's supposed to encompass all scripts used in all living languages (and not a few dead ones) on Earth. This character set is called Unicode. Unicode is a double-byte character set that provides representations of over 40,000 different characters in hundreds of languages. All XML processors are required to understand Unicode, even if they can't fully display it.

As you learned in Chapter 6, an XML document is divided into text and binary entities. Each text entity has an encoding. If the encoding is not explicitly specified in the entity's definition, then the default is UTF-8 – a compressed form of Unicode which leaves pure ASCII text unchanged. Thus, XML files only containing the common ASCII characters can be edited with tools that are unaware of the complications with multibyte character sets like Unicode.

ASCII

ASCII, the American Standard Code for Information Interchange, is by far the most common character set. One of the original character sets, ASCII forms a sort of lowest common denominator for character set support requirements. It only defines all the characters needed to write U.S. English. In fact, it even lacks some characters you might want for writing English like the copyright symbol, curly quotes, and various mathematical symbols. The ASCII characters are mapped to the numbers 0–127. You'll find a complete list of the ASCII characters and their numeric codes in Table A-1 of Appendix A.

Most other common character sets are supersets of ASCII. In other words, they define 0 though 127 exactly the same as ASCII, but add additional characters from 128 on up.

The ISO Alphabet Soup

The A in ASCII stands for American, so it shouldn't surprise you that ASCII is only adequate for writing American English. ASCII contains no £, ü, ©, or other characters for writing in other languages or locales.

ASCII can be extended by assigning additional characters to numbers above 128. The International Standards Organization (ISO) has defined a number of different character sets based on ASCII that add additional characters needed for other languages and locales. The most prominent character set is ISO-8859-1, commonly called Latin-1. Latin-1 includes enough additional characters to write essentially all western European languages. Characters 0 through 127 match ASCII definitions, while characters 128 through 255 are given in Table A-3 of Appendix A.

Latin-1 still omits many useful characters, including those needed for Greek, Cyrillic, Chinese, and many other scripts and languages. Although you may think these additional characters could just be moved into the numbers beyond 256, there's a catch. A single byte can only hold values from 0 to 255. To go beyond that limit, you need to use a multibyte character set. For historical reasons, most programs are written with the assumption that characters and bytes are identical and tend to break when faced with multibyte character sets. Therefore, most current operating systems (Windows NT being the notable exception) use different, single-byte character sets rather than one large multibyte set. Latin-1 is the most common single-byte set, but other sets are needed to handle additional languages.

ISO-8859 defines nine other sets suitable for different scripts, with four more sets in active development. Table 8-1 lists the ISO character sets and the languages and scripts for which they can be used. All sets share the same ASCII characters from 0 to 127 and include additional characters from 128 to 255.

TABLE 8-1 THE ISO CHARACTER SETS

Character Set	Script	Languages
ISO-8859-1	Latin-1	ASCII plus the characters required for most western European languages including Albanian, Afrikaans, Basque, Catalan, Danish, Dutch, English, Faroese, Finnish, Flemish, Galician, German, Icelandic, Irish, Italian, Norwegian, Portuguese, Scottish, Spanish, and Swedish. It omits the ligatures IJ (Dutch), Œ (French), and German quotation marks, however.
ISO-8859-2	Latin-2	ASCII plus the characters required for most central European languages including Czech, English, German, Hungarian, Polish, Romanian, Croatian, Slovak, Slovene, and Sorbian.
ISO-8859-3	Latin-3	ASCII plus the characters required for English, Esperanto, German, Maltese, and Galician.
ISO-8859-4	Latin-4	ASCII plus the characters required for the Baltic languages Latvian, Lithuanian, German, Greenlandic, and Lappish; superseded by ISO 8859-10, Latin-6.
ISO-8859-5		ASCII plus Cyrillic characters required for Byelorussian, Bulgarian, Macedonian, Russian, Serbian, and Ukrainian.
ISO-8859-6		ASCII plus Arabic.
ISO-8859-7		ASCII plus Greek.
ISO-8859-8		ASCII plus Hebrew.
ISO-8859-9	Latin-5	Latin-1 except that the Turkish letters ğ, ş, and ı take the place of the Icelandic letters ð, þ, and ý
ISO-8859-10	Latin-6	ASCII plus characters for the Nordic languages Latvian, Lithuanian, Inuit (Greenlandic Eskimo), non-Skolt Sami (Lappish), and Icelandic.
ISO-8859-11		ASCII plus Thai.
ISO-8859-12	Latin-7	ASCII plus Celtic.
ISO-8859-13	Latin-8	ASCII plus the Baltic Rim.
ISO-8859-14	Latin-9	ASCII plus Sami.
ISO-8859-15	Latin-10	A slight variation of Latin-1 that includes a Euro currency sign and a few extra accented letters for Finnish and French.

Because the character sets overlap, several languages (most notably English and German) can be written in more than one set. To some extent, the different sets are designed to allow different combinations of languages. For instance, Latin-1 can combine most Western languages and Icelandic, whereas Latin-6 combines most Western languages with Turkish instead of Icelandic. Thus, if you needed a document in English, French, and Icelandic, you'd use Latin-1. A document with English, French, and Turkish would use Latin-6, however. A document that required English, Hebrew, and Turkish would have to use Unicode because no single-byte character set handles all three languages and scripts.

This single-byte approach is still insufficient for Chinese, Japanese, and Korean. These languages have more than 256 characters apiece. Therefore, they must use multibyte character sets.

Standards Are Bad! (Apple Version)

The MacOS predates Latin-1 by several years. (The ISO-8859-1 standard was first adopted in 1987. The first Mac was released in 1984.) Unfortunately, this means that Apple had to define its own extended character set called MacRoman, which has most of the same extended characters as Latin-1 (except for the Icelandic letters Þ, þ, and ð) assigned to different numbers. MacRoman matches ASCII and Latin-1 in the lower 127 characters. As a result, text files that use extended characters often look funny when moved from a PC to a Mac or vice versa. Table A-4 in Appendix A lists the upper half of the MacRoman character set.

Standards Are Bad! (Microsoft Version)

The first version of Windows to achieve any sort of widespread adoption followed the Mac by a few years, so it could adopt the Latin-1 character set. Windows replaced the nonprinting control characters between 130 and 159 with more printing characters to stretch the available range, however. This modified version of Latin-1 is generally called Windows ANSI. Table A-5 in Appendix A lists the Windows ANSI characters that differ from Latin-1.

Unicode

Using different character sets for different scripts and languages works well enough provided you satisfy these two conditions:

1. You don't need to work in more than one script at once.

2. You never trade files with anyone using a different character set.

Because Macs and PCs use different character sets, these criteria aren't commonly satisfied.

Obviously, a multibyte character set that everyone agrees upon and encodes all characters in all the world's scripts is necessary. Creating such a set is difficult, because it requires a detailed understanding of hundreds of languages and their scripts. Getting software developers to agree to use one universal set once it's been created is even harder. Nonetheless, work continues on such a set (called Unicode) and the major vendors (Microsoft, Apple, IBM, Sun, and many others) are slowly moving toward compliance. XML specifies Unicode as its default character set.

Unicode encodes each character as a two-byte unsigned number with a value between 0 and 65,535. Currently, more than 40,000 different Unicode characters are defined. The extra 25,000 spaces are reserved for future extensions. The Han ideographs use about 20,000 characters while the Korean Hangul syllabary uses about 11,000 characters. The remaining characters encode most of the world's other languages. Unicode characters 0 through 255 are identical to Latin-1 characters 0 through 255.

To learn more about the specific encodings of the different characters in Unicode, get a copy of *The Unicode Standard*, second edition, ISBN 0-201-48348-9, from Addison-Wesley. This 950-page book includes the complete Unicode 2.0 specification, including character charts for all the different characters defined in Unicode 2.0. Tables A-6 through A-9 in Appendix A list the ranges of the different scripts encoded by Unicode to give you some picture of its versatility.

UTF 8

Because Unicode uses two bytes for each character, files of mostly English text written in Unicode are about twice as large as they would be in ASCII or Latin-1. UTF-8 is a compressed version of Unicode that uses only a single byte for the most common characters (ASCII characters 0–127), while using three bytes for the less common characters (particularly the Hangul symbols and Han ideographs). If you're writing mostly English, UTF-8 can reduce your file sizes by as much as 50 percent. On the other hand, if you're writing mostly Chinese, Korean, or Japanese files, UTF-8 can increase your file size by as much as 50 percent – use it with caution. UTF-8 has little effect on non-Roman, non-CJK scripts like Greek, Arabic, Cyrillic, and Hebrew.

Unless otherwise specified, XML processors assume text data is in the UTF-8 format. In this configuration, XML processors can read ASCII files as is, but other formats like MacRoman or Latin-1 cause trouble. You'll see how to remedy this shortcoming in a following section.

UCS

Unicode has been criticized for its limitations, especially in regard to east Asian languages. It only defines about 20,000 Han ideographs of over 80,000 ideographs used between Chinese, Japanese, Korean, and historical Vietnamese. (Modern Vietnamese uses a Roman alphabet.)

UCS, the Universal Character System, also known as ISO-10646, uses four bytes per character (more precisely, 31 bits) to provide space for over two billion different characters. This approach easily covers every character used in any language in any script on Earth. Among other things, UCS allows a full set of characters to be assigned to each language — for example, the French *e* is not the same as the English *e* is not the same as the German *e*, and so forth.

Like Unicode, UCS defines a number of different variants and compressed forms. Pure Unicode is sometimes referred to as UCS-2 (two-byte UCS). UTF-16 is a special encoding that maps some of the UCS characters into byte strings of varying length in such a fashion that Unicode (UCS-2) data is unchanged.

At this point, the advantage of UCS as opposed to Unicode is mostly theoretical. The only characters actually defined in UCS precisely match those defined in Unicode. UCS does provide more room for expansion in the future, however.

Writing in Unicode

Although Unicode is the native character set of XML and XML browsers should successfully display Unicode to the limits of the available fonts, few text editors support the full range of Unicode. Consequently, you'll probably have to hack the problem in one of the following ways:

1. Write in a localized character set like Latin-1 and then convert your file to Unicode.

2. Include Unicode character references in the text that numerically identify particular characters.

The first option is preferable when you have a large amount of text to enter in one script, or one script plus ASCII. The second approach works best when you need to mix small portions of multiple scripts into your document.

Unicode Character References

Every Unicode character is a number between 0 and 65,535. If you do not have a text editor that can write in Unicode, you can always use a character reference to insert the character in your XML file instead.

A Unicode character reference consists of two characters &#, the character code, and a semicolon. For instance, the Greek letter π has Unicode value 960 so it can be inserted in an XML file as π. The Cyrillic character Ч has Unicode value 1206 so it can be included in an XML file with the character reference Ҷ.

Unicode character references may also be specified in hexadecimal (base 16). Although most humans are more comfortable with decimal numbers, *The Unicode Specification* gives character values as two-byte hexadecimal numbers. It's often easier to use hex values directly rather than converting them to decimal.

Just include an *x* after the &# to signal that you're using a hexadecimal value. For example, π has hexadecimal value 3C0 so it can be inserted in an XML file as π. The Cyrillic character Ч has hexadecimal value 4B6 so it can be included in an XML file with the escape sequence Ҷ. Because two bytes always produce exactly four hexadecimal digits, it's customary (though not required) to include leading zeroes in hexadecimal character references to round them out to four digits.

Unicode character references, both hexadecimal and decimal, may be used to embed characters that would otherwise be interpreted as markup. For instance, the ampersand (&) is encoded as & or &. The less than sign (<) is encoded as < or <.

Converting to and from Unicode

Application software that exports XML files, such as Adobe FrameMaker, handles the conversion to Unicode or UTF-8 automatically. Microsoft Word 97 and later can save files as Unicode text. Otherwise, you'll need to use a conversion tool. Sun's freely available Java Development Kit (JDK) includes a simple command-line utility called native2ascii that converts between many common and uncommon localized character sets and Unicode.

For example:

```
C:\> native2ascii myfile.txt myfile.uni
```

This example assumes the text file uses the platform's default encoding. You can specify a different encoding with the -encoding option:

```
C:> native2ascii -encoding Big5 chinese.txt chinese.uni
```

You can also reverse the process to go from Unicode to a local encoding with the -reverse option:

```
C:> native2ascii -encoding Big5 -reverse chinese.uni chinese.txt
```

If the output file is left off, the converted file is printed out.

The native2ascii program also processes Java-style Unicode escapes, which are characters embedded as \u09E3. These escapes are not the same format as XML numeric character references, though they're similar. If you convert to Unicode using native2ascii, you can still use XML character references. The viewer will still recognize them.

Writing XML in Other Character Sets

Unless told otherwise, an XML processor assumes that text entity characters are encoded in UTF-8. Because UTF-8 includes ASCII as a subset, ASCII text is easily parsed by XML processors as well.

Other than UTF-8, an XML processor is only required to understand raw Unicode. An XML processor distinguishes between UTF-8 and raw Unicode by looking at a byte order mark at the beginning of the text entity. A byte order mark can be either of the following two-byte characters: `&#xFEFF;` or `&#xFFFE;`.

These numbers (65,279 and 65,534) are not assigned to characters. Each pair of hexadecimal digits forms a byte. One of these numbers is formed from the other if the byte order is swapped. This approach allows a processor to determine whether it's dealing with big endian or little endian data, because the Unicode specification does not single out a preferred endianness. The two bytes FF and FE are unlikely to start a random file of text in most encodings and are guaranteed not to do so in Unicode (except as a byte order mark).

If you cannot convert your text into either UTF-8 or raw Unicode, you can leave it in its native character set and tell the XML processor what set that is. Because arbitrary XML processors aren't guaranteed to process other encodings, you should only use this approach as a last resort. Nonetheless, Navigator and Internet Explorer usually do a pretty good job of interpreting the common character sets.

To warn the XML processor that you're using a non-Unicode encoding, include an encoding attribute in the XML declaration at the start of the file. For example, to specify that the entire document uses Latin-1 by default (unless overridden by another processing instruction in a nested entity), use the following XML declaration:

```
<?xml version="1.0" encoding="ISO-8859-1" ?>
```

Table 8-2 lists the canonical names of the most common character sets used today, as they would be given in XML encoding attributes. For encodings not found in this list, consult the official list maintained by the Internet Assigned Numbers Authority (IANA) at `http://www.isi.edu/in-notes/iana/assignments/character-sets`.

TABLE 8-2 ENCODING NAMES

Canonical Name	Languages/Countries
US-ASCII	English
UTF-8	Compressed Unicode
UTF-16	Compressed UCS
ISO-10646-UCS-2	Raw Unicode
ISO-10646-UCS-4	Raw UCS
ISO-8859-1	Latin-1, western Europe

Continued

TABLE 8-2 ENCODING NAMES *(Continued)*

Canonical Name	Languages/Countries
ISO-8859-2	Latin-2, eastern Europe
ISO-8859-3	Latin-3, southern Europe
ISO-8859-4	Latin-4, northern Europe
ISO-8859-5	ASCII plus Cyrillic
ISO-8859-6	ASCII plus Arabic
ISO-8859-7	ASCII plus Greek
ISO-8859-8	ASCII plus Hebrew
ISO-8859-9	Latin-5, Turkish
ISO-2022-JP	Japanese
Shift_JIS	Japanese, Windows
EUC-JP	Japanese, UNIX
Big5	Chinese, Taiwan
GB2312	Chinese, mainland China
KOI8-R	Russian
ISO-2022-KR	Korean
EUC-KR	Korean, UNIX
ISO-2022-CN	Chinese

Summary

In this chapter, you learned the following concepts:

◆ Why international text is good

◆ What a script is, and how it relates to languages

◆ How scripts are used in computers with character sets, fonts, and input methods

◆ What character sets are commonly used on different platforms

- ◆ How to write XML in Unicode

- ◆ How to write XML in other encodings

In the next chapter, you are introduced to XLinks and XPointers, which support hyperlinks between XML documents, including links to an arbitrary position in a document and multidirectional links.

Chapter 9

XLinks and XPointers

IN THIS CHAPTER

- ◆ Why XLL?
- ◆ XLinks
- ◆ Extended links
- ◆ Out-of-line links and link groups
- ◆ XPointers

XLL, THE EXTENSIBLE Linking Language, is a new means of linking between documents. In addition to offering URL-based hyperlinks and anchors, XLL also supports linking to an arbitrary position in a document and multidirectional links. These features make XLL suitable for many new uses as well as many traditional uses that are problematic in pure HTML such as cross-references, footnotes, end notes, interlinked data, and more.

XLL is designed for use in XML documents. In particular, all XLL tags and content are well-formed XML. XLL is divided into two parts: XLink and XPointer. XLink, the XML Linking Language, defines how one document links to another document. XPointer, the XML Pointer Language, defines how individual parts of a document are addressed. An XLink points to a URL that specifies a particular resource. This URL may include an XPointer part that more specifically identifies the desired part or section of the targeted resource or document.

Why XLL?

The Web conquered the more established gopher protocol for one main reason: hypertext links could be embedded in documents. These links could embed images or enable the user to jump from inside one document to another document or another part of the same document. To the extent that XML is rendered into other formats like HTML for viewing, XML documents can use traditional HTML linking syntax. Alternate syntaxes can be converted into HTML syntax using XSL, as you've seen in preceding chapters.

HTML linking has limits, however. URLs are mostly limited to pointing out a single document. Increased granularity, such as linking to the third sentence of the seventeenth paragraph in the document, requires manually inserting named anchors in the targeted file. You can't link to a particular part of a document in HTML without changing the document.

Furthermore, HTML links don't maintain any sense of history or relations between documents. Although browsers may track the path you've followed through a series of documents, such tracking isn't reliable. From inside the HTML, you cannot discern where the reader came from. Links are purely one-way. The linking document knows where it's linking to, but the linked document does not know where it's linked from.

XLL is designed to solve these problems and allow full, multidirectional linking where the links run in more than one direction. XLL is based around two fundamental technologies: XLinks for making the links and XPointers for addressing the links. Furthermore, XLL assumes the URL/URI specification.

At the time of this writing (spring 1998), XLL is still undergoing significant development and modification. Although it is beginning to stabilize, some bits and pieces are likely to change by the time you read this chapter.

Furthermore, no general purpose applications currently support arbitrary XLL. That's because XLL has a much broader base of applicability than HTML links. XLinks are not used just for hypertext connections and embedding images in documents. They can be used by any custom application that needs to establish connections between documents and parts of documents for any reason. Thus, even when XLinks are fully implemented in browsers, they may not always be blue underlined text that you click to jump to another page. They can be that, but they can also be both more and less depending on your needs.

XLinks

In HTML, a link is defined with the <A> tag. However, just as XML is more flexible than HTML with tags that describe elements, it is also more flexible with tags that refer to external resources. In XML, almost any tag can be a link. Elements that include links are called *linking elements.*

Linking elements are identified by an xlink:form attribute with either the value "simple" or "extended". Furthermore, each linking element contains an href attribute whose value is the URI of the linked resource. For example, three linking elements follow:

```
<footnote xlink:form="simple" href="footnote7.xml">7</footnote>
<composer xlink:form="simple"
    href="http://www.users.interport.net/~beand/">
    Beth Anderson
</composer>
<image xlink:form="simple" href="logo.gif"/>
```

Notice that the tags have semantic names describing their content, rather than describing the function of the tags. The information that these elements are links is included in the attributes of the tags.

The three preceding examples are all simple XLinks. Simple links are similar to standard HTML links, and are likely to be supported by application software before the more complex (and more powerful) extended links. (Extended links will be taken up in a following section.)

In the preceding footnote example, the link target attribute's name is href. Its value is the relative URL footnote7.xml. The protocol, host, and directory of this file will be taken from the protocol, host, and directory of the file in which this link appears.

In the preceding composer example, the link target attribute's name is href. The value of the homepage attribute is the absolute URL http://www.users.interport.net/~beand/.

In the third preceding example, the link target attribute's name is href. The value of the href attribute is the relative URL logo.gif. Again, the protocol, host, and directory of this file will be taken from the protocol, host, and directory of the file in which this link appears.

If your document possesses a DTD, these attributes must be declared like any other attribute. For example, declarations of the footnote, composer, and image elements may look like the following:

```
<!ELEMENT footnote (#PCDATA)>
<!ATTLIST footnote
     xlink:form    CDATA    #FIXED "simple"
     href          CDATA    #REQUIRED
>
<!ELEMENT composer (#PCDATA)>
<!ATTLIST composer
     xlink:form    CDATA    #FIXED "simple"
     href          CDATA    #REQUIRED
>
<!ELEMENT image EMPTY>
<!ATTLIST image
     xlink:form    CDATA    #FIXED "extended"
     href          CDATA    #REQUIRED
>
```

With these declarations, the xlink:form attribute has a fixed value. Therefore, it does not need to be included in the instances of the elements, which may now be more compactly written as follows:

```
<footnote href="footnote7.xml">7</footnote>
<composer href="http://www.users.interport.net/~beand/">
  Beth Anderson
</composer>
<image href="logo.gif"/>
```

Making an element a link element doesn't impose restrictions on other attributes or contents of the element. A link element may contain arbitrary children or other attributes, which are subject to the restrictions of the DTD. The following example shows a more realistic declaration of the image element. Note that most of the attributes don't have anything to do with linking.

```
<!ELEMENT image EMPTY>
<!ATTLIST image
     xlink:form    CDATA    #FIXED "extended"
     href          CDATA    #REQUIRED
     alt           CDATA    #REQUIRED
     height        CDATA    #REQUIRED
     width         CDATA    #REQUIRED
>
```

Descriptions of the Local Link

A linking element may contain two optional attributes that further describe the purpose of the link inside the document in which it appears. These optional attributes are content-role and content-title. For example:

```
<author href="http://www.macfaq.com/personal.html"
  content-title="author of the page"
  content-role="whom to contact for questions about this page">
    Elliotte Rusty Harold
</author>
```

The content-role and content-title attributes describe the local element — not the remote resource. Thus, this example says that Elliotte Rusty Harold has the title "author of the page" and the role "person to contact for questions about this page". The title and role do not necessarily have any relation to the document found at http://www.macfaq.com/personal.html.

The content-title attribute is generally used by an application reading the XML to show a bit of extra information to the user, perhaps in the browser's status bar or via a tooltip, when the user moves the mouse over the linked element. The application is not required to show this information to the user, however. It may simply do so if it chooses.

The content-role attribute indicates the purpose of the linked element in the document. The content-role attribute is similar to a processing instruction — it's intended to pass data to the application reading the XML. This attribute has no purpose as XML, though, and applications are free to ignore it.

Like all other attributes, content-title and content-role should be declared in the DTD for each element to which they belong. For example, the following example is a reasonable declaration for the preceding author element:

```
<!ELEMENT author (#PCDATA)>
<!ATTLIST author
```

```
        xlink:form      CDATA     #FIXED     "simple"
        href            CDATA     #REQUIRED
        content-title   CDATA     #IMPLIED
        content-role    CDATA     #IMPLIED
>
```

Descriptions of the Remote Resource

The link element may also contain optional role and title attributes describing the remote resource, which is the document or other resource to which the link points. For example:

```
<author href="http://www.macfaq.com/personal.html"
  title="Elliotte Rusty Harold's personal home page"
  role="further information about the author of this page">
  content-title="author of the page"
  content-role="whom to contact for questions about this page">
  Elliotte Rusty Harold
</author>
```

The role and title attributes describe the remote resource – not the local element. Although not required, the title attribute often matches the contents of the <title> element of the linked page.

The application reading the XML might use these two attributes to show a bit of extra information to the user. The application is not required to show this information to the user or do anything with it all, for that matter.

The content-role attribute indicates the purpose of the linked element in the document. For example, it might distinguish between footnotes, endnotes, and citations.

Like all other attributes, title and role should be declared in the DTD for as many elements as they belong to. For example, this is a reasonable declaration for the preceding author element:

```
<!ELEMENT author (#PCDATA)>
<!ATTLIST author
        xlink:form      CDATA     #FIXED "simple"
        href            CDATA     #REQUIRED
        content-title   CDATA     #IMPLIED
        content-role    CDATA     #IMPLIED
        title           CDATA     #IMPLIED
        role            CDATA     #IMPLIED
>
```

Link Policies

Link elements can contain the following three optional attributes that suggest to applications how the remote resource is connected to the current page:

- show

- actuate

- behavior

The show attribute suggests how the content should be displayed when the link is activated (for example, by opening a new window). The actuate attribute suggests whether the link should be traversed automatically or whether a specific user request is required. The behavior attribute can provide detailed information to the application about exactly how the link is to be traversed (for instance, a time-delay). These attributes are all application-dependent, however, and applications are free to ignore these suggestions.

SHOW

The show attribute has three legal values: replace, new, and embed.

With a value of replace, the target of the link replaces the current document in the same window when the link is activated (generally, in GUI browsers, by clicking it). This functionality is the default behavior of HTML links. For example:

```
<composer href="http://www.users.interport.net/~beand/"
 show="replace">
  Beth Anderson
</composer>
```

With a value of new, traversing the link opens a new window in which the targeted resource is displayed. This functionality is similar to the behavior of HTML links when the target attribute is set to _blank. For example:

```
<website href="http://www.microsoft.com/" show="new">
  Check this out, but don't leave our site completely!
</website>
```

With a value of embed, traversing the link inserts the targeted resource into the existing document. Exactly what this means is application dependent. However, you can use it to provide tree-like structures in Web pages. For example:

```
<family>
  <husband href="Frank.xml" show="embed"/>
  <wife href="Sally.xml" show="embed"/>
  <child href="Dick.xml" show="embed"/>
  <child href="Jane.xml" show="embed"/>
  <dog href="spot.xml" show="embed"/>
</family>
```

Like all attributes in valid documents, show must be declared in <!ATTLIST> declarations for the link element. For example:

```
<!ELEMENT website (#PCDATA)>
<!ATTLIST website
        xlink:form    CDATA    #FIXED "simple"
        href          CDATA    #REQUIRED
        show          CDATA    ("new" | "replace" | "embed") "new"
>
```

ACTUATE

The actuate attribute of a link element has two possible values: user and auto. The default value user specifies that the link is only to be traversed when and if the user requests it. On the other hand, an auto attribute is traversed anytime one of the other targeted resources of the same link element is traversed. This functionality will be useful when link groups are discussed in a following section.

Like all attributes in valid documents, the actuate attribute must be declared in <!ATTLIST> declarations for the link elements in which it appears. For example:

```
<!ELEMENT website (#PCDATA)>
<!ATTLIST website
        xlink:form    CDATA    #FIXED "simple"
        href          CDATA    #REQUIRED
        show          CDATA    ("new" | "replace" | "embed") "new"
        actuate       CDATA    ("user" | "auto") "user"
>
```

BEHAVIOR

The behavior attribute passes arbitrary data in an arbitrary format to the application reading the data. The application is expected to use this data to make additional determinations about how the link behaves. For example, if you want to specify that the sound file fanfare.au be played when a link is traversed, you might write the following example:

```
<composer xlink:form="simple"
    href="http://www.users.interport.net/~beand/"
    behavior="sound: fanfare.au">
    Beth Anderson
</composer>
```

This example requires that the application reading the XML file understand that a behavior attribute with the value "sound: fanfare.au" means that the sound file fanfare.au should be played when the link is traversed. Most, probably all, applications won't understand this statement. They may use the behavior attribute as a convenient place to store nonstandard information that they do understand, however.

Like all attributes in valid documents, the behavior attribute must be declared in <!ATTLIST> declarations for the link elements in which it appears. For example, the preceding composer element would probably be declared as follows:

```
<!ELEMENT composer (#PCDATA)>
<!ATTLIST composer
    xlink:form    CDATA    #FIXED "simple"
    href          CDATA    #REQUIRED
    behavior      CDATA    #IMPLIED
>
```

Extended Links

Simple links behave more or less like the standard links you're accustomed to from HTML. Each simple link contains a single local resource and a reference to a single remote resource. The local resource is the content of the link element. The remote resource is the target of the link.

Extended links, however, go substantially beyond what you can do with an HTML link to include multidirectional links between many documents and out-of-line links. As shown in the following example, extended links are identified by an xlink:form attribute with the value extended:

```
<website xlink:form="extended">
```

Extended links can point to more than one target. To enable these extended links, store the targets in child locator elements of the linking element rather than in a single href attribute of the linking element, as simple links do. For example:

```
<website xlink:form="extended">Cafe au Lait
  <locator href="http://sunsite.univie.ac.at/jcca/mirrors/javafaq/">
    Austria
  </locator>
  <locator href="http://sunsite.icm.edu.pl/java-corner/faq/">
    Poland
  </locator>
  <locator href="http://sunsite.uakom.sk/javafaq/">
    Slovakia
  </locator>
  <locator href="http://sunsite.cnlab-switch.ch/javafaq/">
    Switzerland
  </locator>
  <locator href="http://sunsite.unc.edu/javafaq/">
    North Carolina
  </locator>
</website>
```

Both the linking element itself, website in this example, and the individual locator children may have attributes. The linking element only has attributes that apply to the entire link and to the local resource, such as content-title and content-role. The locator elements have attributes that apply to the particular remote resource to which they link, such as role and title. For example:

```
<website xlink:form="extended" content-title="Cafe au Lait"
   content-role="Java news">
  <locator href="http://sunsite.univie.ac.at/jcca/mirrors/javafaq/"
     title="Cafe au Lait" role=".at"/>
  <locator href="http://sunsite.icm.edu.pl/java-corner/faq/"
     title="Cafe au Lait" role=".pl"/>
  <locator href="http://sunsite.uakom.sk/javafaq/"
     title="Cafe au Lait" role=".sk"/>
  <locator href="http://sunsite.cnlab-switch.ch/javafaq/"
     title="Cafe au Lait" role=".ch"/>
   <locator href="http://sunsite.unc.edu/javafaq/"
     title="Cafe au Lait" role=".us"/>
</website>
```

A Shortcut in DTDs

Because the attribute names and types are standardized, if you have more than one
link element in a document, it's often convenient to make the attribute declarations a
parameter entity reference, and simply repeat that in the declaration of each linking
element. For example,

```
<!ENTITY % link-attributes
    "xlink:form      CDATA      #FIXED 'simple'
    href            CDATA      #REQUIRED
    behavior        CDATA      #IMPLIED
    content-role    CDATA      #IMPLIED
    content-title   CDATA      #IMPLIED
    role            CDATA      #IMPLIED
    title           CDATA      #IMPLIED
    show            CDATA      ('new' | 'replace' | 'embed') 'new'
    actuate         CDATA      ('user' | 'auto') 'user'
    behavior        CDATA      #IMPLIED"
>
<!ELEMENT composer (#PCDATA)>
<!ATTLIST composer
    %link-attributes;
>
<!ELEMENT author (#PCDATA)>
<!ATTLIST composer
    %link-attributes;
>
<!ELEMENT website (#PCDATA)>
<!ATTLIST composer
    %link-attributes;
>
```

If present, the `actuate`, `behavior`, and `show` attributes belong to the individual locator elements.

As in the previous example, where the individual locators point to mirror copies of the same page, remote resource attributes for individual locator elements may be the same across the linking element. In this case, you can use remote resource attributes in the linking element itself. These attributes are applied to each locator child that does not declare a conflicting value for the same attribute. For example:

```
<website xlink:form="extended" content-title="Cafe au Lait"
   content-role="Java news" title="Cafe au Lait">
 <locator href="http://sunsite.univie.ac.at/jcca/mirrors/javafaq/"
   role=".at"/>
 <locator href="http://sunsite.icm.edu.pl/java-corner/faq/"
   role=".pl"/>
 <locator href="http://sunsite.uakom.sk/javafaq/" role=".sk"/>
 <locator href="http://sunsite.cnlab-switch.ch/javafaq/"
   role=".ch"/>
  <locator href="http://sunsite.unc.edu/javafaq/" role=".us"/>
</website>
```

In valid documents, as always, the link elements and all their possible attributes must be declared in the DTD. For example, the following declares the `website` and `locator` elements used in the preceding examples, as well as their attributes:

```
<!ELEMENT website (locator*)>
<!ATTLIST website
    xlink:form      CDATA      #FIXED "extended"
    content-title   CDATA      #IMPLIED
    content-role    CDATA      #IMPLIED
    title           CDATA      #IMPLIED
>
<!ELEMENT locator EMPTY>
<!ATTLIST locator
    xlink:form      CDATA      #FIXED "locator"
    href            CDATA      #REQUIRED
    role            CDATA      #IMPLIED
>
```

Out-of-Line Links and Link Groups

The links considered so far, both simple and extended, have all been inline links. XLL also supports out-of-line links in which the links between documents may not actually be present in the documents themselves. Instead, the links are stored in a separate linking document.

For example, this approach may be useful to maintain a slide show in which each slide requires next and previous links. By changing the order of the slides in the linking document, you could change the targets of the previous and next links on each page without having to edit the slides themselves.

An extended link group element contains a list of links connecting a particular group of documents. Each document in the group is targeted by an extended link document element. It is the responsibility of the application to understand how to activate and understand the connections between the members of the group.

Application support for out-of-line links is at best hypothetical at the time of this writing, however. While this section shows you how to write such links, their actual implementation and support is still forthcoming. Some details remain to be defined and are likely to be implemented in vendor-specific fashions, at least initially. Still, out-of-line links hold the promise of allowing more sophisticated linking than can be achieved through HTML.

For example, I've placed a number of my class notes for a Java course I teach on the Web. Figure 9-1 shows the introductory page. This particular course consists of 13 weeks of notes, each containing between 20 and 40 individual pages. A table of contents is provided for each class week. Each of the site's several hundred pages have links to the previous document, the next document, and the table of contents for the week as shown in Figure 9-2. All told, there are over a thousand interconnections among this set of documents.

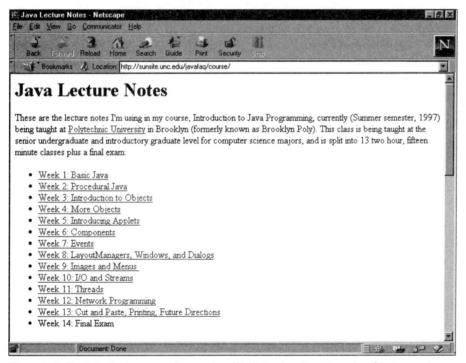

Figure 9-1: The introductory page for my class Web site showing 13 weeks of lecture notes

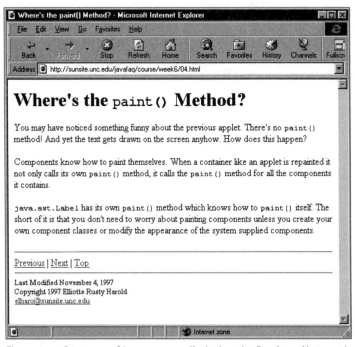

Figure 9-2: One page of lecture notes displaying the Previous, Next, and Top links

The possible interconnections grow exponentially with the number of documents. Every time a single document is moved, renamed, or divided into smaller pieces, the links need to be adjusted on that page, on the page before it and after it in the set, and on the table of contents for the week. The amount of work involved tends to discourage necessary modifications and updates to the course notes.

The sensible thing to do, if HTML supported it, would be to store the connections in a separate document such that only that document needed to be edited in order to reorder or rename a page. HTML links don't support that, but XLinks do. Instead of storing the links inline in HTML files, they can be stored out-of-line in group elements. For example:

```
<course xlink:form="group">
    <class xlink:form="document" href="week1/index.xml"/>
    <class xlink:form="document" href="week2/index.xml"/>
    <class xlink:form="document" href="week3/index.xml"/>
    <class xlink:form="document" href="week4/index.xml"/>
    <class xlink:form="document" href="week5/index.xml"/>
    <class xlink:form="document" href="week6/index.xml"/>
    <class xlink:form="document" href="week7/index.xml"/>
    <class xlink:form="document" href="week8/index.xml"/>
    <class xlink:form="document" href="week9/index.xml"/>
```

```
    <class xlink:form="document" href="week10/index.xml"/>
    <class xlink:form="document" href="week11/index.xml"/>
    <class xlink:form="document" href="week12/index.xml"/>
    <class xlink:form="document" href="week13/index.xml"/>
</course>
```

Steps

One thing an application may choose to do with a link group is preload all the documents in the link group. These documents may contain link groups of their own. For example, each of the preceding document tags refers to one of the site's table of contents pages for a specific week, as shown in Figure 9-3. These documents would then also be loaded. For example, the file `week6/index.xml` might contain the following link group:

```
<class xlink:form="group">
    <document xlink:form="document" href="01.xml"/>
    <document xlink:form="document" href="02.html"/>
    <document xlink:form="document" href="06.html"/>
    <document xlink:form="document" href="12.html"/>
    <document xlink:form="document" href="13.html"/>
    <document xlink:form="document" href="16.html"/>
    <document xlink:form="document" href="17.html"/>
    <document xlink:form="document" href="19.html"/>
    <document xlink:form="document" href="21.html"/>
    <document xlink:form="document" href="22.html"/>
    <document xlink:form="document" href="24.html"/>
</class>
```

Individual documents in this list may contain link groups of their own. Suppose one of these documents refers back to the original document. This reference might trigger an infinite regression in which the same documents are loaded repeatedly until the application runs out of memory. To prevent recursion, the `group` element can contain a `steps` attribute that specifies the number of levels to follow link groups. For example, to specify that you shouldn't go more than three levels deep from the current document, write the following:

```
<group xlink:form="group" steps="3">
```

To be honest, this precaution may not be necessary. An application can note when it's already followed a document and not process the document a second time. Placing the requirement for preventing recursion with the XML processor, rather than with the page author, would probably be a better solution.

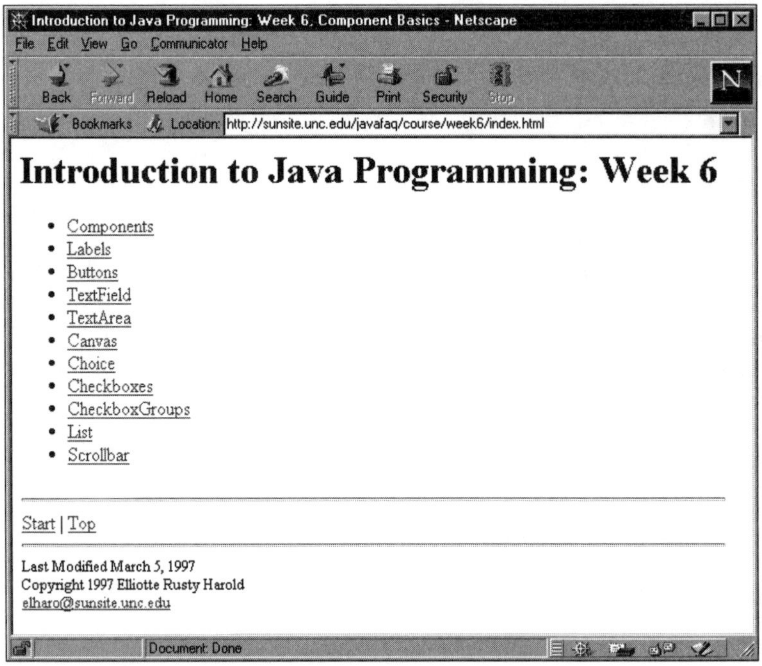

Figure 9-3: A page showing the first week's lecture notes

The `steps` attribute can also be used to limit the amount of preloading that occurs. For instance, in the course example, students will probably not read through the entire set of course notes at one sitting, though perhaps they might want to print or copy the set. In either case, setting `steps` to 1 limits the depth of the traversal to the named pages rather than the entire course notes set.

DTDs

As always, these elements and their attributes must be declared in the DTD of any valid document in which they appear. In practice, the `xlink:form` attribute is fixed so that it need not actually be included in instances of the element, as follows:

```
<!ELEMENT group (document*)>
<!ATTLIST group
    xlink:form    CDATA    #FIXED    "group"
    steps         CDATA    #IMPLIED
  >
<!ELEMENT document EMPTY>
<!ATTLIST document
    xlink:form    CDATA    #FIXED    "document"
    href          CDATA    #REQUIRED
  >
```

XPointers

HTML links generally point to a particular document. Additional granularity (pointing to a particular section, chapter, or paragraph of a particular document) is not well-supported. Provided you control both the linking and the linked document, you can insert a named anchor into an HTML file at the position to which you want to link. For example:

```
<h2><a name="xpointers">XPointers</a></h2>
```

You can then link to this particular position in the file by adding a # and the name of the anchor into the link. For example, you might see the following in a table of contents:

```
<a href="#xpointers">XPointers<a/>
```

In practice, this solution is kludgy. You can't always modify the target document merely so the source can link to it. The target document may be on a different server and controlled by someone other than the author of the source. The target document may also change or move without notice to the author of the source.

Furthermore, named anchors violate the separation of markup from content. Placing a named anchor in a document says nothing about the document or its content – it's just a reference marker for other documents that does not add anything to the document's own content.

XLL allows much more sophisticated connections between documents through the use of XPointers. An XPointer can refer to a particular element of a document: to the first, the second, or the seventeenth such element, to the first element that's a child of a given element, and so forth. XPointers provide extremely powerful connections between documents without requiring the targeted document to contain additional markup just so its individual pieces can be linked to.

Unlike HTML anchors, XPointers don't just point to a point in a document. They can point to ranges or spans. An XPointer might be used to select a particular part of a document, perhaps so that it can be copied or loaded into a program. A few examples of XPointers follow:

```
root()
id(xtocid1087)
origin()
html(xtocid1087)
id(p12)
```

Each of these examples selects a particular element in a document. The document is not specified in the XPointer; rather, the document is specified by the XLink. The preceding XLinks do not contain XPointers, but adding XPointers isn't hard. Often, you'll simply append the XPointer to the URL separated by a #, just as with named anchors in XML. For example, if the preceding XPointers were to select elements from the page `http://www.w3.org/TR/REC-xml`, the complete URLs would look like the following:

```
http://www.w3.org/TR/REC-xml#root()
http://www.w3.org/TR/REC-xml#id(xtocid1087)
http://www.w3.org/TR/REC-xml#html(xtocid0987)
http://www.w3.org/TR/REC-xml#id(p2)
```

Normally, these URLs would be used as values of the `href` attribute of a locator element. For example:

```
<locator

 href = "http://sunsite.unc.edu/javafaq/javafaq.html#id(xtocid1087)">
 Austria</locator>
```

You can also use a vertical bar (|) instead of a # to indicate that you do not necessarily want the entire document. Instead, you want only the part of the document referenced by the XPointer. For example:

```
http://www.w3.org/TR/REC-xml|root()
http://www.w3.org/TR/REC-xml|id(xtocid1087)
http://www.w3.org/TR/REC-xml|id(xtocid0989).child(1,|text)
http://www.w3.org/TR/REC-xml|html(xtocid1087))
http://www.w3.org/TR/REC-xml|id(p2)
```

Whether or not the client is actually able to retrieve only a piece of the document is protocol-dependent. Most current Web browsers and servers won't be able to handle the sophisticated requests these XPointers imply. However, this strategy can be extremely useful for custom protocols that use XML as an underlying document format.

Absolute Location Terms

XPointers are built from location terms. Each *location term* specifies a point in the targeted document generally relative to another well-known point, such as the start of the document or another location term. The type of location term is given by a keyword like root, child, or id. Some location terms take arguments.

To demonstrate the point, it's useful to have a concrete example in mind. Listing 9-1 is a simple, valid document that should be mostly self-explanatory. It contains information about two related families and their members. The `root` element is `familytree`, which can contain `person` elements and `family` elements. Each person and family element has a required `id` attribute. `persons` contain a name, a birth date, and a death date, while `family`s contain a husband, a wife, and zero or more children. The individual persons are referred to from the `family` by reference to their IDs. Any `child` element may be omitted from any element. This data and its DTD will be revisited in Chapter 11. For now, take a minute to look it over and understand the different elements.

Listing 9-1: A family with people, children, and parents

```
<?xml version="1.0"?>
<!DOCTYPE familytree [

  <!ELEMENT familytree (person | family)*>

  <!-- person elements -->
  <!ELEMENT person (name*, born*, died*, spouse*)>
  <!ATTLIST person
    id      ID     #REQUIRED
    father  CDATA  #IMPLIED
    mother  CDATA  #IMPLIED
  >
  <!ELEMENT name (#PCDATA)>
  <!ELEMENT born (#PCDATA)>
  <!ELEMENT died (#PCDATA)>
  <!ELEMENT spouse EMPTY>
  <!ATTLIST spouse idref IDREF #REQUIRED>

  <!--family-->
  <!ELEMENT family (husband?, wife?, child*) >
  <!ATTLIST family id ID #REQUIRED>

]>
<familytree>

  <person id="p1">
    <name>Domeniquette Celeste Baudean</name>
    <born>11 Feb 1858</born>
    <died>12 Apr 1898</died>
    <spouse idref="p2"/>
  </person>

  <person id="p2">
    <name>Jean Francois Bellau</name>
    <spouse idref="p1"/>
  </person>

  <person id="p3" father="p2" mother="p1">
    <name>Elodie Bellau</name>
    <born>11 Feb 1858</born>
    <died>12 Apr 1898</died>
    <spouse idref="p4"/>
  </person>

  <person id="p4" father="p2" mother="p1">
    <name>John P. Muller</name>
```

```
      <spouse idref="p3"/>
  </person>

  <person id="p7">
    <name>Adolf Eno</name>
    <spouse idref="p6"/>
  </person>

  <person id="p6" father="p2" mother="p1">
    <name>Maria Bellau</name>
    <spouse idref="p7"/>
  </person>

  <person id="p5" father="p2" mother="p1">
    <name>Eugene Bellau</name>
  </person>

  <person id="p8" father="p2" mother="p1">
    <name>Louise Pauline Bellau</name>
    <born>29 Oct 1868</born>
    <died>11 May 1879</died>
    <spouse idref="p9"/>
  </person>

  <person id="p9">
    <name>Charles Walter Harold</name>
    <born>about 1861</born>
    <died>about 1938</died>
    <spouse idref="p8"/>
  </person>

  <person id="p10" father="p2" mother="p1">
    <name>Victor Joseph Bellau</name>
    <spouse idref="p11"/>
  </person>

  <person id="p11">
    <name>Ellen Gilmore</name>
    <spouse idref="p10"/>
  </person>

  <person id="p12" father="p2" mother="p1">
    <name>Honore Bellau</name>
  </person>

  <family id="f1">
    <husband idref="p2"/>
    <wife idref="p1"/>
    <child idref="p3"/>
    <child idref="p5"/>
    <child idref="p6"/>
    <child idref="p8"/>
    <child idref="p10"/>
    <child idref="p12"/>
```

```
    </family>

    <family id="f2">
      <husband idref="p7"/>
      <wife idref="p6"/>
    </family>

  </familytree>
```

In following sections, this document will be assumed to be present at the URL `http://www.theharolds.com/familytree.xml`. This address isn't a real URL, but in any case the emphasis here is on selecting individual parts of the document rather than the document as a whole.

ID

The `id` location term is one of the most simple and useful location terms. The term selects the document element that has an ID-type attribute with a specified value. For example, the following URI refers to Honore Bellau's person element:

`http://www.theharolds.com/familytree.xml#id(p12)`

The disadvantage of using the `id` location term is that it requires assistance from the targeted document. If the element to which you want to point does not have an ID-type attribute, you're out of luck. If other elements in the document have ID-type attributes, you may be able to point to one of them and use a relative XPointer (discussed in a following section) to point to the one you really want. Nonetheless, ID attributes work optimally when you control both the targeted document and the linking document so you can ensure that the IDs match the links, even as the documents evolve and change.

In some cases, such as a document without a DTD, the targeted document may not have ID-type attributes, although it may have attributes named `id`. In this case, the application may (or may not) try to make a good guess as to which element you were pointing to. Generally, it selects the first element in the document with an attribute of any type and name whose value matches the requested ID. On the other hand, the application is also free to select no elements.

ROOT

The `root()` location term selects the `root` element of the document and takes no arguments. For example, you could use the following URL to select the `html` element of the file `http://sunsite.unc.edu/javafaq/index.html`:

`http://sunsite.unc.edu/javafaq/index.html#root()`

Primarily, the `root()` location term is useful in compound XPointers as a basis from which to start. However, it can also be used to select the entire document in a URL that uses | to indicate that only part of the document is normally loaded.

HTML

The `html` location term selects named anchors in HTML documents. It has a single argument: the name of the anchor to which it refers. For example, the following named anchor exists in the file `http://sunsite.unc.edu/javafaq/javatutorial.html`:

```
<h4><A NAME="xtocid5004">Unix Installation Instructions</A></h4>
```

The XPointer that refers to this element follows:

```
http://sunsite.unc.edu/javafaq/javatutorial.html#html(xtocid5004)
```

The `html` location term exists primarily for backwards compatibility (to allow XML documents to link to HTML documents). Named anchors may also be used in XML documents, provided all attribute values are quoted, the `<A>` element and its attributes are declared in the DTD, and all other well-formedness criteria are met. In general, however, XML has better ways of identifying locations than named anchors.

ORIGIN

The fourth absolute location term, `origin`, is only useful when used in conjunction with one or more relative location terms. In intradocument links, which are links from one point in the document to another point in the same document, it's often necessary to refer to "the next element after this one" or "the parent element of this element". The `origin` location term refers to the current element so that such references are possible.

Relative Location Terms

`id`, `root`, `html`, and `origin` are absolute location terms, which can find a particular element in a document regardless of what else is in the document. Oftentimes, however, you want to find the first element of a given type, the last element of a given type, the first child of a particular type, the next element of a given type, and so forth. You can accomplish these tasks by attaching a relative location term to an absolute term to form a compound locator.

For example, suppose you want to link to the first person in the document `http://www.theharolds.com/familytree.xml`. The following URL accomplishes this task:

```
http://www.theharolds.com/familytree.xml#root().child(1,person)
```

This URL says to look at the document `http://www.theharolds.com/familytree.xml`, find its `root` element, and then find the first person element that's an immediate child of the `root` element. In Listing 9-1, the first person element is Domeniquette Celeste Baudean, my great-great-grandmother.

Although `familytree.xml` includes ID attributes on most elements, and although those are certainly convenient, these attributes are not required for simply linking into the document. You can select any element in the document by counting down from the `root` element. A number of other powerful selection techniques are discussed in this section.

Including `child()`, there are seven relative location terms, which are described in the following list. Each relative location term is relative to one of the four absolute terms discussed in the previous section (`id`, `root`, `html`, or `origin`) or to another relative term. Each relative location term serves to select a particular subset of the elements in the document. For instance, `following` selects all the elements that come after the target element. The `preceding` location term selects all the elements that come before the target element.

- `child` — The `child` locator element selects only the immediate children of the source element. For example, consider the following URL:

    `http://www.theharolds.com/familytree.xml#root().child(6,name)`

    This points to nowhere because there are no name elements in that document that are direct, immediate children of the `root`. There are a dozen name elements that are indirect children. If you'd like to refer to these, you should use the `descendant` relative locator element instead of `child`.

- `descendant` — The `descendant` locator element searches through all the descendants of the source, not just the immediate children. For example, `root().descendant(3, born)` selects the second born element encountered in a depth-first search of the document tree. (If you simply read through the XML document from top to bottom, the resulting order is depth-first.) In this example, `root().descendant(3, born)` selects Louise Pauline Bellau's birthday, `<born>29 Oct 1868</born>`.

- `ancestor` — The `ancestor` locator element searches through all the ancestors of the source, starting with the nearest, until it finds the requested element. For example, `root().descendant(2, born).ancestor(1)` selects the `person` element, which contains the second born element. In this example, that will select Louise Pauline Bellau's `person` element.

- `preceding` — The `preceding` locator element searches through all elements that occur before the source element. `preceding` has no respect for hierarchy. When it first encounters an element's start tag, end tag, or empty tag, `preceding` counts that element. For example, consider the following rule:

    `root().descendant(3, born).preceding(5)`

This rule says go to Louise Pauline Bellau's birthday, `<born>29 Oct 1868</born>`, and then move back five elements, thereby landing on Marie Bellau's `person` element.

◆ `following` — The `following` locator element searches through all elements that occur after the source element in the document. Like `preceding`, `following` has no respect for hierarchy. The first time it encounters an element's start tag, end tag, or empty tag, `following` counts that element. For example, consider the following rule:

```
root().descendant(2, born).following(4)
```

This rule says go to Elodie Bellau's birthday, `<born>11 Feb 1858</born>`, and then move forward five elements. This rule lands on John P. Muller's `name` element, `<name>John P. Muller</name>` after passing through Elodie Bellau's `died` element, Elodie Bellau's `spouse` element, Elodie Bellau's `died` element, Elodie Bellau's `person` element, and John P. Muller's `person` element, in that order.

◆ `psibling` — The `psibling` relative locator element selects the element that precedes the source element in the same parent element. For example, `root().descendant(2, born).psibling(1)` selects Elodie Bellau's `name` element, `<name>Elodie Bellau</name>`. `root().descendant(2, born).psibling(2)` doesn't point to anything because there's only one sibling before Elodie Bellau's `name` element.

◆ `fsibling` — The `fsibling` relative locator element selects the element that follows the source element in the same parent element. For example, `root().descendant(2, born).fsibling(1)` selects Elodie Bellau's `died` element, `<died>12 Apr 1898</died>`. `root().descendant(2, born).fsibling(2)` doesn't point to anything because there's only one sibling following Elodie Bellau's `name` element.

Because a relative location term alone is generally not enough to specify the targeted element uniquely, additional arguments further specify the targeted element by instance number, node type, or attribute. The possible arguments are the same for all seven relative keywords.

The most general XPointer is a single absolute term, followed by any number of relative terms. Each term in the list is relative to the one that precedes it, except of course for the first absolute term. Terms are separated from each other in the list by periods.

For example, the following fragment selects the first `name` element of the sixth person in the `root` document.

```
root().child(6,person).child(1,name)
```

In Listing 9-1, the fragment selects `<name>Maria Bellau</name>`.

Selection Rules

XPointers provide many ways to choose among particular elements in a given subset, including number, type, and attributes. You can also point to particular positions in a document by its string contents, though this approach generally does not guarantee a complete element will be selected.

SELECTION BY NUMBER

The simplest form of selection is by number. You can pass the number of the element you're seeking. For example, the following fragment selects the seventh element after the `root` element:

```
root().following(7)
```

In Listing 9-1, this fragment selects `<name>Jean Francois Bellau</name>`.

The argument may be either a positive or a negative integer. Negative integers count backwards from the target element. For example, the following fragment selects the element that immediately precedes the family with the ID `f1`.

```
id(f1).following(-1)
```

In Listing 9-1, this fragment selects the `person` element for Honore Bellau. In general, however, you should avoid negative numbers when possible and use an alternate selector. For example, the following fragment selects the same element:

```
id(f1).preceding(1)
```

In tree-oriented selectors like `child` and `descendant`, negative numbers indicate that one should start counting from the end of the parent rather than the beginning. The following example points at the last `person` element in the document:

```
http://www.theharolds.com/familytree.xml#root().child(-1,person)
```

The following points at the penultimate `person` element in the document:

```
http://www.theharolds.com/familytree.xml#root().child(-2,person)
```

SELECTION BY TYPE

If the document changes, selecting by instance number alone can lead to error. The addition or deletion of a single element in the wrong place can misalign all links that rely only on instance numbers.

Most selection rules include the type of the desired element. You've already seen examples in which `root().child(6, person)` selects the sixth `person` child of `root`. This example may still refer to the wrong person if a person element is added or deleted, but at least it will be a `person` element instead of something else like a family element.

You can also specify only a type and omit the instance number; for example, `root().child(person)`. This example selects all the `person` elements in the document.

Exactly what the application does when all `person` elements are targeted is up to the application. In general, something more complex than merely loading the document and positioning it at the targeted element is suggested, because there is in fact more than one targeted element. If the application is using this fragment to decide which parts of a document to load, it would obviously load all the elements of the specified type.

However, this scenario is relatively unusual. Generally, selection by type is used only to restrict further the elements selected until a single one remains targeted.

In addition to targeting elements of a given type, six wild cards target particular constructs that may occur in XML documents. The wild cards are listed in Table 9-1.

TABLE 9-1 WILD CARDS FOR SELECTION RULES

Wild card	Meaning
#element	Any XML element. #element is the default if no type is specified.
#pi	An XML processing instruction.
#comment	An XML comment.
#text	A text region directly inside an element or a CDATA section.
#cdata	A text region inside a CDATA section.
#all	All of the above: elements, processing instructions, comments, text, or CDATA sections.

SELECTION BY ATTRIBUTE

You can target elements according to their attributes by including the attribute name and value after the instance number and the type (which must be included). For example, to find the first element in the document `http://www.theharolds.com/familytree.xml` whose father is Jean Francois Bellau (ID p2), you could write the following:

```
root().child(1, person, father, p2)
```

You can use an asterisk (*) to indicate that any name or value is allowed. For example, the following rule selects the first person element in the document that has a father attribute:

```
root().child(1, #element, father, *)
```

In Listing 9-1, the rule selects Elodie Bellau's person element.

The following rule selects the first person element in the document that has an attribute value of p2, regardless of whether that attribute appears as a father, a mother, an ID, or another value.

```
root().child(1, person, *, *)
```

In Listing 9-1, the rule selects Jean Francois Bellau's person element.

You can use the #IMPLIED keyword to hunt for attributes that aren't specified. For instance, the following rule finds the first person element that doesn't have a father:

```
root().child(1, person, father, #IMPLIED)
```

In Listing 9-1, the rule selects Domeniquette Celeste Baudean's person element.

SELECTION BY STRING

Selecting a particular element is almost always good enough for pointing into well-formed XML documents. On occasion, however, you need to point into non-XML data or into XML data in which large chunks of non-XML text is embedded via CDATA sections, comments, processing instructions, or other means. In these cases, you may need to refer to particular ranges of text in the document that don't map onto any particular markup element. You can use a string selector for such cases.

A string selector selects the specified occurrence of a given string. Unlike most other selectors, a string selector can point to locations inside comments, CDATA, and so forth. For example, the following fragment finds the first occurrence of the string "Harold" in the document:

```
root().string(1, "Harold")
```

In familytree.xml, this fragment would target the position immediately preceding the *H* in Harold in Charles Walter Harold's name element. This targeting is not the same as pointing at the entire name element, as an element-based selector would likely do.

You can also add an optional third position argument to specify how many characters to the right of the beginning of the matched string you want to target. For example, the following fragment targets whatever immediately follows the first occurrence of the string `"Harold"`:

```
root().string(1, "Harold", 6)
```

An optional fourth argument specifies the number of characters to be selected. For example, the following fragment selects the first occurrence of the entire string `"Harold"`:

```
root().string(1, "Harold", 1, 6)
```

You can use string selectors with the empty string ("") to specify particular characters in the document. For example, the following fragment targets the 256th character in the document:

```
root().string(256, "")
```

(To be precise, the fragment targets the position between the 255th and 256th element in the document).

When matching strings, case and white space are considered, but markup characters are ignored. Instead of requesting a particular instance of a particular string match, you can ask for all instances by using the keyword `all` as the first argument. For example, the following rule selects all occurrences of the string `"Bellau"` in the document:

```
root.string(all, "Bellau")
```

This rule generally results in a discontiguous selection, which many applications may not know how to handle.

Spanning Locations

Some applications may need to specify a range of text rather than a particular point in a document. This capability can be accomplished via a span. A span begins at one XPointer and continues until another XPointer.

For example, suppose you wanted to select everything between the first `person` element and the last `person` element in `familytree.xml`. The following fragment accomplishes that:

```
root().span(child(1,person), child(-1,person))
```

Summary

In this chapter, you learned about XLL, XLinks, and XPointers. In particular, you learned the following concepts:

- ◆ Although XLinks can do everything HTML links can do and quite a bit more, they aren't supported by current applications.

- ◆ Simple links behave much like HTML links, but are not restricted to a single `<A>` tag.

- ◆ Link elements are identified by an `xlink:form` and `href` attributes.

- ◆ Link elements can describe the local resource with `content-title` and `content-role` attributes.

- ◆ Link elements can describe the remote document to which they're linking with `title` and `role` attributes.

- ◆ Link elements can use the `show`, `behavior`, and `actuate` attributes to suggest to the application how the link should be activated.

- ◆ Extended links can include more than a single URI in a linking element. Currently, the application decides how to choose between different alternatives.

- ◆ XPointers refer to particular parts of or locations in XML documents.

- ◆ XPointers can select the element they refer to via element names, attributes, string values, or position of element in the document.

- ◆ Different selectors can be combined to make more sophisticated compound selectors.

The next chapter examines one of the first real-world applications to use XML as the underlying data format: Microsoft's Channel Definition Format (CDF), which is used by Internet Explorer to push Web pages to subscribers.

Part III

Practical XML

Chapter 10

Pushing Web Sites with CDF

IN THIS CHAPTER

- ◆ Creating channels
- ◆ Channel attributes
- ◆ Channel children
- ◆ Advanced CDF
- ◆ Pushing software updates

THE CHANNEL DEFINITION FORMAT (CDF) is an XML-based markup language for defining channels. Channels allow Web sites to notify readers of changes to critical information automatically. Similar to subscription services, this method is alternately called *Webcasting* or *push*.

A CDF file is an XML document separate from, but linked to the HTML documents in a site. The channel defined in the CDF document establishes the parameters for a connection between the readers and the content on the site. The data can be transferred through *push* (sending notifications or even whole Web sites to registered readers) or *pull* (readers choose to load the page in their Web browser and get the update information).

There are three types of channels: a pull channel that readers see on their desktop, a push channel that notifies readers of updates via e-mail, and a push channel that sends the updated pages to readers to browse offline.

You do not need to rewrite your site to take advantage of CDF. The CDF file is simply one more file added to the site. A link to a CDF file, generally found on a site's home page, downloads a copy of the channel index to the reader's machine. This download enables the reader to access the current data – as defined in the channel – with a click of an icon.

Creating Channels

A CDF document identifies the content to be pushed to readers using the URLs of selected pages. To establish a channel, you need to complete the following tasks:

◆ Determine channel content

◆ Create the channel definition file

◆ Create a link from the page to the channel

Determining Channel Content

Before you get bogged down in the nitty-gritty technical details of creating a channel with CDF, you first have to decide what content belongs in the channel and how it should be delivered.

When using existing sites, consider the span of each layer in the hierarchy you want to present. The top layer of the channel probably should not have more than eight items. Do you want to use your existing site structure? Do you want to select particular pages out of the site and arrange them in a hierarchy specific to the channel?

Next, select the delivery method for channel content. Automatic messages can be e-mailed to registered readers. You can use Microsoft's notification, which highlights your active channel logo in Explorer, or provide a navigational map for readers. You can also take advantage of offline browsing, in which the page contents are cached on the reader's machine for later viewing.

After choosing your structure, you can create the actual CDF file with all necessary instructions.

Creating CDF Documents

A CDF document contains descriptions of and identifying information about the channel's contents, scheduling information, and logos to link the channel contents to the reader's desktop or browser. All of this information is marked up using a particular set of XML tags. The resulting document is a well-formed XML file. This document will eventually be placed on the Web server for clients to download.

A CDF document begins with an XML declaration, because a CDF document is an XML document and follows all XML document rules.

```
<?xml version="1.0"?>
```

The root element of a CDF document is <CHANNEL>. The channel element must have an HREF attribute that specifies the page being monitored for changes. The root channel element usually identifies the key page in the channel. For example, the following channel points to a newsletter that is updated monthly.

```
<CHANNEL HREF="http://www.writelivelihood.com/newscover.html">
 </CHANNEL>
```

The channel element may itself contain other channels to create a hierarchy, as shown in Listing 10-1.

Listing 10-1: A hierarchical channel

```
<?xml version="1.0"?>
<CHANNEL HREF="http://www.writelivelihood.com/newscover.html">
  <CHANNEL HREF="http://www.writelivelihood.com/column.html">
  </CHANNEL>
      <CHANNEL HREF="http://www.writelivelihood.com/tips.html">
  </CHANNEL>
</CHANNEL>
```

This channel definition creates a hierarchy of pages using nested channel definitions. The two pages, column.html and tips.html, are at the same level as children elements of the page newscover.html.

The channel content does not have to be restricted to a single site. You can include links to remote sites that contain relevant information for your readers, as demonstrated in Listing 10-2:

Listing 10-2: A channel definition that covers multiple sites

```
<?xml version="1.0"?>
<CHANNEL HREF="http://www.writelivelihood.com/newscover.html">
  <CHANNEL HREF="http://www.writelivelihood.com/column.html">
  </CHANNEL>
  <CHANNEL HREF="http://www.writelivelihood.com/tips.html">
  </CHANNEL>
  <CHANNEL HREF="http://www.stceo.org/stimulus.htm">
  </CHANNEL>
</CHANNEL>
```

In Listing 10-2, the second tier of content includes a reference to an external Web site where another periodical is available for download.

Passive channels – channels without push schedules – like Listings 10-1 and 10-2 don't do much. To make the push aspects work, you need to include scheduling information for updates. The scheduling information could be for the entire channel or individual items within the channel.

Linking the Page to the Channel

The third step in channel creation is to make the CDF file available to the reader. To complete this step, you must establish a link from the Web pages to the CDF file.

The basic option uses a simple anchor reference to add a link on the page. The Active Channel subscription feature expands on this option to identify the channel with logos, but requires some JavaScript to make the process work.

The link can be a simple anchor in the HTML, generally enclosing some text or an image that asks the user to subscribe to the channel, as demonstrated in Listing 10-3. When the reader activates this link in a CDF-enabled browser (a fancy way of saying Internet Explorer 4.0 and later), the browser downloads the file information and establishes the channel connection between the client and the server. Other browsers will probably ask the user to save the document.

Listing 10-3: HTML code that links to the CDF file `write_channel.cdf`

```
<a href="write_channel.cdf">
  <img src="channel_subscribe.gif" width=120 height=120
  border=0 alt="Subscribe to UserAble Write Livelihood's
  Monthly 'zine">
</a>
```

When readers activate the link, they download the CDF file to their machine and thereby create an index on their machine. Depending on their choices and your CDF options, they can either respond to notification from the channel or check the channel manually.

If you've added logos to your CDF, those logos appear on the reader's machine in one of two locations: on the desktop or in their browser's channel list.

Channel Attributes

In addition to the required HREF attribute, channel elements may contain four other attributes:

- ◆ BASE
- ◆ LASTMOD
- ◆ PRECACHE
- ◆ LEVEL

The general form of a channel tag follows:

```
<CHANNEL BASE="url" HREF="url" LASTMOD="yyyy-mm-dd" LEVEL="n"
  PRECACHE="yes|no">
</CHANNEL>
```

The BASE attribute is a URL to which relative URLs in the channel can be relative. For instance, if the BASE is set to "http://sunsite.unc.edu/javafaq/", then the HREF attribute may simply be "books.html" instead of "http://sunsite.unc.edu/javafaq/books.html". Subchannels can have their own BASE, which overrides the BASE set in the parent channel. Otherwise, the parent's BASE is used.

The LASTMOD attribute tells the reader's browser whether a download is required by specifying the date (in a year-month-day form like 1998-03-23) when the page referenced by the HREF attribute was last changed. The browser detects and compares the LASTMOD date given in the CDF file with the last modified date provided by the Web server. When the content on the Web server has changed, the cache is updated with the current contents. Readers can also refresh the channel manually.

The PRECACHE attribute instructs the browser to download the channel contents and cache the pages on the reader's machine. When you design the channel, remember that some readers use the cache method almost exclusively. As a result, any links in the channel contents are (effectively) dead or cause the reader to log on to be able to access them. If you are pushing documents across an intranet, the cache option doesn't make a lot of sense, as you'll be duplicating the same files on disks across the corporation. If you are delivering content to readers who pay for online time, you may want to construct content that can be cached and easily browsed offline. Also, embedded content like sound and Java applets do not cache with the content.

The LEVEL attribute only has meaning if the PRECACHE attribute is set to yes. LEVEL indicates how far down into the link hierarchy you want the browser to dig when caching the content. The hierarchy is the abstract hierarchy defined by the document links, not by the directory structure of files on the Web server. Frame pages are considered to be part of the same level as the frameset page, even though an additional link is required with the former.

Channel Children

In addition to other channels, each CHANNEL element can contain various child elements. Table 10-1 lists the possible children and their meanings.

TABLE 10-1 POSSIBLE CHILDREN OF CHANNEL

Tag	Meaning
TITLE	A name for the channel
ABSTRACT	A brief description of the channel
LOGO	An image that can be displayed to the user to indicate the channel
A	The page being pushed, deprecated in favor of the HREF attribute
SCHEDULE	Information telling a browser when a channel should be refreshed
LOGTARGET	A URL to which the log file should be uploaded
LOGIN	Indicates that the browsers should ask the user for a user name and password before updating the content

Let's look at these elements in more detail.

Content Descriptions

Each channel that you define can have a title and an abstract. The title of the channel is not the same as the title of the page. The channel title appears in the channel guide, the channel list, and the channel bar, as shown in Figure 10-1. The title element contains PCDATA.

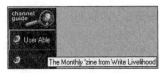

Figure 10-1: The title UserAble appears in the Channel Guide.

If included, the reader can view a description of the channel. Descriptions are contained in an <ABSTRACT> child of the channel element. The abstract also contains PCDATA. Each channel and item can have its own title and description. The description appears in a tool tip window as shown in Figure 10-1, which is based on Listing 10-4. Because tool tips have limited space, keep your abstracts to 200 characters or less. This length limitation cannot be required in a DTD, however.

Listing 10-4: Channels with titles and abstracts

```
<?xml version="1.0"?>
<CHANNEL HREF="http://www.writelivelihood.com/newscover.html">
   <TITLE>UserAble</TITLE>
   <ABSTRACT>The Monthly 'zine from Write Livelihood</ABSTRACT>

   <CHANNEL HREF="http://www.writelivelihood.com/column.html">
   <TITLE>Currents and Trends</TITLE>
   <ABSTRACT>A look at current concerns, trends,
and issues in the technical communication field.</ABSTRACT>
   </CHANNEL>
   <CHANNEL HREF="http://www.writelivelihood.com/tips.html">
   <TITLE>Tip of the Month Club</TITLE>
   <ABSTRACT>
      Clearing stumbling blocks from the field of
      endeavour. Contributions from various sources.
   </ABSTRACT>
   </CHANNEL>
</CHANNEL>
```

Logos

The LOGO element associates a graphic image with your channel. This element is a child of the <CHANNEL> it represents. You can add up to three logos to each channel and item element.

Logos can be used in a number of different ways within your channel: icons on the desktop, icons in the program launcher, and logos in the MS channel guide and channel bar. Internet Explorer supports GIF, JPEG, and ICO format images for logos – but not animated GIFs. Because icons may appear against a whole range of colors and patterns on the desktop, use GIFs with a transparent background for icons. With channel logos that match your Web site's look and feel, you can maintain that trademark appearance on your reader's desktop, channel bar, and channel guide.

The LOGO element has two attributes: HREF and STYLE. The style attribute enables you to have ICON, IMAGE, and IMAGE-WIDE logos. These logos are different sizes and types of images, as given in Table 10-2.

TABLE 10-2 VALUES FOR THE STYLE ATTRIBUTE OF THE LOGO ELEMENT

Image Type	Description
ICON	A 16 wide by 16 high pixel icon displayed in the file list and in the channel bar next to the child elements in a hierarchy, as shown in Figure 10-2.
IMAGE	An 80 wide by 32 high pixel image displayed in the desktop channel bar.
IMAGE-WIDE	A 194 wide by 32 high pixel image displayed in the browser's channel bar. If a hierarchy of channels are nested underneath, they appear when the reader clicks this logo, as shown in Figure 10-3.

Figure 10-2: The channel icons

Figure 10-3: The logo element of each channel defined in the hierarchy of UserAble and Currents and Trends

The CDF document for nested channels in Listing 10-5 uses various sizes of logos.

Listing 10-5: A channel with logos

```
<?xml version="1.0"?>
<CHANNEL HREF="index.html"
 BASE="http://www.writelivelihood.com/">
  <TITLE>Write Livelihood</TITLE>
  <ABSTRACT>Write Livelihood provides technical documentation
    solutions for companies large and small.</ABSTRACT>
  <LOGO HREF="logo_icon.gif" STYLE="ICON"/>
  <LOGO HREF="corp_logo_regular.gif" STYLE="IMAGE"/>
  <LOGO HREF="corp_logo_wide.gif" STYLE="IMAGE-WIDE"/>
  <CHANNEL>
     <TITLE>UserAble</TITLE>
     <ABSTRACT>Write Livelihood's Monthly magazine with product
       reviews, industry news, and personal views.</ABSTRACT>
     <LOGO HREF="logo_icon.gif" STYLE="ICON"/>
     <ITEM HREF="editorial.html">
       <TITLE>Currents and Trends</TITLE>
       <ABSTRACT>The view from our perch or is that
         porch?</ABSTRACT>
       <LOGO HREF="logo_icon.gif" STYLE="ICON"/>
     </ITEM>
  </CHANNEL>
</CHANNEL>
```

The bold lines determine the appearance of the channel bar entries. If the channel called UserAble had a wide image, that wide image would appear in place of the text.

When building channels, you can define the IMAGE and IMAGE-WIDE logos for the uppermost channel only or for any channel or item defined in the CDF. You are not guaranteed that the IMAGE-WIDE logos will be used for the secondary elements of the hierarchy.

When designing logos for the browser channel bar, keep in mind that changes to the content can result in a highlight gleam in the upper-left corner of the logo image. This gleam hides anything in the upper-left corner.

Also, if readers want more flexibility in the presentation of their browser window to stretch the window width beyond the recommended 194 pixels, the browser uses the top right pixel to fill the expanded logo.

Advanced CDF

So far, you have a visible connection that your readers can use to pilot themselves quickly to your site, but you don't have a way to push content or indicators to the readers. With the CHANNEL attributes and the TITLE and ABSTRACT elements, you can remedy this problem by building a working channel. In addition, you can add a number of features to your channel to make it work harder.

For example, readers would be unaware of a channel update – even if they refresh their channel – unless you change the LASTMOD date in the CDF file on your

Web server. You add functionality to the basic channel definition by scheduling updates, logging reader access, identifying pages in a channel, and creating usage attributes.

Scheduling Updates

The SCHEDULE element specifies when the channel is updated. The uppermost channel definition is the only child element that SCHEDULE may possess. Listing 10-6 shows a channel that will be updated weekly between March 29, 1998, and March 29, 1999.

Listing 10-6: A scheduled channel

```
<CHANNEL BASE="http://www.writelivelihood.com/">
  <TITLE>Quality In Development</TITLE>
  <ABSTRACT>TQ100 takes students through the software
    development cycle and shows key documents and
    operations, such as testing.
  </ABSTRACT>
  <LOGO HREF="tune_in_logo_icon.gif" STYLE="ICON"/>
  <LOGO HREF="tune_in_logo_image.jpg" STYLE="IMAGE"/>
  <LOGO HREF="tune_in_logo_image-wide.jpg" STYLE="IMAGE-WIDE"/>
  <SCHEDULE STARTDATE="1998-03-29" STOPDATE="1999-03-29"
    TIMEZONE="-0500">
    <INTERVALTIME DAY="7"/>
    <EARLIESTTIME DAY="1" HOUR="0"/>
    <LATESTTIME DAY="2" HOUR="12"/>
  </SCHEDULE>
</CHANNEL>
```

The SCHEDULE element has three attributes: STARTDATE, STOPDATE, and TIME-ZONE. The STARTDATE indicates when the scheduling begins and STOPDATE indicates when it should end; target the period between your usual site overhauls. If you change the structure of your Web site on a regular interval, use that interval. You'll need to write a new CDF that reflects the new structure.

The STARTDATE and STOPDATE use the same date structure: full numeric year, two-digit numeric month, and two-digit day of month (yyyy-mm-dd).

The TIMEZONE attribute shows the difference in hours between the server's time zone and Greenwich Mean Time. If the tag does not include the TIMEZONE attribute, the scheduled update occurs according to the reader's time zone – not the server's time zone.

The schedule can have up to three child elements: INTERVALTIME, which is a required element, and EARLIESTTIME and LATESTTIME, which are optional elements.

The channel in Listing 10-6 contains class notes, with the schedule indicating that the browser should update the channel once a week (INTERVALTIME DAY="7"). The update should be executed between Sunday midnight (EARLIESTTIME DAY="1" HOUR="0") and noon Monday (LATESTTIME DAY="2" HOUR="12").

The range of earliest and latest times for the update distributes the server load over time. In this case, the class is held on Mondays in the early afternoon, thus giving students time to update and review the contents before class.

The preceding schedule uses the reader's time zone to determine the update schedule. To force the update to a particular time zone, include the optional TIMEZONE attribute in the EARLIESTTIME and LATESTTIME tags:

```
<EARLIESTTIME DAY="1" HOUR="0" TIMEZONE="-0500"/>
    <LATESTTIME DAY="2" HOUR="12" TIMEZONE="-0500"/>
```

With LAN-connected users, you can control the span and force the system to update during slack server times. For example, to push an update across a LAN, you can choose the day of the week (for example, Sunday) and the time span (midnight to five in the morning). All browsers update during that five hour period. If you update across Internet connections, your readers have to be connected to the Internet for the browser to update the channel.

In the preceding example, the students know that the notes for Monday afternoon class are posted on the weekend, so they log on and get the update before class.

When the scheduled update occurs, readers are notified according to their subscription selections. There are two types of updates, changes to the CDF file and changes to the content. Internet Explorer adds a notification mark, called a *gleam*, to the channel logo in the browser channel bar when the LASTMOD date in the CDF file changes. This gleam may or may not reflect a change in the channel content, but you do not need to change the CDF file each time you update the content.

When subscribing to the site by using the link on the page, the reader can choose from three change notification methods, as shown in Figure 10-4.

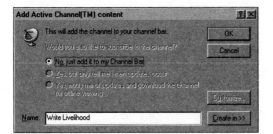

Figure 10-4: This dialog box enables the user to select how to be notified of changes.

If the reader selects the first option, the channel is added to the browser and active desktop channel bars. The reader must then select the channel to get the update. If the reader selects the second option, the browser performs the channel update check and notifies the reader of the change via e-mail. If the reader selects the third option, they will receive the channel contents, cached for offline viewing.

If you use the LEVEL attribute in the CHANNEL and ITEM tags and set it to a value higher than zero, the browser will go Web crawling during updates. Web crawling lets the browser collect more pages than listed in the channel. For example, the page listed in a channel contains a number of links to related topics. If the site has a fairly even hierarchy, like the one shown in Figure 10-5, you can safely add a LEVEL attribute to the topmost channel tag and allow the crawl to include all the pages at the subsequent levels. You can set LEVEL from zero to three.

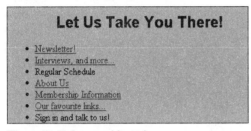

Figure 10-5: An even hierarchy

You can set the level for each subchannel you identify. The maximum level of three won't reach from index.html down to the artist bios in Figure 10-6 (bob_summers.html and alex_miesner.html) because the bios are four levels down. In this situation, you could create two subchannels: events and newsletter. With these subchannels, you can set the crawl level in these tags and thereby gather the entire site without listing every page.

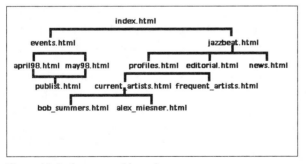

Figure 10-6: An uneven hierarchy

If you only want to select particular pages, create a CHANNEL or ITEM definition for each page and set LEVEL to zero in all the tags.

When the reader launches the browser, it checks the channel information for an update schedule. When the update schedule is found, the browser updates the channel and notifies the reader. Readers can wait for the gleam in the browser channel bar, receive e-mail, or get the channel contents downloaded to their machine.

Logging Reader Access

The LOG and LOGTARGET elements allow the Web server to track the reader's passage through the channel contents. The information is saved on the reader's machine, so even offline browsing can be captured. During a channel update, the reader's machine receives the new channel contents while you receive the log file, as shown in Listing 10-7.

Listing 10-7: A logged channel

```
<CHANNEL HREF="index.html" BASE="http://www.writelivelihood.com/">
  <TITLE>Write Livelihood</TITLE>
  <ABSTRACT>Write Livelihood provides technical documentation
    solutions for companies large and small.</ABSTRACT>
  <LOGO HREF="logo_icon.gif" STYLE="ICON"/>
  <LOGO HREF="logo_regular.gif" STYLE="IMAGE"/>
  <LOGO HREF="corp_logo_wide.gif" STYLE="IMAGE-WIDE"/>
  <LOG VALUE="document:view"/>
  <LOGTARGET HREF="c:\work\loghits.txt" METHOD="POST" SCOPE="ALL">
    <PURGETIME HOUR="12"/>
  </LOGTARGET>
  <SCHEDULE STARTDATE="1998-03-29" ENDDATE="1999-03-29"
    TIMEZONE="-0500">
    <INTERVALTIME DAY="1"/>
  </SCHEDULE>
</CHANNEL>
```

The LOG element specifies what will be saved in the log file. The CDF logging information can be stored in the Extended File Log format. The document:view value makes a log entry every time the reader browses the page associated with the LOG element.

The LOGTARGET element determines the use of the log file generated by the reader's activities. I require a destination identified with the HREF attribute, the transfer method, and scope. The HREF should identify a file location on your server and include the full file location. The METHOD attribute identifies how the information gets to the HREF location. POST is the first available METHOD. The last attribute, SCOPE, identifies the views to be logged; you can use OFFLINE, ONLINE, or ALL.

How the log file is handled is inherited through the channel. Therefore, the LOG-TARGET element should appear as a child of the top level CHANNEL tag. Logging is not inherited — each CHANNEL and ITEM element that you want included in the log must include a log element.

Identifying Pages in a Channel

CDF offers several methods for identifying the location of the content in a channel. Browsers resolve the HREF attribute first and then tackle the anchor tag inside the channel. Both HREF and the anchor tag use the full URL of the referenced page.

Whichever location you use for the link to the content, you can use a relative URL in the child elements if you specify a BASE attribute in the parent channel tag. You can also use the BASE attribute to change the behavior of the hierarchy display in Microsoft Internet Explorer. The base page will display in the browser window when child elements do not have an associated page. For example, you can declare the topmost channel as follows:

```
<CHANNEL BASE="http://www.writelivelihood.com/sdc/index.html">
```

You then create a hierarchy of child elements:

```
<CHANNEL>
<TITLE>Gathering Information</TITLE>
  <ITEM HREF="class01.html">
    <TITLE>Product Ideas</TITLE>
```

The page in the browser window does not change until the reader chooses the child element Product Ideas.

Using Microsoft Usage Attributes

Usage attributes extend the presence of your channel on the reader's desktop. The usage options consist of: desktop item, e-mail, screen saver, and precaching.

You can include a desktop item for readers to include in their Active Desktop (a Microsoft Internet Explorer extension), thus enabling you to put your name and information on the backdrop of the reader's monitor screen. To complete this desktop item, you need a separate CDF file containing the following elements: USAGE, OPENAS, HEIGHT, WIDTH, and CANRESIZE. These elements are Microsoft extensions to the base CDF standard that may or may not achieve popular adoption.

For an Active Desktop item, the USAGE attribute is set to DesktopComponent. Using the OPENAS tag, you can indicate the type for the location in the item HREF attribute. This may be an HTML file or an image. If you do not use the OPENAS tag, Microsoft assumes it is an HTML file. The HEIGHT and WIDTH specify the pixel space on the desktop that the item requires. The CANRESIZE tag indicates whether the reader can change your height and width on the fly.

The reader must have the Active Desktop up and running to see any desktop items you have included.

For the screen saver option, create a separate CDF with the screen saver, which can be an HTML page, as an item in the top level channel. If you include a screen saver, which can include links to content, readers are prompted to replace their current screen saver. Thus, readers may not see your screen saver.

If you include a CDF with the channel usage set to Email, you can specify an HTML page to be the source of the e-mail content. If you do not use the Email usage, readers who choose to receive e-mail notifications will receive the top channel content.

Readers can decide to receive notifications of channel updates via e-mail. To activate the e-mail options, readers must set up their subscription specifying their e-mail address.

Precaching channel content is useful for including items – such as sound and video clips – that you want to move to the reader's machine for use by channel pages. You can precache a single item or a series of items by defining a channel that includes the set of precached items, as in the following example:

```
<CHANNEL>
  <USAGE="none">
    <ITEM HREF="http://www.writelivelihood.com/welcome.wav"
      PRECACHE="yes">
    <ITEM HREF="http://www.writelivelihood.com/blowhorn.wav"
      PRECACHE="yes">
  </USAGE>
</CHANNEL>
```

This example pushes two sound files used at the site, thereby avoiding the difficulties associated with offline viewing.

Pushing Software Updates

Software update channels can both notify users of updates to software and deliver the product across the Internet. The delivery can also be extended to include installation.

To create a software push channel, create a CDF with the channel usage set to "SoftwareUpdate". As with any other channel, you can include the title, abstract, icon, logos, and schedule.

Within the software update channel, you need to define the child element for the update information specific to the software package. Attributes of the <SOFTPKG> tag define the package name, location, version, installation options, and style.

- The package name is the unique name for the distribution and a required attribute.

- The location uses the HREF and points to the URL of the page where the product information resides.

- The version is an optional attribute that distinguishes major and minor releases.

◆ The installation options determine whether the package should automatically install on the reader's machine. Using yes in the AUTOINSTALL attribute, you can set the channel to send the software package across the Internet to the reader without further reader action.

◆ The style attribute indicates whether the Microsoft Internet Component Download (MSICD) or ActiveSetup method downloads the files from the Internet. The MSICD option uses the Open Software Description (OSD) for instructions. ActiveSetup uses ActiveX for the download.

Children of the SOFTPKG element include ABSTRACT, IMPLEMENTATION, LOGO, TITLE, and USAGE.

◆ The ABSTRACT child element describes the software and uses the same tags and options as the standard CDF ABSTRACT.

◆ The IMPLEMENTATION element describes the configuration required for the software package. If the requirements described in the implementation tag are not found on the reader's machine, the download and installation do not proceed. IMPLEMENTATION is an optional element with the following children elements: CODEBASE, LANGUAGE, OS, and PROCESSOR.

◆ The CODEBASE element <CODEBASE FILENAME="url" HREF="url" SIZE="n" STYLE="ActiveSetup|MSCID"> defines the location of the downloadable files for the distribution.

◆ The LANGUAGE element defines the supported language of the interface using the RFC 1766 language codes. If multiple languages are available, separate the list with semicolons.

◆ The OS element can be Mac, Win95, or Winnt, thereby identifying the operating system required for the software. This element can have a child element called OSVERSION that identifies the required release.

◆ The PROCESSOR element can be Alpha, MIPS, PPC, or x86. This element describes the machine requirements for the software.

◆ The software update channel can have a logo, using the same parameters as the standard CDF logos: icon, image, and image-wide.

◆ The title of the software update channel uses the same options as the standard CDF title.

◆ The USAGE tag can also be included as a child element in the software update channel.

Once you've written the CDF file, you need a software description (OSD) file and a distribution unit. The OSD file is also written in XML and contains installation instructions for the reader's machine. The OSD file structure and language is described on the Microsoft Web site at `http://www.microsoft.com/standards/` `osd/`. The distribution unit is a compressed collection of the software and the OSD file. This is compressed using the cabinet (CAB) format and requires a digital signature from a certificate authority.

Summary

In this chapter, you learned:

- The Channel Definition Format (CDF) is an XML application used to describe data pushed from Web sites to Web browsers.

- CDF files are XML files. The root element of a CDF file is `CHANNEL`.

- Each `CHANNEL` element must contain an `HREF` attribute identifying the pushed page.

- `CHANNEL` elements may optionally contain `TITLE`, `ABSTRACT`, `LOGO`, `A`, `SCHEDULE`, `LOGTARGET`, and `LOGIN` elements.

- `CHANNEL` elements may nest to create hierarchical channels.

The next chapter demonstrates an application of XML in the field of genealogy.

Chapter 11

Developing a DTD from Scratch

IN THIS CHAPTER

◆ Organizing the data

◆ The person DTD

◆ The family DTD

◆ The family tree DTD

THE PRECEDING CHAPTER showed you how to use an existing markup language. Using a genealogy example, this chapter shows you how to develop an XML markup language and its associated DTD from scratch. In this chapter, you'll see the gradual development of several DTDs for genealogical data.

Organizing the Data

When developing a DTD from scratch, first organize your data – either in your head or on paper – with three basic steps:

1. Find the elements

2. Identify the fundamental units

3. Relate the elements

An easy way to get started is to explore the forms and reports available from other formats that describe this data. Genealogy is a fairly well-established discipline, and genealogists have determined fairly precisely exactly what information they need to have. This information is often included in a family group sheet, as shown in Figure 11-1.

You'll need to duplicate and organize these fields as necessary in your DTD. Of course, you can supplement or modify them to fit your specific needs.

Family Group Sheet   Page 1 of 1

Name	Samuel English Anderson	
Birth	25 Aug 1871	Sideview
Death	10 Nov 1919	Mt. Sterling, KY
Father	Thomas Corwin Anderson (1845-1889)	
Mother	LeAnah (Lee Anna, Annie) DeMint English (1843-1898)	
Other spouses: Cavanaugh		

Misc. Notes

Samuel English Anderson was known in Montgomery County for his red hair and the temper that went with it. He did once kill a man, but the court found that it was in self-defense. He was shot by a farm worker whom he had fired the day before for smoking in a tobacco barn.

Hamp says this may have been self-defense, because he threatened to kill the workers for smoking in the barn. He also says old-time rumors say they mashed his head with a fencepost.

Beth heard he was cut to death with machetes in the field, but Hamp says they wouldn't be cutting tobacco in Nov., only stripping it in the barn.

Marriage	15 Jul 1892	Cincinnati, Ohio, Central Christian Church

Spouse	Cora Rucker (Blevins?) McDaniel	
Birth	1 Aug 1873	
Death	21 Jul 1909	Sideview, bronchial trouble TB
Burial		Machpelah Cemetery, Mt. Sterling KY , Sideview
Father	Judson McDaniel (1834-1905)	
Mother	Mary E. Blevins (1847-1886)	

Misc. Notes

She was engaged to General Hood of the Confederacy, but she was seeing Mr. Anderson on the side. A servant was posted to keep Mr. Anderson away. However the girl fell asleep, and Cora eloped with Mr. Anderson.

Children

1 M	Judson McDaniel Anderson	
Birth	19 Jul 1894	Montgomery County, KY, 1893
Death	27 Apr 1941	Mt. Sterling, KY
Spouse	Mary Elizabeth Hart	
Marriage	16 Dec 1914	
Spouse	Zelda (Zorah?) Mefford	
2 M	Thomas Corwin Anderson	
Birth	16 Jan 1898	
Death		Probably Australia
3 M	Rodger French Anderson	
Birth	26 Nov 1899	
Death		Birmingham, AL
Spouse	Ruby McDaniel	
4 F	Mary English Anderson	
Birth	8 Apr 1902	August 4, 1902? , Sideview, KY
Death	19 Dec 1972	Mt. Sterling, KY
Spouse	Clark Hagan (Hazen?) Mitchell Major	
Marriage	4 Dec 1939	Fort Knox, KY
Spouse	Carl Edwin (Cully) Berg	
Marriage	1921	
Spouse	Burton Prewitt	

Figure 11-1: A family group sheet

Object-oriented programmers should note similarities between the techniques described in this section and the means they use to gather user requirements. In part, these similarities are the result of the author's own experience and prejudices as an object-oriented programmer, but the majority is due to the similarity of the tasks involved. Gathering user requirements for software is not dissimilar from gathering user requirements for markup languages. Database designers will probably also notice similarities between this section and what they do when starting a new database.

Finding the Elements

The first step in developing DTDs for a domain is to decide what the elements are. This isn't hard; it mostly consists of brainstorming to determine all the different things that may be included in your domain. As an exercise, write down all the different elements that may be part of genealogical information. To keep the problem manageable only include genealogy data. Assume you have a DTD available for standard text information like paragraphs, page titles, and so forth. Only include elements that specifically apply to genealogy.

Don't be shy. You can easily take elements out later if they're too much or don't seem useful. At this stage, you should expect to have some redundant elements as well as elements you'll throw away after further thought.

My assembled list follows. Your list is almost certainly different – you may have used different names for the same things. That's perfectly all right. There's no one right answer (which isn't to say that all answers are created equal, or that some answers aren't better than others).

father	mother	person	family	son	daughter
parent	child	baby	birthday	death date	marriage
baptism	occupation	religion	burial	grandfather	date
note	grave site	sex	surname	given name	middle name
aunt	niece	grandparent	grandmother	uncle	nephew

Finding the Fundamental Units

The preceding list has some effective duplicates, some unnecessary elements, and is probably missing a few elements. That's perfectly normal. Developing a DTD is an iterative process. Some time and additional thought are normally required before you feel comfortable with your results.

Next you must determine the fundamental units of your problem. These units are likely to be those elements that appear as immediate children of the root, rather than contained in some other element. The preceding list has two possibilities: family and person. Most of the other items in the list are either characteristics of a person or family (occupation, birthday, and marriage) or a kind of family or person (uncle, parent, and baby).

At this stage, most people say that family is the fundamental unit and families contain people. This approach is certainly consistent with the usage of the terms *parent* and *child* to describe the relationships of XML elements (a usage from which I temporarily eschew to avoid confusion with the human parents and children modeled in this chapter). For example, you may imagine that a family looks like the following:

```
<family>
  <husband>Samuel English Anderson</husband>
  <wife>Cora Rucker McDaniel</wife>
  <child>Judson McDaniel Anderson</child>
  <child>Thomas Corwin Anderson</child>
  <child>Rodger French Anderson</child>
  <child>Mary English Anderson</child>
</family>
```

This approach has a problem, however. A single person probably belongs to more than one family. I am both the child of my parents and the husband of my wife – that's two different families. Perhaps you can think of this situation as one extended family, but how far back should you go? Are my grandparents part of the same family? My great-grandparents? My in-laws? For the purposes of keeping records, genealogists generally agree that a family consists of a mother, a father, and their children.

Of course, the real world is more complicated. Some people have both adoptive and biological parents. Many people have more than one spouse over a lifetime. My father-in-law, Sidney Hart Anderson, was married fifteen separate times to twelve different women. Admittedly, Sidney is an extreme case. He was only three marriages away from tying the world record for serial marriage when he died. (Since then, someone has pushed the record to 28 consecutive marriages.) Nonetheless, you need to account for the same people who belong to different families.

The standard family group sheets used by the Latter Day Saints account for this problem by repeating the same people and data on different sheets. (Figure 11-1 shows a variation on this approach.) For computer applications, however, you should avoid storing the same information more than once. Among other issues, this approach avoids problems where data stored in one place is updated while data stored in another remains unchanged. Instead, connections can be made between different elements using ID and IDREF attributes.

Rather than the family, the fundamental unit of genealogy is the person. Each person is unique, with a single birthday, a single death date, (usually but not always) a single name, and various other data. Families are composed of different collections of persons. By defining the persons who make up a family and their roles inside the family, you define the family.

In real life, you may think of your family as an extended family including grandparents, daughters-in-law, uncles, aunts, and cousins, and perhaps completely unrelated individuals who happen to live in the same house. According to most genealogy standards, however, a family is a single pair of parents and their children. In some cases the names of these people may not be known, and in many cases there may be no children or spouses (a single individual qualifies as a family of one). A family does not include more distant relationships, however. A large part of genealogy establishes actual, biological, or adoptive relationships between people. In one's research, the Cousin Puss or Aunt Moot referred to in old letters may not be a relation at all! Such people should certainly be included in your records, but confusing their actual connections only leads to disorder further down the road.

Establishing Relationships

The third and final step before the actual writing of the DTD is to identify how the different pieces of information you want to track are connected.

Your two fundamental elements are the person and the family. You now must decide what you want to include in these two fundamental elements. A family is generally composed of a husband, a wife, and zero or more children. Either the husband or the wife is optional. If you wish to account for gay marriages (something most genealogy software couldn't do until recently), you can simply require one or two parents or spouses without specifying gender. Gender may then be included as an attribute of the person, which is where it probably belongs in any case.

What other information is associated with a family as opposed to individuals in the family? I can think of one major item important to genealogists: marriage information. The dates and places a couple was married (if any) and divorced (again, if any) are important information. While you could include such dates as part of each of the married individuals, it really makes sense to make it part of the family. As a result, a `family` will look something like this:

```
<family>
  <marriage>
    <date>...</date>
    <place>...</place>
  </marriage>
  <divorce>
    <date>...</date>
    <place>...</place>
  </divorce>
  <husband/>
  <wife/>
```

```
<child/>
<child/>
<child/>
</family>
```

Irrelevant or missing information can be omitted (for example, if a couple never divorced, their family would not include a divorce element).

The person element is likely to be more complex. The following list reviews the standard information you should store about a person:

- name

- birth

- baptism

- death

- burial

- occupation

- religion

- residence

- father

- mother

Of the preceding list, name, birth, death, burial, occupation, religion, and residence are likely to be elements contained inside a person. Father and mother are likely to be attributes of the person that refer back to the person elements for those people. Furthermore, a person needs an ID attribute to be referenced by family and other person elements.

The occupation, religion, and residence elements are likely to simply be CDATA (though residence could be modified to use a full address element as developed in Chapter 5). The other elements could be more complex, however.

For example, names are generally divided into family name and given name. This division enables you to develop a style sheet that boldfaces all people with the last name Harold, for example.

Birth, death, burial (and possibly baptism, because sometimes only baptismal records are available for an individual) can all be divided into a date (possibly including a time) and a place. Again, the place may simply be CDATA or a full address element. In most cases, full and meaningful addresses are not available.

Dates can either be stored as CDATA or broken up into day, month, and year. In general, it's easier to break them into day, month, and year than to stick to a common format for dates. On the other hand, allowing arbitrary text inside a date element also allows for dates like "1919–20", "before 1753", or "about 1800".

This section has not yet addressed the most interesting piece of all: notes. A note about a person may contain simple data (such as "first Eagle Scout in Louisiana") or a complete story (such as how Sam Anderson was killed in the field). The note may be personal information (such as religious affiliation) or medical information (such as which ancestors died of stomach cancer). If you have an interest in particular information like religion or medical history, you can make that interest a separate element of its own. Still, you should include some element that can hold arbitrary information of interest you dig up during your research.

You could include many other items in a person, photographs for instance, but let's stop here. Now you can move on to writing the DTD.

The Person DTD

By using external entity references, it's possible to store individual people in separate files, then pull them together into families and family trees later. Therefore let's begin with a DTD that works for a single person. We'll merge this into a DTD for families and family trees in the next section.

In developing a DTD, it's often useful to work backwards – first write out the XML markup you want to see using a real example and then write the DTD that matches the data. This section uses my great-grandfather-in-law Samuel English Anderson as an example, because I have enough information about him to serve as a good example and also because he's been dead long enough that no one should be upset about anything I say about him. (You'd be amazed at the scandals and gossip you dig up during genealogical research.) My information about Samuel English Anderson follows:

Name: Samuel English Anderson

Birth: 25 Aug 1871   Sideview

Death: 10 Nov 1919   Mt. Sterling, KY

Father: Thomas Corwin Anderson (1845–1889)

Mother: LeAnah (Lee Anna, Annie) DeMint English (1843–1898)

Misc. Notes

Samuel English Anderson was known in Montgomery County for his red hair and the temper that went with it. He did once kill a man, but the court found that it was in self-defense. He was shot by a farm worker whom he had fired the day before for smoking in a tobacco barn.

Hamp says this may have been self-defense, because he threatened to kill the workers for smoking in the barn. He also says old-time rumors say they mashed his head with a fence post.

Beth heard he was cut to death with machetes in the field, but Hamp says they wouldn't be cutting tobacco in Nov., only stripping it in the barn.

Now reformat this information into XML, as shown in Listing 11-1:

Listing 11-1: Samuel English Anderson

```
<?xml version="1.0"?>
<person id="p37" sex="M">
  <name>
    <given>Samuel English</given>
    <surname>Anderson</surname>
  </name>
  <birth>
    <place>Sideview</place>
    <date>25 Aug 1871</date>
  </birth>
  <death>
   <place>Mt. Sterling, KY</place>
   <date>
     <day>10 Nov 1919</date>
  </death>
  <spouse id="p1099"/>
  <spouse id="p2660"/>
  <father id="p1035"/>
  <mother id="p1098"/>
  <note>
    Samuel English Anderson was known in Montgomery County for his
  red hair and the temper that went with it. He did once kill a man,
  but the court found that it was in self-defense. He was shot by a
  farm worker whom he had fired the day before for smoking in a
  tobacco barn.
  </note>
  <note>
    Hamp says this may have been self-defense, because he threatened
  to kill the workers for smoking in the barn. He also says old-time
  rumors say they mashed his head with a fencepost.
  </note>
  <note>
    Beth heard he was cut to death with machetes in the field, but
  Hamp says they wouldn't be cutting tobacco in November, only
  stripping it in the barn.
  </note>
</person>
```

The information about other people has been removed and replaced with references to them. The ID numbers are provided by the database used to store this information (Reunion 5.0 for the Mac from Leister Productions).

Now construct a DTD for this example. The first element is `person`. This element may contain names, births, deaths, burials, baptisms, notes, spouses, fathers, mothers, occupation, and residence. I'm going to enable zero or more of each item in any order.

```
<!ELEMENT person (name | birth | death | burial | baptism |
   note | spouse | father | mother | occupation | residence)*>
```

At first glance, it may seem strange not to require a birth or some of the other elements – after all, everybody has exactly one birthday. Keep in mind, however, that what's being described here is more our knowledge of the person than the person him or herself. You often know about a person without knowing the exact day or year they were born. Similarly, you may sometimes have conflicting sources that give different values for birthdays or other information. Therefore, you may need to include extra data.

The `person` element has two attributes, an `ID`, which we'll require, and a `sex` which we'll make optional. (Old records often contain children of unspecified gender, who may or may not be named.)

```
<!ATTLIST person
    id  ID       #REQUIRED
    sex (M | F) #IMPLIED>
```

Next, the child elements must be declared. Four – `birth`, `death`, `burial`, and `baptism` – consist of a place and a date; this is a good place for a parameter entity reference:

```
<!ENTITY % event    "(place?, date?)*">
<!ELEMENT  birth   %event;>
<!ELEMENT  baptism %event;>
<!ELEMENT  death   %event;>
<!ELEMENT  burial  %event;>
```

A `place` contains only text while a `date` contains a date string. The example does not require a separate year, date, and month to allow less certain dates common in genealogy, such as "about 1876" or "sometime before 1920":

```
<!ELEMENT  place (#PCDATA)>
<!ELEMENT  date  (#PCDATA)>
```

`occupation`, `residence`, `religion`, and `note` all contain arbitrary text:

```
<!ELEMENT  occupation (#PCDATA)>
<!ELEMENT  religion   (#PCDATA)>
<!ELEMENT  residence  (#PCDATA)>
<!ELEMENT  note       (#PCDATA)>
```

spouse, father, and mother simply contain a link to the ID of a person. Again, this is a good opportunity to use a parameter entity reference:

```
<!ENTITY % personref "id NMTOKEN #REQUIRED">
<!ELEMENT   spouse   EMPTY>
<!ATTLIST   spouse   %personref;>
<!ELEMENT   father   EMPTY>
<!ATTLIST   father   %personref;>
<!ELEMENT   mother   EMPTY>
<!ATTLIST   mother   %personref;>
```

Ideally, the ID attribute would have type IDREF. However, as long as the person being identified may reside in another file the best you can do is require a name token type.

The name may contain surname and given elements; each element may contain text:

```
<!ELEMENT   name      (given?, surname?)>
<!ELEMENT   given     (#PCDATA)>
<!ELEMENT   surname   (#PCDATA)>
```

Listing 11-2 shows the complete DTD.

Listing 11-2: The person DTD

```
<!ELEMENT person (name | birth | death | burial | baptism |
   note | spouse | father | mother | occupation | residence)*>
<!ATTLIST person id   ID #REQUIRED>
<!ATTLIST person sex (M | F) #IMPLIED>

<!ENTITY % event    "(place?, date?)">
<!ELEMENT   birth    %event;>
<!ELEMENT   baptism %event;>
<!ELEMENT   death    %event;>
<!ELEMENT   burial   %event;>

<!ELEMENT   place (#PCDATA)>
<!ELEMENT   date  (#PCDATA)>

<!ELEMENT   occupation (#PCDATA)>
<!ELEMENT   religion    (#PCDATA)>
<!ELEMENT   residence   (#PCDATA)>
<!ELEMENT   note        (#PCDATA)>

<!ENTITY % personref "id NMTOKEN #REQUIRED">
<!ELEMENT   spouse   EMPTY>
<!ATTLIST   spouse   %personref;>
<!ELEMENT   father   EMPTY>
<!ATTLIST   father   %personref;>
<!ELEMENT   mother   EMPTY>
```

```
<!ATTLIST  mother  %personref;>

<!ELEMENT  name    (given?, surname?)>
<!ELEMENT  given   (#PCDATA)>
<!ELEMENT  surname (#PCDATA)>
```

The Family DTD

In the next step, you write a DTD for a family. As before, begin with a sample `family` element as shown in Listing 11-3:

Listing 11-3: Samuel English Anderson's family

```
<?xml version="1.0" standalone="no"?>
<!DOCTYPE family SYSTEM "family.dtd">
<family>
  <husband id="p37"/>
  <wife id="p1099"/>
  <child id="p23"/>
  <child id="p36"/>
  <child id="p1033"/>
  <child id="p1034"/>
  <marriage>
    <place>Cincinatti, OH</place>
    <date>15 Jul 1892</date>
  </marriage>
</family>
```

Here, only references to the members of the family are needed, not the actual family members themselves. The reference IDs are once again provided from the database where this information is stored. As long as the IDs are reliably unique and stable, their exact values aren't important.

Now that you have a sample family, prepare the DTD for all families. Listing 11-4 shows one example. Don't forget to include items needed for some families, such as a divorce. Listing 11-4 uses a parameter entity reference to pull in the information from the person DTD of Listing 11-2.

Listing 11-4: A DTD that describes a family

```
<!ENTITY % person SYSTEM "person.dtd">
%person;

<!ELEMENT family (husband?, wife?, marriage*, divorce*, child*)>

<!ELEMENT husband EMPTY>
<!ATTLIST husband %personref;>
<!ELEMENT wife    EMPTY>
<!ATTLIST wife    %personref;>
```

```
<!ELEMENT   child     EMPTY>
<!ATTLIST   child     %personref;>
<!ELEMENT   divorce   %event;>
<!ELEMENT   marriage  %event;>
```

Listing 11-4 assumes no more than one husband or wife per `family` element — a fairly standard assumption in genealogy, even in cultures where plural marriage is common, because it helps to keep the children sorted out. When documenting genealogy in a polygamous society, the same husband may appear in multiple family elements. When documenting genealogy in a polyandrous society, the same wife may appear in multiple family elements. Aside from overlapping dates, this is essentially the same procedure that's followed when documenting serial marriages. Of course there's nothing in the DTD that requires people to be married to have children (any more than there's anything in biology that requires it).

Overall, this scheme is more flexible than if a `family` needed to contain individual people rather than merely references to them. That approach would almost certainly require duplication of data across many different elements and files. Although this DTD doesn't handle gay marriages well, you can fix this deficiency by changing the `family` declaration to the following:

```
<!ELEMENT family (husband*, wife*, marriage*, divorce*, child*)>
```

Allowing multiple marriages and divorces in a single family may seem a little shaky, but these uncommon events do happen. (My mother-in-law married and divorced my father-in-law three separate times.)

The Family Tree

You can now combine the various families and people into a single grouping that includes everyone. The root element of this document, `familytree`, includes persons and families.

```
<!ELEMENT familytree (person | family)*>
```

Once again, it's not necessary to redeclare the `person` and `family` elements and their children. Instead, import these items by importing the `family` DTD with an external parameter entity reference. The family DTD then imports the person DTD:

```
<!ENTITY % family SYSTEM "family.dtd">
%family;
```

At this point, you should switch from using NMTOKEN types for spouses and parents to actual ID types. A `family` element that is part of a family tree should include all necessary person elements. You can do that by overriding the `personref` parameter entity declaration in the DTD for the family tree:

```
<!ENTITY % personref "id IDREF #REQUIRED">
```

That's all you need. Everything else is contained in the imported `person` and `family` DTDs. Listing 11-5 shows a complete family tree document with twelve people and one family.

Listing 11-5: A family tree

```
<?xml version="1.0" standalone="no"?>
<!DOCTYPE familytree [
  <!ENTITY % personref "id IDREF #REQUIRED">
  <!ELEMENT familytree (person | family)*>
  <!ENTITY % family SYSTEM "family.dtd">
  %family;
]>
<familytree>

<person id="p23" sex="M" father="p37" mother="1099">
  <name>
    <given>Judson McDaniel</given>
    <surname>Anderson</surname>
  </name>
  <birth>
    <place>Montgomery County, KY, 1893</place>
    <date>19 Jul 1894</date>
  </birth>
  <death>
    <place>Mt. Sterling, KY</place>
    <date>27 Apr 1941</date>
  </death>
</person>

<person id="p36" sex="F" father="p37" mother="1099">
  <name>
    <given>Mary English</given>
    <surname>Anderson</surname>
  </name>
  <birth>
    <place>August 4, 1902? , Sideview, KY</place>
    <date>8 Apr 1902</date>
  </birth>
  <death>
    <place>Mt. Sterling, KY</place>
    <date>19 Dec 1972</date>
  </death>
</person>

<person id="p37" sex="M" father="p1035" mother="1098">
```

```
    <name>
      <given>Samuel English</given>
      <surname>Anderson</surname>
    </name>
    <birth>
      <place>Sideview</place>
      <date>25 Aug 1871</date>
    </birth>
    <death>
      <place>Mt. Sterling, KY</place>
      <date>10 Nov 1919</date>
    </death>
  </person>

  <person id="p1033" sex="M" father="p37" mother="1099">
    <name>
      <given>Thomas Corwin</given>
      <surname>Anderson</surname>
    </name>
    <birth>
      <date>16 Jan 1898</date>
    </birth>
    <death>
      <place>Probably Australia</place>  </death>
  </person>

  <person id="p1034" sex="M" father="p37" mother="1099">
    <name>
      <given>Rodger French</given>
      <surname>Anderson</surname>
    </name>
    <birth>
      <date>26 Nov 1899</date>
    </birth>
    <death>
      <place>Birmingham, AL</place>
    </death>
  </person>

  <person id="p1035" sex="M">
    <name>
      <given>Thomas Corwin</given>
      <surname>Anderson</surname>
    </name>
    <birth>
      <date>24 Aug 1845</date>
    </birth>
    <death>
      <place>Mt. Sterling, KY</place>
      <date>18 Sep 1889</date>
    </death>
  </person>
```

```
<person id="p1098" sex="F">
  <name>
    <given>LeAnah (Lee Anna, Annie) DeMint</given>
    <surname>English</surname>
  </name>
  <birth>
    <place>Louisville, KY</place>
    <date>1 Mar 1843</date>
  </birth>
  <death>
    <place>acute Bright's disease, 504 E. Broadway</place>
    <date>31 Oct 1898</date>
  </death>
</person>

<person id="p1099" sex="F" father="p1100" mother="p1101">
  <name>
    <given>Cora Rucker (Blevins?)</given>
    <surname>McDaniel</surname>
  </name>
  <birth>
    <date>1 Aug 1873</date>
  </birth>
  <death>
    <place>Sideview, bronchial trouble TB</place>
    <date>21 Jul 1909</date>
  </death>
</person>

<person id="p1100" sex="M">
  <name>
    <given>Judson</given>
    <surname>McDaniel</surname>
  </name>
  <birth>
    <date>21 Feb 1834</date>
  </birth>
  <death>
    <date>9 Dec 1905</date>
  </death>
</person>

<person id="p1101" sex="F">
  <name>
    <given>Mary E.</given>
    <surname>Blevins</surname>
  </name>
  <birth>
    <date>1847</date>
  </birth>
  <death>
```

```
    <date>1886</date>
  </death>
</person>


  <family id="f25">
    <husband id="p37"/>
    <wife id="p1099"/>
    <child id="p23"/>
    <child id="p36"/>
    <child id="p1033"/>
    <child id="p1034"/>
  </family>

</familytree>
```

Summary

In this chapter, you developed a DTD from scratch. Along the way, you learned:

◆ Always begin a new DTD by considering the domain you're describing.

◆ Try to find the fundamental units of the domain that live at the root level. Everything else is likely to be a child or an attribute of one of these units.

◆ Try to avoid including the same data in more than one place. Use ID and IDREF and attributes to establish pointers from one element to another.

◆ Be sure to consider special cases. Don't base your entire design on the most obvious cases.

Quick Reference

Prolog Tags

XML Declaration

Every XML document should begin with an XML declaration, though for compatibility's sake this is not absolutely required. An XML declaration has the following form:

```
<?xml version="version_num" encoding="encoding_name"
 standalone="standalone_state"?>
```

- ◆ version – currently this is always 1.0, but it may be changed in future versions of XML

- ◆ encoding – one of the encoding names listed in Table A-10 of Appendix A, such as US-ASCII or UTF-8; default is UTF-8

- ◆ standalone – yes if this document does not use external DTDs or entities, no otherwise; default is no

Following are some example XML declarations:

- ◆ `<?xml version="1.0"?>`
- ◆ `<?xml version="1.0" standalone="yes"?>`
- ◆ `<?xml version="1.0" standalone="yes" encoding="Unicode"?>`
- ◆ `<?xml version="1.0" encoding="Unicode"?>`
- ◆ `<?xml version="1.0" encoding="ISO-8859-1"?>`
- ◆ `<?xml version="1.0" encoding="GB2312"?>`

Document Type Declaration

The three types of document type declarations are internal, external, and combined.

Internal Document Type Declaration

An internal document type declaration has the following form:

```
<!DOCTYPE root_element_name [
declarations
]>
```

The pieces are elucidated in the following:

- `root_element_name` – the name of the root element of the document
- `declarations` – element declarations, attribute declarations, entity declarations, notation declarations, processing instructions, comments

External Document Type Declaration

The two kinds of external document type declarations are SYSTEM and PUBLIC. The SYSTEM type locates the DTD via a URL. The PUBLIC type locates the DTD by name from a known repository of DTDs.

SYSTEM

A SYSTEM DOCTYPE declaration has the following syntax:

```
<!DOCTYPE root_element_name SYSTEM DTD_URL>
```

- `root_element_name` – the name of the root element of the document
- `DTD_URL` – the absolute or relative URL where the declarations of the document's elements can be found

Following are some examples of SYSTEM document type declarations:

- `<!DOCTYPE document   SYSTEM "http://sunsite.unc.edu/xml/dtds/publishers.dtd">`
- `<!DOCTYPE familytree SYSTEM "familytree.dtd">`
- `<!DOCTYPE mol       SYSTEM "http://www.venus.co.uk/omf/cml/doc/dtd/cml.dtd">`

PUBLIC

A PUBLIC DOCTYPE declaration has the following syntax:

```
<!DOCTYPE root_element_name PUBLIC "DTD_name" "DTD_URL">
```

◆ `root_element_name` – the name of the root element of the document

◆ `DTD_name` – the name by which the DTD can be located in a common repository

◆ `DTD_URL` – the absolute or relative URL where the declarations of the document's elements can be found

Following are some examples of `PUBLIC` document type declarations:

◆
```
<!DOCTYPE document PUBLIC  "-//Elliotte Rusty Harold//DTD
music publishers//EN"
"http://sunsite.unc.edu/xml/dtds/publishers.dtd">
```

◆
```
<!DOCTYPE HTML PUBLIC "-//W3C//DTD HTML//EN">
```

Combined Document Type Declaration

The combined DTD uses both internal markup declarations and declarations pulled in from an external DTD. It may use either a SYSTEM or a PUBLIC external DTD.

SYSTEM COMBINED:

A combined `DOCTYPE` declaration with `SYSTEM` has the following syntax:

```
<!DOCTYPE root_element_name SYSTEM DTD_URL [
   internal markup declarations
]>
```

An example of a combined document type declaration follows:

```
<!DOCTYPE familytree SYSTEM "genealogy.dtd" [
  <!ENTITY % personref "id IDREF #REQUIRED">
  <!ELEMENT familytree (person | family)*>
  <!ENTITY % family SYSTEM "family.dtd">
  %family;
]>
```

PUBLIC COMBINED:

A combined `DOCTYPE` declaration with `PUBLIC` has the following syntax:

```
<!DOCTYPE root_element_name PUBLIC "DTD_name" "DTD_URL" [
   internal markup declarations
]>
```

An example follows:

```
<!DOCTYPE document PUBLIC  "-//Elliotte Rusty Harold//DTD music
publishers//EN" "http://sunsite.unc.edu/xml/dtds/publishers.dtd" [
<!ELEMENT score(note)*>

]>
```

The ELEMENT Markup Declaration

All ELEMENT declarations have the following form:

`<!ELEMENT name content_type>`

The primary difference in these declarations is the content type, which may be one of three keywords (EMPTY, ANY, #PCDATA) or a list of the child elements.

◆ name — a unique XML name

◆ content_type — EMPTY, ANY, #PCDATA, child list

Following are some examples of element declarations:

◆ `<!ELEMENT  document ANY>`

◆ `<!ELEMENT street (#PCDATA)>`

◆ `<!ELEMENT city (#PCDATA)>`

◆ `<!ELEMENT state (#PCDATA)>`

◆ `<!ELEMENT zip (#PCDATA)>`

◆ `<!ELEMENT country (#PCDATA)>`

◆ `<!ELEMENT  husband  EMPTY>`

◆ `<!ELEMENT  marriage (place?, date?)>`

◆ `<!ELEMENT familytree (person | family)*>`

◆ `<!ELEMENT  family (husband?, wife?, marriage*, divorce*, child*)>`

◆ `<!ELEMENT publisher (name, email?, homepage?, address?, voice?, fax?)>`

◆ `<!ELEMENT address (street+, city, state, zip, country?)>`

The ATTLIST Markup Declaration

The `<!ATTLIST>` markup declaration declares the attributes of a specified element. This declaration's syntax follows:

`<!ATTLIST element_name attribute_name type "default value">`

- ◆ `element_name` – the name of the element to which this attribute applies

- ◆ `attribute_name` – any valid XML name unique among the element's attributes

- ◆ `type` – an enumerated list enclosed in parentheses and separated by vertical bars or one of the nine keywords (CDATA, ID, IDREF, IDREFS, ENTITY, ENTITIES, NMTOKEN, NMTOKENS, NOTATION) or an enumerated list as shown in Table Q-1

- ◆ `default` – the value the attribute takes on if no value is specified for the attribute; either a quoted string or one of the three keywords (#REQUIRED, #IMPLIED, or #FIXED) as given in Table Q-2

TABLE Q-1 ATTRIBUTE TYPE KEYWORDS

Keyword	Meaning
CDATA	character data; that is, nonmarkup text
ID	a unique name not shared by any other ID type attribute in the document
IDREF	the value of an ID type attribute of an element in the document
IDREFS	multiple IDs of elements separated by white space
ENTITY	the name of an entity declared in the DTD
ENTITIES	the names of multiple entities declared in the DTD, separated by white space
NMTOKEN	an XML name
NMTOKENS	multiple XML names separated by white space
NOTATION	the name of a notation declared in the DTD

TABLE Q–2 ATTRIBUTE DEFAULT KEYWORDS

Keyword	Meaning
#REQUIRED	each instance of the element must supply a value for this attribute
#IMPLIED	an instance of the element may omit the value of this attribute
#FIXED	the value of this attribute always has the specified value

---

Following are some examples of ATTLIST declarations:

- `<!ATTLIST greeting language CDATA "English">`
- `<!ATTLIST author name CDATA #REQUIRED>`
- `<!ATTLIST author email CDATA #REQUIRED>`
- `<!ATTLIST author extension CDATA #IMPLIED>`
- `<!ATTLIST image alt CDATA #REQUIRED>`
- `<!ATTLIST image width CDATA #REQUIRED>`
- `<!ATTLIST image height CDATA #REQUIRED>`
- `<!ATTLIST rect length CDATA "15px" width CDATA "34pt">`
- `<!ATTLIST author company   CDATA #FIXED "TIC">`
- `<!ATTLIST person id  ID #REQUIRED>`
- `<!ATTLIST person sex (M | F) #IMPLIED>`
- `<!ATTLIST family id ID  #REQUIRED>`
- `<!ATTLIST  spouse  id NMTOKEN #REQUIRED>`
- `<!ATTLIST  father  id IDREF #REQUIRED>`

The ENTITY Markup Declaration

The two kinds of entity declarations are general entity declarations and parameter entity declarations. General entity references are used inside the main body of the document or in a DTD section that becomes part of the document main body. Parameter entity references are used only inside a DTD.

These declarations can be further subdivided into internal parameter entities, external parameter entities, internal general entities, and external general entities.

Internal General Entity Declarations

Internal general entity declarations have the following syntax:

```
<!ENTITY name "replacement text">
```

- ◆ `name` – a unique XML name
- ◆ `replacement text` – the text that will be substituted for the entity reference

Following are some examples of general internal entity declarations:

- ◆ `<!ENTITY copy98 "Copyright 1998">`
- ◆ `<!ENTITY email "elharo@sunsite.unc.edu">`
- ◆ `<!ENTITY lm "last modified: ">`

External General Entity Declarations

External general entity declarations have the following syntax:

```
<!ENTITY name "URL">
```

- ◆ `name` – a unique XML name
- ◆ `URL` – a relative or absolute URL where the replacement text can be found

Following are some examples of general external entity declarations:

- ◆ `<!ENTITY copy98 "copyright.xml">`
- ◆ `<!ENTITY bio "http://www.macfaq.com/personal/bio.html">`

Internal Parameter Entity Declarations

Internal parameter entity declarations have the following syntax:

```
<!ENTITY % name "replacement text">
```

- ◆ `name` – a unique XML name
- ◆ `replacement text` – the text which will be substituted for the entity reference

Following are some examples of internal parameter entity declarations:

- ◆ `<!ENTITY % personref 'id IDREF #REQUIRED'>`

- ◆ `<!ENTITY % event   "(place?, date?)">`

External Parameter Entity Declarations

External parameter entity declarations have the following syntax:

`<!ENTITY % name SYSTEM "URL">`

- ◆ name – a unique XML name
- ◆ URL – a relative or absolute URL where the replacement text can be found

Following are some examples of external parameter entity declarations:

- ◆ `<!ENTITY % person SYSTEM "person.dtd">`

- ◆ `<!ENTITY % chemml SYSTEM`
  `"http://www.venus.co.uk/omf/cml/doc/dtd/cml.dtd">`

The NOTATION Markup Declaration

Notation declarations have the following syntax:

`<!NOTATION name SYSTEM "externalID">`

- ◆ name – a unique XML name
- ◆ externalID – EMPTY, ANY

Following is an example of notation declarations:

- ◆ `<!NOTATION hqx SYSTEM "StuffIt Expander">`

Appendixes

Appendix A

International Text

The ASCII Character Set

ASCII, the American Standard Code for Information Interchange, is by far the most common character set. As one of the original character sets, ASCII forms a sort of lowest common denominator for character set support requirements. It only defines all the characters needed to write U.S. English. These characters are mapped to the numbers 0–127. Table A-1 presents the ASCII character set.

TABLE A-1 THE ASCII CHARACTER SET

Code	Character	Code	Character	Code	Character	Code	Character
0	null	32	Space	64	@	96	`
1	start of heading (soh)	33	!	65	A	97	a
2	start of text (stx)	34	"	66	B	98	b
3	end of text (etx)	35	#	67	C	99	c
4	end of transmission (eot)	36	$	68	D	100	d
5	enquiry (enq)	37	%	69	E	101	e
6	acknowledge (ack)	38	&	70	F	102	f
7	bell (bel)	39	'	71	G	103	g
8	backspace (bs)	40	(	72	H	104	h
9	tab (\t)	41	)	73	I	105	i

Continued

TABLE A-1 THE ASCII CHARACTER SET *(Continued)*

Code	Character	Code	Character	Code	Character	Code	Character
10	linefeed (\n)	42	*	74	J	106	j
11	vertical tab	43	+	75	K	107	k
12	formfeed (\f)	44	,	76	L	108	l
13	carriage return (\r)	45	-	77	M	109	m
14	shift out (so)	46	.	78	N	110	n
15	shift in (si)	47	/	79	O	111	o
16	data link escape (dle)	48	0	80	P	112	p
17	device control 1 (dc1)	49	1	81	Q	113	q
18	device control 2 (dc2)	50	2	82	R	114	r
19	device control 3 (dc3)	51	3	83	S	115	s
20	device control 4 (dc4)	52	4	84	T	116	t
21	negative acknowledge (nak)	53	5	85	U	117	u
22	synchronous idle (syn)	54	6	86	V	118	v
23	end of transmission block (etb)	55	7	87	W	119	w
24	cancel (can)	56	8	88	X	120	x

Continued

Code	Character	Code	Character	Code	Character	Code	Character
25	end of medium (em)	57	9	89	Y	121	y
26	substitute (sub)	58	:	90	Z	122	z
27	escape (esc)	59	;	91	[	123	{
28	file separator (is4)	60	<	92	\	124	|
29	group separator (is3)	61	=	93	]	125	}
30	record separator (is2)	62	>	94	^	126	~
31	unit separator (is1)	63	?	95	_	127	delete

Characters 0–31 and character 127 are nonprinting control characters. These characters include the space, the carriage return, the line feed, the tab, the bell, and other similar characters. Many of these characters are leftovers from the days of paper-based teletype terminals. For instance, carriage return used to literally move the carriage back to the left margin, like on a typewriter. Linefeed moved the platen up one line. Aside from the few control characters previously mentioned, these characters aren't commonly used anymore.

Most other character sets you're likely to encounter are supersets of ASCII. In other words, they define 0–127 exactly the same as ASCII, but add additional characters from 128 on up.

ISO-8859

ISO-8859 defines ten eight-bit character encodings (based on ASCII) suitable for different scripts, with five more in active development. Table A-2 lists the ISO character sets with the most common languages and scripts for which they can be used. All sets share the same ASCII characters from 0 to 127 and include additional characters from 128 to 255.

TABLE A-2 THE ISO CHARACTER SETS

Character Set	Script	Languages
ISO-8859-1	Latin-1	ASCII plus the characters required for most Western European languages including Albanian, Afrikaans, Basque, Catalan, Danish, Dutch, English, Faroese, Finnish, Flemish, Galician, German, Icelandic, Irish, Italian, Norwegian, Portuguese, Scottish, Spanish, and Swedish. Omits the ligatures Ĳ (Dutch), Œ (French), and German quotation marks, however.
ISO-8859-2	Latin-2	ASCII plus the characters required for most Central European languages including Czech, English, German, Hungarian, Polish, Romanian, Croatian, Slovak, Slovene, and Sorbian.
ISO-8859-3	Latin-3	ASCII plus the characters required for English, Esperanto, German, Maltese, and Galician.
ISO-8859-4	Latin-4	ASCII plus the characters required for the Baltic languages Latvian, Lithuanian, German, Greenlandic, and Lappish; superseded by ISO-8859-10, Latin-6.
ISO-8859-5		ASCII plus Cyrillic characters required for Byelorussian, Bulgarian, Macedonian, Russian, Serbian, and Ukrainian.
ISO-8859-6		ASCII plus Arabic.
ISO-8859-7		ASCII plus Greek.
ISO-8859-8		ASCII plus Hebrew.
ISO-8859-9	Latin-5	Latin-1 except that the three Turkish letters ğ, ş, and ı take the place of the three Icelandic letters ð, þ, and ý.
ISO-8859-10	Latin-6	ASCII plus characters for the Nordic languages Latvian, Lithuanian, Inuit (Greenlandic Eskimo), non-Skolt Sami (Lappish), and Icelandic.
ISO-8859-11		ASCII plus Thai.
ISO-8859-12	Latin-7	ASCII plus Celtic.
ISO-8859-13	Latin-8	ASCII plus the Baltic Rim.
ISO-8859-14	Latin-9	ASCII plus Sami.
ISO-8859-15	Latin-10	A slight variation of Latin-1 that includes the Euro currency sign and a few extra French and Finnish characters.

ISO-8859-1 (Latin-1)

Latin-1 includes enough additional characters to write essentially all western European languages. Characters 0–127 are identical to ASCII characters 0–127 and are given in Table A-1. Characters 128–255 are given in Table A-3. The first 32 characters are mostly unused, nonprinting control characters.

TABLE A-3 THE ISO-8859-1 LATIN-1 CHARACTER SET

Code	Character	Code	Character	Code	Character	Code	Character
128		160	non-breaking space	192	À	224	à
129		161	¡	193	Á	225	á
130	bph	162	¢	194	Â	226	â
131	nbh	163	£	195	Ã	227	ã
132		164	¤	196	Ä	228	ä
133	nel	165	¥	197	Å	229	å
134	ssa	166	¦	198	Æ	230	æ
135	esa	167	§	199	Ç	231	ç
136	hts	168	¨	200	È	232	è
137	htj	169	©	201	É	233	é
138	vts	170	ª	202	Ê	234	ê
139	pld	171	«	203	Ë	235	ë
140	plu	172	¬	204	Ì	236	ì
141	ri	173	discretionary hyphen	205	Í	237	í
142	ss2	174	®	206	Î	238	î
143	ss3	175	¯	207	Ï	239	ï
144	dcs	176	°	208	Ð	240	?
145	pu1	177	±	209	Ñ	241	ñ

Continued

TABLE A-3 THE ISO-8859-1 LATIN-1 CHARACTER SET *(Continued)*

Code	Character	Code	Character	Code	Character	Code	Character
146	pu2	178	²	210	Ò	242	ò
147	sts	179	³	211	Ó	243	ó
148	cch	180	´	212	Ô	244	ô
149	mw	181	µ	213	Õ	245	õ
150	spa	182	¶	214	Ö	246	ö
151	epa	183	·	215	x	247	÷
152	sos	184	‚	216	Ø	248	ø
153		185	¹	217	Ù	249	ù
154	sci	186	º	218	Ú	250	ú
155	csi	187	»	219	Û	251	û
156	st	188	¼	220	Ü	252	ü
157	osc	189	½	221	Ý	253	ý
158	pm	190	¾	222	Þ	254	þ
159	apc	191	¿	223	ß	255	ÿ

MacRoman

The MacOS predates Latin-1 by several years. (The ISO-8859-1 standard was first adopted in 1987. The first Mac was released in 1984.) Unfortunately, this means that Apple had to define its own extended character set called MacRoman, which has most of the same extended characters as Latin-1 (except for the Icelandic letters Þ, þ, and ð) assigned to different numbers. MacRoman matches ASCII and Latin-1 in the lower 127 characters. As a result, text files that use extended characters often look funny when moved from a PC to a Mac or vice versa. Table A-4 lists the upper half of the MacRoman character set.

Table A-4 THE MACROMAN CHARACTER SET

Code	Character	Code	Character	Code	Character	Code	Character
128	Â	160	†	192	¿	224	‡
129	Å	161	°	193	¡	225	·
130	Ç	162	¢	194	¬	226	,
131	É	163	£	195	√	227	„
132	Ñ	164	§	196	ƒ	228	‰
133	Ö	165	·	197	˜	229	Â
134	Û	166	¶	198	?	230	Ê
135	á	167	ß	199	«	231	Á
136	à	168	®	200	»	232	Ë
137	â	169	©	201	…	233	È
138	ä	170	™	202	non-breaking space	234	Í
139	ã	171	´	203	À	235	Î
140	å	172	¨	204	Ã	236	Ï
141	ç	173	≠	205	Õ	237	Ì
142	é	174	Æ	206	Œ	238	î
143	è	175	Ø	207	œ	239	Ó
144	ê	176	8	208	-	240	Ô
145	ë	177	±	209	_	241	
146	í	178	=	210	"	242	Ò
147	ì	179	=	211	"	243	Ú
148	î	180	¥	212	'	244	Û
149	ï	181	µ	213	'	245	ı
150	ñ	182	∂	214	÷	246	ˆ
151	ó	183	Σ	215	?	247	˜

Continued

TABLE A-4 THE MACROMAN CHARACTER SET *(Continued)*

Code	Character	Code	Character	Code	Character	Code	Character
152	ò	184	Π	216	ÿ	248	¯
153	ô	185	π	217	Ÿ	249	˘
154	ö	186	∫	218	/	250	˙
155	õ	187	ª	219	¤	251	°
156	ú	188	º	220	‹	252	¸
157	ù	189	Ω	221	›	253	˝
158	û	190	æ	222	fi	254	˛
159	ü	191	ø	223	fl	255	ˇ

Windows ANSI

The standard American English Windows character set replaces the nonprinting control characters between 130 and 159 in Latin-1 with additional printing characters to stretch the available range. This modified version of Latin-1 is generally called Windows ANSI. Table A-5 lists the Windows ANSI characters that differ from Latin-1.

TABLE A-5 THE WINDOWS ANSI CHARACTER SET

Code	Character	Code	Character	Code	Character	Code	Character
128	undefined	136	^	144	undefined	152	~
129	undefined	137	‰	145	'	153	™
130	,	138	Š	146	'	154	š
131	ƒ	139	‹	147	"	155	›
132	"	140	Œ	148	"	156	œ
133	...	141	undefined	149	•	157	undefined
134	†	142	undefined	150	–	158	undefined
135	‡	143	undefined	151	—	159	Ÿ

Unicode

Unicode encodes each character as a two-byte unsigned number with a value between 0 and 65,535. Currently, more than 40,000 different Unicode characters are defined. The extra 25,000 spaces are reserved for future extensions. The Han ideographs use about 20,000 characters while the Korean Hangul syllabary uses about 11,000 characters. The remaining characters encode most of world's other languages. Unicode characters 0 through 255 are identical to Latin-1 characters 0 through 255.

A complete Unicode character table would occupy this entire book. To discover more information about the specific encodings of the different characters in Unicode, get a copy of *The Unicode Standard*, second edition, ISBN 0-201-48348-9, from Addison-Wesley. This 950-page book includes the complete Unicode 2.0 specification, including character charts for all the different characters defined in Unicode 2.0.

Unicode is divided into character blocks. Most languages require concurrent use of more than one of these blocks. Tables A-6 through A-9 list the ranges of the different scripts encoded by Unicode and provide a picture of its versatility.

TABLE A-6 UNICODE GENERAL SCRIPT BLOCKS

Character Blocks	Range	Languages	Notes
Basic Latin	0–127	U.S. English	Same as ASCII, see Table A-1.
Latin-1 Supplement	128–255	Most western European languages including Albanian, Afrikaans, Basque, Catalan, Danish, English, Faroese, Finnish, Flemish, Galician, Icelandic, Irish, Italian, Norwegian, Portuguese, Scottish, Spanish, and Swedish.	Same as characters 128–255 of Latin-1, see Table A-2.

Continued

TABLE A-6 UNICODE GENERAL SCRIPT BLOCKS *(Continued)*

Character Blocks	Range	Languages	Notes
Latin Extended-A	256–383	Most central European languages including Afrikaans, Breton, Basque, Catalan, Croatian, Czech, Esperanto, Estonian, French, Frisian, German, Greenlandic, Hungarian, Latin, Latvian, Lithuanian, Maltese, Polish, Provençal, Romansh, Romanian, Romany, Sami, Slovak, Slovenian, Sorbian, Turkish, and Welsh.	These languages also require the Basic Latin and Latin-1 blocks. Latin Extended-A adds the additional characters in Latin-2, Latin-3, Latin-4, and Latin-5 not included in Latin-1.
Latin Extended-B	383–591	Chinese and Japanese in Pinyin Latin transcription, Croatian, and Sami.	Mostly characters used to extend Latin scripts to handle additional languages.
IPA Extensions	592–687	Some African languages have adopted IPA symbols in part to represent sounds that aren't in the Roman alphabet.	The International Phonetic Alphabet, a language-independent standard for representing speech sounds.
Spacing Modifier Letters	688–767		Assorted symbols that indicate modification of the preceding or following letter.
Combining Diacritical Marks	768–879		Generally a character that appears above another character (for example, the squiggle above the õ).

Continued

Character Blocks	Range	Languages	Notes
Greek	880–1023	Modern Greek and Coptic.	Combined with the diacritical marks of the previous block, this block also includes ancient Greek.
Cyrillic	1024–1279	Russian, Ukrainian, Byelorussian, Moldovan, Serbian, and many languages of the former Soviet Union.	Many languages can be written in either the Cyrillic or the Roman alphabet. For instance, Croatian is essentially Serbian written in the Roman alphabet.
Armenian	1328–1423	Armenian	
Hebrew	1424–1535	Hebrew, Yiddish, and Judezmo.	
Arabic	1536–1791	Arabic, Kurdish, Pashto, Persian, Sindhi, and Urdu.	
Devanagari	2304–2431	Hindi, Sanskrit, and many other Indian languages.	This block is also used for parts of many other languages that require additional characters.
Bengali	2432–2559	Assamese, Bengali, and various other languages of northeastern India.	
Gurmukhi	2560–2687	Punjabi	
Gujarati	2688–2815	Gujarati	
Oriya	2816–2943	Oriya, Khandi, and Santali.	
Tamil	2944–3071	Tamil and Badaga.	
Telugu	3072–3199	Telugu, Gondi, and Lambadi.	
Kannada	3200–3327	Kannada and Tulu.	

Continued

TABLE A-6 UNICODE GENERAL SCRIPT BLOCKS *(Continued)*

Character Blocks	Range	Languages	Notes
Malalayam	3328–3455	Malalayam	
Thai	3584–3711	Thai, Kuy, Lavna, and Pali.	
Lao	3712–3839	Lao	
Tibetan	3840–4031	Tibetan, Ladakhi, and Lahuli.	
Georgian	4256–4351	Georgian	
Hangul Jamo	4352–4607	Korean	A syllabic script.
Latin Extended Additional	7680–7935	Vietnamese	Latin characters with unusual combinations of diacritical marks.
Greek Extended	7936–8191	Polytonic Greek	Greek characters with unusual combinations of diacritical marks.

TABLE A-7 UNICODE SYMBOL BLOCKS, 8192–10175

Block	Range	Examples	Notes
General Punctuation	8192–8303	‰, ', ", <, >, !!	Variations on hyphens, semicolons, periods, quotation marks, and so forth.
Superscripts and Subscripts	8304–8351	^{1}, ^{2}, ^{3}, ^{n}	
Currency Symbols	8352–8399	£	Currency symbols not contained in other blocks.
Combining Marks Symbols	8400–8447		Used to combine diacritical marks with for multicharacter groups.

Continued

Block	Range	Examples	Notes
Letter like Symbols	8448–8527	℅, ™, Ω	Symbols that look like or are formed out of letters (for example, the Angstrom symbol Å).
Number Forms	8528–8591	1/3, 2/3, 1/5, 3/8, I, II, III, IV, V, VI, i, ii, iii, iv, X, L, C, D, M	Vulgar fractions and Roman numerals.
Arrows	8592–8703	⇐, ⇓, ↑, ↓	Assorted arrows.
Mathematical Operators	8704–8959	⊃, ∈, √, Π, Σ	Various mathematical symbols.
Miscellaneous Technical	8960–9039	❷, →, ↔	Cropping symbols, APL symbols, bra-ket notation, and various others.
Control Pictures	9216–9279	NUL, SOH, STX, ETX, EOT, ENQ	Pictures of the ASCII control codes between 0 and 31.
Optical Character Recognition	9280–9311		Non-ASCII OCR characters plus the MICR characters used on checks.
Enclosed Alphanumerics	9312–9471	1., 2., (a), (b), ①, ②, ③	Circled and parenthesized letters and numbers, and numbers followed by a period.
Box Drawing	9472–9599	┘, ├, ┤, ┬, ┴, ┼, ═	Originated with DOS for spreadsheet-like graphics on character terminals.
Block Elements	9600–9631	■, ▪, ▌, ▏	
Geometric Shapes	9632–9727	■, ❑, ●, ◂, ○, ◗ ▲, ▶, ◀	Squares, triangles, and so forth.
Miscellaneous Symbols	9728–9983	♉, ♀, ♂, ♠, ♣, ♪	Signs of the Zodiac, chess pieces, musical notes, card suits, and assorted icons.
Dingbats	9984–10175	✂, ✩, ★, ↔, ➍, ➋	The Zapf Dingbats character set popularized by PostScript.

TABLE A-8 UNICODE CHINESE, JAPANESE, AND KOREAN BLOCKS, CHARACTERS 12288–55203

Block	Range	Language	Notes
CJK Symbols and Punctuation	12288–12351	Chinese, Japanese, and Korean.	Punctuation marks for Han ideographic representations.
Hiragana	12352–12447	Japanese	Cursive syllabic alphabet.
Katakana	12448–12543	Japanese	Noncursive syllabic alphabet.
Bopomofo	12544–12591	Mandarin Chinese	Phonetic characters used in dictionaries and for teaching. If Paris is French for London, then Bopomofo is Chinese for ABCs.
Hangul Compatibility Jamo	12592–12687	Korean	Syllabic alphabet.
Kanbun	12688–12703	Japanese	Used to indicate the reading order of classical Chinese in Japanese texts.
Enclosed CJK Letters and Months	12800–13055	Chinese, Japanese, and Korean.	
CJK Compatibility	13056–13311	Chinese and Japanese.	Squared Katakana words.
CJK Unified Ideographs	19968–40959	Chinese, Japanese, and Korean.	The Han ideographic characters.
Hangul Syllables	44032–55203	Korean	A syllabic alphabet.

Characters in the range 55296–65535 are mostly intended to maintain compatibility with other character encodings. Often, they are duplicate representations of characters present elsewhere in the Unicode space.

TABLE A-9 SURROGATES, PRIVATE USE, AND COMPATIBILITY
FORMS, 55296–65535

Block	Range	Language	Notes
Surrogates	55296–57343		This block will eventually be used to expand Unicode to the four-byte character set UCS.
Private Use	57344–63743		Applications may put extra characters here such as corporate logos.
CJK Compatibility Ideographs	63744–64255	Korean	268 duplicate encodings of ideographs that denote different pronunciations of the same word.
Alphabetic Presentation Forms	64256–64335	Latin, Armenian, and Hebrew.	Alternative glyphs for certain letters.
Arabic Presentation Forms	64336–65023	Arabic	Alternative glyphs for certain letters.
Combining Half Marks	65056–65071		Half diacritical marks that cross multiple characters.
CJK Compatibility Forms	65072–65103	Chinese used in Taiwan.	
Small Form Variants	65104–65135	Chinese used in Taiwan.	Smaller variants of standard ASCII punctuation characters.
Additional Arabic Presentation Forms	65136–65279	Arabic	Arabic letters with diacritical marks and contextual variants.
Half-width and Full-width Forms	65280–65519	Chinese, Japanese, and Korean.	Different widths of various ideographs.
Specials	65520–65535		The byte order mark and its reverse.

Encoding Names

Table A-10 lists the canonical names of the most common character sets used today, as given in the encoding attribute of an XML declaration. For encodings not found in this list, consult the official list maintained by the Internet Assigned Numbers Authority (IANA) at `http://www.isi.edu/in-notes/iana/assignments/character-sets`.

TABLE A-10 ENCODING NAMES

Canonical name	Languages/Countries
US-ASCII	English
UTF-8	Compressed Unicode
UTF-16	Compressed UCS
ISO-10646-UCS-2	Raw Unicode
ISO-10646-UCS-4	Raw UCS
ISO-8859-1	Latin-1, western Europe
ISO-8859-2	Latin-2, eastern Europe
ISO-8859-3	Latin-3, southern Europe
ISO-8859-4	Latin-4, northern Europe
ISO-8859-5	ASCII plus Cyrillic
ISO-8859-6	ASCII plus Arabic
ISO-8859-7	ASCII plus Greek
ISO-8859-8	ASCII plus Hebrew
ISO-8859-9	Latin-5, Turkish
ISO-2022-JP	Japanese
Shift_JIS	Japanese, Windows
EUC-JP	Japanese, UNIX
Big5	Chinese, Taiwan
GB2312	Chinese, mainland China

Continued

Canonical name	Languages/Countries
KOl8-R	Russian
ISO-2022-KR	Korean
EUC-KR	Korean, UNIX
ISO-2022-CN	Chinese

ISO-639 Two-Letter Language Codes

Table A-11 lists the ISO-639 two-letter language codes, which are used as part of public names for DTDs (as discussed in Chapter 6) and as a value of the xml:lang attribute (as discussed in Chapter 7).

TABLE A-11 THE ISO-639 LANGUAGE CODES

Code	Language	Code	Language	Code	Language
aa	Afar	ab	Abkhazian	af	Afrikaans
am	Amharic	ar	Arabic	as	Assamese
ay	Aymara	az	Azerbaijani	ba	Bashkir
be	Byelorussian	bg	Bulgarian	bh	Bihari
bi	Bislama	bn	Bengali	bo	Tibetan
br	Breton	ca	Catalan	co	Corsican
cs	Czech	cy	Welsh	da	Danish
de	German	dz	Bhutani	el	Greek
en	English	eo	Esperanto	es	Spanish
et	Estonian	eu	Basque	fa	Persian
fi	Finnish	fj	Fiji	fo	Faroese
fr	French	fy	Frisian	ga	Irish

Continued

Table A-11 THE ISO-639 LANGUAGE CODES *(Continued)*

Code	Language	Code	Language	Code	Language
gd	Scots Gaelic	gl	Galician	gn	Guarani
gu	Gujarati	gv	Manx Gaelic	ha	Hausa
he	Hebrew	hi	Hindi	hr	Croatian
hu	Hungarian	hy	Armenian	ia	Interlingua
id	Indonesian	ie	Interlingue	ik	Inupiak
is	Icelandic	it	Italian	iu	Inuktitut
ja	Japanese	jw	Javanese	ka	Georgian
kk	Kazakh	kl	Greenlandic	km	Cambodian
kn	Kannada	ko	Korean	ks	Kashmiri
ku	Kurdish	kw	Cornish	ky	Kirghiz
la	Latin	lb	Luxemburgish	ln	Lingala
lo	Laothian	lt	Lithuanian	lv	Latvian
mg	Malagasy	mi	Maori	mk	Macedonian
ml	Malayalam	mn	Mongolian	mo	Moldavian
mr	Marathi	ms	Malay	mt	Maltese
my	Burmese	na	Nauru	ne	Nepali
nl	Dutch	no	Norwegian	oc	Occitan
om	Oromo	or	Oriya	pa	Punjabi
pl	Polish	ps	Pashto, Pushto	pt	Portuguese
qu	Quechua	rm	Rhaeto-Romanic	rn	Kirundi
ro	Romanian	ru	Russian	rw	Kinyarwanda
sa	Sanskrit	sd	Sindhi	se	Northern Sámi
sg	Sangho	sh	Serbo-Croatian	si	Singhalese
sk	Slovak	sl	Slovenian	sm	Samoan

Continued

Code	Language	Code	Language	Code	Language
sn	Shona	so	Somali	sq	Albanian
sr	Serbian	ss	Siswati	st	Sesotho
su	Sundanese	sv	Swedish	sw	Swahili
ta	Tamil	te	Telugu	tg	Tajik
th	Thai	ti	Tigrinya	tk	Turkmen
tl	Tagalog	tn	Setswana	to	Tonga
tr	Turkish	ts	Tsonga	tt	Tatar
tw	Twi	ug	Uigur	uk	Ukrainian
ur	Urdu	uz	Uzbek	vi	Vietnamese
vo	Volapük	wo	Wolof	xh	Xhosa
yi	Yiddish	yo	Yoruba	za	Zhuang
zh	Chinese	zu	Zulu		

If no appropriate ISO code is available, you can use one of the codes registered with the IANA instead, though currently IANA only adds four codes. These codes can be found in Table A-12. The most current list can be found on the Web at `http://www.isi.edu/in-notes/iana/assignments/languages/tags`.

TABLE A-12 THE IANA LANGUAGE CODES

Code	Language
no-bok	Norwegian "Book language"
no-nyn	"New Norwegian"
i-navajo	Navajo
i-mingo	Mingo

If neither the ISO nor the IANA has a code for the language you need (Klingon perhaps?), you may define new language codes. These "x-codes" must begin with the string x- or X- to be identified as user-defined, private use codes. For example:

```
<p xml:lang="x-klingon">
```

ISO-3166 Two-Letter Country Codes

The value of the xml:lang attribute may include additional subcode segments, which are separated from the primary language code by a hyphen. Most often, the first subcode segment is a two-letter country code specified by ISO-3166, as listed in Table A-13. You can retrieve the most current list from http://www.isi.edu/in-notes/iana/assignments/country-codes.

For example:

```
<p xml:lang="en-US">Put the body in the trunk of the car.</p>
<p xml:lang="en-GB">Put the body in the boot of the car.</p>
```

TABLE A-13 ISO-3166 TWO-LETTER COUNTRY CODES

Code	Country	Code	Country	Code	Country
AF	Afghanistan	AL	Albania	DZ	Algeria
AS	American Samoa	AD	Andorra	AO	Angola
AI	Anguilla	AQ	Antarctica	AG	Antigua and Barbuda
AR	Argentina	AM	Armenia	AW	Aruba
AU	Australia	AT	Austria	AZ	Azerbaijan
BS	Bahamas	BH	Bahrain	BD	Bangladesh
BB	Barbados	BY	Belarus	BE	Belgium
BZ	Belize	BJ	Benin	BM	Bermuda
BT	Bhutan	BO	Bolivia	BA	Bosnia and Herzegovina
BW	Botswana	BV	Bouvet Island	BR	Brazil
IO	British Indian Ocean Territory	BN	Brunei Darussalam	BG	Bulgaria

Continued

Code	Country	Code	Country	Code	Country
BF	Burkina Faso	BI	Burundi	KH	Cambodia
CM	Cameroon	CA	Canada	CV	Cape Verde
KY	Cayman Islands	CF	Central African Republic	TD	Chad
CL	Chile	CN	China	CX	Christmas Island
CC	Cocos Islands	CO	Colombia	KM	Comoros
CG	Congo	CD	Democratic Republic of the Congo	CK	Cook Islands
CR	Costa Rica	CI	Côte d'Ivoire	HR	Croatia
CU	Cuba	CY	Cyprus	CZ	Czech Republic
DK	Denmark	DJ	Djibouti	DM	Dominica
DO	Dominican Republic	TP	East Timor	EC	Ecuador
EG	Egypt	SV	El Salvador	GQ	Equatorial Guinea
ER	Eritrea	EE	Estonia	ET	Ethiopia
FK	Falkland Islands	FO	Faroe Islands	FJ	Fiji
FI	Finland	FR	France	FX	Metropolitan France
GF	French Guyana	PF	French Polynesia	TF	French Southern Territories
GA	Gabon	GM	Gambia	GE	Georgia
DE	Germany	GH	Ghana	GI	Gibraltar
GR	Greece	GL	Greenland	GD	Grenada
GP	Guadaloupe	GU	Guam	GT	Guatemala
GN	Guinea	GW	Guinea–Bissau	GY	Guyana
HT	Haiti	HM	Heard Island and McDonald Islands	HN	Honduras
HK	Hong Kong	HU	Hungary	IS	Iceland
IN	India	ID	Indonesia	IR	Iran

Continued

TABLE A-13 ISO-3166 TWO-LETTER COUNTRY CODES *(Continued)*

Code	Country	Code	Country	Code	Country
IQ	Iraq	IE	Ireland	IL	Israel
IT	Italy	JM	Jamaica	JP	Japan
JO	Jordan	KZ	Kazakhstan	KE	Kenya
KI	Kiribati	KP	North Korea	KR	South Korea
KW	Kuwait	KG	Kyrgyzstan	LA	Laos
LV	Latvia	LB	Lebanon	LS	Lesotho
LR	Liberia	LY	Libya	LI	Liechtenstein
LT	Lithuania	LU	Luxembourg	MO	Macao
MK	Macedonia	MG	Madagascar	MW	Malawi
MY	Malaysia	MV	Maldives	ML	Mali
MT	Malta	MH	Marshall Islands	MQ	Martinique
MR	Mauritania	MU	Mauritius	YT	Mayotte
MX	Mexico	FM	Micronesia	MD	Moldova
MC	Monaco	MN	Mongolia	MS	Montserrat
MA	Morocco	MZ	Mozambique	MM	Myanmar
NA	Namibia	NR	Nauru	NP	Nepal
NL	Netherlands	AN	Netherlands Antilles	NC	New Caledonia
NZ	New Zealand	NI	Nicaragua	NE	Niger
NG	Nigeria	NU	Niue	NF	Norfolk Island
MP	Northern Mariana Islands	NO	Norway	OM	Oman
PK	Pakistan	PW	Palau	PA	Panama
PG	Papua New Guinea	PY	Paraguay	PE	Peru
PH	Philippines	PN	Pitcairn	PL	Poland
PT	Portugal	PR	Puerto Rico	QA	Qatar

Continued

Code	Country	Code	Country	Code	Country
RE	Reunion	RO	Romania	RU	Russian Federation
RW	Rwanda	SH	Saint Helena	KN	Saint Kitts and Nevis
LC	Saint Lucia	PM	Saint Pierre and Miquelon	VC	Saint Vincent and the Grenadines
WS	Samoa	SM	San Marino	ST	São Tomé and Príncipe
SA	Saudi Arabia	SN	Senegal	SC	Seychelles
SL	Sierra Leone	SG	Singapore	SK	Slovakia
SI	Slovenia	SB	Solomon Islands	SO	Somalia
ZA	South Africa	GS	South Georgia and the South Sandwich Islands	ES	Spain
LK	Sri Lanka	SD	Sudan	SR	Suriname
SJ	Svalbard and Jan Mayen	SZ	Swaziland	SE	Sweden
CH	Switzerland	SY	Syria	TW	Taiwan
TJ	Tajikistan	TZ	Tanzania	TH	Thailand
TG	Togo	TK	Tokelau	TO	Tonga
TT	Trinidad and Tobago	TN	Tunisia	TR	Turkey
TM	Turkmenistan	TC	Turks and Caicos Islands	TV	Tuvalu
UG	Uganda	UA	Ukraine	AE	United Arab Emirates
GB	United Kingdom	US	United States	UM	United States Minor Outlying Islands
UY	Uruguay	UZ	Uzbekistan	VU	Vanuatu
VA	Vatican City	VE	Venezuela	VN	Vietnam
VG	British Virgin Islands	VI	U.S. Virgin Islands	WF	Wallis and Fortuna Islands
EH	Western Sahara	YE	Yemen	YU	Yugoslavia
ZM	Zambia	ZW	Zimbabwe		

If the first subcode segment is not a two-letter ISO country code, it should be a character set subcode for the language registered with the IANA, such as csDECMCS, roman8, mac, cp037, or ebcdic-cp-ca. The current list is available from `ftp://ftp.isi.edu/in-notes/iana/assignments/character-sets`. For example:

```
<p xml:lang="en-mac">
```

Finally, the first subcode could be another x-code that begins with `x-` or `X-`. For example:

```
<p xml:lang="en-x-tic">
```

By convention, language codes are written in lowercase and country codes are written in uppercase. However, this is merely a convention. This is one of the few parts of XML that is case-insensitive.

Appendix B

Extensible Markup Language (XML) 1.0

THIS APPENDIX DUPLICATES the Extensible Markup Language specifications found at `http://www.w3.org/TR/REC-xml`.

W3C Recommendation 10-February-1998
  This version:

```
http://www.w3.org/TR/1998/REC-xml-19980210
http://www.w3.org/TR/1998/REC-xml-19980210.xml
http://www.w3.org/TR/1998/REC-xml-19980210.html
http://www.w3.org/TR/1998/REC-xml-19980210.pdf
http://www.w3.org/TR/1998/REC-xml-19980210.ps
```

  Latest version:

```
http://www.w3.org/TR/REC-xml
```

  Previous version:

```
http://www.w3.org/TR/PR-xml-971208
```

Editors:

Tim Bray (Textuality and Netscape) `tbray@textuality.com`

Jean Paoli (Microsoft) `jeanpa@microsoft.com`

C. M. Sperberg-McQueen (University of Illinois at Chicago) `cmsmcq@uic.edu`

Abstract

The Extensible Markup Language (XML) is a subset of SGML that is completely described in this document. Its goal is to enable generic SGML to be served, received, and processed on the Web in the way that is now possible with HTML. XML has been designed for ease of implementation and for interoperability with both SGML and HTML.

341

Status of this document

This document has been reviewed by W3C Members and other interested parties and has been endorsed by the Director as a W3C Recommendation. It is a stable document and may be used as reference material or cited as a normative reference from another document. W3C's role in making the Recommendation is to draw attention to the specification and to promote its widespread deployment. This enhances the functionality and interoperability of the Web.

This document specifies a syntax created by subsetting an existing, widely used international text processing standard (Standard Generalized Markup Language, ISO 8879:1986(E) as amended and corrected) for use on the World Wide Web. It is a product of the W3C XML Activity, details of which can be found at `http://www.w3.org/XML`. A list of current W3C Recommendations and other technical documents can be found at `http://www.w3.org/TR`.

This specification uses the term URI, which is defined by Berners-Lee et al., a work in progress expected to update IETF RFC1738 and IETF RFC1808.

The list of known errors in this specification is available at `http://www.w3.org/XML/xml-19980210-errata`.

Please report errors in this document to `xml-editor@w3.org`.

1. Introduction

Extensible Markup Language, abbreviated XML, describes a class of data objects called XML documents and partially describes the behavior of computer programs which process them. XML is an application profile or restricted form of SGML, the Standard Generalized Markup Language ISO 8879. By construction, XML documents are conforming SGML documents.

XML documents are made up of storage units called entities, which contain either parsed or unparsed data. Parsed data is made up of characters, some of which form character data, and some of which form markup. Markup encodes a description of the document's storage layout and logical structure. XML provides a mechanism to impose constraints on the storage layout and logical structure.

A software module called an XML processor is used to read XML documents and provide access to their content and structure. It is assumed that an XML processor is doing its work on behalf of another module, called the application. This specification describes the required behavior of an XML processor in terms of how it must read XML data and the information it must provide to the application.

1.1 Origin and Goals

XML was developed by an XML Working Group (originally known as the SGML Editorial Review Board) formed under the auspices of the World Wide Web Consortium (W3C) in 1996. It was chaired by Jon Bosak of Sun Microsystems with the active participation of an XML Special Interest Group (previously known as the SGML Working Group) also organized by the W3C. The membership of the XML Working Group is given in an appendix. Dan Connolly served as the WG's contact with the W3C.

The design goals for XML are:

1. XML shall be straightforwardly usable over the Internet.

2. XML shall support a wide variety of applications.

3. XML shall be compatible with SGML.

4. It shall be easy to write programs which process XML documents.

5. The number of optional features in XML is to be kept to the absolute minimum, ideally zero.

6. XML documents should be human-legible and reasonably clear.

7. The XML design should be prepared quickly.

8. The design of XML shall be formal and concise.

9. XML documents shall be easy to create.

10. Terseness in XML markup is of minimal importance.

This specification, together with associated standards (Unicode and ISO/IEC 10646 for characters, Internet RFC 1766 for language identification tags, ISO 639 for language name codes, and ISO 3166 for country name codes), provides all the information necessary to understand XML Version 1.0 and construct computer programs to process it.

This version of the XML specification may be distributed freely, as long as all text and legal notices remain intact.

1.2 Terminology

The terminology used to describe XML documents is defined in the body of this specification. The terms defined in the following list are used in building those definitions and in describing the actions of an XML processor:

may
Conforming documents and XML processors are permitted to but need not behave as described.

must
Conforming documents and XML processors are required to behave as described; otherwise they are in error.

error
A violation of the rules of this specification; results are undefined. Conforming software may detect and report an error and may recover from it.

fatal error
An error which a conforming XML processor must detect and report to the application. After encountering a fatal error, the processor may continue processing the data to search for further errors and may report such errors to the application. In order to support correction of errors, the processor may make unprocessed data from the document (with intermingled character data and markup) available to the application. Once a fatal error is detected, however, the processor must not continue normal processing (i.e., it must not continue to pass character data and information about the document's logical structure to the application in the normal way).

at user option
Conforming software may or must (depending on the modal verb in the sentence) behave as described; if it does, it must provide users a means to enable or disable the behavior described.

validity constraint
A rule which applies to all valid XML documents. Violations of validity constraints are errors; they must, at user option, be reported by validating XML processors.

well-formedness constraint
A rule which applies to all well-formed XML documents. Violations of well-formedness constraints are fatal errors.

match
(Of strings or names:) Two strings or names being compared must be identical. Characters with multiple possible representations in ISO/IEC 10646 (e.g. characters with both precomposed and base+diacritic forms) match only if they have the same representation in both strings. At user option, processors may normalize such characters to some canonical form. No case folding is performed. (Of strings and rules in the grammar:) A string matches a grammatical production if it belongs to the language generated by that production. (Of content and content models:) An element matches its declaration when it conforms in the fashion described in the constraint "Element Valid".

for compatibility
A feature of XML included solely to ensure that XML remains compatible with SGML.

for interoperability
A non-binding recommendation included to increase the chances that XML documents can be processed by the existing installed base of SGML processors which predate the WebSGML Adaptations Annex to ISO 8879.

2. Documents

A data object is an XML document if it is well-formed, as defined in this specification. A well-formed XML document may in addition be valid if it meets certain further constraints.

Each XML document has both a logical and a physical structure. Physically, the document is composed of units called entities. An entity may refer to other entities to cause their inclusion in the document. A document begins in a "root" or document entity. Logically, the document is composed of declarations, elements, comments, character references, and processing instructions, all of which are indicated in the document by explicit markup. The logical and physical structures must nest properly, as described in 4.3.2, "Well-Formed Parsed Entities."

2.1 Well-Formed XML Documents

A textual object is a well-formed XML document if:

1. Taken as a whole, it matches the production labeled `document`.

2. It meets all the well-formedness constraints given in this specification.

3. Each of the parsed entities which is referenced directly or indirectly within the document is well-formed.

Document

```
[1]document::= prolog element Misc*
```

Matching the `document` production implies that:

1. It contains one or more elements.

2. There is exactly one element, called the root, or document element, no part of which appears in the content of any other element. For all other elements, if the start-tag is in the content of another element, the end-tag is in the content of the same element. More simply stated, the elements, delimited by start- and end-tags, nest properly within each other.

As a consequence of this, for each non-root element `C` in the document, there is one other element `P` in the document such that `C` is in the content of `P`, but is not in the content of any other element that is in the content of `P`. `P` is referred to as the parent of `C`, and `C` as a child of `P`.

2.2 Characters

A parsed entity contains text, a sequence of characters, which may represent markup or character data. A character is an atomic unit of text as specified by ISO/IEC 10646. Legal characters are tab, carriage return, line feed, and the legal graphic characters of Unicode and ISO/IEC 10646. The use of "compatibility characters", as defined in section 6.8 of Unicode, is discouraged.

Character Range

```
[2]Char::= #x9 | #xA | #xD | [#x20-#xD7FF]
 | [#xE000-#xFFFD] | [#x10000-#x10FFFF]
/* any Unicode character, excluding the surrogate blocks, FFFE, and
 FFFF. */
```

The mechanism for encoding character code points into bit patterns may vary from entity to entity. All XML processors must accept the UTF-8 and UTF-16 encodings of 10646; the mechanisms for signaling which of the two is in use, or for bringing other encodings into play, are discussed later, in 4.3.3, "Character Encoding in Entities."

2.3 Common Syntactic Constructs

This section defines some symbols used widely in the grammar.

S (white space) consists of one or more space (#x20) characters, carriage returns, line feeds, or tabs.

White Space

```
[3] S::= (#x20 | #x9 | #xD | #xA)+
```

Characters are classified for convenience as letters, digits, or other characters. Letters consist of an alphabetic or syllabic base character possibly followed by one or more combining characters, or of an ideographic character. Full definitions of the specific characters in each class are given in B, "Character Classes."

A Name is a token beginning with a letter or one of a few punctuation characters, and continuing with letters, digits, hyphens, underscores, colons, or full stops, together known as name characters. Names beginning with the string "xml", or any string which would match (('X'|'x') ('M'|'m') ('L'|'l')), are reserved for standardization in this or future versions of this specification.

Note: The colon character within XML names is reserved for experimentation with name spaces. Its meaning is expected to be standardized at some future point, at which point those documents using the colon for experimental purposes may need to be updated. (There is no guarantee that any name-space mechanism adopted for XML will in fact use the colon as a name-space delimiter.) In practice, this means that authors should not use the colon in XML names except as part of name-space experiments, but that XML processors should accept the colon as a name character.

An `Nmtoken` (name token) is any mixture of name characters.

Names and Tokens

```
[4] NameChar::= Letter | Digit | '.' | '-' | '_' | ':' |
 CombiningChar | Extender
[5] Name::= (Letter | '_' | ':') (NameChar)*
[6] Names::= Name (S Name)*
[7] Nmtoken::= (NameChar)+
[8] Nmtokens::= Nmtoken (S Nmtoken)*
```

Literal data is any quoted string not containing the quotation mark used as a delimiter for that string. Literals are used for specifying the content of internal entities (`EntityValue`), the values of attributes (`AttValue`), and external identifiers (`SystemLiteral`). Note that a `SystemLiteral` can be parsed without scanning for markup.

Literals

```
[9] EntityValue::= '"' ([^%&"] | PEReference | Reference)* '"'
 | "'" ([^%&'] | PEReference | Reference)* "'"
[10] AttValue::= '"' ([^<&"] | Reference)* '"'
 | "'" ([^<&'] | Reference)* "'"
[11] SystemLiteral::= ('"' [^"]* '"') | ("'" [^']* "'")
[12] PubidLiteral::= '"' PubidChar* '"' | "'" (PubidChar - "'")* "'"
[13] PubidChar::= #x20 | #xD | #xA | [a-zA-Z0-9] | [-
 '()+,./:=?;!*#@$_%]
```

2.4 Character Data and Markup

Text consists of intermingled character data and markup. Markup takes the form of start-tags, end-tags, empty-element tags, entity references, character references, comments, CDATA section delimiters, document type declarations, and processing instructions.

All text that is not markup constitutes the character data of the document.

The ampersand character (&) and the left angle bracket (<) may appear in their literal form only when used as markup delimiters, or within a comment, a processing instruction, or a CDATA section. They are also legal within the literal entity value of an internal entity declaration; see 4.3.2, "Well-Formed Parsed Entities". If they are needed elsewhere, they must be escaped using either numeric character references or the strings "&" and "<" respectively. The right angle bracket (>) may be represented using the string ">", and must, for compatibility, be escaped using ">" or a character reference when it appears in the string "]]>" in content, when that string is not marking the end of a CDATA section.

In the content of elements, character data is any string of characters which does not contain the start-delimiter of any markup. In a CDATA section, character data is any string of characters not including the CDATA-section-close delimiter, "]]>".

To allow attribute values to contain both single and double quotes, the apostrophe or single-quote character (') may be represented as "'", and the double-quote character (") as """.

Character Data

```
[14] CharData::= [^<&]* - ([^<&]* ']]>' [^<&]*)
```

2.5 Comments

Comments may appear anywhere in a document outside other markup; in addition, they may appear within the document type declaration at places allowed by the grammar. They are not part of the document's character data; an XML processor may, but need not, make it possible for an application to retrieve the text of comments. For compatibility, the string "--" (double-hyphen) must not occur within comments.

Comments

```
[15] Comment::= '<!--' ((Char - '-') | ('-' (Char - '-')))* '-->'
```

An example of a comment:

```
<!-- declarations for <head> & <body> -->
```

2.6 Processing Instructions

Processing instructions (PIs) allow documents to contain instructions for applications.

Processing Instructions

```
[16] PI::= '<?' PITarget (S (Char* - (Char* '?>' Char*)))? '?>'
[17] PITarget::= Name - (('X' | 'x') ('M' | 'm') ('L' | 'l'))
```

PIs are not part of the document's character data, but must be passed through to the application. The PI begins with a target (PITarget) used to identify the application to which the instruction is directed. The target names "XML", "xml", and so on are reserved for standardization in this or future versions of this specification. The XML Notation mechanism may be used for formal declaration of PI targets.

2.7 CDATA Sections

CDATA sections may occur anywhere character data may occur; they are used to escape blocks of text containing characters which would otherwise be recognized as markup. CDATA sections begin with the string `<![CDATA[` and end with the string `]]>`:

CDATA Sections

```
[18] CDSect::= CDStart CData CDEnd
[19] CDStart::= '<![CDATA['
[20] CData::= (Char* - (Char* ']]>' Char*))
[21] CDEnd::= ']]>'
```

Within a CDATA section, only the `CDEnd` string is recognized as markup, so that left angle brackets and ampersands may occur in their literal form; they need not (and cannot) be escaped using `"&lt;"` and `"&amp;"`. CDATA sections cannot nest.

An example of a CDATA section, in which `"<greeting>"` and `"</greeting>"` are recognized as character data, not markup:

```
<![CDATA[<greeting>Hello, world!</greeting>]]>
```

2.8 Prolog and Document Type Declaration

XML documents may, and should, begin with an XML declaration which specifies the version of XML being used. For example, the following is a complete XML document, well-formed but not valid:

```
<?xml version="1.0"?>
<greeting>Hello, world!</greeting>
```

and so is this:

```
<greeting>Hello, world!</greeting>
```

The version number `1.0` should be used to indicate conformance to this version of this specification; it is an error for a document to use the value `1.0` if it does not conform to this version of this specification. It is the intent of the XML working group to give later versions of this specification numbers other than `1.0`, but this intent does not indicate a commitment to produce any future versions of XML, nor if any are produced, to use any particular numbering scheme. Since future versions are not ruled out, this construct is provided as a means to allow the possibility of automatic version recognition, should it become necessary. Processors may signal an error if they receive documents labeled with versions they do not support.

The function of the markup in an XML document is to describe its storage and logical structure and to associate attribute-value pairs with its logical structures. XML provides a mechanism, the document type declaration, to define constraints on the logical structure and to support the use of predefined storage units. An XML document is valid if it has an associated document type declaration and if the document complies with the constraints expressed in it.

The document type declaration must appear before the first element in the document.

Prolog

```
[22] prolog::= XMLDecl? Misc* (doctypedecl Misc*)?
[23] XMLDecl::= '<?xml' VersionInfo EncodingDecl? SDDecl? S? '?>'
[24] VersionInfo::= S 'version' Eq (' VersionNum ' | " VersionNum ")
[25] Eq::= S? '=' S?
[26] VersionNum::= ([a-zA-ZO-9_.:] || '-')+
[27] Misc::= Comment | PI | S
```

The XML document type declaration contains or points to markup declarations that provide a grammar for a class of documents. This grammar is known as a document type definition, or DTD. The document type declaration can point to an external subset (a special kind of external entity) containing markup declarations, or can contain the markup declarations directly in an internal subset, or can do both. The DTD for a document consists of both subsets taken together.

A markup declaration is an element type declaration, an attribute-list declaration, an entity declaration, or a notation declaration. These declarations may be contained in whole or in part within parameter entities, as described in the well-formedness and validity constraints below. For fuller information, see 4. "Physical Structures".

Document Type Definition

```
[28] doctypedecl::= '<!DOCTYPE' S Name (S ExternalID)? S? ('['
(markupdecl | PEReference | S)* ']' S?)? '>'
[ VC: Root Element Type ]
[29] markupdecl::= elementdecl | AttlistDecl | EntityDecl |
NotationDecl | PI | Comment
[ VC: Proper Declaration/PE Nesting ]
[ WFC: PEs in Internal Subset ]
```

The markup declarations may be made up in whole or in part of the replacement text of parameter entities. The productions later in this specification for individual nonterminals (elementdecl, AttlistDecl, and so on) describe the declarations after all the parameter entities have been included.

VALIDITY CONSTRAINT: ROOT ELEMENT TYPE The Name in the document type declaration must match the element type of the root element.

VALIDITY CONSTRAINT: PROPER DECLARATION/PE NESTING   Parameter-entity replacement text must be properly nested with markup declarations. That is to say, if either the first character or the last character of a markup declaration (markupdecl above) is contained in the replacement text for a parameter-entity reference, both must be contained in the same replacement text.

WELL-FORMEDNESS CONSTRAINT: PES IN INTERNAL SUBSET   In the internal DTD subset, parameter-entity references can occur only where markup declarations can occur, not within markup declarations. (This does not apply to references that occur in external parameter entities or to the external subset.)

Like the internal subset, the external subset and any external parameter entities referred to in the DTD must consist of a series of complete markup declarations of the types allowed by the non-terminal symbol markupdecl, interspersed with white space or parameter-entity references. However, portions of the contents of the external subset or of external parameter entities may conditionally be ignored by using the conditional section construct; this is not allowed in the internal subset.

External Subset

```
[30] extSubset::= TextDecl? ExtSubsetDecl
[31] extSubsetDecl::= ( markupdecl | conditionalSect | PEReference |
 S )*
```

The external subset and external parameter entities also differ from the internal subset in that in them, parameter-entity references are permitted within markup declarations, not only between markup declarations.

An example of an XML document with a document type declaration:

```
<?xml version="1.0"?>
<!DOCTYPE greeting SYSTEM "hello.dtd">
<greeting>Hello, world!</greeting>
```

The system identifier "hello.dtd" gives the URI of a DTD for the document.
The declarations can also be given locally, as in this example:

```
<?xml version="1.0" encoding="UTF-8" ?>
<!DOCTYPE greeting [
  <!ELEMENT greeting (#PCDATA)>
]>
<greeting>Hello, world!</greeting>
```

If both the external and internal subsets are used, the internal subset is considered to occur before the external subset. This has the effect that entity and attribute-list declarations in the internal subset take precedence over those in the external subset.

2.9 Standalone Document Declaration

Markup declarations can affect the content of the document, as passed from an XML processor to an application; examples are attribute defaults and entity declarations. The standalone document declaration, which may appear as a component of the XML declaration, signals whether or not there are such declarations which appear external to the document entity.

Standalone Document Declaration

```
[32] SDDecl::= S 'standalone' Eq (("'" ('yes' | 'no') "'") | ('"'
  ('yes' | 'no') '"')) [ VC: Standalone Document Declaration ]
```

In a standalone document declaration, the value "yes" indicates that there are no markup declarations external to the document entity (either in the DTD external subset, or in an external parameter entity referenced from the internal subset) which affect the information passed from the XML processor to the application. The value "no" indicates that there are or may be such external markup declarations. Note that the standalone document declaration only denotes the presence of external declarations; the presence, in a document, of references to external entities, when those entities are internally declared, does not change its standalone status.

If there are no external markup declarations, the standalone document declaration has no meaning. If there are external markup declarations but there is no standalone document declaration, the value "no" is assumed.

Any XML document for which standalone="no" holds can be converted algorithmically to a standalone document, which may be desirable for some network delivery applications.

VALIDITY CONSTRAINT: STANDALONE DOCUMENT DECLARATION   The standalone document declaration must have the value "no" if any external markup declarations contain declarations of:

◆ attributes with default values, if elements to which these attributes apply appear in the document without specifications of values for these attributes, or

◆ entities (other than amp, lt, gt, apos, quot), if references to those entities appear in the document, or

◆ attributes with values subject to normalization, where the attribute appears in the document with a value which will change as a result of normalization, or

◆ element types with element content, if white space occurs directly within any instance of those types.

An example XML declaration with a standalone document declaration:

```
<?xml version="1.0" standalone='yes'?>
```

2.10 White Space Handling

In editing XML documents, it is often convenient to use "white space" (spaces, tabs, and blank lines, denoted by the nonterminal S in this specification) to set apart the markup for greater readability. Such white space is typically not intended for inclusion in the delivered version of the document. On the other hand, "significant" white space that should be preserved in the delivered version is common, for example in poetry and source code.

An XML processor must always pass all characters in a document that are not markup through to the application. A validating XML processor must also inform the application which of these characters constitute white space appearing in element content.

A special attribute named xml:space may be attached to an element to signal an intention that in that element, white space should be preserved by applications. In valid documents, this attribute, like any other, must be declared if it is used. When declared, it must be given as an enumerated type whose only possible values are "default" and "preserve". For example:

```
<!ATTLIST poem   xml:space (default|preserve) 'preserve'>
```

The value "default" signals that applications' default white-space processing modes are acceptable for this element; the value "preserve" indicates the intent that applications preserve all the white space. This declared intent is considered to apply to all elements within the content of the element where it is specified, unless overriden with another instance of the xml:space attribute.

The root element of any document is considered to have signaled no intentions as regards application space handling, unless it provides a value for this attribute or the attribute is declared with a default value.

2.11 End-of-Line Handling

XML parsed entities are often stored in computer files which, for editing convenience, are organized into lines. These lines are typically separated by some combination of the characters carriage-return (#xD) and line-feed (#xA).

To simplify the tasks of applications, wherever an external parsed entity or the literal entity value of an internal parsed entity contains either the literal two-character sequence "#xD#xA" or a standalone literal #xD, an XML processor must pass to the application the single character #xA. (This behavior can conveniently be produced by normalizing all line breaks to #xA on input, before parsing.)

2.12 Language Identification

In document processing, it is often useful to identify the natural or formal language in which the content is written. A special attribute named xml:lang may be inserted in documents to specify the language used in the contents and attribute values of any element in an XML document. In valid documents, this attribute, like any other, must be declared if it is used. The values of the attribute are language identifiers as defined by IETF RFC 1766, "Tags for the Identification of Languages":

Language Identification

```
[33] LanguageID::= Langcode ('-' Subcode)*
[34] Langcode::= ISO639Code | IanaCode | UserCode
[35] ISO639Code::= ([a-z] | [A-Z]) ([a-z] | [A-Z])
[36] IanaCode::= ('i' | 'I') '-' ([a-z] | [A-Z])+
[37] UserCode::= ('x' | 'X') '-' ([a-z] | [A-Z])+
[38] Subcode::= ([a-z] | [A-Z])+
```

The Langcode may be any of the following:

◆ a two-letter language code as defined by ISO 639, "Codes for the representation of names of languages"

◆ a language identifier registered with the Internet Assigned Numbers Authority (IANA); these begin with the prefix "i-" (or "I-")

◆ a language identifier assigned by the user, or agreed on between parties in private use; these must begin with the prefix "x-" or "X-" in order to ensure that they do not conflict with names later standardized or registered with IANA

There may be any number of Subcode segments; if the first subcode segment exists and the Subcode consists of two letters, then it must be a country code from ISO 3166, "Codes for the representation of names of countries." If the first subcode consists of more than two letters, it must be a subcode for the language in question registered with IANA, unless the Langcode begins with the prefix x- or X-.

It is customary to give the language code in lower case, and the country code (if any) in upper case. Note that these values, unlike other names in XML documents, are case insensitive.

For example:

```
<p xml:lang="en">The quick brown fox jumps over the lazy dog.</p>
<p xml:lang="en-GB">What colour is it?</p>
<p xml:lang="en-US">What color is it?</p>
<sp who="Faust" desc='leise' xml:lang="de">
  <l>Habe nun, ach! Philosophie,</l>
```

```
<l>Juristerei, und Medizin</l>
<l>und leider auch Theologie</l>
<l>durchaus studiert mit heißem Bemüh'n.</l>
</sp>
```

The intent declared with xml:lang is considered to apply to all attributes and content of the element where it is specified, unless overridden with an instance of xml:lang on another element within that content.

A simple declaration for xml:lang might take the form

```
xml:lang   NMTOKEN   #IMPLIED
```

but specific default values may also be given, if appropriate. In a collection of French poems for English students, with glosses and notes in English, the xml:lang attribute might be declared this way:

```
<!ATTLIST poem   xml:lang NMTOKEN 'fr'>
<!ATTLIST gloss  xml:lang NMTOKEN 'en'>
<!ATTLIST note   xml:lang NMTOKEN 'en'>
```

3. Logical Structures

Each XML document contains one or more elements, the boundaries of which are either delimited by start-tags and end-tags, or, for empty elements, by an empty-element tag. Each element has a type, identified by name, sometimes called its "generic identifier" (GI), and may have a set of attribute specifications. Each attribute specification has a name and a value.

Element

```
[39] element::= EmptyElemTag| STag content Etag
[ WFC: Element Type Match ]
[ VC: Element Valid ]
```

This specification does not constrain the semantics, use, or (beyond syntax) names of the element types and attributes, except that names beginning with a match to (('X'|'x')('M'|'m')('L'|'l')) are reserved for standardization in this or future versions of this specification.

WELL-FORMEDNESS CONSTRAINT: ELEMENT TYPE MATCH   The Name in an element's end-tag must match the element type in the start-tag.

VALIDITY CONSTRAINT: ELEMENT VALID   An element is valid if there is a declaration matching elementdecl where the Name matches the element type, and one of the following holds:

1. The declaration matches EMPTY and the element has no content.

2. The declaration matches children and the sequence of child elements belongs to the language generated by the regular expression in the content model, with optional white space (characters matching the nonterminal S) between each pair of child elements.

3. The declaration matches Mixed and the content consists of character data and child elements whose types match names in the content model.

4. The declaration matches ANY, and the types of any child elements have been declared.

3.1 Start-Tags, End-Tags, and Empty-Element Tags

The beginning of every non-empty XML element is marked by a start-tag.

Start-tag

```
[40] STag::= '<' Name (S Attribute)* S? '>'
[ WFC: Unique Att Spec ]
[41] Attribute::= Name Eq AttValue
[ VC: Attribute Value Type ]
[ WFC: No External Entity References ]
[ WFC: No < in Attribute Values ]
```

The Name in the start- and end-tags gives the element's type. The Name-AttValue pairs are referred to as the attribute specifications of the element, with the Name in each pair referred to as the attribute name and the content of the AttValue (the text between the ' or " delimiters) as the attribute value.

WELL-FORMEDNESS CONSTRAINT: UNIQUE ATT SPEC   No attribute name may appear more than once in the same start-tag or empty-element tag.

VALIDITY CONSTRAINT: ATTRIBUTE VALUE TYPE   The attribute must have been declared; the value must be of the type declared for it. (For attribute types, see 3.3, "Attribute-List Declarations".)

WELL-FORMEDNESS CONSTRAINT: NO EXTERNAL ENTITY REFERENCES   Attribute values cannot contain direct or indirect entity references to external entities.

WELL-FORMEDNESS CONSTRAINT: NO < IN ATTRIBUTE VALUES   The replacement text of any entity referred to directly or indirectly in an attribute value (other than "<") must not contain a <.

An example of a start-tag:

```
<termdef id="dt-dog" term="dog">
```

The end of every element that begins with a start-tag must be marked by an end-tag containing a name that echoes the element's type as given in the start-tag:

End-tag
```
[42] ETag::= '</' Name S? '>'
```

An example of an end-tag:

```
</termdef>
```

The text between the start-tag and end-tag is called the element's content:

Content of Elements
```
[43] content::= (element | CharData | Reference | CDSect | PI |
 Comment)*
```

If an element is empty, it must be represented either by a start-tag immediately followed by an end-tag or by an empty-element tag. An empty-element tag takes a special form:

Tags for Empty Elements
```
[44] EmptyElemTag::= '<' Name (S Attribute)* S? '/>'
[ WFC: Unique Att Spec ]
```

Empty-element tags may be used for any element which has no content, whether or not it is declared using the keyword EMPTY. For interoperability, the empty-element tag must be used, and can only be used, for elements which are declared EMPTY.

Examples of empty elements:

```
<IMG align="left"
 src="http://www.w3.org/Icons/WWW/w3c_home" />
<br></br>
<br/>
```

3.2 Element Type Declarations

The element structure of an XML document may, for validation purposes, be constrained using element type and attribute-list declarations. An element type declaration constrains the element's content.

Element type declarations often constrain which element types can appear as children of the element. At user option, an XML processor may issue a warning when a declaration mentions an element type for which no declaration is provided, but this is not an error.

An element type declaration takes the form:

Element Type Declaration

```
[45] elementdecl::= '<!ELEMENT' S Name S contentspec S? '>'
[ VC: Unique Element Type Declaration ]
[46] contentspec::= 'EMPTY' | 'ANY' | Mixed | children
```

where the Name gives the element type being declared.

VALIDITY CONSTRAINT: UNIQUE ELEMENT TYPE DECLARATION   No element type may be declared more than once.

Examples of element type declarations:

```
<!ELEMENT br EMPTY>
<!ELEMENT p (#PCDATA|emph)* >
<!ELEMENT %name.para; %content.para; >
<!ELEMENT container ANY>
```

3.2.1 ELEMENT CONTENT

An element type has element content when elements of that type must contain only child elements (no character data), optionally separated by white space (characters matching the nonterminal S). In this case, the constraint includes a content model, a simple grammar governing the allowed types of the child elements and the order in which they are allowed to appear. The grammar is built on content particles (cps), which consist of names, choice lists of content particles, or sequence lists of content particles:

Element-content Models

```
[47] children::= (choice | seq) ('?' | '*' | '+')?
[48] cp::= (Name | choice | seq) ('?' | '*' | '+')?
[49] choice::= '(' S? cp ( S? '|' S? cp )* S? ')'
[ VC: Proper Group/PE Nesting ]
[50] seq::= '(' S? cp ( S? ',' S? cp )* S? ')'
[ VC: Proper Group/PE Nesting ]
```

where each Name is the type of an element which may appear as a child. Any content particle in a choice list may appear in the element content at the location where the choice list appears in the grammar; content particles occurring in a sequence list must each appear in the element content in the order given in the list. The optional character following a name or list governs whether the element or the content particles in the list may occur one or more (+), zero or more (*), or zero or one times (?). The absence of such an operator means that the element or content particle must appear exactly once. This syntax and meaning are identical to those used in the productions in this specification.

The content of an element matches a content model if and only if it is possible to trace out a path through the content model, obeying the sequence, choice, and repetition operators and matching each element in the content against an element type in the content model. For compatibility, it is an error if an element in the document can match more than one occurrence of an element type in the content model. For more information, see "E. Deterministic Content Models".

VALIDITY CONSTRAINT: PROPER GROUP/PE NESTING   Parameter-entity replacement text must be properly nested with parenthetized groups. That is to say, if either of the opening or closing parentheses in a choice, seq, or Mixed construct is contained in the replacement text for a parameter entity, both must be contained in the same replacement text. For interoperability, if a parameter-entity reference appears in a choice, seq, or Mixed construct, its replacement text should not be empty, and neither the first nor last non-blank character of the replacement text should be a connector (| or ,).

Examples of element-content models:

```
<!ELEMENT spec (front, body, back?)>
<!ELEMENT div1 (head, (p | list | note)*, div2*)>
<!ELEMENT dictionary-body (%div.mix; | %dict.mix;)*>
```

3.2.2 MIXED CONTENT

An element type has mixed content when elements of that type may contain character data, optionally interspersed with child elements. In this case, the types of the child elements may be constrained, but not their order or their number of occurrences:

Mixed-content Declaration

```
[51] Mixed::= '(' S? '#PCDATA' (S? '|' S? Name)* S? ')*' | '(' S?
'#PCDATA' S? ')'
[ VC: Proper Group/PE Nesting ]
[ VC: No Duplicate Types ]
```

where the Names give the types of elements that may appear as children.

VALIDITY CONSTRAINT: NO DUPLICATE TYPES   The same name must not appear more than once in a single mixed-content declaration.

Examples of mixed content declarations:

```
<!ELEMENT p (#PCDATA|a|ul|b|i|em)*>
<!ELEMENT p (#PCDATA | %font; | %phrase; | %special; | %form;)* >
<!ELEMENT b (#PCDATA)>
```

3.3 Attribute-List Declarations

Attributes are used to associate name-value pairs with elements. Attribute specifications may appear only within start-tags and empty-element tags; thus, the productions used to recognize them appear in 3.1, "Start-Tags, End-Tags, and Empty-Element Tags." Attribute-list declarations may be used:

◆ To define the set of attributes pertaining to a given element type.

◆ To establish type constraints for these attributes.

◆ To provide default values for attributes.

Attribute-list declarations specify the name, data type, and default value (if any) of each attribute associated with a given element type:

Attribute-list Declaration

```
[52] AttlistDecl::= '<!ATTLIST' S Name AttDef* S? '>'
[53] AttDef::= S Name S AttType S DefaultDecl
```

The `Name` in the `AttlistDecl` rule is the type of an element. At user option, an XML processor may issue a warning if attributes are declared for an element type not itself declared, but this is not an error. The `Name` in the `AttDef` rule is the name of the attribute.

When more than one `AttlistDecl` is provided for a given element type, the contents of all those provided are merged. When more than one definition is provided for the same attribute of a given element type, the first declaration is binding and later declarations are ignored. For interoperability, writers of DTDs may choose to provide at most one attribute-list declaration for a given element type, at most one attribute definition for a given attribute name, and at least one attribute definition in each attribute-list declaration. For interoperability, an XML processor may at user option issue a warning when more than one attribute-list declaration is provided for a given element type, or more than one attribute definition is provided for a given attribute, but this is not an error.

3.3.1 ATTRIBUTE TYPES

XML attribute types are of three kinds: a string type, a set of tokenized types, and enumerated types. The string type may take any literal string as a value; the tokenized types have varying lexical and semantic constraints, as noted:

Attribute Types

```
[54] AttType::= StringType | TokenizedType | EnumeratedType
[55] StringType::= 'CDATA'
[56] TokenizedType::= 'ID'
[ VC: ID ]
```

```
[ VC: One ID per Element Type ]
[ VC: ID Attribute Default ]
| 'IDREF'
[ VC: IDREF ]
| 'IDREFS'
[ VC: IDREF ]
| 'ENTITY'
[ VC: Entity Name ]
| 'ENTITIES'
[ VC: Entity Name ]
| 'NMTOKEN'
[ VC: Name Token ]
| 'NMTOKENS'
[ VC: Name Token ]
```

VALIDITY CONSTRAINT: ID   Values of type ID must match the Name production. A name must not appear more than once in an XML document as a value of this type; i.e., ID values must uniquely identify the elements which bear them.

VALIDITY CONSTRAINT: ONE ID PER ELEMENT TYPE   No element type may have more than one ID attribute specified.

VALIDITY CONSTRAINT: ID ATTRIBUTE DEFAULT   An ID attribute must have a declared default of #IMPLIED or #REQUIRED.

VALIDITY CONSTRAINT: IDREF   Values of type IDREF must match the Name production, and values of type IDREFS must match Names; each Name must match the value of an ID attribute on some element in the XML document; i.e. IDREF values must match the value of some ID attribute.

VALIDITY CONSTRAINT: ENTITY NAME   Values of type ENTITY must match the Name production, values of type ENTITIES must match Names; each Name must match the name of an unparsed entity declared in the DTD.

VALIDITY CONSTRAINT: NAME TOKEN   Values of type NMTOKEN must match the Nmtoken production; values of type NMTOKENS must match Nmtokens.

Enumerated attributes can take one of a list of values provided in the declaration. There are two kinds of enumerated types:

Enumerated Attribute Types

```
[57] EnumeratedType::= NotationType | Enumeration
[58] NotationType::= 'NOTATION' S '(' S? Name (S? '|' S? Name)* S?
')'
[ VC: Notation Attributes ]
[59] Enumeration::= '(' S? Nmtoken (S? '|' S? Nmtoken)* S? ')'
[ VC: Enumeration ]
```

A NOTATION attribute identifies a notation, declared in the DTD with associated system and/or public identifiers, to be used in interpreting the element to which the attribute is attached.

VALIDITY CONSTRAINT: NOTATION ATTRIBUTES   Values of this type must match one of the notation names included in the declaration; all notation names in the declaration must be declared.

VALIDITY CONSTRAINT: ENUMERATION   Values of this type must match one of the Nmtoken tokens in the declaration.

For interoperability, the same Nmtoken should not occur more than once in the enumerated attribute types of a single element type.

3.3.2 ATTRIBUTE DEFAULTS

An attribute declaration provides information on whether the attribute's presence is required, and if not, how an XML processor should react if a declared attribute is absent in a document.

Attribute Defaults

```
[60] DefaultDecl::= '#REQUIRED' | '#IMPLIED' | (('#FIXED' S)?
 AttValue)
[ VC: Required Attribute ]
[ VC: Attribute Default Legal ]
[ WFC: No < in Attribute Values ]
[ VC: Fixed Attribute Default ]
```

In an attribute declaration, #REQUIRED means that the attribute must always be provided, #IMPLIED that no default value is provided. If the declaration is neither #REQUIRED nor #IMPLIED, then the AttValue value contains the declared default value; the #FIXED keyword states that the attribute must always have the default value. If a default value is declared, when an XML processor encounters an omitted attribute, it is to behave as though the attribute were present with the declared default value.

VALIDITY CONSTRAINT: REQUIRED ATTRIBUTE   If the default declaration is the keyword #REQUIRED, then the attribute must be specified for all elements of the type in the attribute-list declaration.

VALIDITY CONSTRAINT: ATTRIBUTE DEFAULT LEGAL   The declared default value must meet the lexical constraints of the declared attribute type.

VALIDITY CONSTRAINT: FIXED ATTRIBUTE DEFAULT   If an attribute has a default value declared with the #FIXED keyword, instances of that attribute must match the default value.

Examples of attribute-list declarations:

```
<!ATTLIST termdef
          id      ID      #REQUIRED
          name    CDATA   #IMPLIED>
<!ATTLIST list
          type    (bullets|ordered|glossary)   "ordered">
<!ATTLIST form
          method  CDATA   #FIXED "POST">
```

3.3.3 ATTRIBUTE-VALUE NORMALIZATION

Before the value of an attribute is passed to the application or checked for validity, the XML processor must normalize it as follows:

- ♦ a character reference is processed by appending the referenced character to the attribute value

- ♦ an entity reference is processed by recursively processing the replacement text of the entity

- ♦ a whitespace character (#x20, #xD, #xA, #x9) is processed by appending #x20 to the normalized value, except that only a single #x20 is appended for a "#xD#xA" sequence that is part of an external parsed entity or the literal entity value of an internal parsed entity

- ♦ other characters are processed by appending them to the normalized value

If the declared value is not CDATA, then the XML processor must further process the normalized attribute value by discarding any leading and trailing space (#x20) characters, and by replacing sequences of space (#x20) characters by a single space (#x20) character.

All attributes for which no declaration has been read should be treated by a non-validating parser as if declared CDATA.

3.4 Conditional Sections

Conditional sections are portions of the document type declaration external subset which are included in, or excluded from, the logical structure of the DTD based on the keyword which governs them.

Conditional Section

```
[61] conditionalSect::= includeSect | ignoreSect
[62] includeSect::= '<![' S? 'INCLUDE' S? '[' extSubsetDecl ']]>'
[63] ignoreSect::= '<![' S? 'IGNORE' S? '[' ignoreSectContents*
 ']]>'
[64] ignoreSectContents::= Ignore ('<![' ignoreSectContents ']]>'
 Ignore)*
[65] Ignore::= Char* - (Char* ('<![' | ']]>') Char*)
```

Like the internal and external DTD subsets, a conditional section may contain one or more complete declarations, comments, processing instructions, or nested conditional sections, intermingled with white space.

If the keyword of the conditional section is INCLUDE, then the contents of the conditional section are part of the DTD. If the keyword of the conditional section is IGNORE, then the contents of the conditional section are not logically part of the DTD. Note that for reliable parsing, the contents of even ignored conditional sections must be read in order to detect nested conditional sections and ensure that the end of the outermost (ignored) conditional section is properly detected. If a conditional section with a keyword of INCLUDE occurs within a larger conditional section with a keyword of IGNORE, both the outer and the inner conditional sections are ignored.

If the keyword of the conditional section is a parameter-entity reference, the parameter entity must be replaced by its content before the processor decides whether to include or ignore the conditional section.

An example:

```
<!ENTITY % draft 'INCLUDE' >
<!ENTITY % final 'IGNORE' >

<![%draft;[
<!ELEMENT book (comments*, title, body, supplements?)>
]]>
<![%final;[
<!ELEMENT book (title, body, supplements?)>
]]>
```

4. Physical Structures

An XML document may consist of one or many storage units. These are called entities; they all have content and are all (except for the document entity, see below, and the external DTD subset) identified by name. Each XML document has one entity called the document entity, which serves as the starting point for the XML processor and may contain the whole document.

Entities may be either parsed or unparsed. A parsed entity's contents are referred to as its replacement text; this text is considered an integral part of the document.

An unparsed entity is a resource whose contents may or may not be text, and if text, may not be XML. Each unparsed entity has an associated notation, identified by name. Beyond a requirement that an XML processor make the identifiers for the entity and notation available to the application, XML places no constraints on the contents of unparsed entities.

Parsed entities are invoked by name using entity references; unparsed entities by name, given in the value of ENTITY or ENTITIES attributes.

General entities are entities for use within the document content. In this specification, general entities are sometimes referred to with the unqualified term entity when this leads to no ambiguity. Parameter entities are parsed entities for use within the DTD. These two types of entities use different forms of reference and are recognized in different contexts. Furthermore, they occupy different namespaces; a parameter entity and a general entity with the same name are two distinct entities.

4.1 Character and Entity References

A character reference refers to a specific character in the ISO/IEC 10646 character set, for example one not directly accessible from available input devices.

Character Reference

```
[66] CharRef::= '&#' [0-9]+ ';' | '&#x' [0-9a-fA-F]+ ';'
[ WFC: Legal Character ]
```

WELL-FORMEDNESS CONSTRAINT: LEGAL CHARACTER   Characters referred to using character references must match the production for Char.

If the character reference begins with "&#x", the digits and letters up to the terminating ; provide a hexadecimal representation of the character's code point in ISO/IEC 10646. If it begins just with "&#", the digits up to the terminating ; provide a decimal representation of the character's code point.

An entity reference refers to the content of a named entity. References to parsed general entities use ampersand (&) and semicolon (;) as delimiters. Parameter-entity references use percent-sign (%) and semicolon (;) as delimiters.

Entity Reference

```
[67] Reference::= EntityRef | CharRef
[68] EntityRef::= '&' Name ';'
[ WFC: Entity Declared ]
[ VC: Entity Declared ]
[ WFC: Parsed Entity ]
[ WFC: No Recursion ]
[69] PEReference::= '%' Name ';'
[ VC: Entity Declared ]
[ WFC: No Recursion ]
[ WFC: In DTD ]
```

WELL-FORMEDNESS CONSTRAINT: ENTITY DECLARED   In a document without any DTD, a document with only an internal DTD subset which contains no parameter entity references, or a document with "standalone='yes'", the Name given in the entity reference must match that in an entity declaration, except that well-formed documents need not declare any of the following entities: amp, lt, gt, apos, quot. The declaration of a parameter entity must precede any reference to it.

Similarly, the declaration of a general entity must precede any reference to it which appears in a default value in an attribute-list declaration. Note that if entities are declared in the external subset or in external parameter entities, a non-validating processor is not obligated to read and process their declarations; for such documents, the rule that an entity must be declared is a well-formedness constraint only if `standalone='yes'`.

VALIDITY CONSTRAINT: ENTITY DECLARED   In a document with an external subset or external parameter entities with `"standalone='no'"`, the Name given in the entity reference must match that in an entity declaration. For interoperability, valid documents should declare the entities `amp`, `lt`, `gt`, `apos`, `quot`, in the form specified in 4.6, "Predefined Entities". The declaration of a parameter entity must precede any reference to it. Similarly, the declaration of a general entity must precede any reference to it which appears in a default value in an attribute-list declaration.

WELL-FORMEDNESS CONSTRAINT: PARSED ENTITY   An entity reference must not contain the name of an unparsed entity. Unparsed entities may be referred to only in attribute values declared to be of type `ENTITY` or `ENTITIES`.

WELL-FORMEDNESS CONSTRAINT: NO RECURSION   A parsed entity must not contain a recursive reference to itself, either directly or indirectly.

WELL-FORMEDNESS CONSTRAINT: IN DTD   Parameter-entity references may only appear in the DTD.

Examples of character and entity references:

```
Type <key>less-than</key> (&#x3C;) to save options.
This document was prepared on &docdate; and
is classified &security-level;.
```

Example of a parameter-entity reference:

```
<!-- declare the parameter entity "ISOLat2"... -->
<!ENTITY % ISOLat2
        SYSTEM "http://www.xml.com/iso/isolat2-xml.entities" >
<!-- ... now reference it. -->
%ISOLat2;
```

4.2 Entity Declarations

Entities are declared thus:

Entity Declaration

```
[70] EntityDecl::= GEDecl | PEDecl
[71] GEDecl::= '<!ENTITY' S Name S EntityDef S? '>'
```

```
[72] PEDecl::= '<!ENTITY' S '%' S Name S PEDef S? '>'
[73] EntityDef::= EntityValue | (ExternalID NDataDecl?)
[74] PEDef::= EntityValue | ExternalID
```

The Name identifies the entity in an entity reference or, in the case of an unparsed entity, in the value of an ENTITY or ENTITIES attribute. If the same entity is declared more than once, the first declaration encountered is binding; at user option, an XML processor may issue a warning if entities are declared multiple times.

4.2.1 INTERNAL ENTITIES

If the entity definition is an EntityValue, the defined entity is called an internal entity. There is no separate physical storage object, and the content of the entity is given in the declaration. Note that some processing of entity and character references in the literal entity value may be required to produce the correct replacement text: see 4.5, "Construction of Internal Entity Replacement Text".

An internal entity is a parsed entity.

Example of an internal entity declaration:

```
<!ENTITY Pub-Status "This is a pre-release of the
 specification.">
```

4.2.2 EXTERNAL ENTITIES

If the entity is not internal, it is an external entity, declared as follows:

External Entity Declaration
```
[75] ExternalID::= 'SYSTEM' S SystemLiteral| 'PUBLIC' S PubidLiteral
 S SystemLiteral
[76] NDataDecl::= S 'NDATA' S Name
[ VC: Notation Declared ]
```

If the NDataDecl is present, this is a general unparsed entity; otherwise it is a parsed entity.

VALIDITY CONSTRAINT: NOTATION DECLARED   The Name must match the declared name of a notation.

The SystemLiteral is called the entity's system identifier. It is a URI, which may be used to retrieve the entity. Note that the hash mark (#) and fragment identifier frequently used with URIs are not, formally, part of the URI itself; an XML processor may signal an error if a fragment identifier is given as part of a system identifier. Unless otherwise provided by information outside the scope of this specification (e.g. a special XML element type defined by a particular DTD, or a processing instruction defined by a particular application specification), relative URIs are relative to the location of the resource within which the entity declaration occurs. A URI might thus be relative to the document entity, to the entity containing the external DTD subset, or to some other external parameter entity.

An XML processor should handle a non-ASCII character in a URI by representing the character in UTF-8 as one or more bytes, and then escaping these bytes with the URI escaping mechanism (i.e., by converting each byte to %HH, where HH is the hexadecimal notation of the byte value).

In addition to a system identifier, an external identifier may include a public identifier. An XML processor attempting to retrieve the entity's content may use the public identifier to try to generate an alternative URI. If the processor is unable to do so, it must use the URI specified in the system literal. Before a match is attempted, all strings of white space in the public identifier must be normalized to single space characters (#x20), and leading and trailing white space must be removed.

Examples of external entity declarations:

```
<!ENTITY open-hatch
    SYSTEM "http://www.textuality.com/boilerplate/OpenHatch.xml">
<!ENTITY open-hatch
    PUBLIC "-//Textuality//TEXT Standard open-hatch boilerplate//EN"
    "http://www.textuality.com/boilerplate/OpenHatch.xml">
<!ENTITY hatch-pic
    SYSTEM "../grafix/OpenHatch.gif"
    NDATA gif >
```

4.3 Parsed Entities

4.3.1 THE TEXT DECLARATION
External parsed entities may each begin with a text declaration.

Text Declaration

```
[77] TextDecl::= '<?xml' VersionInfo? EncodingDecl S? '?>'
```

The text declaration must be provided literally, not by reference to a parsed entity. No text declaration may appear at any position other than the beginning of an external parsed entity.

4.3.2 WELL-FORMED PARSED ENTITIES
The document entity is well-formed if it matches the production labeled document. An external general parsed entity is well-formed if it matches the production labeled extParsedEnt. An external parameter entity is well-formed if it matches the production labeled extPE.

Well-Formed External Parsed Entity

```
[78] extParsedEnt::= TextDecl? Content
[79] extPE::= TextDecl? extSubsetDecl
```

An internal general parsed entity is well-formed if its replacement text matches the production labeled content. All internal parameter entities are well-formed by definition.

A consequence of well-formedness in entities is that the logical and physical structures in an XML document are properly nested; no start-tag, end-tag, empty-element tag, element, comment, processing instruction, character reference, or entity reference can begin in one entity and end in another.

4.3.3 CHARACTER ENCODING IN ENTITIES

Each external parsed entity in an XML document may use a different encoding for its characters. All XML processors must be able to read entities in either UTF-8 or UTF-16.

Entities encoded in UTF-16 must begin with the Byte Order Mark described by ISO/IEC 10646 Annex E and Unicode Appendix B (the ZERO WIDTH NO-BREAK SPACE character, #xFEFF). This is an encoding signature, not part of either the markup or the character data of the XML document. XML processors must be able to use this character to differentiate between UTF-8 and UTF-16 encoded documents.

Although an XML processor is required to read only entities in the UTF-8 and UTF-16 encodings, it is recognized that other encodings are used around the world, and it may be desired for XML processors to read entities that use them. Parsed entities which are stored in an encoding other than UTF-8 or UTF-16 must begin with a text declaration containing an encoding declaration:

Encoding Declaration

```
[80] EncodingDecl::= S 'encoding' Eq ('"' EncName '"' |   "'" EncName
  "'" )
[81] EncName::= [A-Za-z] ([A-Za-z0-9._] | '-')
*/* Encoding name contains only Latin characters */
```

In the document entity, the encoding declaration is part of the XML declaration. The EncName is the name of the encoding used.

In an encoding declaration, the values "UTF-8", "UTF-16", "ISO-10646-UCS-2", and "ISO-10646-UCS-4" should be used for the various encodings and transformations of Unicode / ISO/IEC 10646, the values "ISO-8859-1", "ISO-8859-2", ... "ISO-8859-9" should be used for the parts of ISO 8859, and the values "ISO-2022-JP", "Shift_JIS", and "EUC-JP" should be used for the various encoded forms of JIS X-0208-1997. XML processors may recognize other encodings; it is recommended that character encodings registered (as charsets) with the Internet Assigned Numbers Authority (IANA), other than those just listed, should be referred to using their registered names. Note that these registered names are defined to be case-insensitive, so processors wishing to match against them should do so in a case-insensitive way.

In the absence of information provided by an external transport protocol (e.g. HTTP or MIME), it is an error for an entity including an encoding declaration to be presented to the XML processor in an encoding other than that named in the declaration, for an encoding declaration to occur other than at the beginning of an external entity, or for an entity which begins with neither a Byte Order Mark nor an encoding declaration to use an encoding other than UTF-8. Note that since ASCII is a subset of UTF-8, ordinary ASCII entities do not strictly need an encoding declaration.

It is a fatal error when an XML processor encounters an entity with an encoding that it is unable to process.

Examples of encoding declarations:

```
<?xml encoding='UTF-8'?>
<?xml encoding='EUC-JP'?>
```

4.4 XML Processor Treatment of Entities and References

The table below summarizes the contexts in which character references, entity references, and invocations of unparsed entities might appear and the required behavior of an XML processor in each case. The labels in the leftmost column describe the recognition context:

REFERENCE IN CONTENT   as a reference anywhere after the start-tag and before the end-tag of an element; corresponds to the nonterminal content.

REFERENCE IN ATTRIBUTE VALUE   as a reference within either the value of an attribute in a start-tag, or a default value in an attribute declaration; corresponds to the nonterminal AttValue.

OCCURS AS ATTRIBUTE VALUE   as a Name, not a reference, appearing either as the value of an attribute which has been declared as type ENTITY, or as one of the space-separated tokens in the value of an attribute which has been declared as type ENTITIES.

REFERENCE IN ENTITY VALUE   as a reference within a parameter or internal entity's literal entity value in the entity's declaration; corresponds to the nonterminal EntityValue.

REFERENCE IN DTD   as a reference within either the internal or external subsets of the DTD, but outside of an EntityValue or AttValue.

	Entity Type				Character
	Parameter	**Internal General**	**External Parsed General**	**Unparsed**	
Reference in Content	Not recognized	Included	Included if validating	Forbidden	Included
Reference Attribute Value	Not recognized	Included in literal	Forbidden	Forbidden	Included
Occurs as Attribute Value	Not recognized	Forbidden	Forbidden	Notify	Not recognized
Reference in Entity Value	Included in literal	Bypassed	Bypassed	Forbidden	Included
Reference in DTD	Included as PE	Forbidden	Forbidden	Forbidden	Forbidden

4.4.1 NOT RECOGNIZED

Outside the DTD, the % character has no special significance; thus, what would be parameter entity references in the DTD are not recognized as markup in content. Similarly, the names of unparsed entities are not recognized except when they appear in the value of an appropriately declared attribute.

4.4.2 INCLUDED

An entity is included when its replacement text is retrieved and processed, in place of the reference itself, as though it were part of the document at the location the reference was recognized. The replacement text may contain both character data and (except for parameter entities) markup, which must be recognized in the usual way, except that the replacement text of entities used to escape markup delimiters (the entities amp, lt, gt, apos, quot) is always treated as data. (The string "AT&T;" expands to "AT&T;" and the remaining ampersand is not recognized as an entity-reference delimiter.) A character reference is included when the indicated character is processed in place of the reference itself.

4.4.3 INCLUDED IF VALIDATING

When an XML processor recognizes a reference to a parsed entity, in order to validate the document, the processor must include its replacement text. If the entity is external, and the processor is not attempting to validate the XML document, the processor may, but need not, include the entity's replacement text. If a non-validating parser does not include the replacement text, it must inform the application that it recognized, but did not read, the entity.

This rule is based on the recognition that the automatic inclusion provided by the SGML and XML entity mechanism, primarily designed to support modularity in authoring, is not necessarily appropriate for other applications, in particular document browsing. Browsers, for example, when encountering an external parsed entity reference, might choose to provide a visual indication of the entity's presence and retrieve it for display only on demand.

4.4.4 FORBIDDEN

The following are forbidden, and constitute fatal errors:

- the appearance of a reference to an unparsed entity.

- the appearance of any character or general-entity reference in the DTD except within an `EntityValue` or `AttValue`.

- a reference to an external entity in an attribute value.

4.4.5 INCLUDED IN LITERAL

When an entity reference appears in an attribute value, or a parameter entity reference appears in a literal entity value, its replacement text is processed in place of the reference itself as though it were part of the document at the location the reference was recognized, except that a single or double quote character in the replacement text is always treated as a normal data character and will not terminate the literal. For example, this is well-formed:

```
<!ENTITY % YN '"Yes"' >
<!ENTITY WhatHeSaid "He said &YN;" >
```

while this is not:

```
<!ENTITY EndAttr "27'" >
<element attribute='a-&EndAttr;'>
```

4.4.6 NOTIFY

When the name of an unparsed entity appears as a token in the value of an attribute of declared type `ENTITY` or `ENTITIES`, a validating processor must inform the application of the system and public (if any) identifiers for both the entity and its associated notation.

4.4.7 BYPASSED

When a general entity reference appears in the `EntityValue` in an entity declaration, it is bypassed and left as is.

4.4.8 INCLUDED AS PE

Just as with external parsed entities, parameter entities need only be included if validating. When a parameter-entity reference is recognized in the DTD and included, its replacement text is enlarged by the attachment of one leading and one following space (#x20) character; the intent is to constrain the replacement text of parameter entities to contain an integral number of grammatical tokens in the DTD.

4.5 Construction of Internal Entity Replacement Text

In discussing the treatment of internal entities, it is useful to distinguish two forms of the entity's value. The literal entity value is the quoted string actually present in the entity declaration, corresponding to the non-terminal EntityValue. The replacement text is the content of the entity, after replacement of character references and parameter-entity references.

The literal entity value as given in an internal entity declaration (EntityValue) may contain character, parameter-entity, and general-entity references. Such references must be contained entirely within the literal entity value. The actual replacement text that is included as described above must contain the replacement text of any parameter entities referred to, and must contain the character referred to, in place of any character references in the literal entity value; however, general-entity references must be left as-is, unexpanded. For example, given the following declarations:

```
<!ENTITY % pub    "&#xc9;ditions Gallimard" >
<!ENTITY   rights "All rights reserved" >
<!ENTITY   book   "La Peste: Albert Camus,
&#xA9; 1947 %pub;. &rights;" >
```

then the replacement text for the entity "book" is:

```
La Peste: Albert Camus,
© 1947 Éditions Gallimard. &rights;
```

The general-entity reference "&rights;" would be expanded should the reference "&book;" appear in the document's content or an attribute value.

These simple rules may have complex interactions; for a detailed discussion of a difficult example, see D. "Expansion of Entity and Character References".

4.6 Predefined Entities

Entity and character references can both be used to escape the left angle bracket, ampersand, and other delimiters. A set of general entities (amp, lt, gt, apos, quot) is specified for this purpose. Numeric character references may also be used; they are expanded immediately when recognized and must be treated as character data,

so the numeric character references "<" and "&" may be used to escape <
and & when they occur in character data.

All XML processors must recognize these entities whether they are declared or
not. For interoperability, valid XML documents should declare these entities, like
any others, before using them. If the entities in question are declared, they must be
declared as internal entities whose replacement text is the single character being
escaped or a character reference to that character, as shown below.

```
<!ENTITY lt     "&#38;#60;">
<!ENTITY gt     "&#62;">
<!ENTITY amp    "&#38;#38;">
<!ENTITY apos   "&#39;">
<!ENTITY quot   "&#34;">
```

Note that the < and & characters in the declarations of "lt" and "amp" are doubly
escaped to meet the requirement that entity replacement be well-formed.

4.7 Notation Declarations

Notations identify by name the format of unparsed entities, the format of elements
which bear a notation attribute, or the application to which a processing instruction
is addressed.

Notation declarations provide a name for the notation, for use in entity and
attribute-list declarations and in attribute specifications, and an external identifier
for the notation which may allow an XML processor or its client application to
locate a helper application capable of processing data in the given notation.

Notation Declarations

```
[82] NotationDecl::= '<!NOTATION' S Name S (ExternalID |  PublicID)
     S? '>'
[83] PublicID::= 'PUBLIC' S PubidLiteral
```

XML processors must provide applications with the name and external identi-
fier(s) of any notation declared and referred to in an attribute value, attribute definition, or entity declaration. They may additionally resolve the external identifier
into the system identifier, file name, or other information needed to allow the
application to call a processor for data in the notation described. (It is not an error,
however, for XML documents to declare and refer to notations for which notation-
specific applications are not available on the system where the XML processor or
application is running.)

4.8 Document Entity

The document entity serves as the root of the entity tree and a starting-point for an XML processor. This specification does not specify how the document entity is to be located by an XML processor; unlike other entities, the document entity has no name and might well appear on a processor input stream without any identification at all.

5. Conformance

5.1 Validating and Non-Validating Processors

Conforming XML processors fall into two classes: validating and non-validating.

Validating and non-validating processors alike must report violations of this specification's well-formedness constraints in the content of the document entity and any other parsed entities that they read.

Validating processors must report violations of the constraints expressed by the declarations in the DTD, and failures to fulfill the validity constraints given in this specification. To accomplish this, validating XML processors must read and process the entire DTD and all external parsed entities referenced in the document.

Non-validating processors are required to check only the document entity, including the entire internal DTD subset, for well-formedness. While they are not required to check the document for validity, they are required to process all the declarations they read in the internal DTD subset and in any parameter entity that they read, up to the first reference to a parameter entity that they do not read; that is to say, they must use the information in those declarations to normalize attribute values, include the replacement text of internal entities, and supply default attribute values. They must not process entity declarations or attribute-list declarations encountered after a reference to a parameter entity that is not read, since the entity may have contained overriding declarations.

5.2 Using XML Processors

The behavior of a validating XML processor is highly predictable; it must read every piece of a document and report all well-formedness and validity violations. Less is required of a non-validating processor; it need not read any part of the document other than the document entity. This has two effects that may be important to users of XML processors:

♦ Certain well-formedness errors, specifically those that require reading external entities, may not be detected by a non-validating processor. Examples include the constraints entitled Entity Declared, Parsed Entity, and No Recursion, as well as some of the cases described as forbidden in 4.4, "XML Processor Treatment of Entities and References".

♦ The information passed from the processor to the application may vary, depending on whether the processor reads parameter and external entities. For example, a non-validating processor may not normalize attribute values, include the replacement text of internal entities, or supply default attribute values, where doing so depends on having read declarations in external or parameter entities.

For maximum reliability in interoperating between different XML processors, applications which use non-validating processors should not rely on any behaviors not required of such processors. Applications which require facilities such as the use of default attributes or internal entities which are declared in external entities should use validating XML processors.

6. Notation

The formal grammar of XML is given in this specification using a simple Extended Backus-Naur Form (EBNF) notation. Each rule in the grammar defines one symbol, in the form

```
symbol ::= expression
```

Symbols are written with an initial capital letter if they are defined by a regular expression, or with an initial lower case letter otherwise. Literal strings are quoted.
    Within the expression on the right-hand side of a rule, the following expressions are used to match strings of one or more characters:

```
#xN
```

where N is a hexadecimal integer, the expression matches the character in ISO/IEC 10646 whose canonical (UCS-4) code value, when interpreted as an unsigned binary number, has the value indicated. The number of leading zeros in the #xN form is insignificant; the number of leading zeros in the corresponding code value is governed by the character encoding in use and is not significant for XML.

```
[a-zA-Z], [#xN-#xN]
```

matches any character with a value in the range(s) indicated (inclusive).

`[^a-z]`, `[^#xN-#xN]`

matches any character with a value outside the range indicated.

`[^abc]`, `[^#xN#xN#xN]`

matches any character with a value not among the characters given.

`"string"`

matches a literal string matching that given inside the double quotes.

`'string'`

matches a literal string matching that given inside the single quotes.
These symbols may be combined to match more complex patterns as follows, where A and B represent simple expressions:

`(expression)`

expression is treated as a unit and may be combined as described in this list.

`A?`

matches A or nothing; optional A.

`A B`

matches A followed by B.

`A | B`

matches A or B but not both.

`A - B`

matches any string that matches A but does not match B.

`A+`

matches one or more occurrences of A.

`A*`

matches zero or more occurrences of A.

Other notations used in the productions are:

```
/* ... */
```

comment.

```
[ wfc: ... ]
```

well-formedness constraint; this identifies by name a constraint on well-formed documents associated with a production.

```
[ vc: ... ]
```

validity constraint; this identifies by name a constraint on valid documents associated with a production.

Appendixes

A. References

A.1 NORMATIVE REFERENCES
IANA
(Internet Assigned Numbers Authority) *Official Names for Character Sets*, ed. Keld Simonsen et al. See `ftp://ftp.isi.edu/in-notes/iana/assignments/character-sets`.
IETF RFC 1766
IETF (Internet Engineering Task Force). *RFC 1766: Tags for the Identification of Languages*, ed. H. Alvestrand. 1995.
ISO 639
(International Organization for Standardization). *ISO 639:1988 (E). Code for the representation of names of languages.* Geneva: International Organization for Standardization, 1988.
ISO 3166
(International Organization for Standardization). *ISO 3166-1:1997 (E). Codes for the representation of names of countries and their subdivisions — Part 1: Country codes.* Geneva: International Organization for Standardization, 1997.
ISO/IEC 10646
ISO (International Organization for Standardization). *ISO/IEC 10646-1993 (E). Information technology — Universal Multiple-Octet Coded Character Set (UCS) — Part 1: Architecture and Basic Multilingual Plane.* Geneva: International Organization for Standardization, 1993 (plus amendments AM 1 through AM 7).
Unicode
The Unicode Consortium. *The Unicode Standard, Version 2.0.* Reading, Mass.: Addison-Wesley Developers Press, 1996.

A.2 OTHER REFERENCES

Aho/Ullman

Aho, Alfred V., Ravi Sethi, and Jeffrey D. Ullman. *Compilers: Principles, Techniques, and Tools.* Reading: Addison-Wesley, 1986, rpt. corr. 1988.

Berners-Lee et al.

Berners-Lee, T., R. Fielding, and L. Masinter. *Uniform Resource Identifiers (URI): Generic Syntax and Semantics.* 1997. (Work in progress; see updates to RFC1738.)

Brüggemann-Klein

Brüggemann-Klein, Anne. *Regular Expressions into Finite Automata.* Extended abstract in I. Simon, Hrsg., LATIN 1992, S. 97-98. Springer-Verlag, Berlin 1992. Full Version in Theoretical Computer Science 120: 197-213, 1993.

Brüggemann-Klein and Wood

Brüggemann-Klein, Anne, and Derick Wood. *Deterministic Regular Languages.* Universität Freiburg, Institut für Informatik, Bericht 38, Oktober 1991.

Clark

James Clark. Comparison of SGML and XML. See `http://www.w3.org/TR/NOTE-sgml-xml-971215`.

IETF RFC1738

IETF (Internet Engineering Task Force). *RFC 1738: Uniform Resource Locators (URL)*, ed. T. Berners-Lee, L. Masinter, M. McCahill. 1994.

IETF RFC1808

IETF (Internet Engineering Task Force). *RFC 1808: Relative Uniform Resource Locators*, ed. R. Fielding. 1995.

IETF RFC2141

IETF (Internet Engineering Task Force). *RFC 2141: URN Syntax*, ed. R. Moats. 1997.

ISO 8879

ISO (International Organization for Standardization). *ISO 8879:1986(E). Information processing – Text and Office Systems – Standard Generalized Markup Language (SGML).* First edition – 1986-10-15. [Geneva]: International Organization for Standardization, 1986.

ISO/IEC 10744

ISO (International Organization for Standardization). *ISO/IEC 10744-1992 (E). Information technology – Hypermedia/Time-based Structuring Language (HyTime).* [Geneva]: International Organization for Standardization, 1992. Extended Facilities Annexe. [Geneva]: International Organization for Standardization, 1996.

B. Character Classes

Following the characteristics defined in the Unicode standard, characters are classed as base characters (among others, these contain the alphabetic characters of the Latin alphabet, without diacritics), ideographic characters, and combining characters (among others, this class contains most diacritics); these classes combine to form the class of letters. Digits and extenders are also distinguished.

Characters

```
[84] Letter::= BaseChar | Ideographic
[85] BaseChar::= [#x0041-#x005A] | [#x0061-#x007A] | [#x00C0-#x00D6]
 | [#x00D8-#x00F6] | [#x00F8-#x00FF] | [#x0100-#x0131] | [#x0134-
#x013E] | [#x0141-#x0148] | [#x014A-#x017E] | [#x0180-#x01C3] |
[#x01CD-#x01F0] | [#x01F4-#x01F5] | [#x01FA-#x0217] | [#x0250-
#x02A8] | [#x02BB-#x02C1] | #x0386 | [#x0388-#x038A] | #x038C |
[#x038E-#x03A1] | [#x03A3-#x03CE] | [#x03D0-#x03D6] | #x03DA |
#x03DC | #x03DE | #x03E0 | [#x03E2-#x03F3] | [#x0401-#x040C] |
[#x040E-#x044F] | [#x0451-#x045C] | [#x045E-#x0481] | [#x0490-
#x04C4] | [#x04C7-#x04C8] | [#x04CB-#x04CC] | [#x04D0-#x04EB] |
[#x04EE-#x04F5] | [#x04F8-#x04F9] | [#x0531-#x0556] | #x0559 |
[#x0561-#x0586] | [#x05D0-#x05EA] | [#x05F0-#x05F2] | [#x0621-
#x063A] | [#x0641-#x064A] | [#x0671-#x06B7] | [#x06BA-#x06BE] |
[#x06C0-#x06CE] | [#x06D0-#x06D3] | #x06D5 | [#x06E5-#x06E6] |
[#x0905-#x0939] | #x093D | [#x0958-#x0961] | [#x0985-#x098C] |
[#x098F-#x0990] | [#x0993-#x09A8] | [#x09AA-#x09B0] | #x09B2 |
[#x09B6-#x09B9] | [#x09DC-#x09DD] | [#x09DF-#x09E1] | [#x09F0-
#x09F1] | [#x0A05-#x0A0A] | [#x0A0F-#x0A10] | [#x0A13-#x0A28] |
[#x0A2A-#x0A30] | [#x0A32-#x0A33] | [#x0A35-#x0A36] | [#x0A38-
#x0A39] | [#x0A59-#x0A5C] | #x0A5E | [#x0A72-#x0A74] |
[#x0A85-#x0A8B] | #x0A8D | [#x0A8F-#x0A91] | [#x0A93-#x0AA8] |
[#x0AAA-#x0AB0] | [#x0AB2-#x0AB3] | [#x0AB5-#x0AB9] | #x0ABD |
#x0AE0 | [#x0B05-#x0B0C] | [#x0B0F-#x0B10] | [#x0B13-#x0B28] |
[#x0B2A-#x0B30] | [#x0B32-#x0B33] | [#x0B36-#x0B39] | #x0B3D |
[#x0B5C-#x0B5D] | [#x0B5F-#x0B61] | [#x0B85-#x0B8A] | [#x0B8E-
#x0B90] | [#x0B92-#x0B95] | [#x0B99-#x0B9A] | #x0B9C |
[#x0B9E-#x0B9F] | [#x0BA3-#x0BA4] | [#x0BA8-#x0BAA] | [#x0BAE-
#x0BB5] | [#x0BB7-#x0BB9] | [#x0C05-#x0C0C] | [#x0C0E-#x0C10] |
[#x0C12-#x0C28] | [#x0C2A-#x0C33] | [#x0C35-#x0C39] | [#x0C60-
#x0C61] | [#x0C85-#x0C8C] | [#x0C8E-#x0C90] | [#x0C92-#x0CA8] |
[#x0CAA-#x0CB3] | [#x0CB5-#x0CB9] | #x0CDE | [#x0CE0-#x0CE1] |
[#x0D05-#x0D0C] | [#x0D0E-#x0D10] | [#x0D12-#x0D28] | [#x0D2A-
#x0D39] | [#x0D60-#x0D61] | [#x0E01-#x0E2E] | #x0E30 |
[#x0E32-#x0E33] | [#x0E40-#x0E45] | [#x0E81-#x0E82] | #x0E84 |
[#x0E87-#x0E88] | #x0E8A | #x0E8D | [#x0E94-#x0E97] | [#x0E99-
#x0E9F] | [#x0EA1-#x0EA3] | #x0EA5 | #x0EA7 | [#x0EAA-#x0EAB] |
[#x0EAD-#x0EAE] | #x0EB0 | [#x0EB2-#x0EB3] | #x0EBD | [#x0EC0-
#x0EC4] | [#x0F40-#x0F47] | [#x0F49-#x0F69] | [#x10A0-#x10C5] |
[#x10D0-#x10F6] | #x1100 | [#x1102-#x1103] | [#x1105-#x1107] |
#x1109 | [#x110B-#x110C] | [#x110E-#x1112] | #x113C | #x113E |
#x1140 | #x114C | #x114E | #x1150 | [#x1154-#x1155] | #x1159 |
[#x115F-#x1161] | #x1163 | #x1165 | #x1167 | #x1169 | [#x116D-
#x116E] | [#x1172-#x1173] | #x1175 | #x119E | #x11A8 | #x11AB |
[#x11AE-#x11AF] | [#x11B7-#x11B8] | #x11BA | [#x11BC-#x11C2] |
#x11EB | #x11F0 | #x11F9 | [#x1E00-#x1E9B] | [#x1EA0-#x1EF9] |
[#x1F00-#x1F15] | [#x1F18-#x1F1D] | [#x1F20-#x1F45] | [#x1F48-
#x1F4D] | [#x1F50-#x1F57] | #x1F59 | #x1F5B | #x1F5D |
[#x1F5F-#x1F7D] | [#x1F80-#x1FB4] | [#x1FB6-#x1FBC] | #x1FBE |
[#x1FC2-#x1FC4] | [#x1FC6-#x1FCC] | [#x1FD0-#x1FD3] | [#x1FD6-
#x1FDB] | [#x1FE0-#x1FEC] | [#x1FF2-#x1FF4] | [#x1FF6-#x1FFC] |
#x2126 | [#x212A-#x212B] | #x212E | [#x2180-#x2182] | [#x3041-
#x3094] | [#x30A1-#x30FA] | [#x3105-#x312C] | [#xAC00-#xD7A3]
```

```
[86] Ideographic::= [#x4E00-#x9FA5] | #x3007 | [#x3021-#x3029]
[87] CombiningChar::= [#x0300-#x0345] | [#x0360-#x0361] | [#x0483-
#x0486] | [#x0591-#x05A1] | [#x05A3-#x05B9] | [#x05BB-#x05BD] |
#x05BF | [#x05C1-#x05C2] | #x05C4 | [#x064B-#x0652] | #x0670 |
[#x06D6-#x06DC] | [#x06DD-#x06DF] | [#x06E0-#x06E4] | [#x06E7-
#x06E8] | [#x06EA-#x06ED] | [#x0901-#x0903] | #x093C |
[#x093E-#x094C] | #x094D | [#x0951-#x0954] | [#x0962-#x0963] |
[#x0981-#x0983] | #x09BC | #x09BE | #x09BF | [#x09C0-#x09C4] |
[#x09C7-#x09C8] | [#x09CB-#x09CD] | #x09D7 | [#x09E2-#x09E3] |
#x0A02 | #x0A3C | #x0A3E | #x0A3F | [#x0A40-#x0A42] | [#x0A47-
#x0A48] | [#x0A4B-#x0A4D] | [#x0A70-#x0A71] | [#x0A81-#x0A83] |
#x0ABC | [#x0ABE-#x0AC5] | [#x0AC7-#x0AC9] | [#x0ACB-#x0ACD] |
[#x0B01-#x0B03] | #x0B3C | [#x0B3E-#x0B43] | [#x0B47-#x0B48] |
[#x0B4B-#x0B4D] | [#x0B56-#x0B57] | [#x0B82-#x0B83] | [#x0BBE-
#x0BC2] | [#x0BC6-#x0BC8] | [#x0BCA-#x0BCD] | #x0BD7 |
[#x0C01-#x0C03] | [#x0C3E-#x0C44] | [#x0C46-#x0C48] | [#x0C4A-
#x0C4D] | [#x0C55-#x0C56] | [#x0C82-#x0C83] | [#x0CBE-#x0CC4] |
[#x0CC6-#x0CC8] | [#x0CCA-#x0CCD] | [#x0CD5-#x0CD6] | [#x0D02-
#x0D03] | [#x0D3E-#x0D43] | [#x0D46-#x0D48] | [#x0D4A-#x0D4D] |
#x0D57 | #x0E31 | [#x0E34-#x0E3A] | [#x0E47-#x0E4E] | #x0EB1 |
[#x0EB4-#x0EB9] | [#x0EBB-#x0EBC] | [#x0EC8-#x0ECD] | [#x0F18-
#x0F19] | #x0F35 | #x0F37 | #x0F39 | #x0F3E | #x0F3F |
[#x0F71-#x0F84] | [#x0F86-#x0F8B] | [#x0F90-#x0F95] | #x0F97 |
[#x0F99-#x0FAD] | [#x0FB1-#x0FB7] | #x0FB9 | [#x20D0-#x20DC] |
#x20E1 | [#x302A-#x302F] | #x3099 | #x309A
[88] Digit::= [#x0030-#x0039] | [#x0660-#x0669] | [#x06F0-#x06F9] |
[#x0966-#x096F] | [#x09E6-#x09EF] | [#x0A66-#x0A6F] | [#x0AE6-
#x0AEF] | [#x0B66-#x0B6F] | [#x0BE7-#x0BEF] | [#x0C66-#x0C6F] |
[#x0CE6-#x0CEF] | [#x0D66-#x0D6F] | [#x0E50-#x0E59] | [#x0ED0-
#x0ED9] | [#x0F20-#x0F29]
[89] Extender::= #x00B7 | #x02D0 | #x02D1 | #x0387 | #x0640 | #x0E46
| #x0EC6 | #x3005 | [#x3031-#x3035] | [#x309D-#x309E] | [#x30FC-
#x30FE]
```

The character classes defined here can be derived from the Unicode character database as follows:

◆ Name start characters must have one of the categories Ll, Lu, Lo, Lt, Nl.

◆ Name characters other than Name-start characters must have one of the categories Mc, Me, Mn, Lm, or Nd.

◆ Characters in the compatibility area (i.e. with character code greater than #xF900 and less than #xFFFE) are not allowed in XML names.

◆ Characters which have a font or compatibility decomposition (i.e. those with a "compatibility formatting tag" in field 5 of the database – marked by field 5 beginning with a "<") are not allowed.

◆ The following characters are treated as name-start characters rather than name characters, because the property file classifies them as Alphabetic: #x02BB-#x02C1, #x0559, #x06E5, #x06E6.

◆ Characters #x20DD-#x20E0 are excluded (in accordance with Unicode, section 5.14).

◆ Character #x00B7 is classified as an extender, because the property list so identifies it.

◆ Character #x0387 is added as a name character, because #x00B7 is its canonical equivalent.

◆ Characters ':' and '_' are allowed as name-start characters.

◆ Characters '-' and '.' are allowed as name characters.

C. XML and SGML (Non-Normative)

XML is designed to be a subset of SGML, in that every valid XML document should also be a conformant SGML document. For a detailed comparison of the additional restrictions that XML places on documents beyond those of SGML, see Clark.

D. Expansion of Entity and Character References (Non-Normative)

This appendix contains some examples illustrating the sequence of entity- and character-reference recognition and expansion, as specified in 4.4, "XML Processor Treatment of Entities and References".

If the DTD contains the declaration

```
<!ENTITY example "<p>An ampersand (&#38;#38;) may be escaped
numerically (&#38;#38;#38;) or with a general entity
(&amp;amp;).</p>" >
```

then the XML processor will recognize the character references when it parses the entity declaration, and resolve them before storing the following string as the value of the entity "example":

```
<p>An ampersand (&#38;) may be escaped
numerically (&#38;#38;) or with a general entity
(&amp;amp;).</p>
```

A reference in the document to "&example;" will cause the text to be reparsed, at which time the start- and end-tags of the "p" element will be recognized and the three references will be recognized and expanded, resulting in a "p" element with the following content (all data, no delimiters or markup):

```
An ampersand (&) may be escaped
numerically (&#38;) or with a general entity
(&amp;).
```

A more complex example will illustrate the rules and their effects fully. In the following example, the line numbers are solely for reference.

```
1 <?xml version='1.0'?>
2 <!DOCTYPE test [
3 <!ELEMENT test (#PCDATA) >
4 <!ENTITY % xx '&#37;zz;'>
5 <!ENTITY % zz '&#60;!ENTITY tricky "error-prone" >' >
6 %xx;
7 ]>
8 <test>This sample shows a &tricky; method.</test>
```

This produces the following:

◆ in line 4, the reference to character 37 is expanded immediately, and the parameter entity "xx" is stored in the symbol table with the value "%zz;". Since the replacement text is not rescanned, the reference to parameter entity "zz" is not recognized. (And it would be an error if it were, since "zz" is not yet declared.)

◆ in line 5, the character reference "<" is expanded immediately and the parameter entity "zz" is stored with the replacement text "<!ENTITY tricky "error-prone" >", which is a well-formed entity declaration.

◆ in line 6, the reference to "xx" is recognized, and the replacement text of "xx" (namely "%zz;") is parsed. The reference to "zz" is recognized in its turn, and its replacement text ("<!ENTITY tricky "error-prone" >") is parsed. The general entity "tricky" has now been declared, with the replacement text "error-prone".

◆ in line 8, the reference to the general entity "tricky" is recognized, and it is expanded, so the full content of the "test" element is the self-describing (and ungrammatical) string: *This sample shows a error-prone method.*

E. Deterministic Content Models (Non-Normative)

For compatibility, it is required that content models in element type declarations be deterministic.

SGML requires deterministic content models (it calls them "unambiguous"); XML processors built using SGML systems may flag non-deterministic content models as errors.

For example, the content model ((b, c) | (b, d)) is non-deterministic, because given an initial b the parser cannot know which b in the model is being matched without looking ahead to see which element follows the b. In this case, the two references to b can be collapsed into a single reference, making the model read (b, (c | d)). An initial b now clearly matches only a single name in the content model. The parser doesn't need to look ahead to see what follows; either c or d would be accepted.

More formally: a finite state automaton may be constructed from the content model using the standard algorithms, e.g. algorithm 3.5 in section 3.9 of Aho, Sethi, and Ullman. In many such algorithms, a follow set is constructed for each position in the regular expression (i.e., each leaf node in the syntax tree for the regular expression); if any position has a follow set in which more than one following position is labeled with the same element type name, then the content model is in error and may be reported as an error.

Algorithms exist which allow many but not all non-deterministic content models to be reduced automatically to equivalent deterministic models; see Brüggemann-Klein 1991.

F. Autodetection of Character Encodings (Non-Normative)

The XML encoding declaration functions as an internal label on each entity, indicating which character encoding is in use. Before an XML processor can read the internal label, however, it apparently has to know what character encoding is in use — which is what the internal label is trying to indicate. In the general case, this is a hopeless situation. It is not entirely hopeless in XML, however, because XML limits the general case in two ways: each implementation is assumed to support only a finite set of character encodings, and the XML encoding declaration is restricted in position and content in order to make it feasible to autodetect the character encoding in use in each entity in normal cases. Also, in many cases other sources of information are available in addition to the XML data stream itself. Two cases may be distinguished, depending on whether the XML entity is presented to the processor without, or with, any accompanying (external) information. We consider the first case first.

Because each XML entity not in UTF-8 or UTF-16 format must begin with an XML encoding declaration, in which the first characters must be '<?xml', any conforming processor can detect, after two to four octets of input, which of the following cases apply. In reading this list, it may help to know that in UCS-4, '<' is "#x0000003C" and '?' is "#x0000003F", and the Byte Order Mark required of UTF-16 data streams is "#xFEFF".

- 00 00 00 3C: UCS-4, big-endian machine (1234 order)
- 3C 00 00 00: UCS-4, little-endian machine (4321 order)
- 00 00 3C 00: UCS-4, unusual octet order (2143)
- 00 3C 00 00: UCS-4, unusual octet order (3412)
- FE FF: UTF-16, big-endian

- ◆ FF FE: UTF-16, little-endian

- ◆ 00 3C 00 3F: UTF-16, big-endian, no Byte Order Mark (and thus, strictly speaking, in error)

- ◆ 3C 00 3F 00: UTF-16, little-endian, no Byte Order Mark (and thus, strictly speaking, in error)

- ◆ 3C 3F 78 6D: UTF-8, ISO 646, ASCII, some part of ISO 8859, Shift-JIS, EUC, or any other 7-bit, 8-bit, or mixed-width encoding which ensures that the characters of ASCII have their normal positions, width, and values; the actual encoding declaration must be read to detect which of these applies, but since all of these encodings use the same bit patterns for the ASCII characters, the encoding declaration itself may be read reliably

- ◆ 4C 6F A7 94: EBCDIC (in some flavor; the full encoding declaration must be read to tell which code page is in use)

- ◆ other: UTF-8 without an encoding declaration, or else the data stream is corrupt, fragmentary, or enclosed in a wrapper of some kind

This level of autodetection is enough to read the XML encoding declaration and parse the character-encoding identifier, which is still necessary to distinguish the individual members of each family of encodings (e.g. to tell UTF-8 from 8859, and the parts of 8859 from each other, or to distinguish the specific EBCDIC code page in use, and so on).

Because the contents of the encoding declaration are restricted to ASCII characters, a processor can reliably read the entire encoding declaration as soon as it has detected which family of encodings is in use. Since in practice, all widely used character encodings fall into one of the categories above, the XML encoding declaration allows reasonably reliable in-band labeling of character encodings, even when external sources of information at the operating-system or transport-protocol level are unreliable.

Once the processor has detected the character encoding in use, it can act appropriately, whether by invoking a separate input routine for each case, or by calling the proper conversion function on each character of input.

Like any self-labeling system, the XML encoding declaration will not work if any software changes the entity's character set or encoding without updating the encoding declaration. Implementors of character-encoding routines should be careful to ensure the accuracy of the internal and external information used to label the entity.

The second possible case occurs when the XML entity is accompanied by encoding information, as in some file systems and some network protocols. When multiple sources of information are available, their relative priority and the preferred method of handling conflict should be specified as part of the higher-level protocol used to deliver XML. Rules for the relative priority of the internal label and the

MIME-type label in an external header, for example, should be part of the RFC document defining the text/xml and application/xml MIME types. In the interests of interoperability, however, the following rules are recommended.

- If an XML entity is in a file, the Byte-Order Mark and encoding-declaration PI are used (if present) to determine the character encoding. All other heuristics and sources of information are solely for error recovery.

- If an XML entity is delivered with a MIME type of text/xml, then the charset parameter on the MIME type determines the character encoding method; all other heuristics and sources of information are solely for error recovery.

- If an XML entity is delivered with a MIME type of application/xml, then the Byte-Order Mark and encoding-declaration PI are used (if present) to determine the character encoding. All other heuristics and sources of information are solely for error recovery.

These rules apply only in the absence of protocol-level documentation; in particular, when the MIME types text/xml and application/xml are defined, the recommendations of the relevant RFC will supersede these rules.

G. W3C XML Working Group (Non-Normative)

This specification was prepared and approved for publication by the W3C XML Working Group (WG). WG approval of this specification does not necessarily imply that all WG members voted for its approval. The current and former members of the XML WG are:

Jon Bosak, Sun (Chair); James Clark (Technical Lead); Tim Bray, Textuality and Netscape (XML Co-editor); Jean Paoli, Microsoft (XML Co-editor); C. M. Sperberg-McQueen, U. of Ill. (XML Co-editor); Dan Connolly, W3C (W3C Liaison); Paula Angerstein, Texcel; Steve DeRose, INSO; Dave Hollander, HP; Eliot Kimber, ISO-GEN; Eve Maler, ArborText; Tom Magliery, NCSA; Murray Maloney, Muzmo and Grif; Makoto Murata, Fuji Xerox Information Systems; Joel Nava, Adobe; Conleth O'Connell, Vignette; Peter Sharpe, SoftQuad; John Tigue, DataChannel

W3C IPR DOCUMENT NOTICE

Appendix C

Additional Resources

AS YOU PROBABLY GATHERED from the rest of this book, XML is fairly new. Although a great number of payware tools do not yet exist – and the current tools are mostly expensive repurposed SGML tools – there are more than a few excellent freeware tools. In addition, several Web sites and a couple of mailing lists should be noteworthy to anyone following developments in XML. As you'd probably guess, almost all of the good resources are located on the Internet and the Web.

The XML FAQ

Peter Flynn maintains the semiofficial XML FAQ list at http://www.ucc.ie/xml/. The list is an excellent resource for anyone working with or wanting to know more about XML. Like most FAQ lists, it concentrates on the most frequently asked questions about XML – its practical value is enormous.

The FAQ is divided into four sections addressing questions from four different user categories:

- ◆ General
- ◆ User
- ◆ Author
- ◆ Developer

Specifications and Standards

Most of the technologies described in this book, including XML itself, fall under the auspices of the World Wide Web Consortium (http://www.w3.org). The W3C is an industry consortium that establishes standards related to the Web. XML, HTML, XLinks, and XPointers are only some of the specifications W3C has published. The XML specification in Appendix B was created by this organization. Membership is only open to dues-paying companies – not to individuals. Most of its standards documents are freely available to the public, however.

The underlying protocols of the Internet, as well as a few other standards, mostly fall under the auspices of the Internet Engineering Task Force (IETF). The IETF is a relatively free-wheeling organization that works on the basis of rough consensus and running code. Overall, IETF is more open to participation by interested individuals and academics than the W3C. Standards under the auspices of the IETF include URLs. In many cases, standards are developed in the W3C and then moved to the IETF.

In addition, a few de facto standards don't currently fall under the domain of any formal standards organization. The most notable current example is SAX (Simple API for XML), which is currently developed primarily by David Megginson with input from the members of the xml-dev mailing list. Often such specifications are moved to formal standard status in one or more standards bodies after they've had an opportunity to grow and work out the bugs.

Specifications currently available or under development that relate to XML include the following:

- XML 1.0: `http://www.w3c.org/TR/REC-xml`

- XLinks: `http://www.w3c.org/TR/WD-xlink`

- XPointers: `http://www.w3c.org/TR/WD-xptr`

- XLink Design Principles: `http://www.w3c.org/TR/NOTE-xlink-principles`

- XML Namespaces: `http://www.w3c.org/TR/WD-xml-names`

- XML Data: `http://www.w3c.org/TR/1998/NOTE-XML-data/`

- XSL: `http://www.w3c.org/TR/NOTE-XSL.html`

- DOM: `http://www.w3.org/DOM/`

- SAX: `http://www.microstar.com/XML/SAX/`

- CSS Level 1: `http://www.w3.org/pub/WWW/TR/REC-CSS1`

- CSS Level 2: `http://www.w3.org/TR/PR-CSS2/`

- HTML 4.0: `http://www.w3.org/TR/REC-html40`

- URLs: `ftp://ds.internic.net/rfc/rfc1738.txt`

Most of these documents value precision over clarity. Exact specifications are often given in Backus-Naur Form (BNF) grammars with additional explanation in English. These specifications aren't exactly easy to read, but when you need to know exactly what is and isn't allowed, they're often the only place to turn.

Development Tools

This book mostly used the MSXML validating parser and the MSXSL formatting engine, primarily because they have the cleanest interfaces of the early tools. The XML tools market is developing rapidly, however, with many choices available soon. This section reviews a few of the tools to help you with XML development including:

◆ validating parsers

◆ nonvalidating parsers

◆ XML browsers

Validating Parsers

Validating parsers read a document and compare it with its DTD. Available validating parsers include:

◆ MSXML: http://www.microsoft.com/standards/xml/xmlparse.htm

◆ XML for Java: http://www.alphaworks.ibm.com/formula/xml

◆ DXP: http://www.datachannel.com/products/xdk/DXP/index.html

◆ TclXML: http://tcltk.anu.edu.au/XML/

MSXML

I'm not sure whether Microsoft's MSXML is buggier than the other validating parsers or whether I've just spent more time working with it and thus had more opportunity to notice bugs. Regardless, MSXML is one of the few validating parsers that provides an actual application for validating files, rather than just a class library around which you can build your own programs.

XML FOR JAVA

IBM's alphaworks project has produced a lot of interesting cutting edge software, much of it written in Java. The latest release is XML for Java, a validating XML parser Java class library that supports the most recent releases of the DOM and namespace specifications and includes XPointer support.

DXP

DXP is perhaps the most compliant validating processor at the time of this writing. When I encountered problems with my XML files that I thought were MSXML mistakes rather than my own, I'd pass the files through DXP. DataChannel, the owner of DXP, also offers a number of other XML tools of varying utility.

TCLXML

The TclXML parser isn't as up-to-date as the preceding parsers. TclXML has the distinction of being based on TCL rather than Java or C, however.

Nonvalidating Parsers

A nonvalidating parser merely checks the well-formedness of a document and produces the element tree corresponding to the document. These parsers do not check for validity errors. Nonvalidating parsers include:

- ◆ Lark: `http://www.textuality.com/Lark/`
- ◆ XP: `http://www.jclark.com/xml/xp/index.html`

LARK

Tim Bray's Lark is a free, nonvalidating XML processor written in Java with a user interface only a hacker could love. (In essence, it doesn't have one.) Lark was primarily intended to explore the XML specification and will probably be replaced by other processors. Larval is a validating XML processor based on most of the same code as Lark.

XP

James Clark's XP is a fast, nonvalidating, SAX-compliant, XML 1.0 parser class library written in Java 1.1. Although it doesn't validate files, XP does consider DTDs when required for well-formedness checking, as in the case of both internal and external entity references.

XML Browsers

An XML browser should be able to read and display an arbitrary XML document, and possibly format the document according to the rules given in some sort of style sheet. The two general purpose XML browsers follow:

- ◆ Jumbo: `http://vsms.nottingham.ac.uk/vsms/java/jumbo`
- ◆ Mozilla: `http://www.mozilla.org/`

JUMBO

Peter Murray Rust's Jumbo was the first general purpose XML browser. Jumbo displays XML documents in a tree structure and does not attempt to format them via style sheets. Written in Java, it should run on most platforms supporting Java 1.2 or later.

MOZILLA

Netscape has incorporated support for basic XML formatted according to Cascading Style Sheets in Mozilla (and presumably Communicator and Navigator) 5.0. At the time of this writing, Mozilla 5.0 is primarily available in an extremely buggy source code form from `http://www.mozilla.org/`. I average about five pages viewed between crashes. Nonetheless, the bugs are being fixed rapidly, and Mozilla is already much more stable just three weeks after initial release. XML support is receiving special attention from the legions of hackers banging on the source code, so Mozilla should be more usable by the time you read this book. Mozilla's XML abilities will be discussed in more detail in my forthcoming book, *XML Bible,* available from IDG Books Worldwide.

Informational Sites

Several meta-XML sites on the Web include various background information about XML resources and other useful XML information:

◆ XML.com: `http://www.xml.com/`

◆ Microsoft's XML Page: `http://www.microsoft.com/xml/`

◆ Robin Cover's XML Web Page: `http://www.sil.org/sgml/xml.html`

◆ James Clark's XML Resources: `http://www.jclark.com/xml/`

◆ Café con Leche: `http://sunsite.unc.edu/xml/`

XML.com

I tried to register this domain name myself, but I was beaten to the punch. Nonetheless, the folks at `www.xml.com` have an impressive site with many articles about various aspects of XML. The site is most notable for Tim Bray's annotated version of the XML 1.0 specification.

Microsoft's XML Page

Microsoft is committed to XML in a big way. Their Web page features various white papers and tutorials about XML, particularly as it relates to Internet Explorer 4.0. Among other features, this site features a lot of information about Microsoft's version of XSL.

Robin Cover's XML Web Page

Robin Cover has put together what is almost certainly the largest and most comprehensive collection of annotated links to XML pages on the Web. The page was over 400K when last checked (and desperately needs to be broken up into multiple pages). Cover's collection of SGML links is even larger. Topics include an overview of XML, specifications, FAQ lists, other Web sites, applications of XML, articles and papers about XML, books about XML, press releases about XML related technology, XML discussion forums, XML software, and more.

James Clark's XML Resources

James Clark has been instrumental in the early development of XML. His page features a half dozen parsers and parser tools he's developed, including a subset of XML called Canonical XML for testing XML parsers; test cases for XML parsers; a Java program that generates canonical XML; XP, the high-performance XML parser; a C library for parsing XML called Expat used in Perl and Mozilla; and more. This site is primarily of interest to programmers developing XML-based software.

Café con Leche

Café con Leche is my own site featuring lists of XML books, trade shows, mailing lists, links to other sites, and daily news updates about the XML world. You'll also find the complete set of examples from this book as well as any corrections and updates that become necessary as XML grows and evolves.

Discussing XML

Two major mailing lists and one Usenet newsgroup are devoted to XML:

- ◆ xml-dev
- ◆ XML-L
- ◆ comp.text.xml

xml-dev

xml-dev is the granddaddy of XML mailing lists. Many details of early XML versions and related specifications were hashed out on this list. xml-dev is primarily aimed at implementers of XML-based software – that is, XML developers.

To subscribe, send e-mail to majordomo@ic.ac.uk with the phrase "subscribe xml-dev" in the first line of the message body. A complete archive of messages posted to the list during can be found at http://www.lists.ic.ac.uk/hypermail/xml-dev/.

I occasionally post to this mailing list and read most of its contents, as do several other authors of XML books and many developers of XML software and specifications. This list is the main place where the heavies of the XML world converse.

XML-L

The XML-L mailing list is intended for authors of XML documents, as opposed to developers of XML software. Currently there's a lot of overlap with xml-dev, though the two lists are slowly diverging.

To subscribe, send e-mail to listserv@listserv.hea.ie from the account with which you want to subscribe with the command "subscribe XML-L your name" in the body of the message. I occasionally post to this mailing list and read most of its contents, as do several other authors of XML books and many developers of XML software and specifications.

comp.text.xml

As of spring 1998, a Request for Discussion (RFD) has been made for a comp.text.xml Usenet newsgroup, and the newsgroup should be approved by the time you're reading this book. According to the RFD:

- ◆ comp.text.xml shall be an unmoderated newsgroup for the discussion of the Extensible Markup Language (XML) and its application.

- ◆ This includes, but is not limited to the specifications and syntax, document creation and editing, interchange, software, processing and database integration. This applies not only to XML itself but also the Extensible Linking Language (XLL), the Extensible Style Language (XSL), Cascading Style Sheets (CSS) as applied to XML documents, and to document types and applications of XML.

I don't spend much time on Usenet these days, but those readers who do should find this group valuable.

Appendix D

About the CD-ROM

THIS BOOK'S CD-ROM is cross-platform; you should be able to mount it on Macintosh, Solaris, Windows 95, Windows 98, and Windows NT 4.0. There's no fancy installer. You can browse the directories as you would a hard drive.

Given the rapid state of XML development, any XML software placed on the CD-ROM will almost certainly be obsolete by the time you read this book. Therefore, the examples from the book are the main items of interest on the CD-ROM. You'll find these examples in a folder (organized by chapter) called `examples`. Netscape Communicator 4.0 and Microsoft Internet Explorer 4.0 are also included.

Simple HTML indexes are provided for the examples in each chapter. Because most of the examples are raw XML files, however, current Web browsers don't display them very well. You're probably better off opening the directories in Windows Explorer (or the equivalent) on your platform of choice and reading the files with a text editor.

Most of the files are named according to the example number in the book (for example, `10-2.xml`, `10-3.cdf`, and so forth). In a few cases where a specific name is used in the book, such as `family.dtd` or `family.xml`, that name is also used on the CD-ROM. The files on the CD-ROM appear exactly as they appear in the book's listings. If a listing includes only a fraction of a style sheet or XML document, the CD-ROM still only includes the portion listed in the book. Therefore, all of these files cannot necessarily be validated or pass well-formedness tests. In most cases, these fractional files are alternative parts for a complete file in a different listing – you should be able to add the missing pieces.

Glossary

#FIXED: XML keyword used in `<!ATTLIST>` declarations that specifies an attribute always has its default value for all instances of the element.

#IMPLIED: XML keyword used in `<!ATTLIST>` declarations that specifies an attribute value may or may not be provided in each instance of the element.

#REQUIRED: XML keyword used in `<!ATTLIST>` declarations that specifies an attribute value must be provided in each instance of the element.

action: the output of an XSL rule when its pattern is matched.

ActiveX: Microsoft's proprietary component software architecture model for Windows.

ActiveX Control: a software component written in C++, normally for Windows, according to Microsoft's ActiveX specification.

API: application programming interface – the collection of methods and classes that provides access to the host operating system and user interface beyond what's defined in the language itself.

architecture: a set of compatible computer hardware (for instance, X86 PCI bus or PowerPC NuBus).

attribute: a name value pair included inside an XML tag and separated by an equals (=) sign. The name is on the left-hand side of the equals sign. The value is on the right-hand side of the equals sign and enclosed in single or double quotes (for example, `id="xtocid345"`).

attribute declaration: `<!ATTLIST>` construct found in DTDs that specifies a permissible attribute and attribute values for a particular element.

block: block elements generally begin on new lines. Examples include `<P>` and `<DIV>` in HTML.

Cafe con Leche: 1) coffee with heated milk as served in the Caribbean; 2) a Web site at `http://sunsite.unc.edu/xml/` where you'll find updates and corrections to this book as well as links, events, and daily news updates.

CDATA: 1) XML keyword used in `<!ATTLIST>` declarations that specifies an attribute value may be essentially any raw text that doesn't form markup; 2) text enclosed between `<![CDATA[` and `]]>` in which characters normally considered markup like `<`, `>`, and & simply represent themselves.

character: a letter, digit, punctuation mark, white space, or similar unit.

character data: text in a particular encoding as distinguished from binary data.

child: XML element contained inside another XML element. The containing element is called the parent.

CML: Peter Murray-Rust's XML-based Chemical Markup Language for the molecular sciences.

COM: Microsoft's Component Object Model, associated with ActiveX and a competitor of CORBA.

comment: text inserted in an XML document between `<!--` and `-->` delimiters that is not shown to the end user when the document is displayed.

content: everything between an element's start and end tags.

CORBA: The Common Object Request Broker Architecture is a specification promulgated by the OMG for allowing objects written in different languages such as C++ and Java to communicate with each other.

CSS: Cascading Style Sheets – a way of defining the appearance of particular HTML and/or XML elements.

DCOM: Microsoft's Distributed Component Object Model is an extension of COM that allows objects to communicate with each other on different hosts across a network.

document root: the element in an XML document that contains all other elements; this must be the first element in the document.

document type declaration: the `<!DOCTYPE [   ] >` structure that generally contains a document type definition.

Document Type Definition: the collection of markup declarations that describes an XML document's permissible elements and structure.

DSSSL: the Document Style Semantics and Specification Language (pronounced *dissal*, rhymes with *thistle* or *missal*), ISO standard, 10179:1996; an extremely powerful, extensible, and precise means of specifying exactly what you want to see on a printed page – generally used for formatting SGML documents.

DTD: see Document Type Definition.

ECMAScript: the nontrademarked name for JavaScript.

element: a section of text in an XML document delimited by start and end tags; or, in the case of empty elements, indicated by an empty tag.

element declaration: a construct found in DTDs with the form `<!ELEMENT name content_type>` that declares an element and its content.

empty tag: a tag whose element has no content, most commonly indicated by a forward slash before the closing angle bracket; has the form `<element_name/>`.

end tag: the closing delimiter of an element in the form `</element_name>`.

ENTITIES: XML keyword used in `<!ATTLIST>` declarations that specifies an attribute value must be a list of entities declared in the DTD.

entity: an unspecified type of storage unit for data.

ENTITY: XML keyword used in `<!ATTLIST>` declarations that specifies an attribute value must be the name of an entity declared in the DTD.

entity declaration: `<!ENTITY>` construct found in DTDs that specifies a name and either replacement text for that name or a URL where the replacement text can be found.

entity reference: a parameter entity reference or general entity reference.

escape: a means of embedding individual characters in a document that would otherwise be interpreted as markup.

extended link document element: XML link element that's a child of an extended link group element and refers to a particular URI.

extended link group element: XML element that contains a group of extended link document elements and connects the particular group of documents referred to by the extended link document elements.

external document type declaration: a DOCTYPE construct which uses the SYSTEM or PUBLIC keywords to load a DTD from a source other than the current document.

external entity: an entity not contained in the current document.

free: free means you don't have to pay.

free software: open source software.

freeware: software given away (most commonly in compiled form) without a license that permits it to be modified.

flow object: a particular HTML or DSSSL element that is output by an XSL rule action as a result of a matched pattern.

general entity reference: a reference of the form &*name*; that stands for some replacement text in the body of an XML document.

HTML: HyperText Markup Language, a popular text-based format for describing a document's structure and appearance.

IANA: Internet Assigned Numbers Authority, `http://www.iana.org/`; responsible for assigning IP address blocks, certifying top-level registrars in country domains, and maintaining lists of various codes and abbreviations used in Internet communication.

ID: XML keyword used in `<!ATTLIST>` declarations that specifies an attribute value must be a unique XML name.

IDL: the OMG's Interface Definition Language for describing the signatures of classes, fields, and methods.

IDREF: XML keyword used in `<!ATTLIST>` declarations that specifies an attribute value must be the ID of some element in the document.

IDREFS: XML keyword used in `<!ATTLIST>` declarations that specifies an attribute value must be a list of IDs of elements in the document.

IIOP: the OMG's Internet Inter-ORB Protocol for allowing CORBA objects to communicate across TCP/IP networks such as the Internet.

inline: inline elements generally do not begin on new lines (for example, `<STRONG>`, `<CODE>`, and `<A>` in HTML).

ISBN: the International Standard Book Number; a unique number for each published book that identifies the publisher, title, edition, binding, and all other details a bookstore or consumer needs to order the book.

Java: a trademarked name for a programming language invented at Sun Microsystems.

Java 1.0: the version of Java supported by Netscape 2.0 through 4.0 and Internet Explorer 3.0.

Java 1.1: the version of Java in which JavaBeans, reflection, the delegation event model, and serialization were first introduced, supported by Internet Explorer 4.0.

JavaBeans: a specification for writing reusable Java classes whose instances can be manipulated visually in a builder tool.

JavaScript: a scripting language invented at Netscape that can access the elements of a page as objects.

JDK: the Java Development Kit, Sun's bare-bones character mode compiler, runtime, profiler, and other tools for Java development.

JFC: the Java Foundation Classes, based on both the AWT and Netscape's Internet Foundation Classes (IFC), introduced in Java 1.2.

linking element: an element which contains an `xlink:form` attribute (`xml:link` in early drafts of XLL).

margin: space around the edges of an element; a CSS property.

markup: textual description of and formatting instructions for text content.

markup declaration: an element declaration, attribute declaration, entity declaration, or notation declaration.

MathML: the XML-based mathematical markup language for including equations and other math in Web documents.

name: in the context of XML, a string containing only alphanumeric characters and the punctuation marks period, hyphen, underscore, and colon. Names must begin with an underscore, a colon, or a letter, and may not contain white space.

NMTOKEN: XML keyword used in `<!ATTLIST>` declarations that specifies an attribute value must be a valid XML name.

NMTOKENS: XML keyword used in `<!ATTLIST>` declarations that specifies an attribute value must be a list of valid XML names.

notation: an identifier for the format of unparsed entities, the format of elements that bear a notation attribute, or an application to which a processing instruction is addressed.

NOTATION: XML keyword used in `<!ATTLIST>` declarations that specifies an attribute value must be the name of a notation declared in the DTD.

notation declaration: a `<!NOTATION>` construct found in DTDs.

OCX: an old name for an ActiveX control.

OLE: Object Linking and Embedding; a Microsoft technology repositioned as ActiveX to respond to Java.

open: in computer software, an adjective often used to describe proprietary, non-free systems with some documentation and at least limited licensing available to some third parties, as in Open Software Foundation, OpenWindows, or "Java is an open standard."

open source: available at no cost with full source code, along with a license that allows the source to be modified and redistributed under the same conditions; a.k.a. free software.

opening tag: start tag.

orthogonal: unrelated; two quantities are orthogonal if they can be changed independently of each other.

overloaded: used to mean more than one thing, depending on context.

parameter entity reference: a reference of the form *%name;* that stands for some replacement text in a DTD.

parent: the element that contains another element called the child.

parsed character data: text that generally may contain XML markup.

payware: software you must pay for before using. Most software sold at retail is payware.

PCDATA: parsed character data in which XML markup is interpreted, as distinguished from CDATA.

platform: a loosely defined set of hardware architecture and an operating system whose elements can all run the same software (for instance, PowerPC Macs running MacOS 7.6 or SparcStations running Solaris 2.4 and later).

processing instruction: data enclosed between `<?` and `?>` delimiters and intended for the application to which the XML processor passes the XML tree, rather than the processor itself.

prolog: the XML declaration and document type declaration.

PUBLIC: XML keyword used in various markup declarations to indicate a standard name for an external entity is being referenced.

recursion: referring to oneself (for instance, the acronym Gnu, which stands for "Gnu's not UNIX," is recursive).

regular expression: a pattern that matches a certain set of text strings.

relative URL: a partial URL, generally used as part of a link, in which the omitted parts are to be inferred from the document in which the URL is found.

render: convert source code to a format that can be viewed.

RGB: red-green-blue; the color space used by most color computer displays.

root: the outermost element in the XML document; the element that contains all other elements but is not itself contained.

rule: in XSL, a particular pattern or patterns to which an action is to be applied.

SDD: see Standalone Document Declaration.

semantic: concerned with the meaning of a statement as opposed to its structure.

Standalone Document Declaration: an XML declaration which includes a standalone attribute with the value "yes".

start tag: a tag that denotes the beginning of an HTML or XML element; contains the name of the element and zero or more attributes in the form `<name att1="value1" att2="value2"...attN="valueN">`.

style: the formatting applied to an element such as font face, point size, and other aspects of the element's appearance as distinct from its meaning.

SYSTEM: XML keyword used in various markup declarations to indicate an external entity is being referred to by a URI or URL.

tag: a start tag, end tag, or empty tag; generally used to delimit an element's content.

target: the remote end of a link.

tree: a nonempty collection of nodes and edges with a single root node such that there is exactly one unique path from the root to any of the nodes. Each well-formed XML document is a tree in which the elements of a document are the nodes of a tree. The root element is the root node, and the edges are abstract connections between parent nodes and their immediate children.

Unicode: a two-byte character set with representations of most of the world's characters.

unparsed entity: an entity that contains binary data not intended to be interpreted as text.

URI: Uniform Resource Identifier; in practice, a URL.

URL: Uniform Resource Locator such as `http://www.amnesty.org/` or `ftp://ftp.javasoft.com/`.

UTF-8: a compressed form of Unicode that uses one byte for the ASCII characters, two bytes for other common characters, and three bytes for the remaining characters.

valid: well-formed XML documents that satisfy the grammar defined by their DTD and all validity constraints in the XML specification.

validity: whether an XML document satisfies the validity constraints given in the XML specification. Validity is a superset of well-formedness; that is, all valid documents must be well-formed but well-formed documents do not have to be valid.

validity constraints: a set of rules laid out in the XML specification. XML documents that do not violate any of these rules are valid.

W3C: the World Wide Web Consortium, a standards body physically located at MIT and virtually at `http://www.w3.org/` that sets standards for XML, HTML, XSL, and many other Web technologies.

well-formed: satisfies all well-formedness constraints in the XML specification.

well-formedness: whether an XML document satisfies the well-formedness constraints given in the XML specification.

well-formedness constraints: a set of rules laid out in the XML specification. XML documents that do not violate any of these rules are well-formed.

wild card: an expression that can stand for any of a set of items.

Wintel: the part of the computing world that runs the Microsoft Windows operating systems on Intel X86 family processors.

XLink: an XML element that links to one or more documents through `xlink:form` and `href` attributes

XML: eXtensible Markup Language; a W3C standard for semantic and structural tagging of documents.

XML declaration: the processing instruction with the name xml and optional encoding and standalone attributes that should begin all XML documents.

XPointer: a means of addressing specific locations and ranges in XML documents; used inside Xlinks.

XSL: Extensible Style Language (often misspelled eXtensible Style Language to justify the acronym); an XML application for describing how XML elements are to be formatted using either HTML or DSSSL.

zeroth order: to a first approximation.

Index

Symbols

(continued)

IDG BOOKS WORLDWIDE, INC.
END-USER LICENSE AGREEMENT

<u>READ THIS</u>. You should carefully read these terms and conditions before opening the software packet(s) included with this book ("Book"). This is a license agreement ("Agreement") between you and IDG Books Worldwide, Inc. ("IDGB"). By opening the accompanying software packet(s), you acknowledge that you have read and accept the following terms and conditions. If you do not agree and do not want to be bound by such terms and conditions, promptly return the Book and the unopened software packet(s) to the place you obtained them for a full refund.

1. <u>License Grant</u>. IDGB grants to you (either an individual or entity) a nonexclusive license to use one copy of the enclosed software program(s) (collectively, the "Software") solely for your own personal or business purposes on a single computer (whether a standard computer or a workstation component of a multiuser network). The Software is in use on a computer when it is loaded into temporary memory (RAM) or installed into permanent memory (hard disk, CD-ROM, or other storage device). IDGB reserves all rights not expressly granted herein.

2. <u>Ownership</u>. IDGB is the owner of all right, title, and interest, including copyright, in and to the compilation of the Software recorded on the disk(s) or CD-ROM ("Software Media"). Copyright to the individual programs recorded on the Software Media is owned by the author or other authorized copyright owner of each program. Ownership of the Software and all proprietary rights relating thereto remain with IDGB and its licensers.

3. <u>Restrictions On Use and Transfer.</u>

   (a) You may only (i) make one copy of the Software for backup or archival purposes, or (ii) transfer the Software to a single hard disk, provided that you keep the original for backup or archival purposes. You may not (i) rent or lease the Software, (ii) copy or reproduce the Software through a LAN or other network system or through any computer subscriber system or bulletin-board system, or (iii) modify, adapt, or create derivative works based on the Software.

(b) You may not reverse engineer, decompile, or disassemble the Software. You may transfer the Software and user documentation on a permanent basis, provided that the transferee agrees to accept the terms and conditions of this Agreement and you retain no copies. If the Software is an update or has been updated, any transfer must include the most recent update and all prior versions.

4. <u>Restrictions On Use of Individual Programs</u>. You must follow the individual requirements and restrictions detailed for each individual program in Appendix D, "About the CD-ROM," of this Book. These limitations are also contained in the individual license agreements recorded on the Software Media. These limitations may include a requirement that after using the program for a specified period of time, the user must pay a registration fee or discontinue use. By opening the Software packet(s), you will be agreeing to abide by the licenses and restrictions for these individual programs that are detailed in Appendix D, "About the CD-ROM," and on the Software Media. None of the material on this Software Media or listed in this Book may ever be redistributed, in original or modified form, for commercial purposes.

5. <u>Limited Warranty</u>.

(a) IDGB warrants that the Software and Software Media are free from defects in materials and workmanship under normal use for a period of sixty (60) days from the date of purchase of this Book. If IDGB receives notification within the warranty period of defects in materials or workmanship, IDGB will replace the defective Software Media.

(b) IDGB AND THE AUTHOR OF THE BOOK DISCLAIM ALL OTHER WARRANTIES, EXPRESS OR IMPLIED, INCLUDING WITHOUT LIMITATION IMPLIED WARRANTIES OF MERCHANTABILITY AND FITNESS FOR A PARTICULAR PURPOSE, WITH RESPECT TO THE SOFTWARE, THE PROGRAMS, THE SOURCE CODE CONTAINED THEREIN, AND/OR THE TECHNIQUES DESCRIBED IN THIS BOOK. IDGB DOES NOT WARRANT THAT THE FUNCTIONS CONTAINED IN THE SOFTWARE WILL MEET YOUR REQUIREMENTS OR THAT THE OPERATION OF THE SOFTWARE WILL BE ERROR FREE.

(c) This limited warranty gives you specific legal rights, and you may have other rights that vary from jurisdiction to jurisdiction.

6. <u>Remedies</u>.

(a) IDGB's entire liability and your exclusive remedy for defects in materials and workmanship shall be limited to replacement of the

Software Media, which may be returned to IDGB with a copy of your receipt at the following address: Software Media Fulfillment Department, Attn.: *XML: Extensible Markup Language*, IDG Books Worldwide, Inc., 7260 Shadeland Station, Ste. 100, Indianapolis, IN 46256, or call 1-800-762-2974. Please allow three to four weeks for delivery. This Limited Warranty is void if failure of the Software Media has resulted from accident, abuse, or misapplication. Any replacement Software Media will be warranted for the remainder of the original warranty period or thirty (30) days, whichever is longer.

(b) In no event shall IDGB or the author be liable for any damages whatsoever (including without limitation damages for loss of business profits, business interruption, loss of business information, or any other pecuniary loss) arising from the use of or inability to use the Book or the Software, even if IDGB has been advised of the possibility of such damages.

(c) Because some jurisdictions do not allow the exclusion or limitation of liability for consequential or incidental damages, the above limitation or exclusion may not apply to you.

7. <u>U.S. Government Restricted Rights</u>. Use, duplication, or disclosure of the Software by the U.S. Government is subject to restrictions stated in paragraph (c)(1)(ii) of the Rights in Technical Data and Computer Software clause of DFARS 252.227-7013, and in subparagraphs (a) through (d) of the Commercial Computer – Restricted Rights clause at FAR 52.227-19, and in similar clauses in the NASA FAR supplement, when applicable.

8. <u>General</u>. This Agreement constitutes the entire understanding of the parties and revokes and supersedes all prior agreements, oral or written, between them and may not be modified or amended except in a writing signed by both parties hereto that specifically refers to this Agreement. This Agreement shall take precedence over any other documents that may be in conflict herewith. If any one or more provisions contained in this Agreement are held by any court or tribunal to be invalid, illegal, or otherwise unenforceable, each and every other provision shall remain in full force and effect.

my2cents.idgbooks.com

CD-ROM Installation Instructions

THIS BOOK'S **CD-ROM** is cross-platform; you should be able to mount it on Macintosh, Solaris, Windows 95, Windows 98, and Windows NT 4.0. There's no fancy installer. You can browse the directories as you would a hard drive.

Simple HTML indexes are provided for the examples in each chapter. Because most of the examples are raw XML files, however, current Web browsers don't display them very well. You're probably better off opening the directories in Windows Explorer (or the equivalent) on your platform of choice and reading the files with a text editor.

To install Netscape Communicator 4.0 and Microsoft Internet Explorer 4.0, follow each browser's installation instructions.